Building Transnational Archaeologies
Construyendo Arqueologías Transnacionales

The 11th Southwest Symposium
El XI Simposio del Suroeste
Hermosillo, Sonora, México

Editors
Elisa Villalpando and Randall H. McGuire

Arizona State Museum
THE UNIVERSITY OF ARIZONA.

Arizona State Museum Archaeological Series 209

Arizona State Museum
The University of Arizona
Tucson, Arizona 85721-0026
Copyright © 2014 by the Arizona Board of Regents
All rights reserved.
Printed in the United States of America

ISBN (paper): 978-1-889747-94-1
Library of Congress Control Number: 2014933385

ARIZONA STATE MUSEUM ARCHAEOLOGICAL SERIES

General Editor: Richard C. Lange
Technical Editors: Alicia M. Vega

The *Archaeological Series* of the Arizona State Museum, The University of Arizona, publishes the results of research in archaeology and related disciplines conducted in the Greater Southwest. Original, monograph-length manuscripts are considered for publication, provided they deal with appropriate subject matter. Information regarding procedures or manuscript submission and review is given under Research Publications on the Arizona State Museum website: *www.statemuseum.arizona.edu/research/pubs*. Information may be also obtained from the General Editor, *Archaeological Series*, Arizona State Museum, P.O. Box 210026, The University of Arizona, Tucson, Arizona, 85721-0026; Email: langer@email.arizona.edu. Electronic publications and previous volumes in the Arizona State Museum Library or available from the University of Arizona Press are listed on the website noted above. Print-on-demand versions of the latest Arizona State Museum Archaeological Series may be obtained from several booksellers on-line.

The Arizona State Museum *Archaeological Series* is grateful to the many donors and supporters who continue to make this publication possible.

Covers: 11th Southwest Symposium logo.

Contents

Contents   iii
List of Figures   viii
List of Tables   x
Preface: The 11ᵗʰ Southwest Symposium: Building Transnational Archaeologies
    by Elisa Villalpando and Randall H. McGuire   xi
       The Theme of the Symposium   xi
       Archaeology and the Nations of the Southwest/Northwest   xiii
       Expanding the Southwest/Northwest in Space and Time   xvi
       West and North Mexico   xvi
       The Lost Century: A.D. 1450-1540   xvii
       Language   xvii
       Acknowledgments   xviii
Prefacio: El XI Simposio del Suroeste: Construyendo arqueologías transnacionales
    de Elisa Villalpando y Randall H. McGuire   xxi
       El tema del Simposio   xxi
       La arqueología y las naciones en el Suroeste/Noroeste   xxiii
       Expandiendo el Suroeste/Noroeste en espacio y tiempo   xxvii
       Occidente y Norte de México   xxvii
       El siglo perdido: 1450-1540 d.C.   xxvii
       El idioma   xxviii
       Agradecimientos   xxix

Part I, Introduction: West and North Mexico *by Michael A. Ohnersorgen and José Luis Punzo*   3

Part I, Chapter 1: Los materiales de concha en el Occidente de Mesoamérica y su presencia en el
    Suroeste Americano *por José Carlos Beltrán Medina*   11
       Resumen/Abstract   11
       Antecedentes   12
       Playa del Tesoro y Bahía de Banderas   13
       Medio ambiente   14
       Aztatlán, la turquesa y los intercambios con el Suroeste   14
       La concha y sus materiales   16
          Pulseras de *Glycymeris gigantea*   16
          Cuentas de Collar   16
          Colgantes   17
          Pectorales del género *Pecten*   17
          Cascabeles y sonajas de *Olivas y Conus*   18
          Spondylus, la ostra sagrada   18
          Strombus, el caracol bocina   19
          Pinctada mazatlanica   19
          El caracol de tinte   20
       Comentarios finales   21

Part I, Chapter 2: Ni todos nómadas ni todos sedentarios: El sitio de Cerro de Santiago, Aguascalientes
    por M. Nicolás Caretta y Peter C. Kröfges   23
       Resumen/Abstract   23
       Presentación   23
       Planteamiento teórico   25
       Problemática   27
       Antecedentes de investigación   28

Investigaciones regionales   29
El sitio del Cerro de Santiago   33

Part I, Chapter 3: The Prehispanic Occupation of the Río Fuerte Valley, Sinaloa
    by John P. Carpenter   37
    Abstract/Resumen   37
    Introduction   37
    Environmental Characteristics of the Río Fuerte Valley   39
    The Preceramic Occupations   40
    Ceramic Period Traditions   42
        The Huatabampo Tradition   42
            Mochicahui   42
            The Serrana/(Río Sonora) Tradition   44
            La Viuda/Rincón de Buyubampo (SIN A:6:18)   44
            Cerro de la Máscara   46
    Discussion   48
        Early Ceramic period (200 B.C./200 to 500 A.D.)   50
        Intermediate Ceramic period (500 to 1100/1200 A.D.)   50
        Late Ceramic period (1100/1200 to 1532 A.D.)   50
    Conclusions   50

Part I, Chapter 4: Cultural and contextual differentiation of Mesoamerican Iconography in the
    U.S. Southwest Northwest Mexico by Michael T. Searcy   53
    Abstract/Resumen   53
    Perspectives in Symbolic Archaeology   55
    Salado and Casas Grandes Sociopolitical Organization and Social Hierarchy   56
    Summary of Regional Sociopolitical Organization   58
    Mesoamerican Iconography in the SW/NW   61
    Summary of Mesoamerican Iconography   64
    Distribution of Mesoamerican Iconography among Salado and Casas Grandes Sites   66
    Other Mesoamerican Interaction Markers   70
    Discussion   72
    Conclusions   73

Part II, Chapter 1: The Hohokam-Upper Piman Continuum Revisited
    by Patrick D. Lyons, J. Brett Hill and Jeffery J. Clark   77
    Abstract/Resumen   77
    Models of Hohokam-Upper Piman Continuity and Discontinuity   78
        The Direct Descent Model   79
        The O'otam Model   80
        The Replacement Model   81
        The Late Arrival and Absorption Model   82
    Recent Research on the Late Prehispanic and Protohistoric Southern U.S. Southwest   82
        Immigrants from the North, Coalescence, and Population Decline   83
        Tribal Oral Traditions   84
    The Archaeology of the Sobaipuri   85
        Discussion   86
    The Entrada: Clues From the Documentary and Archaeological Records   87
    Summary and Conclusion   89
        Trees, Nets, and Rivers   89

Part II, Chapter 2: Population History of the Zuni Region across the Protohistoric Transition: Migration,
    Gene Flow, and Social Transformation *by Matthew A. Peeples*   93
      Abstract/Resumen   93
      The Protohistoric Transition at Zuni   94
          Explanations for the Changes Marking the Protohistoric Transition   97
      Using Human Skeletal Morphology to Track Population Movement   99
          The Dataset and Data Pretreatment   100
          Multivariate Analysis of Skeletal Variation   102
      Genetic Evidence for Immigration across the Protohistoric Transition   103
      Potential Sources of New Arrivals   105
      Migration, Gene Flow, and the Protohistoric Transition at Zuni   106
      Conclusions   109
      Acknowledgments   109

Part II, Chapter 3: New Light on the Francisco Vásquez de Coronado Expedition of 1540-1542
    by Matthew F. Schmader   111
      Abstract/Resumen   111
      Introduction   112
      Piedras Marcadas Pueblo   120
      Site Structure   122
      Artifact Assemblage and Inventory   124
      Piedras Marcadas Assemblage as a Reference Site   127
      Non-Metal Artifacts   128
      Identifying Piedras Marcadas Pueblo   129
      Conclusions   130

Part II, Chapter 4: Continuidad Cultural en la Periferia Sur del Noroeste/Suroeste: El Periodo Protohistórico
    en el Sur de Sonora y el Norte de Sinaloa *por John Carpenter y Guadalupe Sánchez*   133
      Resumen/Abstract   133
      Introducción   133
      La conquista española de la Planicie Costera   135
      Los sitios de La Viuda y Rincón de Buyubampo en territorio de los Sinaloas   136
      Los sitios de La Botijuela y La Ciénega   143
      El sitio La Playa de Ocoroni, Sinaloa   144
      Integración cultural y permanencia en la Región Cahita del Norte durante el Siglo Perdido   146

Part III, Introducción: Arqueologías Mexicana y Norteamericana: Entre la obligación moral y los shovel bums
    por César Villalobos   151
      Introducción   151
      Arqueología en México y Estados Unidos   151
      La arqueología Mexicana patriotera hasta el agresivismo   152
      La arqueología en los Estados Unidos   154
      ¿Diferencias o Similitudes?   156
      Conclusiones   159

Part III, Chapter 1: Conservación del Patrimonio y Transformación de la Sociedad en las Cordilleras Centrales
    de la Península de Baja California, México *por María de la Luz Gutiérrez M.*   161
      Resumen/Abstract   161
      Introducción   162
      La Sierra de San Francisco   164
          El estilo pictórico Gran Mural   164
          Valoración del significado de la Sierra   166

Gestión del Patrimonio Cultural 167
    Antecedentes 167
    Santa Marta y San Francisco de la Sierra 167
    Implementación del Plan de Manejo 168
    Las principales amenazas 168
    Políticas para el acceso de visitantes 169
La zona arqueológica y el área rupestre 169
    Vías de acceso 169
    Niveles de visita 170
    Vigilancia 171
    Evaluación del plan 172
Problemas recientes 173
    Conclusiones 175

Part III, Chapter 2: Paquimé y el Museo de las Culturas del Norte en la construcción de una "nueva" identidad
    en el noroeste de Chihuahua *por José Luis Punzo Díaz* 177
    Resumen/Abstract 177
    La región noroeste de Chihuahua y sus habitantes 178
    Paquimé antes de la declaratoria de Patrimonio Mundial 178
    Paquimé después de la declaratoria de Patrimonio Mundial 179
        El Museo de las Culturas del Norte y la comunidad 179
    La conformación y el discurso Museo de las Culturas del Norte 180
    El turismo en la región noroeste de Chihuahua 182
    Paquimé en la identidad de los habitantes del noroeste de Chihuahua 182
    Paquimé en la identidad de los Chihuahuenses 184
    Y entonces ¿Para qué sirven las declaratorias de Patrimonio Mundial a nivel comunitario? 185

Part III, Chapter 3: Arqueología, Turismo y Sitios Patrimonio de la Humanidad en México y Estados Unidos
    por César Villalobos 187
    Resumen/Abstract 187
    Introducción 187
    Arqueología para todos y en todos los lugares 188
    UNESCO y Turismo 189
    México y su obsesión por el pasado 191
    Estados Unidos y su distanciamiento con la UNESCO 193
    Discusión 195
    Conclusiones 196

Part III, Chapter 4: Heritage Management in Mexico and the United States
    by Jeffrey H. Altschul and T. J. Ferguson 197
    Abstract/Resumen 197
    Private Property versus National Patrimony 198
    Centralized versus Local Control 201
    Traditional versus Scientific Authority in Archaeological Interpretation 204
    Conclusions 205
    Acknowledgments 205

Part III, Chapter 5: O'odham Heritage, Sovereignty, and the Legal Conundrums of the U.S.-Mexico Boundary
    by Joseph T. Joaquin, Eric J. Kaldahl and Peter Steere 207
    Abstract/Resumen 207
    A Few Historical Facts 209
    O'odham Patrimony 210

The Quitovac Ethnoarchaeological Project   211
The UNAM Project   213
Going Forward   214

Part III, Chapter 6: Patrimonal Wasteland? Expanded Notions of Material Culture in the
    U.S.-Mexico Borderlands *by Maribel L. Alvarez*   217
    Abstract/Resumen   217
    Learning from Archaeologists   218
    Border Artifacts   220
    The Trouble Curios Make   222

References/Bibliografía   225

Figures/Figuras

I.1.1.	Localización de Playa del Tesoro y Bahía de Banderas	13
I.1.2.	Pulsera de *Glycymeris* con cuentas	17
I.1.3.	Pulseras zoomorfas con murciélagos	17
I.1.4.	Collar de *Spondylus*	17
I.1.5.	*Turritellas* con un orificio	18
I.1.6.	Colgantes de *Argopecten circularis*	18
I.1.7.	Cascabeles de *Oliva*	18
I.1.8.	Colgantes zoomorfos de *Spondylus*	20
I.1.9.	Caracol bocina de *Strombus galeatus*	20
I.1.10.	Valvas y anzuelos de *Pinctada mazatlánica*	21
I.1.11.	Caracol de tinte *Hexaplexregius*	21
I.2.1.	Sitio arqueológico de Santiago, Aguascalientes	36
I.3.1.	Area encompassed by the INAH Proyecto Arqueológico Norte de Sinaloa	38
I.3.2.	Locations of the principal sites documented in the Río Fuerte región	39
I.3.3.	Sinaloan thorn forest near El Fuerte, Sinaloa	41
I.3.4.	Approximate geographical distribution of the Huatabampo and Serrana archaeological traditions	43
I.3.5.	Huatabampo/Guasave Red ware recovered from a burial mound in Mochicahui	45
I.3.6.	Guasave Red-on-buff recovered from a burial mound in Mochicahui	45
I.3.7.	Aztatlán Polychrome recovered from a burial mound in Mochicahui	45
I.3.8.	Plan of Residential Unit 2 at Rincón de Buyubampo	47
I.3.9.	Petroglyphs at Cerro de la Máscara	49
I.3.10.	Petroglyphs at Cerro de la Máscara	49
I.3.11.	Preliminary Cahitan Ceramic Scheme	51
I.4.1.	Map of the Salado and Casas Grandes traditions	57
I.4.2.	Sites included in this study	61
I.4.3.	Spade motif which may be the horned/plumed serpent, macaw, or a combination of the two	65
I.4.4.	Comparison of frequency of Mesoamerican motifs between more and less hierarchical sites among the Salado and Chihuahuan traditions	69
II.1.1.	A "braided river channel" model of connections among the Mogollon, Hohokam, Kayenta (Anasazi), and Tusayan (Anasazi) archaeological cultures and the present-day Zuni, O'odham, and Hopi	91
II.2.1.	Major sites in the Zuni region in the Pueblo IV and Protohistoric periods	95
II.2.2.	Approximate locations of the sub-regional samples for the R-matrix analysis	101
II.2.3.	Principal coordinates analysis of the R-matrix for all craniometric data	107
II.3.1.	Map of Hispania Nova ("New Spain")	113
II.3.2.	Route of the expedition led by Fray Marcos de Niza (1539)	115
II.3.3.	Route of the expedition led by Francisco Vázquez de Coronado (1540-1542)	117
II.3.4.	Map of the central Río Grande valley or "Tiguex Province" of Vázquez de Coronado	119
II.3.5.	Map of the Albuquerque metropolitan area showing location of Piedras Marcadas pueblo	121
II.3.6.	Sixteenth century metal artifacts recovered from Piedras Marcadas pueblo	123
II.3.7.	Sixteenth century metal artifacts recovered from Piedras Marcadas pueblo	126
II.4.1.	Provincias Históricas de la Planicie Costera	134
II.4.2.	Localización de los sitios mencionados	137
II.4.3.	Las estructuras habitacionales de Buyubampo y La Viuda	138
II.4.4.	Tipos cerámicos San Miguel en el piso de la estructura 2 de Rincón de Buyubampo	140
II.4.5.	Mayólicas y porcelanas del sitio de Rincón de Buyubampo	141
II.4.6.	Sellos de plomo recuperados abajo del piso de ocupación en la Estructura 3	141
II.4.7.	Fotografía de los sellos de plomo	142

II.4.8.   Unidad habitacional con patio central en el sitio de La Botijuela, Sonora   145
II.4.9.   Unidades habitacionales del sitio La Ciénega, Sonora   145
III.1.1. Las Cordilleras Centrales de la península de Baja California   163
III.1.2. La sierra de San Francisco presenta altas mesas seccionadas por profundos cañones 165
III.1.3. Panel este de Cueva Pintada, Arroyo de San Pablo, Sierra de San Francisco   165
III.1.4. Panel central de Cuesta Palmarito, Arroyo de Santa Marta, Sierra de San Francisco   170
III.1.5. Afortunadamente la Sierra de San Francisco se ubica totalmente dentro de la Reserva de la
          Biosfera El Vizcaíno   171
III.1.6. Sitios Gran Mural en la Sierra de San Francisco   172
III.1.7. Vías de Acceso autorizadas y Niveles de Visita   173
III.1.8. Camino a San Francisco de la Sierra   175
III.6.1. Pig from an antique shop in Tucson, Arizona   221
III.6.2. Pig from the Southwest Indian Art Fair   221
III.6.3. Pig from a curio shop in Nogales, Arizona   221

Tables/Tablas

I.4.1.	Summary of sites	60
I.4.2.	Motif frequencies for more and less hierarchical Salado sites	67
II.2.1.	Craniometric data included in this study	98
II.2.2.	Craniometric variables used in this analysis	101
II.2.3.	Kruskal-Wallis tests for all variables included in the R-matrix analysis	104
II.2.4.	Relethford-Blangero analysis of Zuni craniometric data	104
II.2.5.	Values of F_{st} for comparisons by time period based on Zuni craniometric data	105
II.3.1.	Facts and Figures of the Vázquez de Coronado Expedition	116
III.2.1.	Cifras de visitantes al Museo de las Culturas del Norte	180
III.2.2.	Turismo en Chihuahua por región 2006 expresado en miles	183
III.2.3.	Visitantes mexicanos al Museo de las Culturas del Norte por ciudad de origen	183
III.2.4.	Visitantes norteamericanos al Museo de las Culturas del Norte por ciudad de origen	184

The 11th Biennial Southwest Symposium:
Building Transnational Archaeologies
Hermosillo, Sonora, México
January 8 and 9, 2010

Preface

Elisa Villalpando and Randall H. McGuire

The Centro INAH Sonora hosted the 11th biennial Southwest Symposium in Hermosillo, Sonora, Mexico, January 8th and 9th, 2010. In the tradition of past meetings, the 21st Southwest Symposium provided a forum for archaeologists and other scholars to discuss innovative ideas and to develop networks for anthropological research in the U.S. Southwest and Mexican Northwest. We built the symposium around the theme of building transnational archaeologies. The Hermosillo meeting was the most diverse of the Southwest Symposiums held so far. The participants included U.S., Mexican, and indigenous researchers who worked in museums, universities, governmental agencies and contract archaeology.

The 11th Southwest Symposium had four presented sessions and a series of themed poster sessions on transnational topics. Two of the presented sessions, West and North Mexico, and The Lost Century: A.D. 1450-1540 focused on substantive issues that expand our understanding of the Southwest/Northwest in space and time. The other two presented sessions Collaborating Across Cultures, and Archaeology and Society, discussed methods and goals in transnational archaeologies. The poster sessions included Violence in the Southwest/Northwest, Coastal Archaeology, Relations between the Southwest/ Northwest and Mesoamerica, Cliff Dwellings, and Contract Archaeology. This volume includes 14 chapters from three of the presented sessions.

THE THEME OF THE SYMPOSIUM

The Southwest Symposium began in 1988 and it is the only conference that brings professional archaeologists together to consider pan-regional questions of theory, methods, and aboriginal history for the Southwest/Northwest culture area. In an oft quoted comment, Erik Reed (1964:175) defined the culture area as extending from Durango, Colorado to Durango, Mexico and from Las Vegas, Nevada to Las Vegas, New Mexico. A quick glance at a map will reveal that almost half of this region lies south of the international border in Mexico. The Southwest Symposium has been from its inception the major intellectual forum that has actively transcended that frontier. Mexican archaeologists have participated in the Southwest Symposium from the first meeting in 1988. This was the third Southwest Symposium to be held in Mexico. Hermosillo hosted the 6th Southwest Symposium in 1998 (Villalpando

Elisa Villalpando Centro INAH Sonora
Randall H. McGuire Binghamton University

2002) and Chihuahua City, Chihuahua hosted the 9th Southwest Symposium in 2002 (Webster et al. 2008). Both of these earlier Mexican Southwest Symposiums emphasized crossing borders as their themes. We doubt that the organizers of the first Southwest Symposium in 1988 would have imagined that 20 years later a quarter of the Southwest Symposiums would have been held in Mexico although we know that they are pleased that this is the case.

Many borders crisscross the Southwest/ Northwest culture area dividing it into pieces and creating "communities of practice" (Minar and Crown 2001) within those pieces. These boundaries, divisions and parts clearly had no meaning for the ancient indigenous peoples of the region but they have profound meanings and consequences for the contemporary archaeologists who study those peoples (McGuire 2002). The international border forms the most prominent of these boundaries, but state boundaries in the U.S. and Mexico also significantly shape the practice of archaeology. The descendents of the ancient indigenous peoples of the region define their own territories in defiance of the lines drawn by their conquerors. Indian reservations in the United States and *comunidades indígenas* (indigenous communities) in Mexico have clear demarcations imposed by the modern Nation States but Indigenous Nations embrace territories that extend beyond these modern lines. In the case of the Cocopa, the Tohono O'odham and the Yaqui the international border divides Indian Nations and these nations do not recognize the legitimacy of these divisions. These nations, the United States, Mexico, and the Indian nations, each has their own heritage and archaeology. These national archaeologies present a challenge that requires more than just crossing borders. Archaeologists need to engage in the even more difficult enterprise of building a transnational archaeology. Such an archaeology should recognize and make the most of the diversity of national interests, programs and contexts that we do archaeology in but also find commonalities and shared goals that will facilitate collaboration between national contexts. Southwest/Northwest archaeology has always existed in this multi-national context but scholars largely ignored this reality until the dawn of the 21st century.

For most of the 20th century, a handful of U.S. institutions, their professors and students, dominated archaeology in the southwestern United States. The development of contract archaeology in the 1970s broadened the extent of and altered the practice of archaeology in the southwest U.S. but reinforced it as a nationalist practice. By the beginning of the 21st century, however, a nationalist view of the region had become parochial. Starting in the 1970s, the Instituto Nacional de Antropología e Historia (National Institute of Anthropology and History) of Mexico, established regional centers, museums and expanded research in the northwest of Mexico. At the turn of the 21st century, an Indigenous archaeology developed as Indian Nations established their own archaeological programs, goals, and methods. Each of these "national" archaeologies focus on different regions, make different assumptions, asks different questions, seeks different answers, emphasize different methods and embraces different theories or worldviews.

Transnational archaeologies reach beyond or transcend national boundaries and they do so in numerous ways. They imply a broad vision of historical and cultural processes in the Southwest/ Northwest that is not artificially limited by political, cultural, or linguistic borders. They necessarily entail a multi-sited archaeology where researchers work in different "nations." They stand strong when their foundations rest on collaborations across cultural groups. They require archaeologists to reexamine the contributions that archaeology can make to society. They expand the archaeology of the Southwest/Northwest linguistically, culturally and regionally.

ARCHAEOLOGY AND THE NATIONS OF THE SOUTHWEST/NORTHWEST

The national contexts of archaeology in the Southwest/Northwest differ in terms of wealth, power, heritage and the practice of archaeology. The three contexts overlap and intertwine in complex ways that are necessary to understand if we want our work to be transnational. We give a brief summary of similarities and differences here. Two of our sessions, Collaborating Across Cultures and Archaeology and Society addressed these national contexts and how to work across them.

The United States is clearly the most powerful and wealthy nation in the region. Hundreds of professional archaeologists work in the U.S. southwest (easily over 1,000 in total) and there are hundreds of field projects each year in the region. The number of recorded archaeological sites for the U.S. southwest is in the hundreds of thousands. The amount of money expended annually on archaeology in the region would be measured in the tens of millions of dollars (a best guess would be around $40 million, Jeff Altschul personal communication). Each year there are multiple projects with budgets in the millions of dollars. The vast majority of this money is spent in contract archaeology by private companies, who bid on projects. Federal laws, most notably the National Historic Preservation Act of 1968 (Acuerdo de Preservación Histórico Nacional), mandate this work on federal lands, projects requiring federal permits or projects using federal money. Archeological remains belong to the land owner and thus no legislation requires archaeological work for projects on private lands using private money. Archaeologists from different federal land holding agencies such as the National Park Service, the U.S. Forest Service (Servicio de Bosques Nacionales) and the U.S. Bureau of Land Management (Oficina de Manejo de Tierras) supervise the archaeology on the agencies' lands. A State Historic Preservation Officer oversees compliance with the federal legislation. In addition, states, many counties, and many cities have their own archaeological regulations, and in numerous cases their own staff archaeologists to administer these regulations.

The majority of archaeology done in the U.S. southwest studies the Indigenous past of the region but virtually all of the archaeologists doing this research are Euro-Americans. The United States incorporates Indigenous peoples into the heritage of the United States as the "First Americans." That is, as the first of a series of peoples who entered North America and created the United States (McGuire 1992). The First Americans ideology obscures the fact that Euro-Americans established the United States on land taken from indigenous peoples but does give the descendents of these peoples a place in the heritage of the nation. Archaeology began in the United States as the study of the indigenous other, and the southwest has traditionally been the most intensively studied archaeological region in the U.S. (Fowler 2000). In the last few decades of the 20th century, considerable conflict erupted between Native Americans and archaeologists (McGuire 1992). One of the consequences of this conflict was the federal Native American Graves Protection and Repatriation Act of 1990 (NAGPRA; Acuerdo de Protección y Repatriación de Tumbas de los Nativos Americanos en español) that requires human remains and ritual objects recovered from archaeological projects be returned to contemporary indigenous descendants.

Mexico has a well established and vibrant discipline of archaeology that began in the early part of the 20th century (Bernal 1980; Lorenzo 1998). The total number of professionally employed archaeologists in the country numbers in the hundreds. No more than 15 to 20 of these professionals work in Sonora and Chihuahua. Although researchers have recorded hundreds of thousands of archaeological sites in Mexico, the number of recorded sites in both Sonora and Chihuahua number less than 10 thousand. Funding for archaeology is also far less than in the southwest U.S. As Paul Minnis (2003:2) has noted, the budgets for the largest individual archaeological projects in the southwest U.S. regularly exceed the total amount of money ever spent on archaeology in Chihuahua; the same could be said for Sonora.

For most of the 20th century, the federal Insituto Nacional de Antropología e Historia (INAH) conducted the vast majority of archaeology in Mexico (Bernal 1980; Lorenzo 1998). The Mexican nation claims archaeological remains as national patrimony and archaeological sites belong to the nation not to private land owners. Federal law charges INAH with the protection, investigation and interpretation of archaeological sites. Thus, there is a uniform national patrimony law and individual states, communities and cities do not have separate regulations. All archaeologists working in Mexico (domestic and foreign) must obtain a permit to do research from the INAH. The INAH has its own school, the Escuela Nacional de Antropología e Historia (ENAH; National School of Anthropology and History) that trains students to be archaeologists, anthropologists and historians. No private contract archaeology exists in Mexico, the INAH does the majority of savage archaeology.

At the end of the 20th century, two changes threatened INAH's control of archaeology in Mexico (Vázquez León 2003). Numerous state universities including the Universidad Nacional Autónoma de México (National Autonomous University of Mexico) now train students at the undergraduate and graduate level, conduct archaeological research and provide a career path outside of the INAH. This had led to marked rivalries between INAH and some university archaeologists (Vázquez León 2003). Nonetheless, students from ENAH are better trained to work immediately on substantive institutional tasks mainly because professors are INAH's own archaeologists.

The right-wing party (Partido Acción Nacional, National Action Party) that has controlled the Mexican government for the first decade of the 21st century keeps introducing legislation that would privatize major Mexican archaeological zones as corporate run tourist destinations (McGuire 2008:140-186). Even with these recent changes, Mexican archaeology continues to be much more centralized and uniform in its practice than U.S. archaeology.

Following the Mexican Revolution, archaeology played a major role in the *Indigenismo* (Indianism) movement remaking Mexican national identity and heritage (Bernal 1980). *Indigenismo* embraced the country's glorious indigenous past while assimilating their descendants into a unified *mestizo* or mixed race nation. Mexican archaeologists see themselves as the biological and cultural descendents of the ancient peoples who they study. Contemporary indigenous movements, such as the Zapatistas, commonly reject *Indigenismo*. Increasingly in Mexico, indigenous groups have challenged the treatment of archaeological remains as national patrimony and seek to control them as their heritage.

There are important similarities in the place of Indigenous Nations in Mexico and the United States. These similarities result from the colonial conquests of indigenous peoples that created Mexico and the U.S. In both countries, Indigenous Nations are politically subjugated, economically the poorest of the poor, and their heritages subsumed by the national heritage. Behind these broad similarities rest important differences that affect the practice of a transnational archaeology, especially in the cases where the international border has divided Indigenous Nations.

Indigenous Nations in the United States have a semi-sovereign status that Mexican indigenous peoples largely lack. In the southwest U.S., Indian reservations have their own governments, elected by the members of the indigenous nation. Individual states, such as Arizona or New

Mexico have no authority over reservations and state laws do not apply on reservations. Native American nations have misdemeanor and civil jurisdiction on their own lands but federal environmental and historic preservation laws do apply. In Mexico, indigenous peoples have had far less or no autonomy. Special legislation in the 1930s gave the Yaqui of southern Sonora more autonomy than other Indigenous Nations in Mexico. Changes in Mexican law in 2003 gave all Indigenous Nations more autonomy but they still have less sovereignty than Native American nations.

In a relative sense, the indigenous peoples are the poorest groups in both countries. In absolute terms, however, U.S. indigenous nations have far greater resources and wealth than do Mexican groups. This in part, reflects the greater absolute wealth of the U.S. versus Mexico. The greater wealth of U.S. groups also results from the ability of Native American governments to gain money from the exploitation of natural resources and from federal government programs. Most southwestern Indigenous Nations have set up casino gambling that state laws prohibit but that federal laws allow. Gambling has not made Indian people rich, or even raised standards of living to U.S. averages. Gambling revenues have given indigenous governments more money to provide more services for their people.

The political and economic position of Native American nations gives them more control over their heritage than Mexican indigenous groups. Native American nations own and control the archaeological sites on their reservations. Off the reservation, NAGPRA gives them an active say in archaeological research and repatriation rights to human remains and sacred objects recovered from excavations. Every southwest U.S. indigenous nations has set up cultural committees that oversee these rights. Archaeologists must consult with these committees in order to comply with NAGPRA. Since state laws and government have no

authority on Native American nations, State Historic Preservation Officers cannot oversee compliance with federal historic preservation laws on reservations. Native American nations have Tribal Historic Preservation Officers who have the authority for such oversight. Many southwest nations employ their own archaeologists, have tribal contract archaeology programs, and their own museums. Although primarily Euro-American professionals staff these programs, increasingly tribal governments are hiring Native American professionals in these positions. The greater poverty of Mexican indigenous nations leads these people to be more concerned about economics than heritage issues. Indigenous groups in the Maya area of southeast Mexico who have taken over archaeological zones appear to have been motivated as much by the money to be made by tourism at these sites as control of heritage (McGuire 2008:140-186). None of these nations has their own archaeologists or heritage managers both because of cost but also because Mexican law vests control of all archaeology with the INAH. The legal structure of Mexico does not have legislations comparable to NAGPRA.

The session Collaborating Across Cultures discussed how to work across these differences. Andrew Darling of the Gila River Indian Community, and Davina Two Bears of the Navajo Archaeological Department organized this session. Collaborations that reach beyond or transcend national and cultural boundaries are key to transnational archaeologies. Collaboration implies the integration of goals, interests, and practices between the individuals and/or social groups that work together. It entails a dialogue that goes beyond an instrumentalist concern with resolving a conflict or respecting rights and responsibilities. It requires humility, patience, listening, careful consultation, equality, and respect. Collaboration should be transformative of the parties involved. Each party brings different resources, skills, knowledge, authority and/or interests to a collaborative labor. Collaboration involves the melding of these unique qualities into common goals and practices. This session addressed collaboration both across the international frontier and between scholars and Indian Nations. However, the organizers of this session did not submit chapters for this volume.

The session Archaeology and Society explored these relationships in the United States, in Mexico, and in Indian Nations. Elizabeth Bagwell, of Aspen Environmental Group, and Cesar Villalobos of Instituto de Investigaciones Antropológicas UNAM, organized the session. The papers from this session discussed public programs, education, heritage, and identity. The papers sought to compare and contrast these issues in different nations with the goal of transcending and reaching beyond national interests.

The current volume includes six chapters from this session, one by U.S. researchers, four from Mexico, and one from the Tohono O'odham Nation. Jeffrey H. Altschul of the SRI Foundation in Tucson and T. J. Ferguson of the University of Arizona, begin this section with a highly useful summary and comparison of heritage management in the United States and Mexico. Three of the chapters present case studies of archaeology and society: (1) José Luis Punzo Díaz of Centro INAH Michoacán discusses the role of the Paquimé museum and the construction of identity in Chihuahua, (2) César Villalobos discuss the relationship between UNESCO and archaeological tourism in the United States and Mexico, and (3) María de la Luz Gutiérrez for the Centro INAH Baja California Sur considers the role of heritage and societal transformation in the central mountains of Baja California del Sur. Maribel Alvarez, a cultural anthropologist with the Southwest Center at the University of Arizona, discusses how cultural anthropology benefits from archaeological concepts of culture and materiality, and illustrates her argument with an analysis of modern material culture in northern Mexico. Joseph T. Joaquin of the Tohono O'odham Nation, Eric J. Kaldahl of the Amerind

Foundation, Dragoon, Arizona and Peter Steere with the Tohono O'odham Nation present the Tohono O'odham perspective on heritage and they review how it runs into conflict with both U.S. and Mexican heritage laws and practices.

EXPANDING THE SOUTHWEST/ NORTHWEST IN SPACE AND TIME

The international border has structured archaeological research in ways that nothing to do with the ancient history of aboriginal peoples in the Southwest/Northwest. Diplomats drew the current border in the mid-19th century following lines of latitude and longitude that have no relationship to the cultural or physical geography of the region. This has affected what areas archaeologists emphasize in their research and it has created ambiguous spaces in time and space that do not attract archaeological attention. At the 11th Southwest Symposium we focused on two such ambiguous spaces, West and North Mexico, and the Lost Century: A.D. 1450-1540.

WEST AND NORTH MEXICO

The international border between Mexico and the United States and the culture area border that separates our region from Mesoamerica has long hampered our understanding of the archaeology of the Southwest/Northwest. The archaeology of West and North Mexico does not fit easily into either culture area and the degree of fit changes over time. Developments in these areas had direct impacts on the Southwest/Northwest. Indeed, "Mesoamerican influences" on the north most likely originated in these regions and not the core of Mesoamerica. The discussion allowed scholars working in West and North Mexico to share information and interact with Southwest/ Northwest archaeologists. José Luis Punzo (actually of Centro INAH Michoacán), and

Michael Ohnersorgen, University of Missouri, Saint Louis, organized this session.

This volume includes three chapters from this session, two by Mexican scholars and one by a U.S. scholar. A marked similarity in shell jewelry forms is one of the striking uniformities between the Southwest/Northwest and West Mexico. José Carlos Betrán of the Centro INAH Nayarit discusses the similarities and differences between these assemblages. John Carpenter of the Centro INAH Sonora discusses the Prehispanic occupation of the Río Fuerte. This is a notable addition to the little known frontier between the Southwest/Northwest and West Mexico. Michael Searcy of Brigham Young University provides an overview of cultural and contextual differentiation of Mesoamerican iconography in the Southwest/Northwest.

THE LOST CENTURY: A.D. 1450-1540

In the century A.D. 1450 to A.D. 1540, most of the Southwest/Northwest suffered a significant demographic collapse and transformation of cultures. Scores of regional sequences ended and village based agriculture ceased in areas where it had been practiced for hundreds of years. Outside of the Pueblos, this is a lost century making it difficult to link archaeological traditions and modern Indian Nations, and to understand the processes that created the ethnographically known Southwest/Northwest. The international border has hampered our understanding of this century because it structures research but has no meaning for the historical and cultural processes we wish to understand. Indian Nations hold very different perspectives on this century than either U.S. or Mexican scholars. John Carpenter, Centro INAH Sonora, Hermosillo, and Anna Neuzil, Eco Plan Associates, organized this session.

We have included four chapters from this session in the present volume, three by U.S. scholars and one by a Mexican scholar. Matt Peeples of Archaeology Southwest in Tucson, Arizona, provides us with a succinct summary of the history of Zuni Pueblo between A.D. 1450 and 1540. Patrick D. Lyons of the Arizona State Museum, J. Brett Hill of Hendrix College, and Jeffery J. Clark Archaeology Southwest revisit the issue of a Hohokam to Pima continuum in southern Arizona. They apply a "braided river channel" type model and conclude that there were cultural links between the Hohokam and Piman speaking peoples. Matthew F. Schmader of the City of Albuquerque looks at the 16th century, and examines Coronado's 1540-1542 expedition to New Mexico, its sociopolitical context and organizational details. Finally, John Carpenter of the Centro INAH Sonora and Guadalupe Sánchez of ERNO Instituto de Geología-UNAM take us back to the frontier between the Southwest/ Northwest and West Mexico at the border of Sonora and Sinaloa to discuss the protohistoric in this critical region.

LANGUAGE

National languages, English and Spanish, challenge our attempts to create a transnational archaeology. Language differences present problems for bi-national projects, training students, communication between scholars, and publication of results. Archaeologists usually resolve these problems by using one language rather than the other. Most commonly, that language is English. Researchers and students who want to participate in a transnational archaeology need to be bilingual in English and Spanish. Scholars who are not bilingual cannot master and control the literature and research of the whole of the Southwest/Northwest.

Bilingual competency varies greatly between U.S. and Mexican archaeologists. All archaeologists trained in Mexico are expected to read English and archaeology professors routinely assign readings in English. The actual competence of individual Mexican archaeologists in English varies greatly, but almost all Mexican archaeologists can read articles and books in English. This competency often does not extend to being able to speak and understand the language. Most U.S. graduate programs in anthropology require that their students read a second language, but these requirements are rarely rigorously enforced. Also, we know of no U.S. program that requires students preparing for careers in the archaeology of the Southwest/Northwest to study Spanish. Archaeology professors in the United States do not routinely assign readings in Spanish to classes and seminars.

At every Southwest Symposium, language has limited participation and communication among archaeologists. At the 11th Southwest Symposium, we had simultaneous translation during all presented sessions. All three of the Southwest Symposiums held in Mexico had simultaneous translation but no Southwest Symposium held in the United States has had simultaneous translation. In part, this reflects the fact that services such as simultaneous translation cost far more in the United States than in Mexico. Each session at the 11th Southwest Symposium included papers in both English and Spanish. All authors prepared a long abstract/summary of their paper in both English and Spanish. These summaries were included in the program. We asked all authors to prepare their PowerPoint presentations in the opposite language of their presentation or to use bilingual PowerPoint presentations. Finally we asked that all posters be bilingual or that poster presenters bring a poster in each language.

Two archaeological literatures exist for the Southwest/Northwest. One published in English in the U.S. and a second published in Spanish in Mexico. Presses and institutions distribute these literatures through different networks making it difficult for scholars to learn of, locate and purchase the literature in the other country. The Southwest Symposium has been one of the main loci in the Southwest/Northwest to bring these literatures together, and to aid the distribution of ideas across the international frontier. Both previous Southwest Symposiums in Mexico published their results in English. We decided not to do this because we feel it is a disincentive for U.S. and Canadian researcher to learn Spanish if all-important literature is translated into English. A transnational archaeology must be bilingual and this volume is bilingual. The University of Colorado Press has published most of the proceedings of the Southwest Symposium but they were not willing to publish chapters in Spanish. The Arizona State Museum, however, was willing to publish a bilingual volume in English and Spanish and for this reason; we are publishing the 11th Southwest Symposium in the *Arizona State Museum Archaeological Series*.

The Southwest Symposium has been a major force in shaping the study of Southwestern/Northwestern archaeology. It has also been a key player in transcending the borders, international and state that divide the study of the region. The 11th Southwest Symposium continued these contributions by focusing on the construction of a transnational archaeology. The chapters presented here represent an important step to this goal.

Acknowledgments We first must thank the Board of Directors of the Southwest Symposium for their enthusiastic support for holding the 2010 meeting in Hermosillo, Sonora, especially given security concerns because of drug violence in northern Mexico. We also must heartily thank the Secretaría Técnica del Instituto Nacional de Antropología e Historá for providing institutional resources for the symposium including office supplies, the closing and the closing dinner at the exhibit hall of the Museo de Sonora en la Antigua Penitenciaría. We could not have held the symposium without financial contributions from Archaeology Southwest, the School of Anthropology at the University of Arizona, the School of Human Evolution and Social Change at Arizona State University, Statistical Research Inc., the Department of Anthropology at the University of Colorado, William Self Associates Inc., Department of Anthropology at Binghamton University, and Anthropological Research LLC. We thank Binghamton University, for hosting the symposium web site and the Centro INAH Sonora for providing us with personnel before, during, and after the symposium to mount the posters, set up, and tear down the meeting area at the Centro de las Artes de la Universidad de Sonora. The staff of the Centro de las Artes were very helpful and attentive to our needs throughout the symposium. Last but not least we must thank the Sonoran archaeology students that helped with the logistics and photography during the meeting and the archaeologists from the University of Arizona who drove vans filled with participants from Tucson to Hermosillo.

El XI Simposio del Suroeste:
Construyendo arqueologías transnacionales
Hermosillo, Sonora, México
el 8 y 9 de enero de 2010

Prefacio

Elisa Villalpando y Randall H. McGuire

El Centro INAH Sonora fue el anfitrión del XI Simposio del Suroeste (*11ᵗʰ Southwest Symposium*), en la ciudad de Hermosillo, Sonora, México, el 8 y 9 de enero de 2010. Siguiendo la tradición de los eventos anteriores, este simposio fue un foro de discusión de ideas innovadoras entre arqueólogos y otros profesionistas para desarrollar redes de investigación antropológica en el Suroeste de los Estados Unidos y el Noroeste de México. Organizamos este simposio alrededor del tema de la construcción de arqueologías transnacionales. El evento de Hermosillo fue uno de los *Southwest Symposium* más diversos que se hayan llevado a cabo; los participantes fueron investigadores norteamericanos, mexicanos e indígenas, que se desempeñan profesionalmente en museos, universidades, agencias gubernamentales y proyectos de salvamento arqueológico.

El XI Simposio del Suroeste tuvo cuatro sesiones de presentaciones y dos sesiones que agruparon carteles temáticos sobre tópicos transnacionales. Los participantes en dos de las sesiones de presentaciones, Occidente y Norte de México y El Siglo Perdido: 1450-1540 d.C., se enfocaron en asuntos sustantivos que amplían nuestra comprensión del Suroeste/

Noroeste tanto en espacio como en tiempo. Las ponencias presentadas en las otras dos sesiones Colaboración Entre Culturas y Arqueología y Sociedad discutieron métodos y objetivos de las arqueologías transnacionales. Las sesiones de carteles incluyeron temas como violencia en el Suroeste/Noroeste, Arqueología Costera, Relaciones entre el Suroeste/Noroeste y Mesoamérica, Casas en Acantilado y Arqueología de Salvamento. Este volumen que ahora presentamos, contiene 15 trabajos sobre tres de las sesiones de ponencias.

EL TEMA DEL SIMPOSIO

El *Southwest Symposium* empezó en 1988 y es el único evento que conjunta a arqueólogos profesionales para considerar temas pan-regionales de teoría, métodos e historia aborigen del área cultural que comprende el Suroeste/Noroeste. En un comentario frecuentemente citado, Erik Reed (1964:175) definió el área cultural–a la que preferimos referirnos como Suroeste/Noroeste–con una extensión que comprende desde Durango, Colorado, hasta Durango, México, y desde Las Vegas, Nevada,

Elisa Villalpando Centro INAH Sonora
Randall H. McGuire Binghamton University

hasta Las Vegas, New Mexico. Una rápida ojeada a un mapa revelará que casi la mitad de esta región se encuentra al sur de la frontera internacional entre México, y los Estados Unidos. El Southwest Symposium ha sido desde sus inicios el principal foro intelectual que trasciende activamente dicha frontera. Los arqueólogos mexicanos han participado en el simposio desde su primera realización en 1988 y éste ha sido el tercero que se realiza en México. Hermosillo fue la sede del 6º *Southwest Symposium* en 1998 (Villalpando 2002) y el Centro INAH Chihuahua en la ciudad de Chihuahua organizó el noveno en el 2002 (Webster et al. 2008); ambos simposios enfatizaron en sus temáticas las fronteras. Dudamos que todos los organizadores del primer *Southwest Symposium* en 1988 se habrían llegado a imaginar que veinte años más tarde una cuarta parte de los simposios se hubieran llevado a cabo en México, aunque estamos seguros que se sienten complacidos de que este sea el caso.

Muchas fronteras se entrecruzan en el área cultural del Suroeste/Noroeste dividiéndola en segmentos y creando "comunidades de práctica" (Minar y Crown 2001) dentro de tales fracciones. Estas fronteras, divisiones y partes, carecen definitivamente de significado para los antiguos habitantes nativos de la región, pero ha tenido significados profundos y consecuencias para los arqueólogos contemporáneos que estudian a esas poblaciones (McGuire 2002). La frontera internacional forma la más sobresaliente de tales divisorias, pero los límites estatales tanto en los Estados Unidos como en México también delinean de manera significativa la práctica de la arqueología. Los descendientes de los antiguos habitantes de la región definen sus propios territorios en desafío de las líneas marcadas por sus conquistadores. Las reservaciones indias en los Estados Unidos y las comunidades indígenas en México tienen claras demarcaciones impuestas por los modernos Estados-Nación, pero las naciones indígenas incluyen territorios que se extienden más allá de esas líneas modernas. En

el caso de los Cocopa, los Tohono O'odham y los Yaqui, la frontera internacional divide a las Naciones Indias quienes no reconocen la legitimidad de tales divisiones. Estas naciones, los Estados Unidos, México y las Naciones Indias, tienen su propio patrimonio y arqueología. Estas diversas arqueologías nacionales presentan un reto que requiere para resolverse, más que el cruce de fronteras. Los arqueólogos necesitamos comprometernos en la tarea aún más difícil de construir una arqueología transnacional. Tal arqueología deberá reconocer y llevar al máximo la diversidad de intereses nacionales, programas y contextos que realizamos en arqueología, pero también encontrar los puntos en común y los objetivos compartidos que facilitarán la colaboración entre los diversos escenarios nacionales. La arqueología del Suroeste/Noroeste siempre ha existido en este contexto multinacional, pero los académicos han ignorado ampliamente esta realidad hasta los albores del siglo XXI.

Durante la mayor parte del siglo XX, una decena de instituciones norteamericanas, sus profesores y sus estudiantes dominaron la arqueología del Suroeste de los Estados Unidos. El desarrollo de la arqueología de contrato o de salvamento en la década de los años setenta, extendió y alteró la práctica de la arqueología en el Suroeste, pero la reforzó como una práctica nacionalista. Sin embargo, para el inicio del siglo XXI, una visión nacionalista de la región se ve con tintes provincianos. Empezando en la década de los setenta, el Instituto Nacional de Antropología e Historia estableció centros regionales y museos y expandió la investigación antropológica e histórica del noroeste de México. Con la llegada del siglo XXI, en los Estados Unidos se desarrolló una arqueología Indigenista cuando las Naciones Indias establecieron sus propios programas arqueológicos, con sus objetivos y métodos particulares. Cada una de estas arqueologías "nacionales" se enfocó en diferentes regiones, hizo diferentes suposiciones, formuló distintas preguntas, ofreció respuestas disímiles, enfatizó métodos diferentes y comprendió diferentes teorías o formas de ver el mundo.

Las arqueologías transnacionales trascienden las fronteras nacionales y lo hacen de múltiples formas: Implican una visión amplia de los procesos históricos y culturales que han existido en el Suroeste/Noroeste, espacio que no debería estar artificialmente limitado por fronteras políticas, culturales o lingüísticas. Estas arqueologías transnacionales deberían ser arqueologías de emplazamientos múltiples, no obstante que los investigadores trabajen en diferentes "naciones." Las arqueologías transnacionales tendrán una sólida permanencia cuando sus bases descansan en una colaboración efectiva entre los grupos culturales, para lo cual se requiere de arqueólogos que estén de acuerdo en la necesidad de re-examinar las contribuciones que la disciplina puede aportar a la sociedad y expandir la arqueología del Suroeste/Noroeste lingüística, cultural y regionalmente.

LA ARQUEOLOGÍA Y LAS NACIONES EN EL SUROESTE/NOROESTE

Los contextos nacionales de la arqueología en el Suroeste/Noroeste difieren en términos de riqueza, poder, patrimonio y la práctica de la arqueología. Los tres contextos se sobreponen y entrelazan de maneras complejas que son necesarias de entender si pretendemos que nuestro trabajo sea transnacional. Haremos a continuación un breve resumen de las similitudes y diferencias. Dos de sesiones que se llevaron a cabo en el simposio: Colaboración Entre Culturas y Arqueología y Sociedad, destacan esos contextos nacionales y proponen cómo trabajar entre ellos.

Los Estados Unidos 0son sin lugar a dudas la nación más poderosa y rica en la región. Cientos de arqueólogos profesionales trabajan en el Suroeste (fácilmente más de 1000) y se llevan a cabo cientos de proyectos de campo

cada año. El número de sitios arqueológicos registrados es de cientos de miles. La cantidad de recursos monetarios destinados anualmente a la arqueología de la región puede llegar a las decenas de millones de dólares; un aproximado puede andar alrededor de los \$40 millones (Jeff Altschul, comunicación personal). Cada año existen múltiples proyectos con presupuestos de millones de dólares. La gran mayoría de este dinero se ejerce en la arqueología de salvamento por compañías privadas quienes se hacen cargo de los proyectos. Las leyes federales y de manera más notable, el Acuerdo de Preservación Histórico Nacional de 1968 (National Historic Preservation Act), mandata este trabajo en terrenos federales, por lo que los proyectos ahí realizados requieren de permisos federales o proyectos que usen dinero federal. Ya que las evidencias arqueológicas pertenecen al propietario de la tierra, no hay legislación para el trabajo arqueológico en proyectos en terrenos privados que usan dinero privado. Los arqueólogos de diferentes agencias federales de terrenos federales como el Servicio Nacional de Parques, el Servicio de Bosques Nacionales y la Oficina de Manejo de Tierras, supervisan la arqueología en terrenos de dichas agencias. Un Encargado de Preservación Histórica Estatal supervisa de conformidad con la legislación federal. Además de lo anterior, los estados y muchos condados y ciudades tienen su propio equipo de arqueólogos para administrar tales regulaciones.

La mayoría de la arqueología practicada en el Suroeste de los Estados Unidos estudia el pasado Indígena de la región, pero virtualmente todos los arqueólogos que llevan a cabo las investigaciones son euro-americanos. Los Estados Unidos incorporan a los habitantes Indígenas en su herencia cultural como los "Primeros Americanos"; esto es, como los primeros de una serie de gentes que entraron a Norteamérica y crearon los Estados Unidos (McGuire 2008). La ideología de los Primeros Americanos obscurece el hecho de que los Euro-

Americanos establecieron los Estados Unidos sobre tierras que pertenecían a los indígenas, pero les dan a los descendientes de tales grupos un lugar en el patrimonio cultural de la nación. La arqueología empezó en los Estados Unidos como el estudio de los otros, los indígenas, y el Suroeste ha sido tradicionalmente la región más intensivamente estudiada de todos los Estados Unidos (Fowler 2000). En las últimas décadas del siglo veinte, se presentaron conflictos considerables entre los Nativos Americanos y los arqueólogos (McGuire 1992); una de las consecuencias de este conflicto fue la creación del Acuerdo de Protección y Repatriación de Tumbas de los Nativos Americanos (NAGPRA; Native American Graves Protection and Repatriation Act en inglés), que establece que los restos humanos y los objetos rituales recuperados por los proyectos arqueológicos sean regresados a los descendientes contemporáneos indígenas.

México tiene una muy bien establecida y vibrante disciplina arqueológica que empezó a principios del siglo veinte (Bernal 1980; Lorenzo 1998). El número total de arqueólogos empleados profesionalmente en el país es de algunos cientos. Sin embargo, no más de diez tienen un empleo permanente en la arqueología y unas dos decenas trabajan en proyectos a contrato en Sonora y Chihuahua. Aunque existen cientos de miles de sitios arqueológicos registrados en todo México, el número de sitios registrados en Sonora y Chihuahua es de menos de 10,000. Los recursos destinados a la arqueología en el Noroeste de México es infinitamente menor que el del Suroeste de Estados Unidos. Como Paul Minnis (2003:2) ha señalado, el presupuesto de los más grandes proyectos arqueológicos individuales en el Suroeste de Estados Unidos regularmente excede la cantidad total de dinero jamás ejercido en la arqueología de Chihuahua; lo mismo puede decirse de Sonora.

A lo largo de casi todo el siglo XX, el Instituto Nacional de Antropología e Historia (INAH) como dependencia federal, llevó a cabo la mayor parte de la arqueología en México (Bernal 1980; Lorenzo 1998). La nación mexicana considera los vestigios arqueológicos como patrimonio nacional, por lo que los sitios arqueológicos pertenecen a la nación y no a los dueños particulares de las tierras. La legislación federal le otorga al INAH la protección, investigación y difusión de los sitios arqueológicos. En este sentido existe una legislación federal sobre patrimonio nacional y los estados, municipios, comunidades y ciudades, no tienen reglamentaciones separadas. Todos los arqueólogos que trabajan en México (tanto los nacionales como los extranjeros), deben obtener del mismo INAH (a través del Consejo de Arqueología), un permiso para llevar a cabo investigaciones en el país. El INAH tiene su propia escuela, la Escuela Nacional de Antropología e Historia (ENAH), en donde los estudiantes reciben capacitación para convertirse en arqueólogos, antropólogos, antropólogos físicos, lingüistas, historiadores y etnohistoriadores. En México no existe la arqueología de contrato privada ya que aunque los salvamentos se realicen con recursos procedentes de otras instituciones federales o de agencias privadas, el INAH es el único que puede llevarlos a cabo. Desde las últimas décadas del siglo XX, dos cambios parecen amenazar la hegemonía ejercida por el INAH en la arqueología en México (Vázquez León 2003). Numerosas universidades, incluyendo la Universidad Nacional Autónoma de México, ofrecen posgrados y licenciaturas en arqueología, realizan investigaciones y proporcionan una carrera en el ejercicio profesional fuera del INAH, lo cual en consideración de algunos, ha ocasionado que se presenten rivalidades entre los arqueólogos del INAH y los arqueólogos de las universidades (Vázquez León 2003); sin embargo, los egresados de la ENAH siguen siendo quienes reciben el mejor entrenamiento para llevar a cabo las tareas sustantivas de la institución, ya que la mayoría de quienes imparten los cursos son investigadores del propio INAH. El segundo cambio que enfrenta la arqueología oficial en México proviene de las iniciativas del Partido Acción Nacional (PAN), quienes han controlado el gobierno mexicano por casi todo el presente siglo; desde esa postura política se han presentado iniciativas dentro de la legislación federal que pretenden la privatización de las principales zonas arqueológicas y su incorporación como destinos turísticos con infraestructura procedente de capitales privados (McGuire 2008), o la modificación del estatus de institución de educación del propio INAH destacando la necesidad de inversiones redituables en los sitios arqueológicos con la disminución de los recursos destinados a la investigación y protección de tales sitios. No obstante, aun con todos estos cambios recientes, la arqueología mexicana continúa siendo mucho más centralizada y uniforme en su práctica que la arqueología en los Estados Unidos.

Posteriormente a la revolución mexicana la arqueología jugó un papel fundamental en la construcción de una identidad y un patrimonio nacional mexicano con base en el Indigenismo. El Indigenismo adoptó el discurso de un pasado indígena glorioso y fusionó a sus descendientes en una nación mestiza o de mezcla racial unificada. A diferencia de los arqueólogos de Estados Unidos, los arqueólogos mexicanos se consideran como los descendientes biológicos y culturales de los antiguos habitantes que investigan. En realidad en la actualidad el Indigenismo representa una perspectiva de élite, educada y urbana, que una visión de los mismos grupos indígenas. Los movimientos contemporáneos indígenas como el Zapatismo, rechazan la visión paternalista del Indigenismo. De manera cada vez más frecuente, especialmente en el norte de México, los grupos indígenas cuestionan el tratamiento de los restos arqueológicos como patrimonio nacional y pretenden controlarlos como su patrimonio.

Existen importantes similitudes en el lugar que ocupan las Naciones Indígenas en México y los Estados Unidos. Dichas similitudes resultan de las conquistas coloniales de los grupos indígenas que dieron origen a México y los Estados Unidos, ya que en ambos países las Naciones Indígenas terminaron subyugadas políticamente y desde la perspectiva económica son los más pobres de los pobres y su patrimonio se encuentra subsumido por el patrimonio nacional. Atrás de estas amplias similitudes subyacen importantes diferencias que afectan la práctica de una arqueología transnacional, especialmente en os casos donde la frontera internacional ha dividido el territorio de las Naciones Indígenas.

Las Naciones Indígenas en Estados Unidos tienen un estatus de semi-soberanía que en México no existe. En el suroeste de Estados Unidos, las reservaciones tienen sus propios gobiernos, elegidos por los miembros de cada nación indígena. Los estados, como Arizona o Nuevo México, no tienen autoridad sobre las reservaciones y las leyes estatales no aplican dentro del territorio de la reservación. Las naciones Americanas nativas tienen jurisdicción civil y de ofensas menores dentro de sus propias tierras, aunque si aplican las leyes federales de medio ambiente y preservación histórica. En México, los grupos indígenas tienen una autonomía muy restringida o no tienen. Legislaciones especiales otorgaron en la década de 1930 una mayor autonomía a los Yaquis del sur de Sonora respecto a otros grupos indígenas en México. Los cambios en la legislación mexicana de la primera década del siglo XXI les otorgaron una mayor autonomía aunque tienen aun menor soberanía que las naciones Americanas Nativas.

En un sentido relativo los indígenas constituyen los grupos más pobres en ambos países. Sin embargo, en términos absolutos las naciones indígenas de Estados Unidos tienen muchos más recursos y bienestar que los grupos mexicanos. Esto refleja en parte la mayor riqueza absoluta de los Estados Unidos con respecto a México. El mayor bienestar de los grupos de Estados Unidos también es el resultado de las habilidades que han desarrollado los gobiernos Americanos Nativos para obtener ganancias de la explotación de los recursos naturales que se encuentran dentro de su territorio y de los programas del gobierno federal. La mayoría de las Naciones Indígenas del suroeste de Estados Unidos han instalado casinos dentro de sus reservaciones, casinos que las leyes estatales prohíben pero están autorizados por la legislación federal. El juego no ha vuelto ricos a los indígenas ni ha elevado sus niveles de vida al promedio de los Estados Unidos; el juego y las apuestas únicamente ha permitido a los gobiernos indígenas obtener más dinero para proporcionar más servicios a su gente.

La posición política y económica de las naciones Nativas Americanas les ha dado más control sobre su patrimonio que a los grupos indígenas mexicanos. Las primeras son propietarias y controlan los sitios arqueológicos que se encuentran dentro de sus reservaciones; fuera de ellas, NAGPRA les otorga una voz activa en la investigación arqueológica y en los derechos de repatriación de los restos humanos y objetos sagrados recuperados de las excavaciones. Las naciones del Suroeste han nombrado comités culturales que resguardan tales derechos; los arqueólogos deben consultar con tales comités para cumplir con las disposiciones de NAGPRA. Ya que las leyes estatales y los gobiernos no tienen autoridad sobre las naciones nativas americanas, los oficiales de Conservación Histórica Estatal no pueden supervisar conforme a la ley federal de preservación histórica lo que ocurre dentro de las reservaciones; son los oficiales de Preservación Histórica Tribal de las Naciones Americanas los que se encargan de tal supervisión. Las naciones del Suroeste emplean a sus propios arqueólogos, tienen programas de salvamento arqueológico tribal y sus propios museos. Aunque son principalmente profesionistas euro-americanos los que conforman los equipos para llevar a cabo tales programas, de manera cada vez más creciente los gobiernos tribales están contratando profesionistas nativos americanos en tales posiciones. La mayor pobreza

de las naciones indígenas Mexicanas da por resultado que se encuentren más preocupados en asuntos económicos que en la preservación del patrimonio. Algunos grupos indígenas del área Maya en el sureste mexicano que han tomado el control de las zonas arqueológicas, parecen haber sido motivados más por el dinero que pueden obtener de la presencia del turismo en tales sitios, que realmente sobre el control de su patrimonio. Como sabemos, la legislación federal mexicana le otorga el control de toda la arqueología al INAH.

La sesión Colaboración entre Culturas del XI Southwest Symposium discutió como trabajar pese a tales diferencias. Los organizadores de la sesión fueron Andrew Darling de la Comunidad India del Río Gila y Davina Two Bears del Departamento Arqueológico Navajo. La comunicación que trasciende o va más allá de las fronteras nacionales y culturales es clave en la arqueología transnacional. De igual manera, la colaboración implica la integración de objetivos, intereses y prácticas entre los individuos y/o los grupos sociales que trabajan juntos, conlleva un diálogo que va más allá de un interés instrumentalista para resolver un conflicto o para respetar derechos y responsabilidades. Requiere de humildad, paciencia, saber escuchar, consulta cuidadosa, igualdad y respeto. La colaboración debe ser transformativa de las partes que intervienen, cada una de las cuales aporta diferentes recursos, habilidades, conocimientos, autoridad y/o intereses para un trabajo conjunto. La colaboración implica la declaración de tales cualidades únicas hacia objetivos y prácticas comunes. Esta sesión dirigió sus esfuerzos hacia la colaboración a través de la frontera internacional y entre los escolares y las Naciones Indígenas; sin embargo, los organizadores de esta sesión decidieron no enviar sus trabajos para este volumen.

La sesión Arqueología y Sociedad exploró tales relaciones en los Estados Unidos, en México y ente las Naciones Indígenas. Elizabeth Bagwell de Aspen Environmental Group y César Villalobos del Instituto de Investigaciones Antropológicas UNAM organizaron esta sesión. Las ponencias presentadas en esta sesión discutieron sobre programas públicos, educación, patrimonio e identidad. Buscando comparar y contrastar dichos asuntos en las diferentes naciones con el objetivo de trascender y llegar más allá de los intereses nacionales. El presente volumen incluye seis de las ponencias presentadas que se desarrollaron como artículos: uno de ellos por investigadores de los Estados Unidos, cuatro de México y uno de la Nación Tohono O'odham.

EXPANDIENDO EL SUROESTE/ NOROESTE EN ESPACIO Y TIEMPO

La frontera internacional ha estructurado la investigación arqueológica en una manera que no tiene nada que ver con la historia antigua de los grupos aborígenes nativos del Suroeste/Noroeste. Los diplomáticos dibujaron la actual frontera a mediados del siglo XIX siguiendo líneas de latitud y longitud que no tienen ningún sentido en relación con la cultura o la geografía física de la región. La frontera ha afectado las áreas que enfatizan los arqueólogos en sus investigaciones y ha creado zonas ambiguas en el tiempo y en el espacio, que no tienen que ver con la atención arqueológica. En el XI Southwest Symposium nos enfocamos en dos de tales espacios ambiguos: Occidente y Norte de México y el Siglo Perdido: 1450 -1540 d.C.

OCCIDENTE Y NORTE DE MÉXICO

La frontera internacional entre México y los Estados Unidos y la frontera del área cultural que separa nuestra región de Mesoamérica, por largo tiempo ha obstaculizado la comprensión de la arqueología del Suroeste/Noroeste. La arqueología del Occidente y del Norte de México no cabe totalmente dentro de ninguna de las áreas

culturales y el grado de inclusión definitivamente cambia a través del tiempo. Sin embargo los desarrollos que ocurrieron en tales áreas tuvieron impactos directos en el Suroeste/Noroeste. De hecho las "influencias mesoamericanas" en el norte, de manera más precisa se originaron en esas regiones y no en el núcleo central de Mesoamérica. La sesión dedicada al Occidente y Norte de México permitió el intercambio de información y la interacción entre arqueólogos del Occidente y Norte con los del Suroeste/ Noroeste. José Luis Punzo, adscrito entonces al Centro INAH Durango y Michael Ohnersorgen de University of Missouri, Saint Louis, organizaron esta sesión. Este volumen incluye tres capítulos de esta sesión, dos de colegas mexicanos y uno de un colega norteamericano.

Una notable similitud en las formas de los ornamentos de concha es una de las marcadas consistencias entre el Suroeste/Noroeste y el Occidente de México. José Carlos Beltrán del Centro INAH Nayarit, discute en su capítulo las diferencias y semejanzas entre ambos conjuntos. John P. Carpenter, del Centro INAH Sonora, nos presenta un texto sobre la ocupación prehispánica del Río Fuerte, lo cual constituye una notable incorporación de datos significativos a la poco conocida frontera entre el Suroeste/Noroeste y el Occidente de México. Michael Searcy de Brigham Young University, desarrolla en su texto una revisión de las diferencias culturales y contextuales de la iconografía de Mesoamérica en el Suroeste/Noroeste.

EL SIGLO PERDIDO: 1450-1540 D.C.

Durante el periodo comprendido entre el 1450 y 1540 d.C. gran parte del Suroeste/Noroeste sufrió un colapso demográfico significativo que ocasionó una transformación de las culturas existentes. Muchas de las secuencias regionales terminan en esas fechas y la agricultura sustentada en aldeas cesó en áreas donde había sido practicada por cientos de años. Fuera del área de los Pueblos, este es un siglo que hace difícil ligar las tradiciones arqueológicas y las Naciones Indias modernas, al igual que entender los procesos que originaron el Suroeste/Noroeste etnográficamente. La frontera internacional ha restringido nuestro entendimiento de este siglo, debido a que estructura la investigación, pero no tiene significado dentro de los procesos históricos y culturales que pretendemos entender. Las Naciones Indias tienen diferentes perspectivas sobre este siglo respecto a las de los académicos de Estados Unidos y México. John Carpenter del Centro INAH Sonora y Anna Neuzil de EcoPlan Associates fueron los organizadores de esta sesión en el simposio y se recibieron cinco trabajos para su publicación en el presente volumen, cuatro de académicos norteamericanos y uno de dos colegas mexicanos.

Hemos incluido cuatro capítulos de esta sesión en el presente volumen, tres de investigadores de Estados Unidos y uno de investigadores de México. Matt Peeples de Archaeology Southwest en Tucson, Arizona, nos proporciona una síntesis de la historia de Zuni Pueblo entre 1450 y 1540 d.C., Patrick D. Lyons, director de Arizona State Museum, J. Brett Hill de Hendrix College y Jeffrey J. Clark de Archaeology Southwest revisaron el tema del continuo Hohokam - Pima en el sur de Arizona; aplican un modelo tipo "canal entrelazado" y concluyen que existieron asociaciones culturales entre los hablantes de Hohokam y Pima. Matthew F. Schmader de la Ciudad de Albuquerque se acerca al siglo XVI en New Mexico y examina la expedición de Vázquez de Coronado de 1540-1542, el contecto sociopolítico y los detalles de su organización, además de los impactos de la violencia sobre las poblaciones indígenas durante "El siglo perdido." Finalmente, John P. Carpenter del Centro INAH Sonora y Guadalupe Sánchez de la Estación Regional Noroeste del Instituto de Geología de la UNAM, nos regresan a la frontera entre el Suroeste/Noroeste y el Occidente de

México en el límite entre Sonora y Sinaloa, para discutir el periodo proto-histórico en esta crítica región.

EL IDIOMA

Los idiomas nacionales, inglés y español, son un reto en nuestra intención para crear una arqueología transnacional. Las diferencias de idiomas presentan problemas en los proyectos binacionales, en el entrenamiento de estudiantes, así como en la comunicación entre académicos y la publicación de resultados. Los arqueólogos generalmente resuelven estos problemas usando un idioma más que el otro, y de manera más común tal idioma es el inglés. Los investigadores y estudiantes que desean participar de una arqueología transnacional necesitan ser bilingües en inglés y español, ya que aquellos que no lo son, no pueden tener dominio y revisión de la literatura producida y de la investigación realizada en todo el Suroeste/Noroeste.

La competencia en ambos idiomas varía de manera significativa entre los arqueólogos de Estados Unidos y México. Entre los arqueólogos formados en México se espera que lean en inglés y los profesores de arqueología, generalmente incluyen en sus asignaturas textos en inglés. Aunque la competencia actual de los arqueólogos mexicanos en inglés varía considerablemente, casi todos pueden leer artículos y libros en ese idioma; sin embargo esta competencia no implica necesariamente que puedan hablar y entender el idioma. En los Estados Unidos, la mayoría de los programas en antropología requieren que sus estudiantes lean en un segundo idioma, pero estos requerimientos rara vez se hacen cumplir con rigor. Sabemos también que no hay programa en los Estados Unidos que requiera que los estudiantes en preparación para carreras profesionales en la arqueología del Suroeste/ Noroeste estudien español. Los profesores de arqueología en los Estados Unidos no asignan tampoco de manera rutinaria textos en español en sus clases y seminarios.

En cada *Southwest Symposium* el idioma ha limitado la participación y comunicación entre los arqueólogos, por lo que en el XI Simposio del Suroeste tuvimos traducción simultánea durante las sesiones de ponencias, tal y como ha ocurrido en los dos simposios previamente realizados en México. Ninguno de los *Southwest Simposium* que se han llevado a cabo en los Estados Unidos ha contado con traducción simultánea. Sabemos que esto refleja–en parte–el hecho ineludible de que el costo de tal servicio es mucho más alto en los Estados Unidos que en México, pero explica la participación más numerosa de arqueólogos y estudiantes mexicanos en los eventos realizados en México. Cada sesión del XI *Southwest Symposium* incluyó ponencias en inglés y en español; todos los autores prepararon un resumen amplio de su ponencia en ambos idiomas, los cuales fueron incluidos en el programa. Les fue solicitado a los autores que prepararan su presentación visual en el idioma contrario de su presentación verbal, o que usaran ambos idiomas en su presentación gráfica, lo cual cumplieron prácticamente todos ellos. De igual manera solicitamos que cada cartel fuera bilingüe o que se presentara un cartel en cada idioma, lo cual también se cumplió en todos los casos.

Sin embargo, existen dos literaturas arqueológicas para el Suroeste/Noroeste, una publicada en inglés en los Estados Unidos y otra publicada en español en México. Las editoriales e instituciones distribuyen estas obras a través de diferentes redes, volviendo bastante difícil para los académicos el conocer, localizar y comprar las publicaciones del otro país. El *Southwest Symposium* ha sido uno de los principales lugares en el Suroeste/Noroeste en donde ambas literaturas convergen y en donde se ayuda a la distribución de ideas a través de la frontera internacional. Los simposios realizados en México fueron ambos publicados en inglés. En esta ocasión decidimos no hacerlo para incentivar a los colegas canadienses y norteamericanos a aprender español y no esperar que toda la literatura importante se traduzca al inglés. Una arqueología transnacional debe ser al menos bilingüe y este volumen es por consiguiente, bilingüe. La editorial de la Universidad de Colorado ha publicado la mayoría de los volúmenes de los *Southwest Symposium* anteriores, pero no están posibilitados para publicar textos en español; sin embargo el Museo Estatal de Arizona si puede hacerlo, por lo cual reciben este volumen a través de la Serie Arqueológica del Museo Estatal de Arizona.

El *Southwest Symposium* ha sido un esfuerzo fundamental en el estudio de la arqueología del Suroeste/Noroeste. Ha jugado también un lugar clave para trascender las fronteras internacionales y estatales que dividen el estudio de la región. El XI Southwest Symposium ha continuado tales contribuciones enfocándose en la construcción de una arqueología transnacional. Los capítulos presentados en este libro constituyen un avance importante en el logro de este objetivo.

Agradecimientos Agradecemos en primer lugar a la Mesa Directiva del Southwest Symposium que apoyó entusiastamente la realización de este evento en Hermosillo, pese al clima de inseguridad de Sonora que empezaba a ser conocido al norte de la frontera. De igual manera agradecemos a la Secretaría Técnica del Instituto Nacional de Antropología e Historia que complementó con recursos institucionales los fondos propios del simposio, encargándose de la papelería, impresos y la cena de clausura que se realizó en las instalaciones del Museo de Sonora en la Antigua Penitenciaría. No podríamos haber realizado este evento sin el patrocinio desinteresado de Archaeology Southwest, School of Anthropology de University of Arizona, School of Human Evolution and Social Change de Arizona State University, Statistical Research, Inc., University of Colorado, William Self Associates Inc., Department of Anthropology de Binghamton University y Anthropological Research, L.L.C. Gracias a Binghamton University por haber albergado la página web del simposio y al Centro INAH Sonora por haber proporcionado personal de apoyo previo y durante el evento. El Museo de Sonora destinó personal para el montaje de los carteles en las instalaciones del Centro de las Artes de la Universidad de Sonora, cuyo diligente personal estuvo siempre atento al desarrollo adecuado del evento; a todos ellos les damos las gracias. De manera muy especial tienen nuestro agradecimiento los jóvenes arqueólogos sonorenses que apoyaron en la logística y fotografía durante los días del evento, así como los arqueólogos de la Escuela de Antropología de la Universidad de Arizona que colaboraron manejando las vans en que se transportaron muchos de los asistentes de Tucson a Hermosillo.

West and North Mexico
Occidente y Norte de México

Part I, Introduction
West and North Mexico

Michael A. Ohnersorgen and José Luis Punzo Díaz

West and North Mexico, considered together here as "Northwest Mexico," have held a somewhat ambiguous status within the broader context of New World archaeology. Situated between the intensively studied archaeological culture areas of the American Southwest and Mesoamerica, Northwest Mexico encompasses an expansive, environmentally diverse, but archaeologically ill-defined region that remains poorly understood relative to its neighboring regions to the north and south (Wilcox 1986). Unlike the sharply-defined international political border that readily separates modern Mexico and the southwest United States, the separation between the ancient Southwest and Mesoamerica is not so clear. Rather, it consists of a much broader, fuzzier, and diachronically variant zone of cultural distinctions and overlapping, shared influences spread across northern Mexico. For various reasons, this discrepancy between modern political boundaries and ancient culture areas has hampered our understanding of the archaeology of both the Southwest and Mesoamerica, and, in order to better understand either, we must also improve our understanding of Northwest Mexico.

For the purposes of this symposium, we consider Northwest Mexico as including the modern Mexican states of Jalisco, Nayarit, Aguascalientes, Zacatecas, Durango, Sinaloa, Chihuahua, and Sonora. Our inclusion of these states is merely a reflection of the scope of papers that contributed to our session, not an attempt to define a discrete geographic or archaeological

culture area. Other scholars have attempted to describe and delineate Northwest Mexico as a distinct geographic and/or cultural unit; such definitions have varied according to the purposes of particular scholars and, in part, reflect historical trends in research in the area and changes in theoretical perceptions about Northwest Mexico and its relationships to Mesoamerica and/or the U.S. Southwest (see e.g., Braniff 1993, 2001:7-12; Brown 1985; Di Peso 1968, 1974; Foster 1986; Foster and Gorenstein 2000; Foster and Weigand 1985; Gorenstein and Foster 2000; Mathien and McGuire 1986; Pailes and Whitecotton 1995; Reyman 1995; Riley 2005; Schaafsma and Riley 1999; Wilcox 1986).

The various ways in which Northwest Mexico has been conceptualized contributes considerably to the ambiguity of this area. The northernmost portions of modern Mexico, in particular the northern portions of Chihuahua and Sonora, bear sufficient material culture similarities to the archaeology of the U.S. Southwest that they are generally considered the southern extension of the Southwestern cultural traditions, and frequently considered within the conceptual phrase, "*the Greater Southwest*" (Lister 1961:39; see also Riley 1976, 1987, 2005:1-7). In a similar manner, West and Northwest Mexico (up to the modern U.S.-Mexico border) have been described as "*Greater Mesoamerica*" (Foster and Gorenstein 2000; Gorenstein and Foster 2000). Still other scholars have described Northwest Mexico as a somewhat more autonomous geo-

Michael A. Ohnersorgen University of Missouri, St. Louis
José Luis Punzo Díaz Centro INAH Michoacán

cultural entity, using terms derived from native descriptions such as *"the Gran Chichimeca," "Chichimecatlalli," "the Chichimec Sea,"* (e.g., Di Peso 1968, 1974; Braniff 1993, 2001; Mathien and McGuire 1986; Pohl 2001; Reyman 1995), or *"Aztlan,"* (Fields and Zamudio-Taylor 2001; Riley 2005), concepts that can encompass the Northwest Mexico along with various portions of the more traditionally defined American Southwest or Mesoamerica. But whether we view Northwest Mexico as a culturally independent area, or where exactly the Southwest ends and Mesoamerica begins, and how to explain shared cultural influences among these regions, remains problematic (Foster 1986; Pailes and Whitecotton 1995). As Braniff laments, what constitutes the Southwest, Mesoamerica, and even the Gran Chichimeca, culturally and geographically, "is not at all clear" (1993:66). There exist broad areas of Northwest Mexico that do not "fit" easily into the Southwest or Mesoamerican culture areas, and the degree of fit changes over time. Nonetheless, it can be said that Northwest Mexico formed part of a more broadly integrated landscape of interactions across space and over time, and developments here had direct impacts on the cultures of the American Southwest. Indeed, some "Mesoamerican influences" on the north most likely originated in these regions and not the core of Mesoamerica, or at least moved through these areas and may have been uniquely transformed or reinterpreted in the process.

Theoretical frameworks for understanding Northwest Mexico have changed considerably over time, and the reader is referred to other recent sources for a deeper discussion of this history (e.g., Braniff 1993; Gorenstein and Foster 2000; Mathien and McGuire 1986; Pailes and Whitecotton 1995; Riley 2005; Schaafsma and Riley 1999; Whalen and Minnis 2001; Wilcox 1986). Despite a longstanding acknowledgment of connections between Mesoamerica and the Southwest, the intervening Northwest Mexican region generally has been considered as being somewhat marginal to both culture areas, a real part of neither. Additionally, it is often discussed relative to the Southwest or Mesoamerica – in terms of connections and similarities rather than of indigenous local or regional processes (Wilcox 1986:9), a fact reflected in terms like *"frontier," "periphery," "margin,"* or *"intermediate area,"* which are frequently used to describe it.

Pailes and Whitecotton (1995) note that, historically, Northwest Mexico has not attracted as much research attention as the neighboring areas to its north and south. Further, they summarize historical trends in archaeological thinking among Southwestern and Mesoamerican archaeologists to show how this theoretical history, coupled with the influence of the culture area concept, has tended to isolate the Southwest and Mesoamerica as separate cultural phenomena, leaving the status of the intermediate area (i.e., Northwest Mexico) in a state of limbo. Research during the 1950-1960s in the northwest, in particular at Paquimé, along with a growing body of evidence of Mesoamerican influence from Southwestern sites, made it clear that Northwest Mexico needed to be considered as a significant player in ideas about long-distance interactions between Mesoamerica and the Southwest. Early explanations of such interaction were initially somewhat heavy-handed, emphasizing interregional trade as a form of Mesoamerican political-economic imperialism (e.g., Di Peso 1974; Kelley 1986; Kelley and Kelley 1975). Such interpretations were met with considerable resistance from Southwestern archaeologists, whose initial discounting of the influence of Mesoamerican interactions led to a polarized milieu of competing, isolationist-imperialist perspectives (McGuire 1993; Whalen and Minnis 2001:25-58). Archaeologists have moved past this polarized atmosphere to some degree, generally acknowledging some level of Mesoamerican influence in the Southwest, although the degree, nature, and impact of such influence remains uncertain. In recent years, a variety of models of interaction have been employed to engage our thinking about Mesoamerican-Southwest relationships, productively emphasizing aspects of world systems, interaction spheres, prestige exchange economies, and the role of ideology (see e.g., Foster 1986; Mathien and McGuire 1986; McGuire 1980; Pailes and Whitecotton 1995; Riley 2005; Wilcox 1986). These and newer models are actively being examined as new data accumulates, and explaining Mesoamerican-Southwest interaction is still an active pursuit.

A critical element of our understanding of the relationships between Mesoamerica and the Southwest has been the role of sites in Northwest Mexico, much of which can still be considered *terra incognita*. As the above-described theoretical ideas were being tossed about, it was clear that too many gaps existed in our knowledge of the Northwest, and new information was crucial to examining various models that depended on basic archaeological data about regional settlement patterns and site chronologies, political organization, economy and craft production, relative social complexity of Northwest Mexican populations, and how such sites across the area actually were integrated within broader realms of interregional interaction. As Whalen and Minnis (2001) point out, apart from research at a few isolated sites in Northwest Mexico, there is no regional context to understand to role of this area. During the last three decades, archaeologists have increasingly developed research programs in Northwest Mexico that have targeted these issues through more systematic field research that has stimulated fresh, exciting ideas. As new data and insights are accumulating, Northwest Mexico is becoming recognized in its own right as a region of tremendous cultural diversity and significant cultural accomplishments (for some recent syntheses see Braniff 2001; Ericson and Baugh 1993; Foster and Gorenstein 2000; Reyman 1995; Riley 2005; Schaafsma and Riley 1999; Whalen and Minnis 2001; Woosley and Ravesloot 1993). Further, as Mesoamerican and Southwestern

scholars continue to refine their understanding of their respective areas, and to grapple with the causes and significance of connections between them, it is clear that additional research and data from the West and North Mexican region will be critical to understand local cultural formations and their role in, and influence on, broader cultural developments and interactions.

The papers that were part of this session in no way represent a cohesive effort to address these longstanding issues or to engage a new theoretical paradigm, nor do we even focus in particular on Mesoamerican-Southwest interaction in this section (although some session participants did address this issue). A continuing obstacle to our understanding of the archaeology of Northwest Mexico, one being addressed through this symposium, has been the modern political, cultural, and language differences between the United States and Mexico that have resulted in few Southwest scholars becoming familiar with Mexican research and literature about the area, and few Mexican scholars becoming acquainted with the research and literature of their U.S. Southwestern counterparts (Kelley 1993). The focus of this symposium was to foster communication and the sharing of ideas, and to promote transnational collaboration. Our particular session was designed to highlight new research taking place throughout West and North Mexico and to bring together archaeologists from both sides of the border to interact and share information about ongoing research about which they may not be aware.

The papers presented in the symposium session in Hermosillo covered a variety of topics, time periods, and geographic subregions within Northwest Mexico. Unfortunately, not all of the scheduled presenters were able to attend to the symposium or submit a paper. As a result, the following papers were presented:

José C. Beltrán M. (Centro INAH Nayarit): *Materiales de Concha en el Occidente, el*

Noroeste de México y el Suroeste de los Estados Unidos / Shell Artifacts from West and Northwest Mexico and the American Southwest

Ben A. Nelson (Arizona State University) and Michael Ohnersorgen (University of Missouri – St. Louis):
Mesoamerican-Southwestern Interaction and Local Political Action / Interacción e Acción Política Local entre Mesoamérica y el Suroeste

M. Nicolás Caretta (Universidad Autónoma de San Luis Potosí), Mario Pérez (Geósfera), and Jorge Martinez (Geósfera):
Ni Todos Nómadas, Ni Todos Sedentarios: El Sitio de Cerro de Santiago, Aguascalientes / Not All Nomads, Not All Sedentary: Cerro de Santiago, Aguascalientes

John Carpenter (Centro INAH Sinaloa):
La Ocupación prehispánica del Valle del Río Fuerte, Sinaloa / The Prehispanic Occupation of the Río Fuerte Valley, Sinaloa

Michael Searcy (University of Oklahoma):
Cultural and Contextual Differentiation of Mesoamerican Iconography in the Southwest/ Northwest / Diferencias Culturales y Contextuales de la Iconografía de Mesoamérica en el Suroeste/ Noroeste

Michael Mathiowetz (University of California, Riverside):
"Seeking Sìitukwi (Flower Mountain)": Integrating Indigenous Oral Traditions and Archaeology in Northwest Mexico and the America Southwest/"Buscando Sìitukwi (Montaña Flor)": Integrando las tradiciones orales indígenas en el Noroeste de México y el Suroeste de los Estados Unidos

For various reasons, not all presenters were able to submit papers for publication in this volume. Subsequently, this section includes contributions from José C. Beltrán, Nicolás Caretta and Peter Kröfges, John Carpenter, and Michael Searcy. We hope to see the remaining contributions quickly published elsewhere.

We have identified several major themes that tend to characterize and/or crosscut the presentations: interregional relationships, economy and craft production, iconography, and regional synthesis; some presentations touched on more than one of these. These themes have been developed over the years in numerous prior publications dealing with Northwest Mexico. Perhaps the topic most commonly addressed was that of interregional relationships, a theme that ran through all of the presentations at some level, and one that underscores the important role of Northwest Mexico in broader interregional connections.

Beltrán's study of the role of marine shell, for example, highlights the long-standing role of this fundamental material in exchanges that integrated the cultures of coastal West Mexico with the rest of Mesoamerica, with the U.S. Southwest, and even with coastal Central America and Ecuador. His paper simultaneously addresses themes of economy and craft production, as he discusses the exploitation and multiple uses (sumptuary and utilitarian) of various marine and estuarine species, along with the production and distribution of shell objects, based on his extensive research at coastal sites in Nayarit, Colima and Jalisco. Much of his discussion focuses on exchange networks to the north, with shell ultimately ending up in the U.S. Southwest, most likely in exchange for turquoise. He contextualizes this economic activity culturally as well as chronologically, framing production and exchange within local developments, such as the Aztatlán Tradition florescence, and broader contexts of external demand. His paper is a welcome complement to prior studies of shell in Mesoamerican interactions, such as those by Bradley (1993, 2000), Manzo (1983), and Suárez (1988, 1989, 2007).

The presentations by Nelson and Ohnersorgen, Mathiowetz, and Searcy more specifically addressed the issue of Mesoamerican-Southwest relationships, emphasizing a variety of approaches and bringing new data and perspectives to our understanding of this complex issue. Nelson and Ohnersorgen (whose presentation is not published here) pointed out that many prior attempts to characterize Mesoamerican-Southwest relationships have tended focus on single classes of items (e.g., copper bells, macaws, or turquoise) and to treat interactions as a single phenomenon that could be characterized under general models such as commercialism, mercantilism, or political economy (see e.g., Di Peso 1974, 1979; Ericson and Baugh 1993; Kelley 1986, 2000; Mathien and McGuire 1986; Vargas 2001; Weigand and Weigand 2001). They suggest that such models can be better evaluated by more detailed examinations that tease apart the geographic and temporal distributions of different types of goods and symbols involved in interactions, as well at their unique archaeological contexts. Their evaluation of data about Mesoamerican objects from Pueblo Bonito and other Southwestern sites suggests that most such "goods" derived through long-distance interactions served as sacred objects, likely used to mediate social relations and sanctify local political and religious authority, rather than serve as economic commodities. Their approach complements recently proposed ideas by Pohl (2001) and Schaafsma and Riley (1999) that emphasis the ritual roles of leaders and their manipulation of material culture.

Searcy, whose paper is included in this volume, and Mathiowetz (not included here) both explored religious iconography and ideology to better clarify Mesoamerican-Southwest interactions. Their papers add to a small but growing body of research about the role and influence of Mesoamerican ideology in the American Southwest (see e.g., Farmer 2001; Schaafsma 1994, 1999, 2001; Taube 2001). Searcy examines the occurrences of Mesoamerican symbols on pottery from different cultural contexts in the Southwest to illuminate how such iconography might have functioned in different societies and why foreign symbols may have been adopted in local contexts. Through his study of more than 600 pottery vessels from sites in the Salado and Chihuahuan cultural areas, he identifies 10 Mesoamerican iconographic motifs and assesses their frequency on vessels. In order to help gauge the potential use of Mesoamerican iconography in legitimizing local political authority in these areas, Searcy further compares the distribution of motifs at sites that he categorizes as relatively "more hierarchical" or "less hierarchical," and additionally discusses the distribution of other Mesoamerican interaction markers in the Salado and Chihuahuan areas. Interestingly, he finds a greater frequency of Mesoamerican iconographic motifs in the Chihuahan area, where a number of such motifs occur more frequently at more hierarchical sites. He suggests an adoption of foreign religious symbolism in local political contexts that were somewhat exclusive. In contrast, the Salado area is characterized by a relatively lower frequency and more even distribution of Mesoamerican iconography, suggesting a culturally more inclusive adoption of symbols that were less politically charged than in Chihuahuan contexts.

Mathiowetz additionally explored Mesoamerican religious iconography and sociopolitical organization in the Southwest, focusing on elements of the Mesoamerican Flower World ritual complex manifested at Paquimé, Chihuahua. Through an examination of the relationships between archaeological data at Paquime and various aspects of Southwestern Puebloan culture (oral traditions, migration accounts, and ritual practices), Mathiowetz proposed that the appearance of Mesoamerican symbols and practices at Paquimé marked the introduction of a cohesive religious complex, closely tied to political authority, that may have been introduced by migrants from West Mexico where the related Aztatlán tradition is found. Although previous scholars have similarly proposed a strong, direct connection between the Southwest and West Mexico's Aztatlán tradition (e.g., Foster 1999; Kelley 2000), these largely emphasize economic connections. In contrast, Mathiowetz highlighted the roles of social agency and religion in events that dramatically transformed the sociopolitical landscape of much of northern Mexico and the American Southwest during the Pueblo IV period.

Other contributions synthesize the results of recent fieldwork in Aguascalientes (Caretta and Kröfges) and in Sinaloa (Carpenter), and contextualize these new data as they relate to broader regional and interregional themes in Northwest Mexico. The archaeology of Aguascalientes is not well known, yet as Caretta and Kröfges point out in this volume, it is often discounted as an area on the edge of Mesoamerica's traditional boundaries, occupied by nomadic hunter-gatherers, and marginal to developments in the interior of Mesoamerica or its interactions with the Southwest. They attempt to dispel this characterization through both a review of theoretical literature on Mesoamerican-Southwest interaction, arguing that while some previously proposed models may have relevance; Northwest Mexico has a unique history, or histories, of development that resulted in different forms and intensities of interaction over time among Northwest Mexico, nuclear Mesoamerica, and the Southwest. They review prior research in the state of Aguascalientes and present data from the newly-mapped site of Cerro de Santiago, a large and impressive political center with several platforms, plazas, and a ballcourt. Cerro de Santiago appears to be contemporaneous with several other key centers that developed in Northwest Mexico, in particular La Quemada (Zacatecas), and it provides clear evidence that large, complex sedentary communities were present in Aguascalientes. Such sites, they argue, were critical to interrelationships between

nuclear Mesoamerica and areas to the north (i.e., Northwest Mexico/U.S. Southwest). Future research at Cerro de Santiago should allow us to better understand the roles of such regional centers and provide data to test the relevance of various theoretical models of interaction that pertain to this region.

Carpenter, in his contribution to this volume, summarizes the results of archaeological survey and excavation conducted since 2004 as part of the Instituto Nacional de Antropología e Historia's Proyecto Arqueológico Norte de Sinaloa. The project focuses on collecting new information from the Río Fuerte Valley in northern Sinaloa, a region he describes as being at the margins of the larger West Mexican and Northwest/Southwest cultural traditions. Data from more than 100 sites identified during survey indicate that the Río Fuerte Valley exhibits a long history of occupation and adaptation to diverse environments that include rich coastal zones, fertile river valleys, and forested uplands. Carpenter identifies and describes two related Cahita cultural traditions in the study zone: the lowland/coastal Huatabampo tradition and the upland Serrana (Río Sonora) tradition, whose differences largely reflect distinct environmental adaptations. Data from particular sites within the study zone suggest long-standing cultural affinities with the Southwest's Mogollon tradition, as well as clear evidence of interaction at various times with other parts of West Mexico/Mesoamerica, in particular with West Mexico's Aztatlán tradition. Such periods of broader interaction provided local opportunities for craft production and trade, which Carpenter suggests were most likely associated with a prestige goods economy. The Cahitan cultural traditions, Carpenter argues, are primarily local developments unique to the Río Fuerte Valley, at times influenced by interregional interactions, but never integrated in external political-economic structures.

Collectively, the contributions of the West and North Mexico session to this published volume reflect an active research landscape, in which new data are emerging, new questions are being asked, and new theories are being proposed. This is a good thing for our understanding of the archaeology of the Southwest and for Mesoamerica, and, of course, for the intervening area of Northwest Mexico. Let us hope that such research continues fruitfully, and that the spirit of transnational communication and collaboration fostered by this symposium also continues, to the benefit of us all.

Part I, Chapter 1

Los materiales de concha en el Occidente de Mesoamérica y su presencia en el Suroeste Americano

José Carlos Beltrán Medina

RESUMEN

Esta ponencia presenta información por algunas de las especies de concha y los materiales que aparecen con mayor frecuencia tanto en el Occidente como en el noroeste de México y/o Suroeste norteamericano, los cuales muestran gran parecido tanto en su técnica de manufactura, como en sus formas y acabados. En efecto el litoral costero fue el lugar de origen de la mayoría de las especies y materiales encontrados en el Suroeste. La importancia de la concha se debió a su intenso aprovechamiento como recurso alimenticio, así como por sus diversos usos y funciones, destacando la variedad y calidad de los artefactos elaborados, pero de manera especial por la carga simbólica con la que estaban revestidas algunas especies. Por lo tanto existió una amplia distribución de sus productos, especialmente en las áreas nucleares. La concha es un material arqueológico de importancia para entender los procesos de integración cultural que se dieron entre diversas regiones culturales del continente, ya que junto con el metal, la turquesa, la obsidiana, cerámica de alta calidad así como con otros bienes y artículos de prestigio, la concha desempeñó desde tiempos tempranos un papel fundamental en los sistemas de intercambio mercantil, especialmente con el noroeste del México antiguo o Suroeste norteamericano, lo mismo que con el resto de Mesoamérica y con la costa del Ecuador. Para la realización de este trabajo nos apoyamos en trabajos realizados tanto en bahía de Banderas como en Playa del Tesoro, tratándose de centros portuarios de primera importancia que muestran la magnitud y los alcances logrados por la explotación de los moluscos en el mundo precolombino.

ABSTRACT

The aim of this research is to present data for some of the most important marine mollusks that appear most frequently in Western Mesoamerica and the American Southwest; these materials show certain similarities in manufacture techniques and shapes. The western coast of Mesoamerica was the source of most of the materials found in the Southwest. This research focuses first on the species of mollusks that were collected for their food value and the second one to those species that were selected and transformed into personal ornaments and other utilitarian uses. Shell is an important archaeological material to understand the processes of cultural interaction that occurred between different cultural regions. These materials as well as metal artifacts and other luxury items such as turquoise were distributed along the West Coast and were involved in trade between the West Coast and the American Southwest. These are some of the results on the malacological investigation at Playa del Tesoro, Colima and other coastal sites in the Banderas Bay, Nayarit.

José Carlos Beltrán Medina Centro INAH Colima

Antecedentes

En el mundo precolombino la concha fue un material altamente apreciado y de gran demanda entre diversos pueblos por sus propiedades alimenticias, pero también fue valorada por sus diversos usos y funciones, al igual que por los atributos simbólicos con los que estaba revestida, ya que ciertas especies eran consideradas sagradas. Debido a estas características se tuvo una amplia dispersión y un alto poder de cambio. No es extraño por lo tanto su presencia en sitios diversos del Suroeste norteamericano, donde han sido encontrados desde las primeras excavaciones artefactos de concha y ejemplares completos procedentes principalmente del Pacífico tropical, lo que indica la existencia de intercambios entre estas dos regiones (Gladwin et al. 1937).

En efecto, los pueblos asentados en el litoral del occidente de Mesoamérica, participaron activamente en la milenaria tradición de explotación marina del Pacífico tropical americano, desarrollando una intensa actividad de extracción y transformación de productos, lo que les permitió formar parte de los antiguos sistemas mercantiles. La concha ha sido utilizada como herramienta valiosa para estudiar las antiguas rutas mercantiles, así como los intercambios de materiales y productos, la difusión de conceptos y el grado de interacción cultural que existió entre algunos pueblos y regiones.

Entre los materiales característicos de Occidente y que también se encuentran presentes en el Suroeste, sobresalen las pulseras de una pieza elaboradas en *Glycymeris gigantea*, los cascabeles elaborados de *Oliva* y *Conus* y las cuentas de collar, materiales que se encuentran presentes desde las fases tempranas. También han sido encontrados especímenes de *Turritella* y algunos *Argopecten circularis* y *Lyropecten subnodosus*, utilizados como colgantes, así como *Pecten excavatus* (Gladwin et al. 1937). Sobresalen las placas de concha nácar manufacturadas en *Pinctada mazatlánica*, así como los grandes caracoles bocina en *Strombus*

galeatus, S. peruvianus y *Fasciolaria princeps*. Destaca de manera especial *Spondylus*, la ostra sagrada, su concha fue utilizada como ofrenda principal en ancestrales ritos de la fertilidad, lo mismo que en la elaboración de collares y otros artefactos.

La mayoría de los ejemplares que se encuentran presentes en sitios del Suroeste americano proceden del litoral de Sonora y Sinaloa, como lo sugiere la cercanía con el Golfo de California y la similitud entre los principales materiales de ambas regiones; sin embargo la tecnología para la elaboración de estas manufacturas así como las formas, diseños y tipos básicos parecen haber venido de lugares ubicados más al sur, ya que al menos desde el Clásico en la Bahía de Banderas, en Playa del Tesoro y en otros sitios de Occidente, se encuentran bien representados estos materiales, así como algunas actividades desarrolladas para la obtención y transformación de éstos géneros marinos. Por supuesto que cada región muestra sus propias características específicas en la talla de la concha, pero todas usan las mismas especies y la misma tecnología.

Los datos presentados en este trabajo provienen de un importante sitio de la bahía de Manzanillo, Playa del Tesoro, mientras que en la Bahía de Banderas la información proviene de varios sitios (Punta Mita, Higuera Blanca, Pontoque, Ixtapa y el puerto de Huanacaxte, Figura I.1.1). En estos puntos se encuentran bien representados las diferentes especies, los materiales de concha y los procesos de trabajo, pero es en la bahía de Banderas donde existen materiales procedentes del noroeste durante la tradición Aztatlán.

En ambas bahías se ha encontrado turquesa, tratándose de uno de los bienes de prestigio altamente valorados que aparecieron tardíamente en Mesoamérica. Se trata de una piedra preciosa con atributos simbólicos y emblemáticos que compitió favorablemente con otras piedras preciosas. La extracción e intercambio de la turquesa pudiera ser uno de los principales

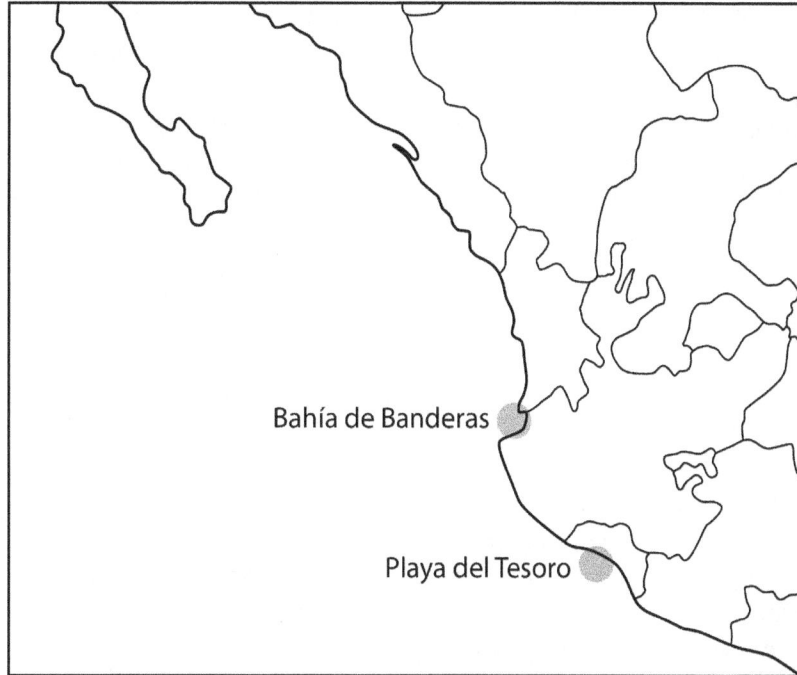

Figura I.1.1. Localización de Playa del Tesoro y Bahía de Banderas.

motivos del desarrollo de las sociedades Pueblo del cañón del Chaco, así como de los sitios Aztatlán ubicados en la frontera norte como Guasave y Mochicahui. Por lo tanto es necesaria una revisión mínima al complejo Aztatlán para contextualizar culturalmente la problemática existente. Paralelamente en este escrito se hace una revisión de las principales especies y materiales de concha que han sido encontrados tanto en el Suroeste como en Occidente.

Playa del Tesoro y Bahía de Banderas

Uno de los sitios importantes de Occidente es Playa del Tesoro que forma parte del puerto de Salagua. Está formado por diversa áreas dispersas que muestran una mayor concentración junto al mar, donde destaca el rico cementerio de Playa del Tesoro, así como el histórico puerto de Salagua, ahora puerto Las Hadas. Presenta tres fases de ocupación, la primera se llama Morett Temprano perteneciente al Preclásico final (300 a.C. al 100 d.C.). La segunda se llama Tesoro

correspondiendo a un período de tiempo que va del 150 d.C. al 750 d.C., muestra una dinámica cultural especial que presenta materiales y rasgos culturales Teotihuacanos. La última ocupación del sitio es denominada Reocupación, extendiéndose del 750 al 1100 d.C., se encuentra asociada con la metalurgia, con materiales Toltecas y Aztatlán. La actividad más intensa del sitio es entre el 200 d.C. y el 670 d.C., como lo indican ocho muestras de radiocarbono, mientras que otra fecha ubica al sitio en el 1090 d.C. (Beltrán 2001). En Morett fueron obtenidas 12 fechas que concuerdan plenamente con las de Playa del Tesoro (Meighan 1972).

El sitio forma parte de la provincia arqueológica de Cihuatlán de gran tradición marinera, ya que se extiende a lo largo de los valles aluviales costeros y de las bahías del sur de Jalisco y Colima caracterizados por figurillas y cerámica rojo sobre bayo o bayo sobre crema.

Bahía de Banderas con sus playas, islas y arrecifes tienen grandes recursos naturales, por lo que no es de extrañar la presencia del hombre desde tiempos tempranos, así como una densa ocupación prehispánica distribuida en el paisaje, con asentamientos cercanos a sus recursos naturales. Existen materiales que indican la presencia humana desde el Formativo hasta la conquista española (Beltrán y González 2007). En estas bahías existieron importantes centros marítimos y portuarios que funcionaron como receptores de productos marinos, desde donde eran procesados y distribuidos hacia otras regiones a través de rutas mercantiles bien establecidas, tanto por mar como por tierra. Destaca la variedad y calidad de objetos suntuarios y utilitarios elaborados de concha, así como la presencia de ciertos implementos y herramientas que fueron utilizadas en el buceo, en sus procesos productivos y en la elaboración de sus manufacturas.

La primera evidencia del uso de concha en Occidente se tiene en Capacha, fechada aproximadamente entre el 1500 a.C. y el 800 a.C. (Kelly 1980), pero en realidad es hasta la tradición Tumbas de Tiro entre el 200 a.C. y el 600 d.C. cuando se intensifica la explotación marina, mientras que entre el 200 d.C. y el año 900 d.C. es Playa del Tesoro la responsable de esta actividad. Desde el 900 d.C. al 1350 d.C. fue Aztatlán quien desarrolló gran parte de la extracción y transformación de mariscos, los intercambios mercantiles y la navegación. Por último son las tradiciones locales herederas de Aztatlán, quienes terminan esta larga tradición de explotación marina, la cual colapsa casi totalmente con la conquista europea (Beltrán 2001). Estas tradiciones culturales son de gran valor para entender el desarrollo de la explotación marina en Occidente y la dispersión de sus productos en otras regiones. La evidencia más notable de esta actividad es la presencia de grandes montículos de concha y de un variado muestrario de artefactos utilitarios y ornamentales de concha.

MEDIO AMBIENTE

Mientras que la Bahía de Banderas se encuentra

en la boca del Golfo de California, Playa del Tesoro y la Bahía de Manzanillo se encuentran un poco más al sur, pero ambas son afectadas por la confluencia de la corriente tropical Norecuatorial procedente del sur, que al interactuar con la corriente fría de California y con el reflujo de la masa de agua subtropical del Golfo de California, provenientes del norte, da por resultado un área de gran biodiversidad perteneciente al ecosistema de costa estuario, uno de los más ricos del planeta. Los trabajos arqueológicos desarrollados permitieron mostrar aspectos de importancia de la explotación marina, donde el buceo y recolección de mariscos constituyó una de las principales actividades.

El grupo zoológico más numeroso y mejor representado fue el de los moluscos, los cuales pertenecen a la provincia malacológica Panameña. La identificación taxonómica de 160 especies diferentes de concha en nuestros muestrarios fue una útil herramienta para poder establecer las relaciones que tuvieron los grupos costeros con su medio ambiente, ya que su identificación permitió conocer los nichos ecológicos de donde proceden y el rango de dispersión de las diferentes comunidades, por lo que fue posible tener una aproximación sobre las formas de organización y técnicas de recolección y buceo que tuvieron que ser implementadas en su captura. En realidad la tradición marina del Pacífico tropical americano empezó desde temprano y fue compartida por los pueblos costeros de la provincia malacológica Panameña que se extiende desde el norte de Perú hasta el Golfo de California (Keen 1971); sin embargo sus materiales muestran un rango de distribución mayor al de esta provincia de la fauna, mostrando las fechas más tempranas en la costa del Ecuador (Marcos 1995).

AZTATLÁN, LA TURQUESA Y LOS INTERCAMBIOS CON EL SUROESTE

La tradición Aztatlán emerge en el Posclásico mostrando dos períodos importantes, el primero asociado al mundo tolteca (900 d.C. al 1100 d.C.), y el otro a la Mixteca Puebla (1100 d.C. al 1350 d.C.), pero con sus propias características. Aportó nuevas tecnologías y un nuevo estilo de vida que se difundió rápidamente en una amplia área, imponiendo fuertes cambios y aportando nuevos componentes a la región de Occidente, entre ellos la metalurgia difundida también en el Suroeste, insertando a la región entera en la edad de los metales.

Mientras que en el Clásico es el puerto de Salagua (Playa del Tesoro) uno de los sitios importantes que se encargó de la producción y distribución de la concha, en el Posclásico es Aztatlán quien continúa con estas actividades, siendo uno de los actores principales de los intercambios con el Suroeste. En Aztatlán concurren claramente varias vigorosas corrientes culturales de la época, entre ellas la norteña, las que junto a las tradiciones locales, formaron la entidad cultural más importante del Occidente en ese momento. Su economía estuvo basada en la explotación intensiva de los productos naturales, en la agricultura de riego, en el control de puertos y bahías así como en la explotación intensiva de los estuarios, lo mismo que en su participación en la selecta red de mercaderes de bienes exóticos, donde los moluscos marinos, la turquesa y los objetos de cobre desempeñaron un papel preponderante.

Mientras que Bahía de Banderas muestra una fuerte ocupación Aztatlán, en Playa del Tesoro fue detectado un entierro con materiales Aztatlán junto con artefactos de filiación tolteca, con una fecha del 1090 d.C. (Beltrán 2009). En ambos sitios fueron encontradas algunas pocas turquesas.

La turquesa y ciertos géneros de conchas fueron los materiales intercambiados por los antiguos pueblos de Occidente y del Suroeste norteamericano. Han sido encontrados en contextos arqueológicos mesoamericanos pertenecientes al Formativo, pero es hasta el Clásico cuando aparecen en mayor cantidad tanto en la margen costera como en el altiplano. Hay evidencias claras que a partir del 500 d.C. durante la fase Alta Vista, la cultura Chalchihuites estuvo bien involucrada en los intercambios de turquesa con los Hohokam de la fase Gila Butte, así como en su posterior distribución hacia Mesoamérica. También estuvo involucrada en la producción intensiva de piedras preciosas extraídas de sus propias minas (Weigand 1995). Sin embargo es durante el Posclásico (900 d.C. a 1350 d.C.) cuando se producen los intercambios entre los productores de turquesa del cañón del Chaco con la cultura Aztatlán, entidades dominantes en este momento. Ha sido encontrada turquesa del yacimiento de Cerillos en Nuevo México, en Guasave, Ixtlán del Río, Zacoalco y Las Cuevas, en niveles contemporáneos con el cañón del Chaco (Weigand 1995). Igualmente en Higuera Blanca (Bahía de Banderas) y en Playa del Tesoro fueron encontradas algunas turquesas.

En el Posclásico temprano fueron desarrollados intercambios importantes entre algunos puntos del Suroeste con sitios de Occidente pertenecientes a la tradición Aztatlán. Es posible que puntos de la frontera norte como Guasave, Culiacán y Mochicahui, hayan sido los que intercambiaron productos costeros hacia el norte a través de los pueblos Cahitas de Sonora, ya que existe similitud entre los materiales de concha de sitios Hohokam con los de Guasave (Ekholm 1942). Aztatlán se caracterizó por elaborar y distribuir materiales de buena calidad, entre ellos artefactos de metal, cerámica fina, plomiza y tipo Códice, obsidiana, piezas de alabastro, textiles y por supuesto conchas enteras y labradas. Aparentemente los bienes que circularon en dirección contraria fueron piedras preciosas como la turquesa, pigmentos y minerales, lo mismo que hachas, plumas, cucharones y probablemente cestería. En ese momento existió una fuerte expansión de los modelos mesoamericanos.

Existe evidencia de la presencia de especies alimenticias en sitios del interior, como Persícula bandera, especie endémica de la región de Banderas; lo mismo sucede con *Ostrea, Anadara, Megapitaria, Chama* y *Strombus gracilior*, pequeño caracol que aparece en sitios alejados como Snaketown (Gladwin et al. 1937).

A la caída del Chaco en el Posclásico final, hay un aumento de la presencia de turquesa en Mesoamérica y entre otros sitios. Paquimé jugó un importante papel como uno de los puntos en el intercambio y distribución de la turquesa entre el Suroeste y Mesoamérica. Presenta abundancia de turquesa junto a materiales del Occidente, como cerámica y concha (Di Peso 1974); parece ser que sirvió de intermediario en la introducción de turquesa a Mesoamérica.

Al igual que lo había hecho antes Playa del Tesoro, Aztatlán participó activamente en el tráfico de larga distancia a través de la red de navegantes que existió a lo largo del Pacífico americano, la cual no tuvo mayor dificultad en llegar hasta el fondo del Golfo de California. Desempeñó un papel central en las rutas mercantiles y en el sistema de intercambios de bienes y productos, generando una amplia dispersión no nada más hacia el Suroeste sino también hacia el interior de Mesoamérica y a otros lejanos lugares como la costa centroamericana y del Ecuador.

La concha y sus materiales

La gran cantidad y variedad de moluscos originó una intensa explotación que generó una floreciente industria de la concha, sobresaliendo dos categorías, una de apropiación de alimentos y otra de transformación de productos. En la primera categoría se encuentra una buena variedad de especímenes utilizados como alimento, representando una gran fuente alimenticia para los pueblos antiguos. La segunda categoría se encuentra vinculada con las actividades de producción y transformación de la concha, mostrando varias ramas artesanales bien definidas: la explotación del tinte púrpura, el buceo de los géneros preciosos, la elaboración de cal y la industria artesanal del tallado de la concha, mostrando gran variedad de productos, tanto utilitarios como suntuarios. Sobresalió

la elaboración de collares, brazaletes, pulseras y ajorcas, lo mismo que cuentas y colgantes, narigueras, aretes, cascabeles, cinceles, punzones, agarraderas de átlatl, botones y otros abalorios, existiendo una gran distribución de estos materiales en diversos sitios del Occidente, principalmente en Sinaloa, Zacatecas, Nayarit, Jalisco, Colima y Michoacán, así como en el Suroeste norteamericano. Entre los materiales más comunes sobresalen los siguientes.

Pulseras de *Glycymeris gigantea*

Uno de los materiales que fueron utilizados con más abundancia en ambas regiones son las pulseras de una sola pieza, elaboradas a partir de *Glycymeris gigantea*, ya que la gran dureza de su borde fue aprovechada para obtener aros de gran belleza. La técnica de trabajo consiste en lograr un orificio por percusión en el centro de la concha, luego se empieza a agrandar hasta llegar al mismo borde del manto, que tiene la forma propia de una pulsera; al obtener el aro se procede a retirar completamente el esmalte para luego ser pulido cuidadosamente. Algunas de estas pulseras son zoomorfas, pero la mayoría son lisas. Estas pulseras aparecen en varias partes de la costa desde Guerrero hasta Sonora y sus conchas fueron llevadas hasta el Suroeste, donde han sido detectadas en ofrendas funerarias (Figuras I.1.2 y I.1.3).

Existen unos aros de mayor tamaño manufacturados en otra especie, los cuales fueron utilizados como brazaletes, provenientes de la gran lapa *Ancistromesus mexicanus*. Fueron elaborados con la misma técnica utilizada en las pulseras.

Cuentas de Collar

En las excavaciones llevadas a cabo en Playa del Tesoro y Bahía de Banderas fueron localizadas varias cuentas de collar con perforación circular o cuadrada, principalmente de *Anadara* y *Spondylus*. Existe cierta variedad en los diseños de las cuentas pero predominan las que tienen forma de rueda, después del 900 d.C. empiezan a ser usadas unas cuentas cuadradas de mayor tamaño (Figura I.1.4).

Colgantes

Los colgantes presentan una gran variedad en sus diseños, los cuales son zoomorfos, fitomorfos o con trazos geométricos. Las especies más utilizadas fueron *Spondylus princeps* y *Pinctada mazatlanica*. Algunos colgantes muestran la forma original de la concha, mientras que otros muestran una transformación total de su forma natural. La mayoría de estos colgantes fueron usados formando parte de collares y pulseras, pero también se encontraron en forma aislada. Los bivalvos muestran un orificio en el umbo o un poco más abajo, mientras que los univalvos tienen el orificio en la parte angosta del cono. El material muestra dos tipos de perforaciones: uno muy delgado y fino por el que solo puede pasar un hilo, y otro que tiene el diámetro más grueso por el que puede pasar una correa; estas perforaciones pueden ser cónicas o paralelas. Los ejemplares que tienen la perforación de diámetro más grande, provienen de *Pseudochama inermis, Argopecten circularis, Placunanomia cumingii, Anadara formosa, Trachycardium consors, Trachycardium procerum* y *Anadara grandis*. Sobresalen 70 ejemplares de *Turritella leucostoma* encontrados en Playa del Tesoro, los cuales presentan como único trabajo una perforación cónica (Figura I.1.5). Con perforación delgada hay ejemplares de *Polymesoda mexicana, Chione californiensis, Pitar lupanaria, Turritella leucostoma, Cassis centiquadrata* y *Chiton* sp.

Pectorales del género *Pecten*

En las bahías fueron trabajadas *Argopecten circularis* y *Lyropecten subnodosus*, el más grande y llamativo de la familia, el cual presenta colores morado, magenta y naranja; llegan a medir hasta 16 cm. Junto con estas dos especies,

Figura I.1.2. Pulsera de Glycymeris *con cuentas.*

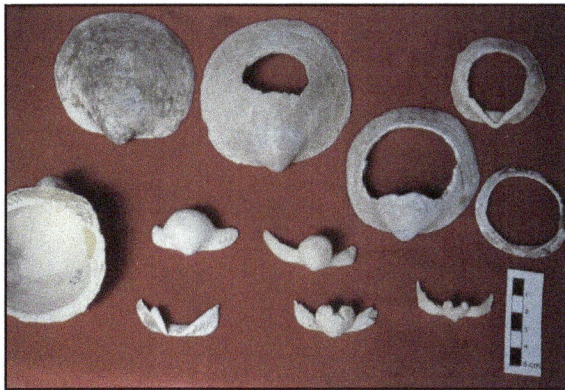

Figura I.1.3. Pulseras zoomorfas con murciélagos.

Figura I.1.4. Collar de Spondylus.

en el Suroeste han sido encontrados también ejemplares de *Pecten excavatus. Argopecten circularis* es una concha más pequeña que la anterior pero de una belleza especial con tonos rojizos y cremas (Figura I.1.6). Fueron encontrados muchos ejemplares sin trabajar y algunos con un pequeño orificio en el umbo, hay algunos casos en que se muestra la concha perforada con una técnica similar a la utilizada para conseguir aros, pulseras y brazaletes.

Cascabeles y sonajas de *Olivas* y *Conus*

Estos artefactos fueron utilizados en sus danzas y bailables como instrumentos musicales de percusión, iban sujetados a los tobillos o a los muslos, funcionando como sonajas con percutor interno, los cuales sonaban al impactarse entre sí marcando de esta manera el ritmo de sus ceremonias. Aparecen desde el Preclásico superior en México. Se trata de los artefactos más abundantes de Punta Mita, ya que fueron obtenidos principalmente de olívidos, y en menor proporción de cónidos; predominando ampliamente los especímenes de *Oliva porphyria* el más grande de la familia, aunque también hay ejemplares de *O. incrassata y Conus vittatus*, uno de los más bellos (Figura I.1.7). En el Suroeste han sido encontrados ejemplares de *Olivella biplicata* (Gladwin et al. 1937). En el Museo de Universitario de Colima (M.A.G.) existe un bello ejemplar de *Conus* de gran tamaño con restos de pintura al fresco de color rosa, verde y azul, procedentes de una tumba de tiro.

Spondylus, la ostra sagrada

De gran importancia fue la captura de *Spondylus princeps*, la ostra sagrada que muestra una vistosa concha de largas espinas con un intenso colorido de tonos rojizos. Se le encuentra adherida firmemente en profundos fondos rocosos y en los arrecifes de coral, por lo que resulta difícil su captura, necesitándose de la presencia de buceadores especializados. También fue capturada

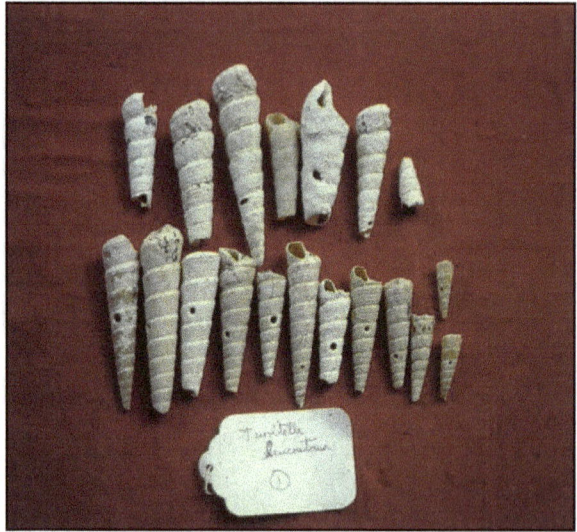
Figura I.1.5. Turritellas *con un orificio.*

Figura I.1.6. Colgantes de Argopecten circularis.

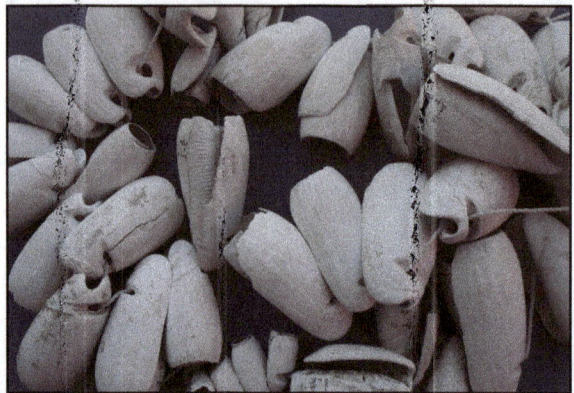
Figura I.1.7. Cascabeles de Oliva.

Spondylus calcifer, una ostra sin espinas pero más grande y pesada. Ambas muestran un borde rojo muy apreciado en la elaboración de artesanías. Era considerada sagrada, por lo que fue objeto de una amplia explotación desde tiempos tempranos. Ambas especies se distribuyen a lo largo de toda la provincia malacológica Panameña, hay otra especie que se le encuentra en el Golfo de California, *Spondylus unicolors*, que se distribuye a lo largo del golfo, por lo que es probable que se le encuentre en el Suroeste. Se trata de un molusco apreciado por su exquisito sabor, pero su verdadero valor radica en la utilización de su concha durante antiguos ritos agrarios de petición de lluvia, pues se le consideraba un símbolo de fertilidad.

También fue utilizado como materia prima para la elaboración de colgantes, cuentas, abalorios y diversos objetos. La presencia del *Spondylus* en Occidente es temprana, ya que aparece en contextos Capacha del Formativo inferior (López-Mestas y Ramos de la Vega 1998). El buceo, acopio, transformación y distribución del *Spondylus* parece haber jugado un importante papel durante la época prehispánica, ya que fue desarrollada una red bien organizada para su explotación. En los sitios de Punta Mita y Litibú fueron encontrados pesas de buceo profundo y talleres de procesamiento de *Spondylus*, donde fueron recuperadas bisagras y partes blancas de la concha, mientras que ningún ejemplar presentaba el borde rojo, el cual fue separado de la concha para ser trabajado y enviado al interior (Figura I.1.8).

Strombus, el caracol bocina

Estos caracoles fueron utilizados como bocinas o trompetas ceremoniales suprimiéndoles el ápex, es decir la última vuelta de su espira para formar la boquilla, servían para dar inicio a las ceremonias, contiendas y batallas, para marcar los ritmos cósmicos y sus tiempos rituales, así como para otros sucesos de importancia. Se trata de un artefacto que tuvo uso músico ceremonial.

En las bahías fueron encontrados fragmentos de diversos tamaños en proceso de trabajo, existen unos artefactos en forma de media luna procedentes de estrómbidos, fueron obtenidos de la última o penúltima vuelta de la columela, ya casi en el vértice del cono. Una vez recortadas eran pulidas para ser utilizados como narigueras o como agarraderas de átlatl (lanza dardo).

Fueron detectados caracoles bocina elaborados de *Strombus Galeatus* y *S. Peruvianus*, asociados a contextos arqueológicos del clásico y posclásico, lo mismo que otras especies utilizadas como *Fasciolaria princeps* el caracol más grande de la provincia Panameña. Existe un ejemplar de *Hexaplex regius* utilizado como trompeta, el cual procede del puerto de Huanacaxte, en la Bahía de Banderas. Igualmente *Malea ringens* ha sido utilizada como bocina. La importancia de los caracoles trompeta es tal que en Occidente aparecen varios ejemplares procedentes del mar Caribe, especialmente *Strombus gigas*, *S. costatus* y *Turbinella angulata*, los que suelen aparecer junto con los grandes caracoles del Pacífico. Esto revela intercambios entre los dos litorales al menos desde el Formativo superior (Figura I.1.9).

Pinctada mazatlanica

Existe una ostra perlífera, *P. mazatlanica*, la gran productora de perlas, explotada a lo largo de la costa del Pacífico tropical americano, proviene de fondos rocosos donde se encuentra adherida firmemente. En las bahías de Banderas y Manzanillo su captura alcanzó gran importancia ya que fueron cotizadas por su concha y por sus perlas. De su concha fueron elaboradas placas de diferentes diseños para ser incrustadas en otros materiales, del margen de la concha fueron obtenidas aros elípticos usados como anteojeras Tlaloc. También fueron elaborados anzuelos señuelo obtenidos de la sección curva que tiene la concha.

Otra especie nacarada que se encuentra presentes son *Atrina maura* y las diferentes especies de *Ostrea*, todas ellas productoras

Figura I.1.8. Colgantes zoomorfos de Spondylus.

Figura I.1.9. Caracol bocina de Strombus galeatus.

de perlas. En el Suroeste la concha nácar fue obtenida de la concha del abulón rojo *Haliotis rufescens* procedente del Pacífico septentrional ya en la alta California. Los conquistadores españoles asociaron el buceo de perlas y la provincia de Cihuatlán (lugar de mujeres), con la leyenda de las amazonas, creyendo que se trataba de la región habitada exclusivamente por mujeres, con abundancia de perlas y de oro. Este fue el motivo principal de la conquista de Occidente y las subsecuentes entradas de los españoles hacia el noroeste (Figura I.1.10).

El caracol de tinte

Existió una importante actividad en Bahía de Banderas y Playa del Tesoro, relacionada con la explotación del caracol de púrpura para teñir hilados y textiles a partir de *Murex y Thais*. Destacaron *Purpura pansa*, *Hexaplex erythrostomus* y *H. regius*, lo mismo que *Thais biserialis*, *Acanthina brevidentata*, *Purpura pansa* y *Neorapana muricata*. En el puerto Cruz de Huanacaxte fueron aprovechados ampliamente, existen claras evidencias de su utilización ya que aparecen al lado de grandes hornos, ollas y vasijas sugiriendo sus procesos productivos. Fue detectado un enorme ejemplar de *Hexaplex erythrostomus* con un orificio en el ápex para ser usado como caracol trompeta.

Los *Murex* son unos caracoles con una compleja estructura que termina en forma de espinas, unos son de boca rosa y otros de boca morada, se encuentran en fondos profundos viviendo en grandes colonias a lo largo de la costa rocosa alimentándose de ostras, mejillones y otros moluscos, por lo tanto para su captura se requieren buzos especialistas. Cuando están en peligro tienen la propiedad de segregar como protección un viscoso líquido que por oxidación con el medio ambiente produce un tinte de color morado índigo permanente y de muy buena calidad, el cual fue utilizado para teñir textiles, llegando a ser muy apreciados ya que las prendas teñidas solo eran utilizadas por la clase dirigente. La abundancia de costa rocosa en la bahía y la existencia de un rico arrecife marino, provocó abundancia de estos caracoles. El tinte púrpura por lo general es recolectado en grandes conchas, en donde se introducen las madejas de algodón para teñirlos, mientras que en la explotación de los murícidos por el contrario, hay que recolectarlos del fondo marino, y es necesario sacrificar al molusco. La intensidad del púrpura, la calidad así como la cantidad vertida depende de cada especie (Figura I.1.11). La presencia de malacates en estos sitios sugiere producción textil, la cual pudo ser teñida en parte con este producto marino.

Figura I.1.10. Valvas y anzuelos de Pinctada mazatlanica.

Figura I.1.11. Caracol de tinte Hexaplex regius.

COMENTARIOS FINALES

Como quedó de manifiesto, la mayoría de las especies de concha que han sido encontrados en el Suroeste norteamericano, así como la tecnología utilizada para la elaboración de sus principales artefactos proceden de la costa oeste mesoamericana donde han sido encontrados desde el Clásico. Los ejemplos más claros son Playa del Tesoro y varios sitios de la Bahía de Banderas como Punta Mita, Litibú, Pontoque y Huanacaxte. De gran importancia fueron la captura y transformación de la concha ya que fue una de las bases del gran mercado de productos exóticos que existió, recorriendo los antiguos caminos prehispánicos tanto en el Suroeste como en Mesoamérica y otras regiones más alejadas, beneficiando ampliamente a los pueblos productores.

Como resulta evidente la concha y la turquesa fueron los principales bienes de intercambio, los cuales fueron acompañados por otros productos de importancia como el cobre. La presencia de estos materiales en un área constituyó una notable empresa, ya que fue producto de grandes esfuerzos parea la captura, transformación y distribución de sus productos.

Los intercambios no consistieron solamente en un trueque sencillo de materiales, sino que involucró a todo un sistema mercantil basado en relaciones de poder bien estructuradas, así como en una serie de símbolos y conceptos ideológicos que se encontraban plasmados en los materiales emblemáticos que hicieron circular, cuya posesión justificaba por si mismo el poder detentado, por lo tanto no podían ser obtenidos o manejados por cualquiera. Todo un tema resulta ser el estudio de los intercambios mercantiles que hicieron posible la presencia de materiales, productos y conceptos culturales entre Occidente y el Suroeste.

Algunas piezas que muestran la integración de diferentes tradiciones culturales, son las máscaras de madera Aztatlán, cubiertas con mosaico de turquesa, con sus rasgos elaborados con *Spondylus*, concha nácar (*Pinctada mazatlanica*) y obsidiana, materiales que proceden de las diferentes tradiciones culturales de la época.

Son necesarios más trabajos para entender mejor el grado de interacción que existió entre estas dos antiguas regiones culturales, lo mismo que para poder avanzar en el conocimiento de los grupos humanos que desarrollaron estas actividades así como en los modelos que fueron implementados. Por lo pronto esperamos que sirva este estudio para reabrir la discusión sobre el tema.

Part 1, Chapter 2

Ni todos nómadas, ni todos sedentarios: El sitio del Cerro de Santiago, Aguascalientes

M. Nicolás Caretta y Peter C. Kröfges

RESUMEN

En este documento se discutirá el sitio arqueológico de Santiago en Aguascalientes, México, el cual sin duda alguna es uno de los asentamientos con mayor perspectiva de investigación en el centro-norte del país. El desarrollo de estudios en dicha zona nos permitirá conocer no sólo los procesos de desarrollo social al interior del sitio, también nos ayudará a comprender cómo es que los grupos de habitantes de esta región establecieron y fortalecieron interacciones sociales con otros grupos de las áreas circunvecinas entre ellas Mesoamérica. Además, el estudio de este asentamiento nos permitirá reafirmar la hipótesis de que la zona del Mar Chichimeca estuvo habitada por diversas sociedades, las cuales mostraron diferencias en su desarrollo social, en particular las actividades económicas.

ABSTRACT

In this document we discuss the archaeological site of Santiago in Aguascalientes, Mexico, site that without any doubt is one of the settlements with greater perspective of research in the Centre-North of the country. The research in this area enable us to understand about the processes of social development to the interior of the site, and also help us to understand how the social group of that inhabited this site established and strengthened their social interactions with other groups in the surrounding areas including Mesoamerica. In addition, this study will allow us to reaffirm the hypothesis that the Chichimec Sea area was inhabited by societies with a different social development, in particular the economic activities.

PRESENTACIÓN

Está por demás decir que el número de investigaciones arqueológicas realizadas en la zona centro norte del México han sido muy limitadas, casi nulas. Lo anterior prioriza la importancia de incrementar el número de investigaciones en esta zona a fin de dar respuesta a las interrogantes existentes sobre la estructura social y el desarrollo cultural de estos pueblos de la misma manera como sucede con los sitios arqueológicos e históricos del centro-sur del país. Uno de estos estados olvidados por la arqueología mexicana es Aguascalientes, estado que por no contar con grandes asentamientos prehispánicos dotados de un amplio y monumental complejo arquitectónico ha sido desdeñado e ignorado tanto por investigadores como por instituciones dedicadas a realizar investigaciones de este tipo. Si bien es cierto que los sitios que hoy se encuentran dentro de la frontera geopolítica de Aguascalientes no sobresalen por sus impactantes

M. Nicolás Caretta Colegio de Ciencias Sociales y Humanidades, Universidad Autónoma de San Luis Potosí
Peter C. Kröfges Colegio de Ciencias Sociales y Humanidades, Universidad Autónoma de San Luis Potosí

dimensiones arqueológicas, ello no quiere decir que no cuenten con una historia compartida con el resto de los pueblos del país y en ello yace su importancia y su aportación al conocimiento de la arqueología nacional. El Ocote, El Cerro de en Medio y Santiago, entre otros, son sitios que participaron en el desarrollo de la región, por tal motivo, su valor como objetos de estudio radica en que las investigaciones que se realicen en estas zonas nos permitirán entender el desarrollo y las interacciones culturales que se dieron entre los grupos que se establecieron en esta gran región y sus vecinos.

Las explicaciones que hasta la fecha se han dado sobre el desarrollo de esta región en relación al resto del Mar Chichimeca están basadas en investigaciones sobre material en superficie y en ocasiones en meras prospecciones por lo tanto se presentan como explicaciones muy exiguas. Lo anterior deja en evidencia la imperiosa necesidad de realizar un mayor número de investigaciones que pongan a prueba las propuestas teóricas existentes y los modelos explicativos que estamos aplicando a nivel regional e incluso macroregional.

La propuesta de investigación arqueológica que a continuación se presenta busca dar respuesta a las interrogantes existentes sobre esta zona, además pretende ayudar a desvanecer los límites territoriales y geopolíticos que con frecuencia aún se manejan y que están basados en la propuesta del modelo de la Mesoamérica marginal de Braniff (1972, 1974).

En primer lugar debemos reconocer que la indiferencia o el poco interés que la arqueología del Norte de México ha tenido en estas zonas se ven reflejada en los vacíos de información o bien en la mala información acerca de la historia de esta región o de los grupos que en ella se establecieron. No obstante, no podemos negar que estas sociedades interactuaron en diferentes grados y formas con grupos pertenecientes a la Mesoamérica nuclear, al Occidente de México y grupos concernientes al Suroeste de los Estados Unidos de América, a pesar de que algunos investigadores les han querido ver desde una perspectiva aislacionistas o difusionistas.

Para nuestra suerte existe un número de investigadores que aun navegando en contra de la corriente aislacionista y/o difusionista, se han dado a la tarea de tratar de explicar el desarrollo cultural de esta vasta extensión territorial denominada *Mar Chichimeca* por el arqueólogo estadounidense J. Charles Kelley (1974).

De esta forma, desde la última década de siglo pasado hasta ahora, los debates sobre esta problemática se están nuevamente evaluando y replanteando a través de la aplicación del modelo de estudio conocido como "World Systems" (Sistemas Mundiales) el cual abarca hasta Mesoamérica (Foster 2000:197-219; Jiménez 1989; Jiménez y Darling 2000:155-180; Le Blanc 1986:105-134; McGuire 1986, 1989; Pailes y Whitecotton 1979; Weigand 1982; Whitecotton y Pailes 1986; entre otros) o bien mediante el modelo de "Peer Polity" (Interacción entre Unidades Equipolentes) este último presenta un alcance de desarrollo más específico ya que básicamente se apoya en relaciones ecológicas de tipo local (Jiménez 1992; Minnis 1989; Minnis y Whalen 1992, 1993; Whalen y Minnis 1996a, 1996b, 1996c, 2001, 2009). Whalen y Minnis (2001) presentan una postura menos extrema a aquella que guardaban con respecto al modelo de "Peer Polity" en sus trabajos previos. De igual forma, estos investigadores presentan algunas precisiones sobre el concepto de Sistemas Regionales y su complejidad.

Gran parte de toda la discusión que se ha originado en torno a estas zonas arqueológicas olvidadas se debe a que éstas no poseen una gran organización social, política, económica e ideológica en comparación con otros pertenecientes a centros mayores ubicados al noroeste del país, ello no quiere decir que el estudio de estas zonas no sea importante.

En el territorio que actualmente le corresponde a la región noroccidental del país existen muchos sitios que se encuentran en lo que se conoce como zona de interface entre la "Mesoamérica nuclear" y la Mesoamérica Mayor, sitios que fueron parte de una red de interacción humana que debió existir entre los grupos del centro de México con sociedades de tradiciones más norteñas orientadas a las de la zona del Bajío y el Occidente. El sitio de La Quemada ha sido considerado, por mucho, como el punto más norteño de la frontera mesoamericana; sin embargo, gran parte de su importancia depende de su relación con otros sitios que se encuentran dentro de su área cultural o más allá de ésta, sitios que actualmente no han sido estudiados. Lamentablemente sólo dos de estas han sido investigadas a profundidad; La Quemada y Alta Vista. En fechas recientes, otros sitios han logrado ser parte del interés científico, estos son conocidos como el sitio de Tepizuasco, Juchipila, Cruz de la Boca y Ojo Caliente, los resultados de tales investigaciones han sido por demás provechosas.

Lo antes dicho, nos permite remarcar que la realización de un proyecto de investigación en otro lugar, como los descritos anteriormente, puede considerarse de gran potencial científico, desde esta perspectiva su estudio aportará datos con los cuales se podrá comprender el desarrollo cultural de la región noroccidental no sólo a nivel regional también a nivel macroregional.

Otra de las zonas que posee el potencial de investigación de las ya mencionadas es el sitio arqueológico de Santiago ubicado en el Municipio del Pabellón de Arteaga en el estado de Aguascalientes; en este sitio arqueológico, nos proponemos estudiar todos los elementos relacionados con la organización social del mismo. Con la finalidad de lograr nuestro objetivo nos proponemos examinar numerosos conjuntos de datos los cuales incluyen la cronología de crecimiento, el tamaño y la permanencia de la población en el sitio de Santiago, la naturaleza de las actividades locales, el papel que jugó la localidad dentro del sistema económico regional e inter-regional, así como la relación que este grupo social mantuvo con su hábitat y las áreas circunvecinas.

La procedencia de los datos sobre los cuales se realizará este estudio es resultado de investigaciones previas que se han realizado en prospección y registro en superficie. Sumado a estos datos también se planea realizar futuras excavaciones a fin de obtener más información, los resultados que se generen de este proyecto de investigación tendrán implicaciones directas en la comprensión de la historia prehispánica regional, igualmente se podrá explicar la dinámica de cambios culturales no sólo en el ámbito espacial, sino a través del tiempo en el Noroeste del país. Por otro lado, este estudio permitirá conocer la viabilidad de la aplicación de los modelos de Sistema Mundiales y de Interacción entre Unidades Equipolentes, modelos que han propiciado debates teóricos sobre la validez de su aplicación en la explicación de cambios culturales en sociedades precolombinas.

PLANTEAMIENTO TEÓRICO

Gracias a diversas investigaciones realizadas por otros estudiosos del tema, no sólo en América sino también en Europa, Asia y África, sabemos que en la medida que las sociedades se relacionan unas con otras, aunque sea en diferentes niveles y en diferentes grados en el consumo y producción de bienes, además del intercambio de ideas (religión y tecnología), es necesario considerar sistemas de relaciones más extensas para explicar su desarrollo y su historia (Abu-Lughod 1989; Chase-Dunn 1998; Chase-Dunn y Hall 1997; Chase-Dunn y Mann 1998; Gunder y Gills 1993; Kristiansen 1998; Peregrine y Feinman 1996). Este requerimiento ha llevado a algunos investigadores a dar uso a teorías generadas por otras disciplinas para dar cuenta de las problemáticas emergentes en el campo de la arqueología.

Entre los postulados teóricos más utilizados

por los arqueólogos en los últimos años podemos citar la Teoría de Sistemas Mundiales o "World System" desarrollada por Emmanuel Wallerstein (1974, 1978, 1980) y aplicada al estudio de sociedades precolombinas en la Mesoamérica nuclear (Blanton et al. 1981; Blanton y Feinman 1984; Ekholm y Friedman 1982; Kohl 1979) así como en el Noroeste de México (Di Peso 1983; Jiménez y Darling 2000; McGuire 2000; Pailes y Whitecotton 1979; Plog et al. 1982; Plog 1983; Upham 1982; Villalpando 2000; Weigand 1982; Whitecotton y Pailes 1986). Es importante considerar que aun cuando algunos investigadores no comulgan con esta postura académica de conexiones inter-regionales, ellos mismos se refieren en sus propuestas explicativas a los grupos del norte de Mesoamérica como componentes de un conjunto y no como entes totalmente aislados. De igual manera, dentro de las propuestas teóricas vistas como alternativas para la explicación de estas sociedades del Norte de México se encuentra el modelo de Interacción entre Unidades Equipolentes o "Peer Polity Interaction" (Minnis 1989; Minnis y Whalen 1992, 1993; Whalen y Minnis 1996a, 1996b, 1996c, 2001, 2009). Este modelo teórico hace énfasis en una escala intermedia de análisis entre lo local y lo inter-regional, centrándose en las relaciones al interior de una región y asumiendo que dichas interacciones son más importantes para el cambio cultural que las interacciones con el exterior.

No obstante, podemos considerar que tanto el modelo de Sistemas Mundiales como el modelo de Interacción entre Unidades Equipolentes no deberían ser considerados como teorías adversas, ya que ambos modelos aportan argumentos y estrategias metodológicas que permiten realizar el análisis a diferentes escalas (ver Wilcox 1986a). La posición teórica que se ha considerado para este proyecto está basada en la interrogante de cómo en casos específicos confluyeron relaciones e interacciones de los grupos endémicos a diferente niveles o estratos para crear patrones y

cambios que actualmente podemos observar. Esta es la misma posición teórica que mantuvimos como directriz para dos de los proyectos en los sitios de Las Ventanas y Cruz de la Boca como parte de las investigaciones arqueológicas de la región, además estas propuestas coinciden con las propuestas de Peter Jiménez para esta región Noroccidental del país (Caretta 2004). Por tal razón, retomamos los argumentos teóricos expuestos en la propuesta de investigación que se presentó ante el Consejo de Arqueología para estos proyectos.

Partiendo de esta interrogante de estudio se planeó ejecutar nuestra investigación en varias etapas de análisis, de esta forma, en la medida como cambiemos la escala de nuestra observación, enmarcaremos diferentes conjuntos de relaciones sociales. La conformación de estas relaciones desaparecerá bajo una escala diferente en tanto un nuevo patrón de disparidad aparezca en el mundo las sociedades humanas se desarrollan en diferentes etapas y escalas, por lo tanto, su posición frente a otros grupos varía en la medida en que se alterare su escala de referencia.

La escala que se elija delimitará un área de estudio lo que permitirá ver un conjunto de relaciones sociales en particular. Así en la medida en que nos situemos en uno u otro nivel de estudio dispondremos de algunos modelos teóricos que nos proporcionaran la información necesaria para cada etapa de análisis en la que nos encontremos. Debemos de recordar que gran parte de la discusión, tanto teórica como descriptiva de esta investigación han girado en torno a estudiar las interacciones sociales y culturales que debieron haber existido entre las sociedades del centro de México, el Occidente y aquellas de las regiones norteñas (Frisbie 1983; Jiménez 1989; Mathien y McGuire 1986b).

Otro punto importante está relacionado con la percepción que distintos grupos de arqueólogos tienen sobre las regiones del norte con respecto a la Mesoamérica, por un lado, algunos sostienen que la parte septentrional de nuestro país era simplemente el límite de la parte norte de la región mesoamericana, donde la incursión de los comerciantes y los eventos acaecidos en esta zona fueron factores determinantes en el progreso de las sociedades que se desarrollaron en estas latitudes del norte (Di Peso 1974; Foster 1986; Kelley y Kelley 1975; Reyman 1978).

Existe otro grupo de académicos que se ha declarado partidario de ver ésta región norte como un territorio de desarrollo autónomo, aunque, ellos mismo reconocen la presencia de elementos de origen mesoamericano (agricultura y cerámica) también consideran que una posible interrelación con las sociedades del centro del país no debería ser considerada como importante (Haury 1976; McGuire 1980; Nelson 1986).

En propuestas más recientes podemos notar posiciones menos radicales y más propensas a enfocarse en la búsqueda de respuestas que den cuenta de la problemática de las interacciones de estos pueblos y el impacto que éstas relaciones pudieron haber provocado en las sociedades que habitaron la parte norte del México y el suroeste Estadounidense (Jiménez 1989; Jiménez y Darling 2000; Kelley 1986; Le Blanc 1986; Lekson 1999, 2005, 2008; Mathien 1986; McGuire 1986; Riley 1986; Upham 1986; Weigand 1982; Whitecotton y Pailes 1986; Wilcox 1986a, 1986b).

Consideramos importante señalar que el problema principal al que se enfrenta la arqueología de esta región es la falta de datos que apoyen o rechacen las propuestas teóricas que hasta ahora se han formulado, y que a su vez den respuesta a las interrogantes referentes al desarrollo de los grupos que se establecieron en esta parte del continente. Existen evidencias que confirman que una cantidad considerable de objetos y de intercambio de conocimiento fueron los que transitaron por las rutas establecidas por diversos grupos a lo largo del territorio que ahora le corresponde al Centro, Bajío, Occidente, Norte de México y el Suroeste Estadounidense.

De igual forma, sabemos que fueron diversas las sociedades que participaron de forma directa o indirecta dentro de estas redes o rutas, y el papel que estos pueblos jugaron en el funcionamiento y/o deterioro de las interrelaciones; sin embargo, es importante entender la naturaleza del establecimiento de las relaciones de estos pueblos, si acaso hubo, además de comprender hasta qué grado se interrelacionaron, lo anterior nos proporcionará la información necesaria para poder hacer reconstrucciones más veraces acerca del desarrollo de estas sociedades tanto en un nivel regional, interregional como pan-regional.

Así dentro de la consideración teórica multi-escala para este proyecto, proponemos enfocar nuestro estudio sobre las relaciones inter-regionales desde un punto de vista más integral. Lo anterior posibilitará la realización de observaciones más concretas que consideren un número mayor de variables y que al mismo tiempo eviten hacer interpretaciones arqueológicas al momento de realizar un estudio en un sitio, un área o una región a partir de un pozo de sondeo.

PROBLEMÁTICA

Para llevar a cabo el seguimiento de una investigación como la que nos proponemos realizar creemos necesario tomar en consideración las siguientes interrogantes básicas las cuales nos permitirán enfocar nuestra propuesta de estudio al sitio de Santiago dado que éste se encuentra dentro de un área de interacción que es necesario entender tanto en su funcionamiento regional como interregional y panregional. Así nos preguntamos ¿Fueron poblaciones humanas asentadas en el norte de México resultado de una expansión de grupos provenientes de la parte nuclear de Mesoamérica? o ¿Fueron estos grupos resultado de proceso centrados en la comunidad local por parte de sus habitantes? En este sentido ¿Cuál fue el papel que jugó el sitio de Santiago dentro del desarrollo de la región?

Con la finalidad de dar respuesta a estas interrogantes buscaremos información de referencia, datos que actualmente no se ha encontrado en otras fuentes. Ello nos motiva a tratar de identificar la cultura material asociada a un grupo en particular al igual que su cronología. Parece más que obvio mencionar que las preguntas son amplias y complejas, por tanto, sabemos de antemano que para dar respuesta a estas interrogantes tendremos que buscar en un sinnúmero de procesos de investigación y tiempos, más allá de su delimitación espacial actual.

ANTECEDENTES DE INVESTIGACIÓN

En este apartado realizaremos un esbozo de las escasas investigaciones previas que se han realizado en el estado de Aguascalientes, tal vez uno de los estados más abandonados del país en relación a estudios arqueológicos. Así en 1926, Moisés Herrera informa de unas ruinas en el Municipio de Calvillo, sitio que es llamado Monte Huma. En este informe Herrera describe varios tipos de estructuras localizadas en este sitio, es importante señalar que esta zona arqueológica nunca ha vuelto a ser ubicada por ningún otro medio o investigador (Valencia 1993:3) a pesar de que El Atlas Arqueológico de la República Mexicana (Valencia 1994:15) hace referencia a los datos presentados por Herrera, además de mencionar los sitios de Jalpa y Tabasco.

Posteriormente Carlos Margain presenta ante la Mesa Redonda de la Sociedad Mexicana de Antropología un trabajo titulado "Zonas Arqueológicas de Querétaro, Guanajuato, Aguascalientes y Zacatecas" en la cual el autor intenta presentar una visión general de la arqueología de esta zona; sin embargo, en este trabajo nunca se hace mención a sitios en el estado de Aguascalientes. En su trabajo de investigación, realizado a mediados de los ochenta, José Luis Lorenzo y Lorena Mirambell (1985) realizan un recorrido en los estados de Aguascalientes, Zacatecas y Durango con el fin de buscar sitios

del arcaico, en su recorrido registraron los sitios del Tepozan I y II, además del sitio de las Raíces (ahora conocido como El Ocote).

A fines del 1986 los arqueólogos Sergio Sánchez y Rosalba Delgadillo del Departamento de Salvamento Arqueológico de México llevaron a cabo una inspección sobre el transecto del área que cubriría un ducto de Pemex, el cual estaba en proceso de construcción y recorría los estados de Aguascalientes y Zacatecas. Estos investigadores no reportan ningún sitio verificado por ellos a no ser por informes de lugareños que les mencionan puntos como Tepezala, Asientos, El Chichimeco, El Chiquihuite y El Tepozan (Valencia 1993:4).

Ante la ausencia de arqueólogos permanentes en el Centro INAH del estado Aguascalientes en ocasiones se pide apoyo a los arqueólogos del Centro INAH ubicado en Zacatecas, así Peter Jiménez y Baudelina García en atención a varias denuncias lograron registrar sitios como El Ocote I y El Ocote II. De acuerdo a las descripciones que se presentaron, estos sitios, al igual que muchos de la zona, exhibían un alto grado de deterioro por causas antrópicas y naturales. En ellos, fueron encontrados artefactos hechos con riolita, pedernal, obsidiana y cuarzo; además de cerámica doméstica.

En 1992, Daniel Valencia registró un total de nueve sitios con petrograbados y pintura rupestre. De igual manera, este investigador realizó una aproximación cronológica basándose en materiales cerámicos principalmente los tipos rojo sobre bayo, negro esgrafiado, negativo, negro sobre naranja y rayas grises. Estos materiales sugieren una larga ocupación que iría desde el año 100 d.C. hasta 1200 d.C. (Fernández 2001:5). Posteriormente otros tres trabajos de tesis sobre pintura rupestre fueron realizados (González Leos y Macías Quintero 2007; Macías Quintero 2006; Palacios Díaz 2010) incrementando las investigaciones sobre este tema.

El arqueólogo Eloy Castellanos durante su periodo de colaboración con el Centro INAH Aguascalientes realizó un recorrido y un registro de sitios entre los años de 1991 y 1992. De hecho en el año de 1992 éste llevó a cabo excavaciones de sondeo en el sitio de Cerro de Enmedio, Cerro del Meco, Plan de Potrerillos y al parecer también en Santiago, aunque no nos ha sido posible confirmar esta información.

En el año de 1993, por invitación del Gobierno del Estado de Aguascalientes el arqueólogo estadounidense John Foster (1994) realizó un recorrido y un registro de sitios en la Sierra Fría pertenecientes a San José de Gracia, Calvillo y Rincón de Romo. Este investigador reportó los sitios de Playa de las Cebolletas, Cueva Barranca del Rico y Agua Escondida, además de otros sitios como Agua Encampanada, Mesa del Águila, Cueva del Chamuco, Barranca del Rico, Puerto del Aire y Cerro de Enmedio.

Ahora bien, en lo que respecta a la zona de Santiago, si bien la existencia y ubicación de este sitio no había pasado desapercibida para muchos de los pobladores de Aguascalientes y otros puntos aledaños, los trabajos de investigación en este lugar han sido nulos, a pesar de haberse realizado muchas visitas por parte de diversos investigadores. Anteriormente se había hecho referencia a la falta de ubicación de este sitio en un mapa histórico así como la escasa existencia de documentación. Entre la poca documentación de este sitio podemos citar al arqueólogo Eloy Castellanos quien en 1991 registró por primera vez este sitio, posteriormente aparecen otras dos cédulas de registro del mismo en 1992, además de unas hojas con observaciones generales.

Este sitio también fue recorrido y reportado a las autoridades del INAH por el biólogo Mario Pérez quien siempre ha mostrado interés por la protección de este sitio, por lo que siempre ha acompañado en sus visitas al personal del INAH. Subsiguientemente el sitio fue estudiado por la arqueóloga Ana María Pelz como parte del trabajo de revisión de sitios bajo responsabilidad del Centro INAH Aguascalientes, debido que el gobierno del estado planea realizar una carretera que ha hecho una línea de traza a unos metros del límite del sitio.

De momento existen investigaciones y excavaciones en áreas muy cercanas como Ojocaliente por el arqueólogo Gerardo Fernández y en El Ocote por la arqueóloga Ana María Pelz, pero definitivamente nada en este sitio. Existe la referencia de un proyecto de recorrido realizado en 2000-2001 por el arqueólogo Christopher Neill de la Universidad Autónoma de Zacatecas, donde supuestamente recorrió y colectó materiales para análisis los cuales sirvieron como material para elaboración de tesis de sus estudiantes; no obstante, no existe referencia de algún proyecto y/o permiso de investigación presentado o autorizado por parte del Consejo de Arqueología que sirva de referencia.

INVESTIGACIONES REGIONALES

El interés por realizar estudios a nivel regional se encuentra no sólo en la falta de información en sitios como estos, sino también en el hecho de que es necesario tratar de entender la dinámica de interacción que llevaron a cabo las sociedades humanas que habitaron esta parte del país. Según nos marcan las fuentes, la región que nos ocupa se encontraba habitada al menos por dos grupos correspondientes a los tan mal comprendidos chichimecas, quienes se distribuían por esta parte de la geografía del país; ellos son los Guachichiles o Cuachichiles y los Caxcanes (Caretta y Motilla 2008).

Wigberto Jiménez Moreno (1943) presentó una división territorial de estos grupos, siguiendo el cauce del río San Pedro de Aguascalientes y definió la extensa expansión territorial de los Guachichiles, gracias a esto se ha podido identificar su movilidad desde Saltillo Coahuila hasta San Felipe Guanajuato, (Valencia 1993:8). Al parecer el epicentro de su desarrollo y distribución era lo que ahora conocemos como el Gran Tunal ubicado en el estado de San Luis Potosí, un territorio que seguramente compartieron con otros grupos entre ellos los

Guamaraes. Según referencias tomadas de los mexicas, De las Casas (1936:589) describe a este grupo como los Guachichiles, llamados de esta manera por traer la cabeza o el cabello pintado de rojo o bien por portar bonetes de cuero pintados de rojo o tocados con plumas del mismo color. Es importante hacer hincapié que los mismos Guachichiles estaban formados por diferentes grupos, para más detalles sobre este grupo véase Galaviz de Capdeville (1967:44).

Acuña (1988:300) ubica a los caxcanes en el actual estado de Zacatecas y en Guadalajara, Jalisco, incluyendo el oeste de Los Altos (Teocaltiche, Mechoacanejo y Teocaltitlán), Huejúcar, Colotán y lo que ahora se conoce como Calvillo Aguascalientes antes valle de Huejúcar. Jiménez Betts (1988) ha llamado a este gran espacio territorial Región de los Cañones o Región Caxcana.

Por lo que se puede apreciar en los restos arqueológicos y por los datos históricos con los que se cuentan, esta zona poseía una amplia extensión territorial así como un largo asentamiento. Juchipila o Xuchupila aparece también como Taltan en las fuentes (Tello 1945: IV:47[1542]), población que fue conquistada por los caxcanes en el siglo XII (Baus Czitrom 1982:97) y estuvo bajo su control hasta la entrada de los españoles en el siglo XVI (Weigand 1985). El Cerro de Las Ventanas es identificado por Weigand (1985:169-170) como el "Peñol de Juchipila" cercano al "Peñol del Mixton" de las Crónica de la Conquista del Reino de Nueva Galicia (Razo Zaragoza 1963:343[1542]), este último también se define como otro centro ceremonial y político del pueblo de los caxcanes.

Parece ser que la lengua de los caxcanes era una variante del Náhuatl similar a la de los mexicas, sin embargo, dada la forma brusca de ser de los caxcanes y su manera de hacer uso de su lengua se les refería como "mexicanos rústicos", "tochos", o "villanos" (Baus 1985:98; Santoscoy 1903:71-72; Tello 1945:IV:40). Inclusive Tello (1942:II:19, 382), hace referencias muy claras

de la relación existente entre los mexicas y los caxcanes no sólo como parte de un mismo grupo lingüístico sino también como adoradores de, al menos, una deidad en común Huitzilopochtli. De la misma información que podemos encontrar en las fuentes y de los restos arqueológicos observados en superficie y análisis de materiales cerámicos se puede asumir una larga ocupación y desarrollo social en este sitio. Phil Weigand, afirma que cuando menos existen cuatro tipos cerámicos pertenecientes al Cerro de Las Ventanas y el valle de Juchipila (Weigand 1985:173-175). El primero de estos tipos cerámicos llamado *Policromo Negativo de las Ventanas,* según Weigand, es una variación local del valle de Juchipila, de los estilos que aparecen en la zona de Chupícuaro durante el preclásico. Entre estos se distinguen las figurillas, las vasijas trípodes, copas y escudillas. Asimismo, este autor menciona que este tipo de material también se ha descubierto hacia el norte de esta región en el Valle de Mal Paso, usualmente asociado a entierros. El segundo tipo, *Bicromo Negativo de Las Ventanas,* se encuentra distribuido tanto en áreas de habitación como entierros. Aquí nos preguntamos ¿cómo sabe Weigand que pertenecían a entierros cuando oficialmente no excavó ninguno? ¿Habrán sido materiales que encontró asociados a entierros saqueados? Entre las cerámicas características de este tipo se encuentran platos, jarros, escudillas, así como vasijas trípodes. Este tipo de elementos son identificados como los mismos que se han recuperado en la región de Chalchihuites (llamado Negativo A), en el valle de Malpaso, en el Cañón de Bolaños y otras áreas de Jalisco. Weigand afirma que el tercer tipo de material (*Policromo de Las Ventanas*), también aparece en sitios preclásicos de Jalisco. Las formas usuales en que aparece este material cerámico son: jarros, platos, figurillas, escudillas y vasijas trípodes. Finalmente, el cuarto tipo fue bautizado como *Negro en Rojo de Las Ventanas,* se encuentra frecuentemente en vasijas y figurillas. Este material se encuentra a lo largo del período Clásico y Postclásico en la zona, por sus semejanzas podría estar asociado a aquellos propios del Suroeste Estadounidense y a los llamados Policromos de St. Johns y Wingate de acuerdo a Weigand.

Durante el diseño del North-Central Frontier of Mesoamerica (Kelley et al.1961-1963:1-37), tanto el valle de Juchipila como el valle de Malpaso se definieron como zonas pertenecientes al Área 4. La definición, mejor dicho, la percepción que Kelley hizo de esta "área arqueológica" estaba basaba en correlaciones observadas en análisis detallados que éste realizó de la colección de materiales del Sr. Sescosse provenientes de la región de Apozol-La Purísima-La Tirisia en Juchipila y su comparación con otras colecciones.

En este sentido, Schöndube (1980:173) ha señalado que la tradición de tumbas de tiro del occidente mexicano y la tradición Chupícuaro mostraban muy poco traslape, a excepción de la zona de Los Altos de Jalisco y Juchipila. Esta confluencia de Preclásico Tardío y Clásico Temprano se manifiesta en el complejo cerámico del valle de Juchipila, a la fecha, los materiales cerámicos identificados en este valle han sido vasijas del grupo Colorines descritas para el complejo Tabachines del valle de Atemajac, una región considerada dentro de la tradición de tumbas de tiro del occidente mexicano (Galván 1991:48-50). En estas tumbas se aprecia la existencia de cuencos trípodes y platos negativos policromos de Apozol y Juchipila los cuales son análogos a los que fueron encontrados en el Cerro Encantado en la región vecina de Los Altos de Jalisco (Bell 1974).

Estas cerámicas están directamente relacionadas a los tipos identificados como componentes del complejo Morales del noroeste de Guanajuato (Braniff 1972, 1998; Jiménez 1988). Estas son las cerámicas tempranas que Kelley definió como tipos de "filiación Chupícuaro." En el Cerro encantado, dichas cerámicas negativas diagnósticas se encontraron asociadas con las figurillas huecas conocidas

como "cornudos", asociación que también se da en la zona de Apozol. De hecho, un reciente trabajo de rescate hecho en Juchipila proporcionó materiales negativos pintados, ollas como las que fueron encontradas por Bell (1974, fig. 7) en Cerro Encantado.

Los nexos existentes con la zona de los Colorines-Tabachines/Morales también han sido definidos en Los Altos de Jalisco como pertenecientes a la fase I (200 a.C.-300 d.C.), al parecer éstos indican la integración del valle de Juchipila a la región del Los Altos desde fechas muy tempranas, sobre todo, dicha convergencia se muestra por la presencia de trompetas de caracolas, espejos de pirita, figuras huecas de "cornudos" y diseños geométricos policromos sobre negativos, algo que puede ser considerado como perteneciente al complejo Morales de Guanajuato.

Una vez que Kelley analizó la colección de Sescosse y los artefactos provenientes de Totoate en el valle de Bolaños, un tercer componente tuvo que ser considerado para esta región, así los cuencos trípode, garras o bulbos huecos, negativos pintados del valle de Juchipila mantienen ciertas analogías directas con elementos recientemente encontrados en una tumba de tiro sellada en el valle de Bolaños, la cual dio fechas radiocarbónicas de entre el II y IV siglo d.C. (Cabrero 2005). Estos elementos culturales pertenecientes al valles de Bolaños sugieren una confluencia dentro del valle de Juchipila de tres de los mayores sistemas culturales regionales del occidente de México.

Es de suponerse que las dinámicas culturales resultantes de estas confluencias de tradiciones del occidente mexicano estuvieron relacionadas de alguna manera a los procesos que produjo la oleada inicial de la expansión mesoamericana hacia el valle de Malpaso y la región de Chalchihuites, las que dieron como resultado el horizonte Canutillo-Malpaso, iniciando al menos con la parte temprana del período Clásico Medio. Las vasijas negras esgrafiadas con rojo son las cerámicas diagnósticas para este valle. Una variedad especial de ellas ha sido previamente identificada como una variante regional del Atoyac inciso de la cuenca de Sayula (Noyola 1994, fig. 5). Otras excavaciones realizadas en el Cerro de Tepisuazco, Jalpa, produjeron una gran cantidad de este material cerámico. También las colecciones de Sescosse y Muro provenientes de Apozol incluían este tipo de variedad. La distribución de este material es continua, se extiende desde el valle de Juchipila al valle de Atemajac (Galván 1976: lams. 11 y 13; Schöndube comunicación personal 1994), a la cuenca de Sayula y hasta la costa de Colima, en lo que Ramírez Urrea (1997) ha propuesto como un marcador cerámico que pertenece a una esfera de interacción mayor, la cual tuvo lugar del 500 al 750 d.C.

El elemento diagnóstico que se dio a través de esta extensa esfera de interacción es la figurilla denominada Clase F de Cerrito de García (Gómez Gastélum y de la Torre 1996:142), Jiménez y Darling (2000:169) han llamado a esta esfera como Jalisco-Colima. Las figurillas de Cerrito de García están presentes en el valle de Juchipila, en las zonas de Apozol y Jalpa, y en el valle de Bolaños, Kelley y Hrdlicka encontraron este tipo de figurillas en su excavación en Totoate incluso Cabrero las ha detectado en el sitio conocido como Piñón en el valle de Bolaños. La cronología para el sitio de las figurillas F de Cerrito de García es de aproximadamente 600-900 d.C. (Ramírez Urrea 1997).

Igualmente, la cerámica negativa pintada de base anular perteneciente al período Epi-Clásico constituye un importante marcador de este horizonte cultural. La distribución de este tipo de material cerámico diagnóstico se extiende desde el valle de Juchipila en el Cerro de Tepisuazco, Jalpa, y Apozol hasta la región de Los Altos (López-Mestas et al. 1994), hacia el Este a León, Guanajuato (López-Mestas y Ramos de la Vega 1998), al Norte a través de la región de Encarnación de Díaz en Jalisco y Aguascalientes hasta la región de Villa García en la parte Este del estado de Zacatecas y el sur del valle de Atemajac (Schöndube y Galván 1978).

Este tipo de material cerámico también ha sido encontrado como componente intrusivo en la cuenca de Sayula (Noyola 1994:79, fig. 4). La cerámica negativa de base anular de Juchipila es considerada una cerámica de elite, contemporánea a la cerámica negativa de Tepozan proveniente del complejo de La Quemada hacia el norte del país. Ambos tipos comparten los mismos diseños iconográficos, aunque la cerámica de base anular aun no ha sido identificada en el valle de Malpaso. La distribución de la cerámica negativa pintada de base anular (cuencos) puede ser considerada como evidencia importante de la esfera de interacción que une a estas dos regiones contiguas, por lo tanto, pueden, tentativamente, ser identificadas como la sub-esfera Altos-Juchipila.

Fragmentos de secciones de moldes faciales de cerámica tipo efigie constituyen otro elemento diagnóstico del valle de Juchipila. Estos han sido encontrados en San Aparicio en la región de Los Altos (Jiménez 1989:14, fig. 2, 1995, fig. IB), en el valle de Atemajac (Schöndube y Galván 1978; Schöndube 1983), y en los sitios de Cerritos Colorados y Atoyac en la cuenca de Sayúla (Noyola 1994:62-63, fig. 2 y 3; Ramírez Urrea 1997).

Entre los componentes arquitectónicos del Epi-Clásico de Tepisuazco se ha recuperado una amplia variedad de vasijas pseudocloisonné, al igual que ornamentos manufacturados en concha, piedras verdes y turquesa. Es de importancia mencionar que una variedad específica de vasija pseudocloisonné decorada hallada en Tepisuazco es del mismo tipo encontrado en La Quemada y Totoate.

Jiménez Betts descubrió en 1991 un complejo circular Guachimonton en el sitio del Cerro de Tepisuazco, en donde el patrón arquitectónico predominante responde a la forma de un complejo pirámide-plaza de tipo rectangular. Desde entonces este ha sido verificado en varias ocasiones por Weigand (Weigand et al. 1999). La presencia de arquitectura de plazas rectangulares con arquitectura circular también ocurre en Totoate (Kelley 1971). Hasta ahora, la fecha y la cronología de las estructuras principales sólo es tentativa. La presencia de cerámica de tipo Gavilán Policromo y Amapa (Meighan 1976), en Tepisuazco podría relacionarse con los fechados de complejos arquitectónicos circulares.

La ocupación de Juchipila durante el Posclásico es limitada y sólo sabemos algo de ella por la información que dan las fuentes históricas, es así como se conoce que durante la época de la conquista y la guerra del Mixtón esta región estuvo habitada por los caxcanes.

El hecho de suponer que el sitio del Cerro de Santiago haya sido ocupado por un grupo social específico, los caxcanes, nos brinda la oportunidad de poder realizar, al igual que en la zona de Las Ventanas, una cronología más larga y detallada. Tal acción nos podrá ayudar a establecer los lazos de interacción social, cultural y económica entre grupos del occidente y sus contrapartes ubicadas más al norte (Caretta y Motilla 2008). El valor no sólo de este sitio, el Cerro de Santiago, sino de la región se encuentra, por un lado, en el hecho de que éste se reconoce como enclave estratégico entre las sociedades que se desarrollaron en lo que ahora son los estados de Aguascalientes, Zacatecas, Guadalajara y sus consecuentes relaciones con grupos que se establecieron hacia el norte, occidente, centro y sur de México (Lelgemann 2001). Por otro lado, debido a que se encuentra en un área semiárida con ojos de agua esta zona se posiciona como ruta de paso o zona de transición ecotonal de grupos sedentarios, semi-sedentarios y cazadores-recolectores del desierto.

En efecto, las preguntas que se hagan acerca del origen, desarrollo y organización interna de los grupos de esta región y los grupos vecinos como El Ocote, La Montesita, La Quemada, Las Ventanas, El Cóporo y la Región del Gran Tunal darán respuesta a muchas de las interrogantes que se tienen en la actualidad sobre estas sociedades pero sobretodo su interacción con otros grupos dentro y más allá de su región y de la Mesoamérica Mayor. Por "Mesoamérica Mayor" nos referimos al área que incluye o considera la parte norte del país y no el concepto monolítico de la Mesoamérica Marginal.

EL SITIO DEL CERRO DE SANTIAGO

El Cerro de Santiago se encuentra ubicado en las coordenadas UTM E773.5000/N2447.400 (Caretta 2006), a unos dos kilómetros del poblado de Santiago en el Municipio de Pabellón de Arteaga, muy cerca de la ciudad de Aguascalientes, a escasa media hora por la autopista hacia Zacatecas. El sitio se encuentra en lo que fuera parte de los terrenos de la antigua Hacienda de Santiago.

La Hacienda de Santiago, actualmente localidad del municipio de Pabellón de Arteaga, históricamente se ubicaba en la jurisdicción de Rincón de Romos. Las primeras referencias documentales a este lugar se remontan a las primeras décadas del siglo XVIII. Hacia 1715, la hacienda de Santiago, entonces con extensión de aproximadamente 1750 dedicados al ganado mayor era propiedad de Margarita de la Escalera, casada entonces con Andrés Tello de Lomas; la hacienda le había sido heredada a ella por su difunto esposo Matías López de Carrasquilla. Hacia 1772 se le señalaba una superficie de dos sitios de ganado mayor, aproximadamente 3,500 hectáreas. En el casco de la hacienda vivían entonces 113 personas, según un recuento de la población de curato de Aguascalientes. Ya en el siglo XIX, la familia De la Vega era propietaria de la hacienda hacia 1875, siendo entonces Patricio de la Vega el dueño de las tierras, mientras que para 1910 los herederos de Gonzalo de la Vega y de María Concepción de la Vega detentaban la posesión; para ese momento la extensión de la hacienda se había reducido a 1829 hectáreas.

La hacienda fue afectada por las dotaciones ejidales debido que la mayor parte de sus tierras fueron repartidas para ejidos en las décadas de los veintes y los treintas del siglo XX (Ramón García. Datos de fichas de Catálogo, Centro INAH-Aguascalientes 2004). Según el régimen de tenencia de la tierra, gran parte de la zona arqueológica pertenece a la Señora Margarita De Loera (Castellanos 1992).

Después de nuestra primera temporada de campo (Caretta 2006) pudimos constatar que la parte más importante y visible del sitio se halla ubicada sobre la cima del cerro, nucleada en, al menos, cuatros sectores. En este sentido, la parte que corresponde a los montículos mayores, incluyendo un posible juego de pelota, se encuentra separada de dos áreas aparentemente destinadas como espacios habitacionales. Desde la cima del cerro se aprecia una excelente vista de los valles en ambos lados así como de la Sierra Fría, además de una buena vista de la Presa Elías Calles y del arroyo que todavía lleva agua en la parte baja de la cañada de Jocoqui. En esta parte todavía se pueden encontrar dos "ojos de agua", uno de ellos llamado el "meco", que aunque muy pequeños aun sirven de abrevaderos para la fauna. En este lugar se halla un arroyo de tipo temporal que baja de la parte alta del cerro y que pasa al lado de una de las concentraciones de estructuras arquitectónicas, cause que sin duda alguna no se manifiesta de manera fortuita.

Debido al abandono que este sitio ha sufrido y al uso que actualmente tiene como terreno de agostadero, dicha zona presenta la proliferación de vegetación muy densa, particularmente la que corresponde a nopaleras, huizaches, sangregado, guapilla, lechuguilla, pastos y palo flojo. Mucha de esta vegetación se concentra particularmente en las esquinas de las estructuras lo cual, por una parte, ha causado el deterioro de las construcciones pero por otro ha permitido que muchas estructuras se mantengan firmes.

Las estructuras, principalmente rectangulares, están conformadas por alineamientos de roca muchos de ellos se desplantan sobre la roca madre y otros se levantan sobre una superficie de suelo muy somero. Existen otras estructuras que forman plataformas de baja altura, 55 cm aproximadamente, a simple vista sólo se puede observar que éstas han sido edificadas con rocas careadas; que al parecer tuvieron algún mortero y que la mayoría de las estructuras expuestas se ha perdido. De hecho la observación del mortero se hizo en la parte expuesta de un pozo de saqueo, aun cuando a simple vista las estructuras parecen estar orientadas, lo cierto es que muchas de ellas siguen la conformación de la topo forma del mismo cerro (Caretta 2006).

La parte de mayor tamaño de las estructuras presenta una altura de no más de tres metros desde el nivel de su desplante, casi todas muestran huellas de saqueo aunque sólo de forma superficial. Se pueden apreciar varias estructuras que aparentemente formarían cuartos de alturas no mayores a 55 cm en promedio y muchas de ellas se encuentran afectadas por saqueo, pastoreo, y daños provocados por la vegetación, la fauna y el alto grado de erosión que ocurre en la zona. La erosión actual es muy marcada en varios puntos de la zona, en donde se puede observar perfectamente los procesos de pérdida de suelos por arrastre debido a la falta de vegetación, como consecuencia de esto se aprecia la intemperización de la roca la cual ha quedado expuesta a los efectos climáticos. En el área cubierta de la Acrópolis se pudieron registrar 71 elementos arquitectónicos: 14 plataformas, 12 montículos, 25 estructuras, dos patios, 17 muros y un juego de pelota (Caretta 2006).

En la parte denominada Alfa Centro de sitio de se encuentra un patio hundido con un altar central, que está rodeado por estructuras rectangulares y otras de tipo piramidal, las cuales sin duda nos evocan precisamente el estilo de construcción mesoamericano. En la parte baja del sitio se encuentra centralizada la mayor parte del asentamiento poblacional del sitio de Santiago, la cual se ha podido mapear en fechas recientes. En esta área se encuentran complejos habitacionales de cuartos aledaños que conforman unidades distribuidas en un área aproximada de 90 hectáreas (Figura I.2.1). Los materiales que se han encontrado en superficie se asemejan a los de sitios aledaños, particularmente con los de la región del Cañón de Juchipila, La Quemada y San Luis Potosí.

Existen restos de más estructuras la cuales se ubican de manera dispersa en los cerros aledaños, en la parte media y alta de los cerros adyacentes en los que es necesario trabajar. El área donde se pueden observar restos de este sitio se expanden a un poco más de 100 hectáreas y la parte donde se nuclean los componentes arquitectónicos son de unas 20 hectáreas según los recorridos hechos en diferentes años por los arqueólogos Castellanos, Pelz, Nicolás Caretta y el biólogo Mario Pérez y Jorge Martínez.

En varias partes del cerro pueden observarse restos de materiales arqueológicos esparcidos sobre la superficie además de muchos otros que han sido removidos por acción natural, fenómeno de arrastre y por acción antrópica, actos de saqueo. Gran parte de los materiales en superficie muestran un alto grado de erosión, entre estos restos de material arqueológico se han detectado tipos cerámicos relacionados con la región del cañón de Juchipila, particularmente los fragmentos de bases anulares, además de material de la región de San Luis Potosí.

Con lo antes mencionado, sin duda salta a la vista la contradicción entre aquellos argumentos que sostienen que este tipo de grupos, quienes se desarrollaron en esta zona del semi-desierto mexicano y su organización social, se caracterizaban como simples sociedades cazadoras-recolectoras con asentamientos estacionales y con todas las atenuantes que esto significa. Lo cierto es que hemos notado con base en las primeras investigaciones hechas en el Cerro de Santiago, y en aquello que han dejado ver sitios aledaños que la diversidad de grupos y su complejidad social es mucha, ésta va desde los asentamientos de tipo campamentos hasta asentamientos de tamaños considerables que implicaban una organización social más compleja, por lo menos de tipo cacical. Cierto es que falta mucho por avanzar en las investigaciones, no solamente en este sitio sino en otros tantos existentes en el Mar Chichimeca de Kelly. Así esta investigación se presenta como una de varias que busca servir de apoyo al conocimiento de la frontera Septentrional de Mesoamérica, donde se ponen a prueba las propuestas teóricas existentes y los modelos explicativos antes señalados para la explicación del desarrollo cultural de sitios de la región. Un mejor entendimiento de la cronología del sitio de Santiago, de sus dimensiones, su arquitectura y sus materiales nos dará pauta para entender mejor su dinámica de interacción regional, interregional y panregional y servirá para dar pie a futuras respuestas acerca del origen, desarrollo y organización interna de estos pueblos, lo que a su vez dará respuesta a muchas de las interrogantes que se tienen en la actualidad sobre estas sociedades y sobre su interacción con otros grupos que se desarrollaron en esta región y más allá de la Mesoamérica Mayor.

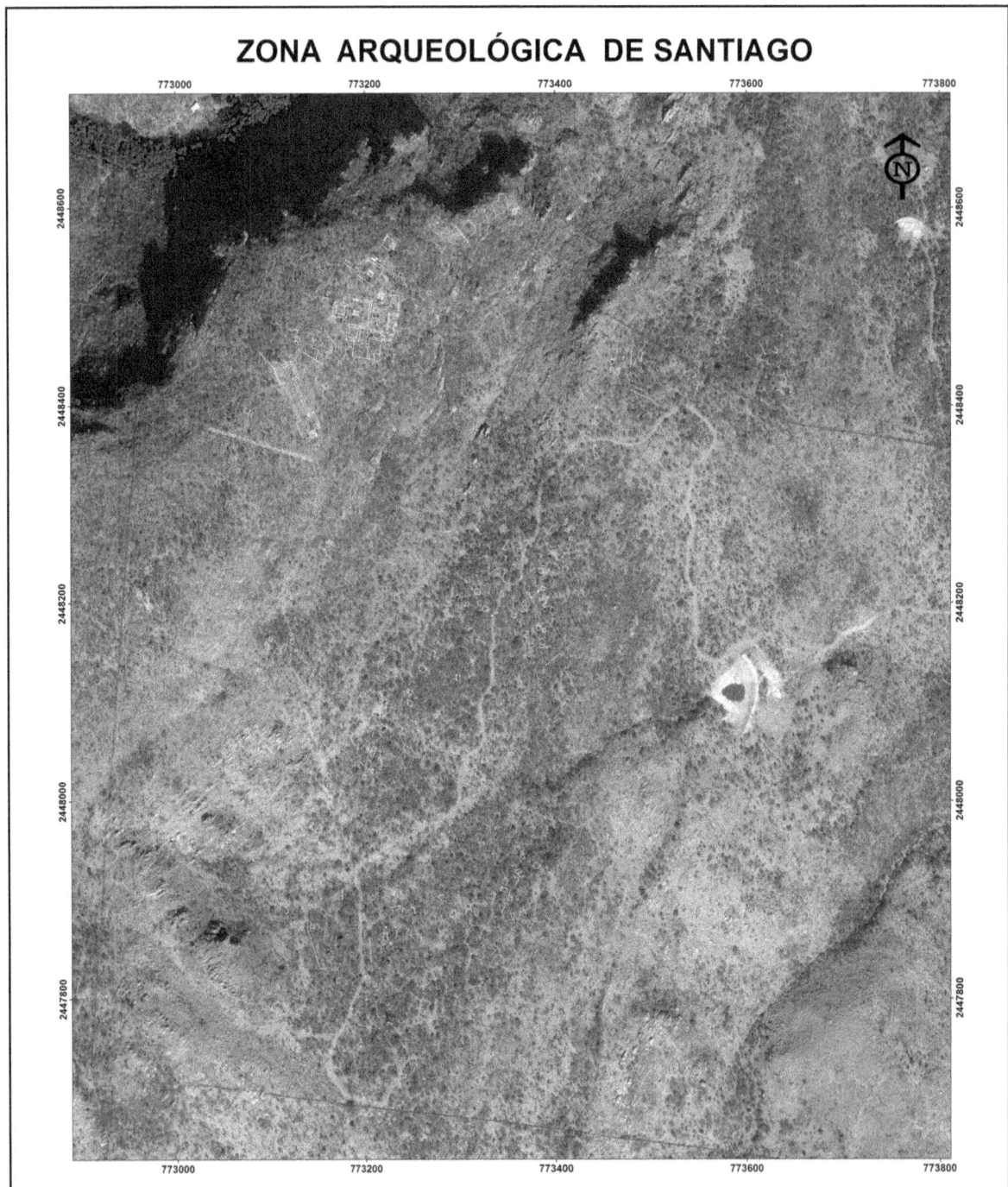

Figura I.2.1. Sitio arqueológico de Santiago, Aguascalientes.

Part I, Chapter 3

The Prehispanic Occupation of the
Río Fuerte Valley, Sinaloa

John Carpenter

ABSTRACT

Geographically, the Río Fuerte, in northern Sinaloa, lies on the margins of both the Northwest/ Southwest and West Mexican macrotraditions. Since 2004, the Proyecto Arqueológico Norte de Sinaloa (INAH) has carried out the first systematic archaeological investigations in this region; the results indicate human occupation since at least the Paleoindian period, and suggest that both the Huatabampo and Serrana (Río Sonora) archaeological traditions most likely represent differing lowland and highland expressions with a shared origin with strong Mogollon affinities. Interaction with the Aztatlán tradition and participation in the long distance exchange network between West Mexico and the Northwest/Southwest is also evident.

RESUMEN

Geográficamente, el río Fuerte en el norte de Sinaloa, cae en las dos macrotradiciones del Noroeste/Suroeste y el Occidente de México. Desde el 2004, el Proyecto Arqueológico Norte de Sinaloa (INAH), ha realizado las primeras investigaciones arqueológicas sistemáticas en la región; los resultados indican una ocupación humana cuando menos desde el periodo Paleoindio y siguieren que las tradiciones arqueológicas Huatabampo y Serrana (Río Sonora) probablemente representan diferentes expresiones, de las tierras bajas y las tierras altas, con un origen compartido (con fuertes afinidades Mogollon). La interacción con la tradición Aztatlán es también evidente.

INTRODUCTION

As a result of Gordon Ekholm's (1939, 1940, 1942) pioneering archaeological investigations in Sonora and northern Sinaloa carried out between 1937 and 1939 for the American Museum of Natural History's Sonora-Sinaloa Archaeological Project, the Río Fuerte Valley has long been suggested as representing the frontier between the West Mexican/Mesoamerican and Northwest/ Southwest archaeological macro-traditions. Despite the potential significance of this region, it remained largely ignored over the years following Ekholm's initial observations and 2004, when the *Proyecto Arqueológico Norte de Sinaloa* (INAH) implemented systematic archaeological research in the region; to date, regional reconnaissance has been conducted within an area of approximately 9,000 km² ranging between the Sea of Cortes and *Cajón de Cancio* in the Sierra Madre Occidental (Figure I.3.1), with systematic surveys carried out in various locations; approximately 100 sites have been documented, with excavations carried out at 15 locations, including the La Viuda,

John Carpenter Centro INAH Sonora

SONORA

CHIHUAHUA

● El Fuerte

Los Mochis

● Guasave

● Guamuchil

DURANGO

Navolato
●

○
Culiacán

↑
N

Mazatlán

Escuinapa
●

60 km

40 mi

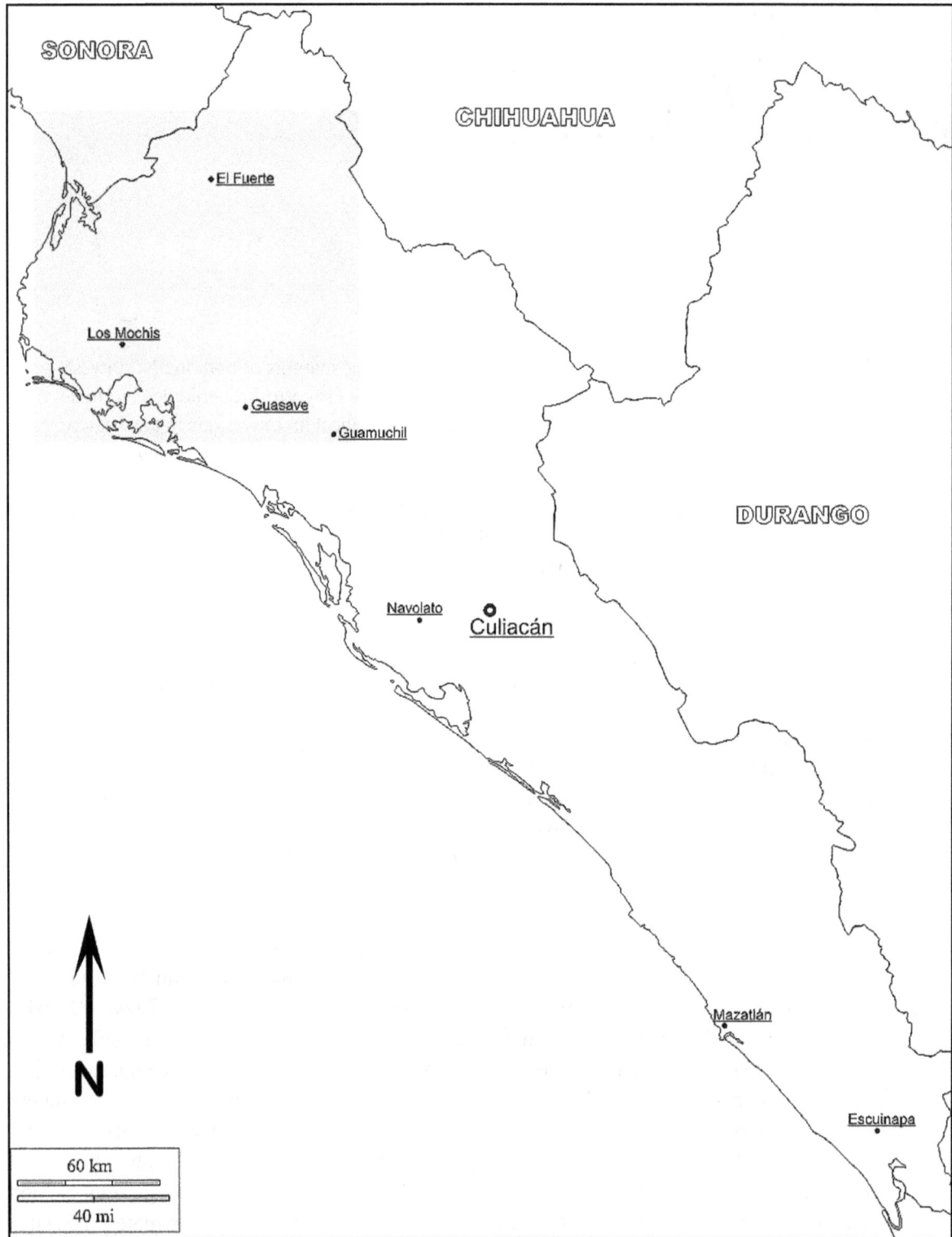

Figure I.3.1. Area encompassed by the INAH Proyecto Arqueológico Norte de Sinaloa.

Rincón de Buyubampo, Cerro de la Máscara, La Botijuela, and La Ciénega sites as well as several localities in and around Mochicahui (Figure I.3.2) (Carpenter 2009; Carpenter and Lopez 2009; Carpenter and Sánchez 2005, 2007; Carpenter et al. 2005, 2006, 2008a, 2008b, 2009a, 2009b).

Environmental Characteristics of the Río Fuerte Valley

The Río Fuerte is recognized as the largest river within Sinaloa, with a drainage basin comprising an area of 33,590 km² and a total discharge of some five million cubic meters (Schmidt 1976:34). The topography in this region of Sinaloa varies from sea level on the Sea of Cortés to some 2,290 m/7,328 ft in the uplands of the Sierra Madre Occidental and encompasses three principal physiographic provinces: 1) the coastal plain; 2) the foothills (*serrana*); and 3) the Sierra Madre Occidental. The Sierra Madre Occidental is composed of the worlds' largest block of rhyolite, along with other volcanic extrusives like andesite and basalt, which were deposited atop Precambrian and Mesozoic

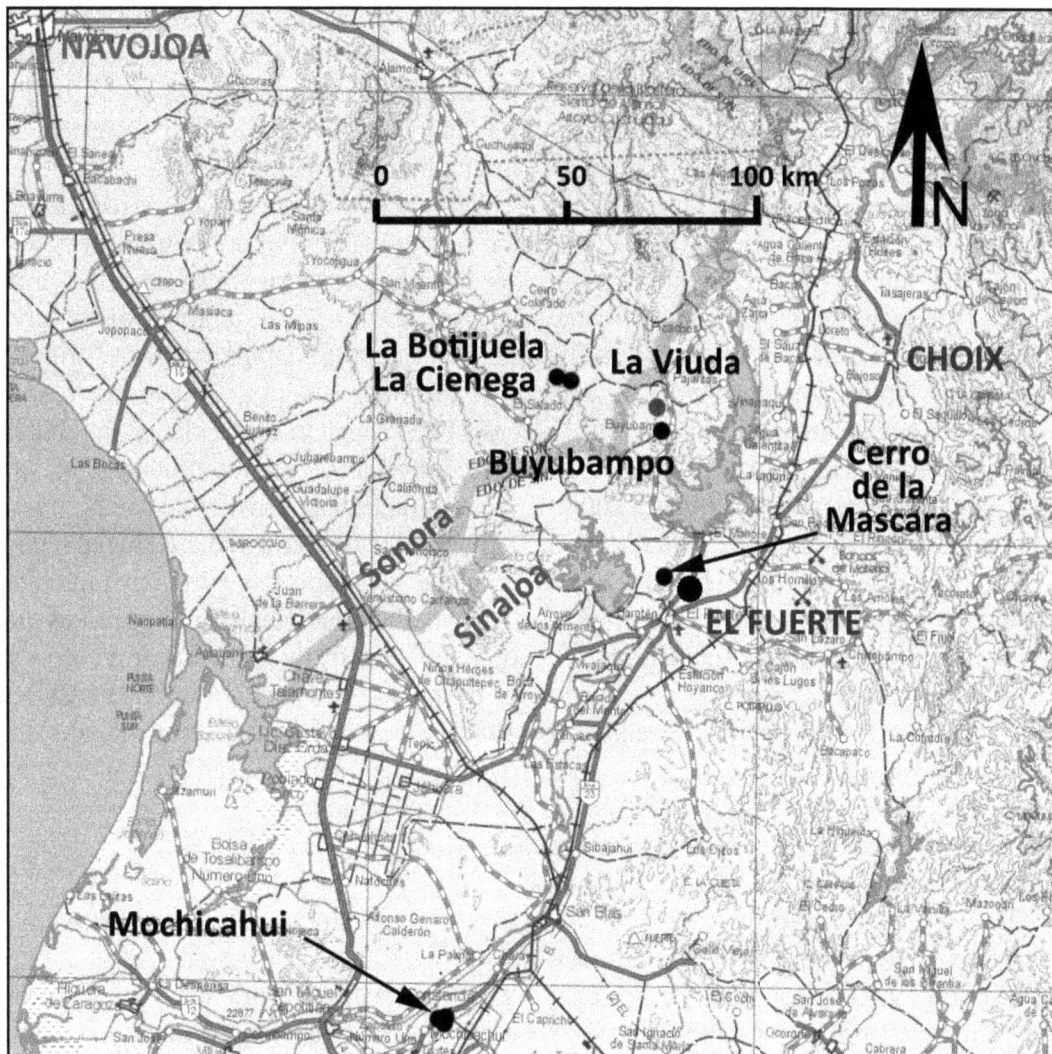

Figure I.3.2. Locations of the principal sites documented in the Río Fuerte region by the INAH Proyecto Arqueológico Norte de Sinaloa.

metamorphic strata (Schmidt 1976:26). Here, peaks rise to approximately 3,000 m/9,600 ft and are punctuated by deep, precipitous canyons, the most spectacular being the renowned Barranca de Cobre (Copper Canyon).

Average temperatures in this region vary from -1.5 °C (29 °F) in the winter, and 47 °C (117 °F) in the summer. The Spanish *conquistadores* christened the coastal lowlands as the "*tierra caliente,*" and early descriptions are rife with complaints of the stifling heat; a temperature of 56 degrees centigrade (133 °F) has been recorded at Huites, along the Río Fuerte (Schmidt 1978:6). Andrés Pérez de Ribas, a Jesuit missionary who spent several years in northern Sinaloa during the early 17th century, claimed the heat to be so excessive that it was due only to sheer luck that animals didn't fall over dead from their own melting fat (Pérez de Ribas 1944 I:122).

Annual average precipitation in the foothill province in Choix is 785 mm, 565 mm for El Fuerte and 302 mm for Ahome (Schmidt1978), and reflects the extreme southern limits of the bimodal distribution pattern characteristic of the Sonoran Desert. To the south of the Río Fuerte Valley, summer precipitation is predominant.

Oak woodlands are found in the foothills province above approximately 1,000 m/3,200 ft, while the highest elevations of the Sierra Madre, between 2,000 and 3,000 m/6,400 ft and 9,600 ft support diverse species of pines (*Pinus arizonica, P. engelmannii, P. ponderosa, P. chihuahuana*), with firs (*Pseudotsuga menziesii*) widely dispersed in the higher elevations (Rzedowski 1981:297).

The vegetation of the coastal plain, in its natural state, presents a dense and exuberant growth characteristic of the Sinaloan thorn forest (Figure I.3.3) (Rzedowski 1981:209). Here, acacia (*A. cymbispina*) is the predominant species (Shreve 1937). Other species associated with the Sinaloan thorn forest include pitahaya (*Stenocereus thurberi*), senita (*Lophocereus schotti*), echo (*Pachycereus pecten-aborignum*), maguey (*Agave schotti* y *A. ocahui*), palo fierro (*Olneya tesota*), torote (*Bursera* sp.), cassias (*Cassia atomaria* y *C. emarginata*), Sonoran ebony (*Pithecellobium sonorae*), palo colorado (*Caesalpinia platyloba*), Lonchocarpus megalanthus, copalillo (*Jatropha cordata*), palo verde (*Cercidium torreyanum*), mesquite (*Prosopis* sp.), mauto (*Lysiloma divaricata*) and palo blanco (*Piscidia mollis*) (Brown 1994:101-104; Rzedowski 1981:210). Riparian vegetation in the Río Fuerte Valley includes cottonwood (*Populus dimorpha*), sycamore (*Platanus* sp.), mesquite (*Prosopis juliflora*), camuchín (*Ficus* sp.), cumbro (*Celtis pallida*), cypress (*Taxodium mucronatum*), desert willow (*Chilopsis linearis*), y aliso (*Salix goodingii*) (Brown 1994:339).

The riparian zones and estuaries of this region comprise an integral part of the Pacific migratory bird flyways, offering seasonal homes to innumerable migratory birds. The Río Fuerte Valley is especially significant as it encompasses the northern limits of some tropical species as well as the southern limits of other northern species and is home to the worlds' greatest number of hummingbird species.

Among the most important resources associated with the coastal plain is the abundance of marine fauna. The combination of various factors, including prevailing winds, tides, sea floor relief and the alluvial and fluvial sediments combine to produce an extremely high biomass of phytoplankton which, in turn, makes the Sea of Cortés one of the richest marine ecosystems on the planet (Brusca 1976:85-93; Pérez Bedolla 1985:171). Important species include shrimp, oyster, clam, lobster, sardine, tuna, snapper, mullet and haddock.

THE PRECERAMIC OCCUPATIONS

Although specific evidence for a Paleoindian occupation remains largely unknown within the Río Fuerte Valley, Clovis tradition sites have been extensively documented throughout the adjacent state of Sonora (Di Peso 1955; Montané 1996

Figure I.3.3. Sinaloan thorn forest near El Fuerte, Sinaloa.

(1985); Robles Ortíz 1974; Sánchez 2001, 2010). Arturo Guevara (1987) previously described two fluted points from the Río Sinaloa Valley. In 2004, we recovered a late Paleoindian projectile point from the vicinity of Balácachi, in the central Fuerte Valley. In addition, presumably locally collected Paleoindian points are included among the artifacts displayed in the Casa de Cultura Conrado Espinoza, in Los Mochis. The remains of several undated mammoth remains have been reported from the *municipios* of El Fuerte and Ahome.

Similarly, information regarding the subsequent Archaic period occupations is practically unknown and is, as yet, restricted to isolated finds of Archaic point styles diagnostic of the Chiricahua phase of the Cochise Archaic (Álvarez et al. 2001). Additionally, several Archaic projectile points are displayed in the Casa de Cultura Conrado Espinoza, and in the Museo de Evora, in Guamúchil.

Based upon Bruce Benz's (1999) model of maize evolution/diffusion and linguistic data (Miller 1983a, 1983b), this region can also be suggested as the probable region where the incipient maize cultivators associated with the Early Agriculture period of the Sonoran Desert originated during, or shortly after, the Altithermal (Carpenter et al. 2002).

CERAMIC PERIOD TRADITIONS

With the emergence of ceramic traditions within Sinaloa, approximately dated to the years between 200 B.C. and 150 A.D., at least three major regional traditions can be discerned: Aztatlán, Huatabampo and Serrana (Río Sonora) along with two minor traditions (Tacuichamona and Rasped Ware). Among these, both the Huatabampo and Serrana traditions figure prominently in the ceramic period of the Río Fuerte region (Figure I.3.4).

The Huatabampo Tradition

The Huatabampo tradition extends along the coastal plain between approximately the Río Mocorito, near Guamúchil, Sinaloa and the margins of the Río Mayo, in southern Sonora, and in the Río Fuerte Valley, extends from the Sea of Cortés upriver to approximately Tehueco. This archaeological component was proposed by Ekholm (1939, 1940, 1942) in defining a complex of sites in the vicinity of the Río Mayo, characterized by coiled-and-scraped, fine-paste red wares with vessel forms including jars, bowls, and double-bodied canteens (Ekholm 1942:25). Additional attributes include ceramic ear spools, modeled spindle whorls, shell ornaments and extended burials with heads oriented to the north. Huatabampo components have been excavated in the vicinity of Huatabampo, Sonora (Álvarez 1990; Ekholm 1939, 1940, 1942), in Mochicahui, (Talavera and Manzanilla López 1991), and Guasave, Sinaloa (Ekholm 1939, 1940, 1942; Carpenter 1996). Based upon 12 radiocarbon dates from the El Ombligo funerary mound (Guasave Site) (Carpenter 1996) and Machomoncobe (Álvarez 1990), the Huatabampo tradition is tentatively dated to between 200 B.C. and 1450 A.D.

The Huatabampo tradition appears to emerge from the local expression of the San Pedro Cochise/Early Agriculture period. The initial ceramic horizon, represented by Huatabampo

Brown/Venadito Brown, developed between 200 B.C. and 200 A.D.; the data suggest that the Huatabampo phase and Batacosa/Cuchujaqui phases of the Serrana tradition, can be attributed to a single early Brown ware ceramic tradition (Álvarez 1982, 1990; Pailes 1972, 1976a). These types were followed shortly thereafter by the appearance of red wares. This general pattern has been observed throughout the regions where San Pedro phase materials have been identified, and may likely include the Río Sonora, Serrana, Loma San Gabriel and Tacuichamona traditions, along with the Mogollon, Trincheras and Hohokam (c.f. Foster 1991). Certain traits, such as modeled spindle whorls, ceramic ear spools and paint cloisonné gourds suggest affinities with West Mexico. Huatabampo pottery, on the other hand, is most often compared to either Mogollon or Hohokam pottery, and is generally included among the Sonoran brown ware series (Braniff 1992; Foster 1988; McGuire and Villalpando 1993; Pailes 1972, 1976a).

Shell ornament production reflects strong similarities to the Trincheras and Hohokam traditions. Marine shell undoubtedly served as an important commodity of exchange, and likely figured prominently in obtaining non-local resources such as turquoise, obsidian, olivine, and vesicular basalt (Álvarez 1990:76). Rare fragments of prismatic obsidian blades are indicative of interaction with their Aztatlán tradition neighbors to the south.

The construction of platform mounds was confirmed in the vicinity of the Arroyo Ocoroni, a tributary of the Río Sinaloa. These platform mounds continue to be incorporated in contemporary Semana Santa rituals by the Ocoroni/Yoreme. The funerary mounds so far documented within northern Sinaloa appear to be restricted to Huatabampo tradition contexts and may be considered as an indigenous trait.

Mochicahui

Mochicahui is located in the lower Río Fuerte

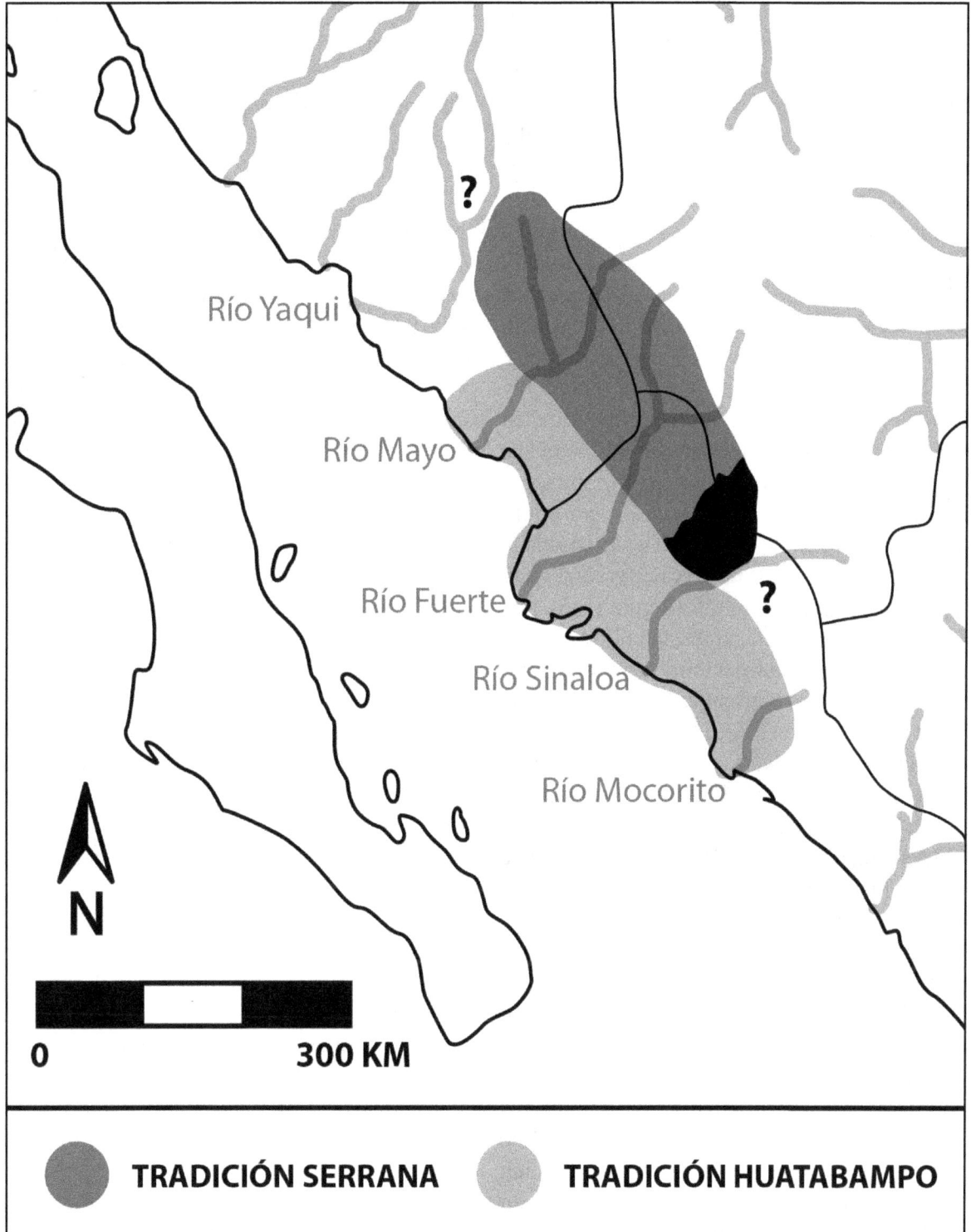

Figure I.3.4. Approximate geographical distribution of the Huatabampo and Serrana archaeological traditions.

Valley some 10 kilometers upriver from modern-day Los Mochis and, in the 16th century, was described by the Spaniards as the principal pueblo of the Zuaque (Pérez de Ribas 1944, I:234), who were recognized as the most powerful of the various Cahitan groups occupying the valley. Here, at least three funerary mounds have been documented. In 1988, Talavera and Manzanilla López (1991) recovered 15 burials from a small funerary mound in Mochicahui. The existence of an additional funerary mound in Mochicahui was documented in 2008 (Carpenter 2009). Unfortunately, this component was thoroughly looted in the late 1970s, producing an estimated 40 burials along with approximately 120 complete vessels, some of which are in the museum collections of the *Universidad Autónoma Indígena de México* (UAIM). This assemblage includes Huatabampo/Guasave red wares (Figure I.3.5), Guasave Red-on-buff (Figure I.3.6), and Aztatlán Red-on-buff and Aztatlán Polychrome (Figure I.3.7). Recently, a third funerary mound was discovered in November 2009 and salvage excavations recovered three burials. Additionally, over 11,000 sherds were recovered, representing 11 ceramic types including eight varieties, of which Guasave Red (33 percent), Guasave Brown (26 percent) and Guasave Buff (22 percent) were predominantly represented in the assemblage, with Guasave Red-on-buff (3 percent) and Guasave Polychrome (3 percent) reflecting the principal decorated wares.

Along with El Ombligo, these represent all of the funerary mounds yet documented in Sinaloa; there is an unconfirmed report of an additional funerary mound in the vicinity of Guamúchil. Geographical distribution and the predominance of local materials suggest that these features can best be considered as an attribute of the Huatabampo tradition. At both the Leyva and Borboa mounds, funerary practices included placing a large mollusk shell beneath the head as a "pillow," and placing a small shell in the mouth. As yet, no urn burials have been documented in the Mochicahui assemblages, and

the funerary offerings are much less elaborate in comparison with the El Ombligo assemblage.

The Serrana/(Río Sonora) Tradition

As initially defined by Richard Pailes (1972, 1976a, 1976b), the Río Sonora tradition encompassed an extremely large region of the western slope of the Sierra Madre Occidental foothills region, ranging from northern Sonora south into Sinaloa for an unknown distance; what was previously often referred to as the southern branch of the Río Sonora tradition has recently been redefined as the Serrana tradition (see Braniff 1976; Carpenter and Vicente 2009), and dated to ca. 200 B.C. and 1500 A.D. Within the Río Fuerte Valley, the Serrana tradition extends upriver from approximately Tehueco into the Sierra Madre Occidental.

Serrana ceramics are characterized by an early brown ware horizon, followed by the presence of red wares and a predilection for surface texturing with punctuate and incised designs. Other artifacts associated modeled spindle whorls, clay whistles, stone cruciforms, shell ornaments, overhanging-end manos and tabular metates (Pailes 1972:367).

Survey data suggests that the earliest communities are likely pit house villages (Carpenter et al. 2008). Later architectural remains are typically indicated by rectangular cobble alignments, and sites generally appear to reflect small *rancherías* of from one to five extended families (Pailes 1972:364).

La Viuda/Rincón de Buyubampo (SIN A:6:18)

Excavations carried out at the La Viuda and Rincón de Buyubampo sites (Carpenter et al. 2006), located near the Arroyo Janalicahui (a tributary drainage of the Río Fuerte) five kilometers south of the border with Sonora in the *municipio* of Choix, confirmed that these adjacent sites represent a significant occupation from

Figure I.3.5. Huatabampo/Guasave Redware recovered from a burial mound in Mochicahui (UAIM).

Figure I.3.6. Guasave Red-on-buff recovered from a burial mound in Mochicahui (UAIM).

Figure I.3.7. Aztatlán Polychrome recovered from a burial mound in Mochicahui (UAIM).

circa 200 to 1750 A.D., and is unquestionably associated with the Sinaloa, one of the many ancestral groups that today comprise the Yoreme (Mayo) community. In the Yoreme language, "Buyubampo" signifies "place of abundant water."

Preliminary investigations in the later Buyubampo component, encompassing some 20,000 m² atop a low hill and extending onto the surrounding eastern edge of the valley, indicate that the late prehispanic-to-historic occupation consisted of between 20 and 30 habitation units, consisting of from two to four or more large rectangular rooms reaching 8 m x 5 m (Figure I.3.8). The foundation walls are predominantly of faced stone masonry, 50-60 cm wide and were built atop rubble-and-trash-filled platforms.

Hearths are double "U"-shaped and reflect pronounced similarities to those used today by the Ocoroni/Yoreme. Post holes were excavated 50 cm or more into the soft bedrock substrate. The roofs were likely constructed with vigas and latillas covered with earth or adobe. Small storage or granary structures are also frequently found in close proximity to the residential units. Several segments of terrace/retaining walls were constructed along the eastern hill slope.

The utilitarian/domestic wares recovered are predominantly associated with the Serrana tradition. Intrusive ceramics are predominantly Guasave Red-on-buff, and include Navolato Polychrome from the Culiacán region, Tuxpan Red-on-orange from Amapa, Nayarit, Arivechi Red-on-brown from east-central Sonora, and Babicora Polychrome from the Paquimé region of Chihuahua. Additional non-local/exotic objects recovered include obsidian blades, a copper bell, a ceramic cylinder seal and several Aztatlán-style spindle whorls. Two small fragments of obsidian prismatic blades, each under 2.0 cm in length, were recovered. Two copper objects, a thin plaque and a type 1C1a crotal (Vargas 1995:17) were also recovered; this crotal type has been reported from Paquimé, Casa Grande, Gila Pueblo and Cherry Creek (Di Peso et al.

1974, v7:225; Vargas 1995:60). The Amapa, Nayarit region, 500 kilometers to the south, marks the northernmost limits of both obsidian prismatic blade production and copper metallurgy (Pendergast 1962); artifacts of both materials are relatively rare within Sinaloa. Cylinder seals are also associated with the Aztatlán complex; Isabel Kelly (1945:127) reported 12 from the Culiacán region, and Ekholm (1942:89) recovered another from Guasave; only two additional cylinder seals are known from Sinaloa north of the Río Mocorito. Lastly, at least eight Aztatlán-style modeled spindle whorls were also present within the assemblage.

Substantial quantities of marine shell, representing both finished ornaments and waste were recovered, including evidence for the onsite production of *Glycymeris* bracelets, along with ornaments of various other species. Marine shell is relatively abundant at even the smaller sites in the region, and includes *Glycymeris* sp., *Venus* sp., *Vermetus* sp., *Laevicardium* sp., *Trachycardium*, *Conus* sp. and *Dosinia* sp. The *Glycymeris* bracelet production techniques are identical to the Huatabampo and Trincheras traditions. Notably, the absence of marine shell in site assemblages is generally a reliable indicator of post-contact occupations. Apparently, shell ornament production ceases abruptly with contact, and presumably is also indicative of the disruption of traditional exchange goods and the dissolution of the long-distance interaction system.

Historic artifacts recovered from Rincón de Buyubampo include majolica, buttons, nails and three textile seals of British origin (see Carpenter and Sánchez, this volume, for a more detailed discussion of the historic period occupation).

Cerro de la Máscara

Located two kilometers from the city of El Fuerte, the Cerro de la Máscara petroglyph site is situated on the northern margins of the Río Fuerte, and consists of a series of outcrops of igneous rocks,

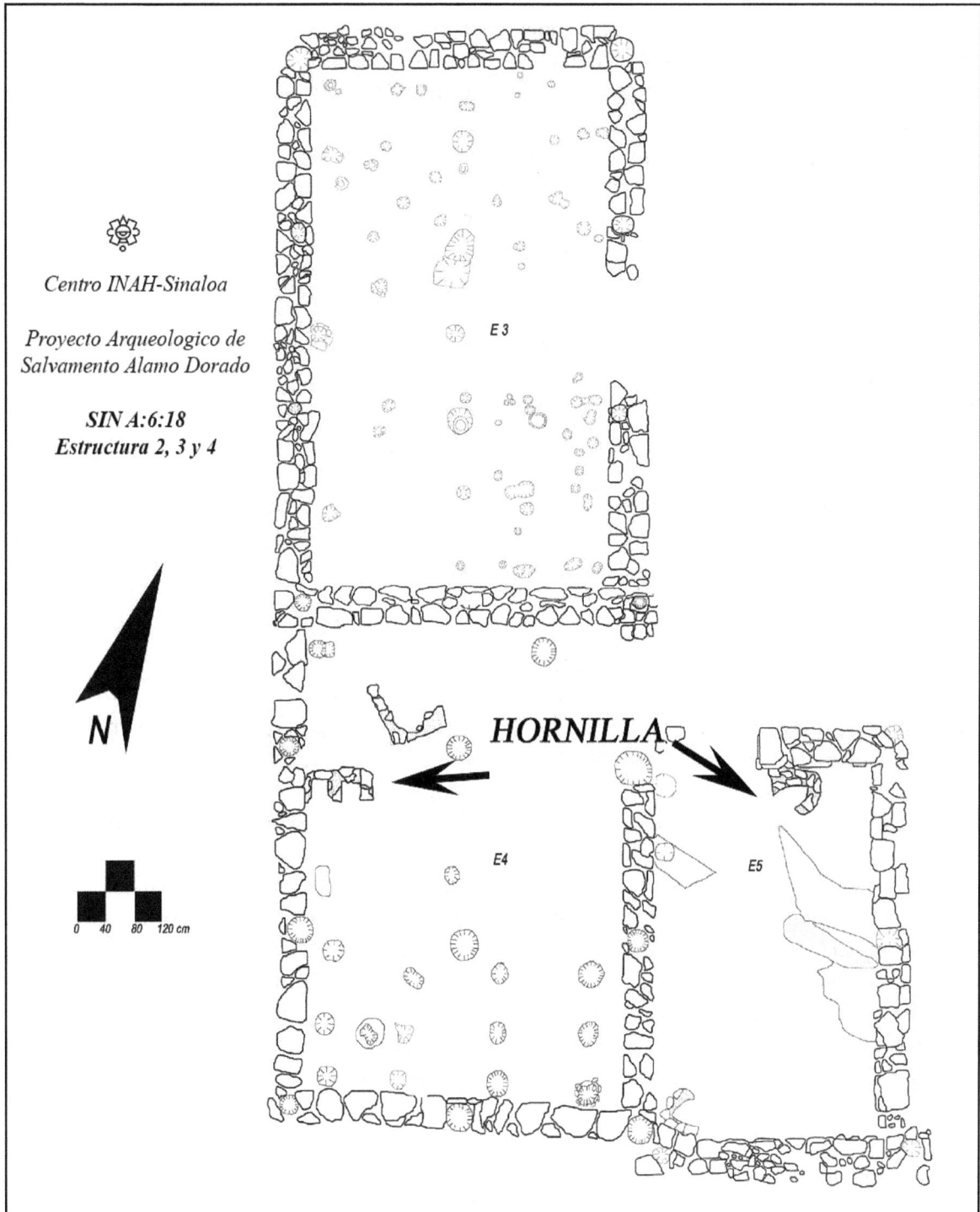

Centro INAH-Sinaloa

Proyecto Arqueologico de
Salvamento Alamo Dorado

SIN A:6:18
Estructura 2, 3 y 4

N

0   40   80   120 cm

E 3

HORNILLA

E4

E5

Figure I.3.8. Plan of Residential Unit 2 at Rincón de Buyubampo.

predominantly of rhyolite, that originates near the rivers' edge and eventually forming a promontory that provides a sweeping panorama of the valley. The various petroglyph locales are comprised of rhyolitic blocks of varying sizes and shapes, upon the faces of which are found diverse panels with petroglyphs composed of simple geometric designs such as circles, squares, rectangles, spirals, and dots, along with other design elements composed of concentric circles, double spirals, square or rectangular elements with interior geometric designs that have been previously described as "cartouches of information" (Figures I.3.9 and I.3.10) (Mendiola 1994:289). Anthropomorphic elements consist of foot and hand prints, faces, and stylized representations of human figures. Phytomorph (botanical) elements include cacti and as yet unidentified fruits. Zoomorphic elements include a probable canid, a possible feline figure, butterflies, and unidentified animal forms. Also present are astronomical motifs depicting both the sun and Venus, and simple strands of dot elements considered to signify astronomical markers. The depictions of masks, headdresses, and weaponry are tentatively classified as fetish elements.

As yet, the preliminary results of our investigations indicate that the Cerro de la Máscara site primarily reflects a role as an important ritual space among the indigenous groups of the region. In considering it's setting in a semi-isolated location, the spatial distributions of the locales, along with the nature of the design elements depicted, all suggest an association with shamanistic ceremonies. A few intrusive ceramics from the Culiacán region indicate (minimal) contact with the northern Aztatlán region. Additionally, a very few glyphs may likely reflect the influence of West Mexican/Mesoamerican symbolism.

Acknowledging the various techniques employed in their production, and considering the variable degree of weathering evinced by the petroglyphs, indications are that the Cerro de la Máscara site was utilized for an extensive period of time. Preliminary analysis of the ceramic assemblage suggests a range between approximately 200 and 1400 A.D. The entire petroglyph assemblage can, unquestionably, be attributed to the Cahita, and more specifically to the Tehueco or Sinaloa groups, who occupied this region from at least 2,000 years prior to the time of Spanish contact in the 16th century.

Discussion

As a result of the research carried out by the INAH *Proyecto Arqueológico Norte de Sinaloa*, we can tentatively confirm that the Río Fuerte Valley has been occupied since the late Pleistocene/ early Holocene. There is no question that the ancestors of the contemporary Yoreme (Mayo) community have occupied this region for at least two thousand years if not considerably more.

These data suggest that the Huatabampo and Serrana traditions can be attributed to a single early plain ware ceramic tradition, with both archaeological traditions sharing a common origin in Venadito Brown (Álvarez 1982, 1990; Pailes 1972, 1976a). Both traditions reflect a strong affinity with the Viejo period of northwestern Chihuahua and northeastern Sonora (Braniff 1992). The Huatabampo tradition predominates on the coastal plain, extending in the Fuerte Valley to a point between San Blas and the Arroyo Sibajauhui. The Serrana tradition predominates from approximately Tehueco to the Sierra Madre Ocidental.

We propose that the eventual bifurcation into the Huatabampo and Serrana traditions can most likely be attributed to regional coastal plain and foothills adaptations of a single panregional prehispanic Cahita ceramic tradition, minimally encompassing the region between the Río Mocorito and the middle Río Yaqui. Our investigations along the margins of the Arroyo Cuchujaqui indicate cultural continuity between the archaeological Serrana tradition and the ethnographic Tehueco. Similarly, the

Figure I.3.9. Petroglyphs at Cerro de la Máscara.

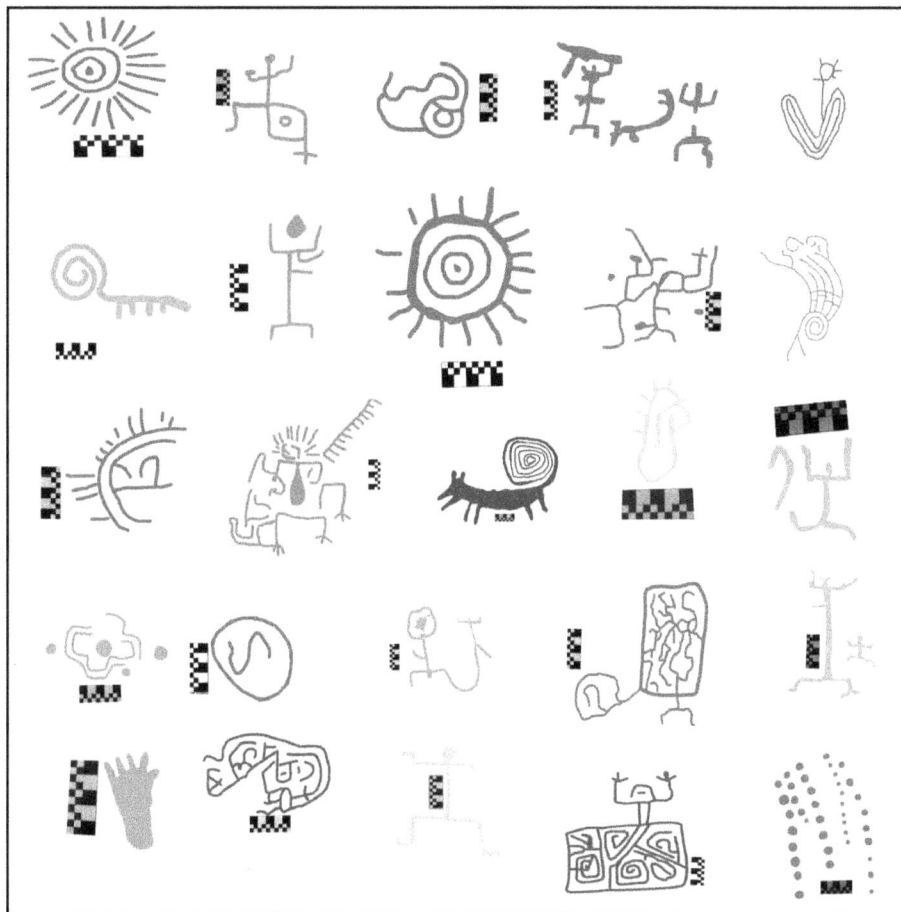

Figure I.3.10. Petroglyphs at Cerro de la Máscara.

La Viuda/Rincón de Buyubampo sites confirm continuity of this same archaeological tradition with the historic period Sinaloa who occupied this region at the moment of contact in the 16th century. The data from La Playa de Ocoroni equally demonstrates cultural continuity from the archaeological Huatabampo tradition to the contemporary Ocoroni/Yoreme.

Regional lithic technologies are also characteristic of Northwest/Southwest traditions, with multi-platform cores, projectile points, scrapers, mescal knives, and utilized flakes. Both shallow basin and tabular metates were utilized, along with rectangular, overhanging-end and cobble manos. Full- and ¾-grooved axes, mauls, and notched, hafted split-cobble "hoes" are common.

Analyses of the regional ceramic assemblages allows for the elaboration of a preliminary Cahitan ceramic sequence divided into early, intermediate and late periods (Figure I.3.11) (Carpenter and Vicente 2009).

Early Ceramic period (200 B.C./200 to 500 A.D.)

The Early Ceramic period, dating from approximately 200 B.C. to 500 A.D., is characterized by plain Brown wares. Venadito Brown, a plain ware with a fine paste and with shell-scraped interior, represents the initial ceramic type in both Huatabampo and Serrana traditions. In general, this initial period is almost indistinguishable from that of the Mogollon, and is particularly reminiscent of the Alma Plain series. Red wares quickly become prevalent in the Huatabampo region, but are absent in the Serrana tradition.

Intermediate Ceramic period (500 to 1100/1200 A.D.)

During the following Intermediate Ceramic period, from 500 to 1100/1200 A.D., regional diversification between the Huatabampo and Serrana traditions is observed. The Batacosa series emerges as the predominant type in the upland zones, where the appearance of red wares may indicate influences from the Huatabampo tradition. Within the lower foothills, Cuchujaqui Red predominates, while in the higher elevations San Bernardo Red, characterized by incised geometric designs, represents the most prevalent pottery type.

Late Ceramic period (1100/1200 to 1532 A.D.)

The Late Ceramic period, dating from ca. 1100/1200 A.D. to Spanish contact, is characterized the appearance of the Los Camotes series, replacing the San Bernardo series in the upper elevations. In the lower foothills región, Cuchujaqui Red continues to represent the predominant pottery type, as does Huatabampo Red in the coastal region. These types persist until shortly after Spanish contact, when they are replaced by the manure-tempered San Miguel types.

With respect to the Huatabampo tradition, Guasave/Huatabampo Red and Guasave Red-on-buff comprise the most common pottery types. Guasave Red-on-Brown design elements occasionally reflect Aztatlán influences, but most commonly present strong parallels with Southwestern motifs, and particularly with Tanque Verde Red-on-Brown from the Tucson region. It also now appears that Guasave Red-on-Brown may have continued in production up to Spanish contact.

CONCLUSIONS

Although direct evidence is lacking, it seems likely that the initial occupation of the Río Fuerte Valley occurred in the late Pleistocene/early Holocene when Paleo-Indian bands no doubt encountered abundant large animals inhabiting a pristine riparian environment. Scant evidence

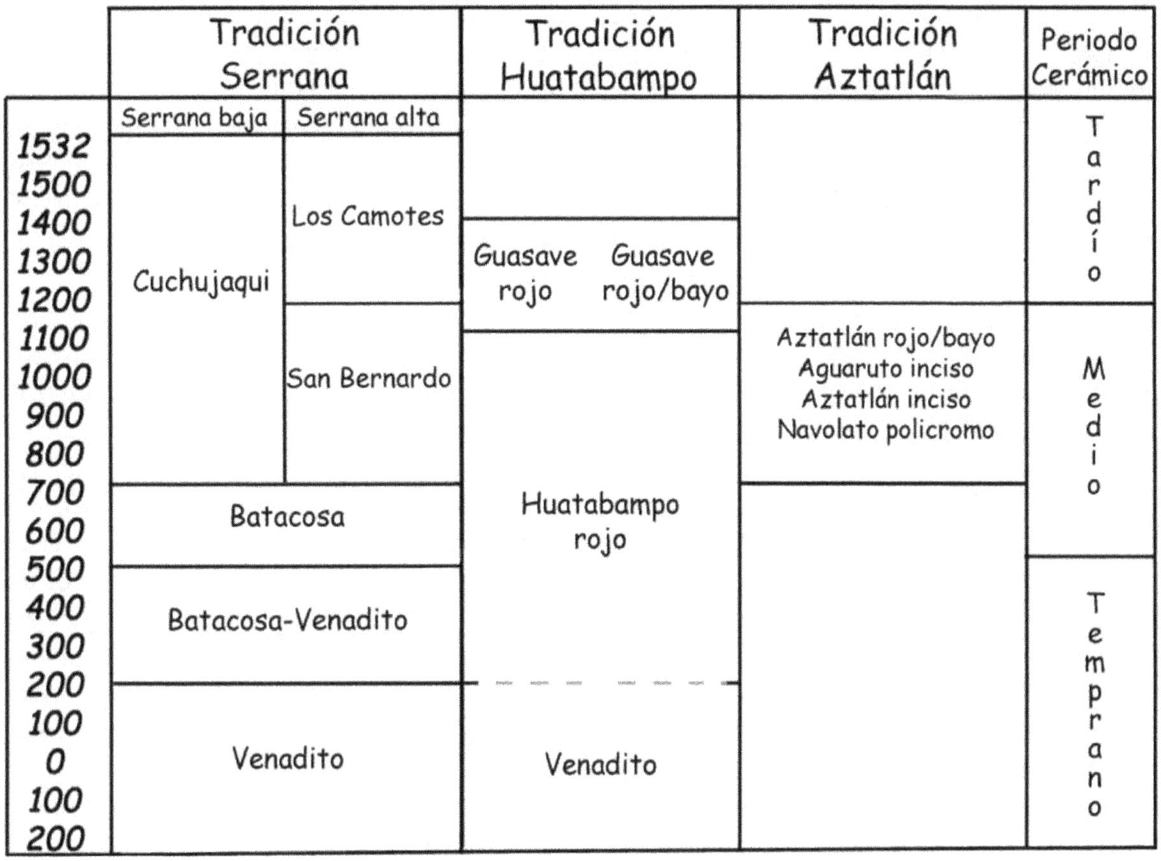

	Tradición Serrana		Tradición Huatabampo		Tradición Aztatlán	Periodo Cerámico
	Serrana baja	Serrana alta				T a r d í o
1532 1500 1400 1300 1200	Cuchujaqui	Los Camotes	Guasave rojo	Guasave rojo/bayo		
1100 1000 900 800		San Bernardo	Huatabampo rojo		Aztatlán rojo/bayo Aguaruto inciso Aztatlán inciso Navolato policromo	M e d i o
700 600	Batacosa					
500 400 300	Batacosa-Venadito					T e m p r a n o
200 100 0 100 200	Venadito		Venadito			

Figure I.3.11. Preliminary Cahitan Ceramic Scheme (from Carpenter and Vincente 2009).

during the subsequent Archaic period suggests the presence of hunters and gatherers affiliated with the Cochise Archaic tradition. If our model is correct, the earliest evidence for maize cultivation in northwest Mexico should also be found within this region; the systematic search for the remains of early maize in rock shelters and caves should be undertaken.

Along the margins of the Río Fuerte, between the *serrana* and the sea, a more-or-less continuous distribution of artifacts confirms the presence of a dense population of prehispanic farmers. Ethnohistoric documents describe extensive fields of maize, bean, squash and cotton (Carpenter 2008). Spindle whorls indicate that the cultivation of cotton began by approximately 1000 A.D. Settlement patterns indicate numerous small *rancherías*, reflecting the conditions described by the 16th century Spaniards. Coastal

groups fished the estuaries and collected mollusks which they exchanged for agricultural produce and ceramics from their farmer neighbors.

Evidence from Mochicahui and the La Viuda and Rincón de Buyubampo sites confirm local participation in the long distance exchange network that connected West Mexico and the Northwest/Southwest. The Mochicahui funerary mound is the northernmost containing Aztatlán Polychrome yet known. Abundant shell remains recovered at Buyubampo indicate that the production of marine shell ornaments was an important activity likely associated with the exchange network. The existence of a Cahitan linguistic continuum has been proposed as having facilitated long distance exchange between the Aztatlán tradition and the Northwest/Southwest (Vicente and Carpenter 2008).

There seems little doubt that the Rincón de

Buyubampo site represents an important node in the long-distance exchange of goods, ideology, and information between the complex societies of West Mexico/Mesoamerica and the sedentary farming communities of northwest Mexico/ Southwest U.S. during the late prehistoric period. The supposed *meseta* central exchange route extending from the Chalchihuites region of southern Durango/northern Zacatecas to the Paquimé region, although widely cited and illustrated on maps, cannot be upheld by the known archaeological data. Along the Pacific slope, however, a few sites, such as Amapa, Nayarit and El Ombligo (Guasave), Sinaloa can be identified as representing probable nodes along a long distance exchange/interaction network; virtually nothing is known of the region between Guasave and the Paquimé region.

We can propose that from Mochicahui, the exchange route traveled east along the Rio Fuerte to the confluence with the Arroyo Cuchujaqui, within Tehueco territory. We have identified two exchange/interaction routes in the region between the Rio Fuerte and southernmost Sonora. One route follows along the Arroyo Cuchujaqui (Arroyo Alamos), from its confluence with the Rio Fuerte north to the vicinity of Alamos, Sonora. The other route departs from the Rio Fuerte some 20 km further to the east, within Sinaloa territory, and follows the Arroyo Janalacahui, which trends approximately parallel to the Cuchujaqui. Both routes were regarded as *caminos reales* during the Colonial period, and appear to converge somewhere in the vicinity of the pueblo of Cuchujaqui, Sonora.

Lastly, there is incontrovertible evidence for cultural continuity linking the Huatabampo tradition with the historic/contemporary groups occupying the coastal plain as well as linking the Serrana tradition with the Tehueco and Sinaloa. The intermediate zone between the Arroyo

Sibajahui and El Fuerte manifests characteristics of both the Huatabampo and Serrana traditions. It now appears that both traditions comprise a single pan-regional prehispanic Cahita tradition; the few distinctions observed between these archaeological traditions likely reflecting differences in adaptations to coastal and foothill environments.

At present, there is no evidence suggesting that any of the late prehispanic communities north of the Río Mocorito were politically or economically integrated with their adjacent Aztatlán neighbors; the documented distribution of the material and cultural traits which can be attributed to the Aztatlán complex can be explained as the results of exchange and/or the diffusion of cultural influences – as in the case of urn burials, for example – and, in our opinion, is most likely associated with a prestige goods economy (cf. Frankenstein and Rowlands 1978; McGuire 1987).

The Cahitan region to the north of the Río Mocorito represents an extensive area where sedentary agriculturalists share closest affinities with the archaeological communities of the Southwestern U.S. but who also, during various centuries lived "face-to-face" with traditions related to broader developments in West Mexico/ Mesoamerica (Beals 1974:63). These various Cahitan groups reflect a cultural diversity that cannot be adequately explained by reference to mainstream developments in the heartlands of the American Southwest or Mesoamerica. Instead, much as Ralph Beals proclaimed almost 70 years ago (1943), this region can be better understood as a complex web of ecological factors and reciprocal relations between social groups which involved a wide range of interaction and varying degrees of integration at the regional and interregional scales.

Part I, Chapter 4

Cultural and Contextual Differentiation of Mesoamerican Iconography in the U.S Southwest/Northwest Mexico

Michael T. Searcy

ABSTRACT

Ample research has documented the long-term interaction between Mesoamerica and the U.S. Southwest/Northwest Mexico (SW/NW). Nelson (2006:345) has used the phrase "Mesoamerican interaction markers" as a way to describe evidence of this contact in the SW/NW. He further defines these as "a variety of archaeological patterns that are reminiscent of Mesoamerican counterparts" including "objects, practices, and styles." Some of the interaction markers that have been studied at length are trade goods such as copper bells, macaws, shell, and iron pyrite mirrors (Bayman 2002; Bradley 1993; Ericson and Baugh 1993; Kelley 1966, 1995; Mathien 1993; McGuire 1993b; Nelson 2000; Riley 2005). Ideological aspects of Mesoamerican culture also have been identified in the form of ceremonial architecture such as ball courts (Harmon 2005, 2006; Nelson 1995, 2000; Scarborough and Wilcox 1991; Wilcox 1985, 1991; Wilkerson 1991). New discoveries like chile seeds at site 315 in the Casas Grandes Valley (Minnis and Whalen 2010) and the use of cacao at Chaco Canyon (Crown and Hurst 2009) provide further evidence that Mesoamerican interaction was significant and wide-spread throughout the SW/NW.

RESUMEN

Amplias investigaciones han documentado la interacción de gran profundidad entre Mesoamérica y el Suroeste de los Estados Unidos/Noroeste de México (SW/NW). Nelson (2006:345) ha usado la frase "marcadores de interacción mesoamericana" como una manera de describir las evidencias de este contacto en el SW/NW, definiéndolos además como "una variedad de patrones arqueológicos que son reminiscentes de sus contrapartes mesoamericanas" incluyendo "objetos, prácticas y estilos". Algunos de los marcadores de interacción que han sido estudiados profusamente son los bienes de intercambio como los cascabeles de cobre, guacamayas, concha y espejos de pirita (Bayman 2002; Bradley 1993; Ericson and Baugh 1993; Kelley 1966, 1995; Mathien 1993; McGuire 1993b; Nelson 2000; Riley 2005). Aspectos ideológicos de la cultura mesoamericana han sido identificados también en la forma de arquitectura ceremonial como juegos de pelota (Harmon 2005, 2006; Nelson 1995, 2000; Scarborough and Wilcox 1991; Wilcox 1985, 1991; Wilkerson 1991). Los descubrimientos recientes de semillas de chile en el sitio 315 en el valle de Casas Grandes Valley (Minnis and Whalen 2010) y el uso del cacao en cañón de Chaco (Crown and Hurst 2009) proporcionan evidencia adicional de que esta interacción mesoamericana fue significativa y ampliamente difundida en todo el SW/NW.

Michael T. Searcy Brigham Young University

Although there is evidence that many SW/NW communities interacted with Mesoamerica, this contact was variable, both regionally and diachronically. In addition, some archaeologists have interpreted this relationship as one where complex Mesoamerican polities "influenced" SW/NW communities (cf. Di Peso 1974; Haury 1976). In contrast, this paper works to understand some of the internal dynamics of SW/NW interaction with Mesoamerica and explores how this long-distance relationship may have shaped local sociopolitical organization in the late prehistoric period (A.D. 1200-1450). I further examine how Mesoamerican objects and ideas were adopted and adapted to fit the needs of local communities in the SW/NW.

In order to investigate these aspects of long-distance interaction, I examine another line of evidence, Mesoamerican iconography, which has been identified on both pottery and rock art in the SW/NW (Creel and McKusick 1994; Crown 1994; Di Peso 1974; Hays-Gilpin and Hill 1999, 2000; Hill 1992; Kelley 1964; Mathiowetz 2008; Riley 2005; Schaafsma 1999, 2001; Thompson 1999, 2000; VanPool 2003; VanPool et al. 2006; VanPool et al. 2008; VanPool and VanPool 2007). These symbols of foreign interaction were also wide-spread, and many appear prominently on polychrome pottery produced in the Salado and Casas Grandes regions during the late prehistoric period (A.D. 1200-1450).

Other studies have looked at these signs as markers of foreign religious ideologies (VanPool 2003; VanPool and VanPool 2007), while some see them as local manifestations of a wide-sweeping religious cult (Crown 1994). While there may have been a link to religious or ideological structures, the role of these symbols in SW/NW societies was likely complex, multifaceted, and warrants reanalysis. I take a different approach by considering the symbolic meaning of Mesoamerican iconography following three perspectives associated with the archaeological study of symbols as described by Robb (1998), who conducted a comprehensive

review of literature focused on the archaeology of symbols. He found that scholars most often saw symbols as tokens, girders, or tesserae (Robb 1998:332), and I use these categories as a way to characterize the political and social implications associated with these Mesoamerican symbols in Salado and Casas Grandes communities.

I analyzed 639 whole vessels with either regional or site-level provenience in order to compare the distribution of Mesoamerican iconography in the Salado and Casas Grandes regions. The vessels were all Salado Polychromes (also called Roosevelt Red Wares) and Chihuahuan Polychromes associated with the Salado and Casas Grandes regions respectively. These vessels are housed at three different repositories: the Arizona State Museum, University of Arizona, in Tucson, Arizona, Eastern Arizona College in Thatcher, Arizona, and the Museum of Indian Arts and Culture in Santa Fe, New Mexico (see Searcy 2010 for a more detailed description of the whole vessels analyzed in this study). The examination of these vessels included an iconographical analysis of their decorated surfaces and the identification of 10 motifs considered to be Mesoamerican. I then compared the distributions of this foreign iconography among Casas Grandes and Salado sites and identified patterns indicating variation in how symbols were distributed among communities with different social and political structures.

The results of the distributional analysis of this iconography among the Salado and Casas Grandes regions show that they were broadly distributed, suggesting that they were being used as ideological girders possessed by all members of the society. Although these general patterns of distribution existed, I found that Mesoamerican iconography was depicted on pottery more frequently at Paquimé and sites around this core polity, suggesting that foreign ideology expressed symbolically may have also been used as tokens of power/authority by elites at the core of the Casas Grandes region.

In order to explore this variation further,

I compared the distribution of Mesoamerican iconography to other Mesoamerican interaction markers. A few of these, including macaws, ballcourts, shell, and copper items, are examined in more detail and provide multiple lines of evidence that further illustrate the differential use of foreign iconography and ideology by these societies in the SW/NW. In particular, this additional evidence supports the results of the iconographical analysis, which indicates that elites associated with Casas Grandes may have been using their links to Mesoamerica as a way to legitimize their authority. They also indicate that the Salado region was not as actively engaged with Mesoamerica as was the Casas Grandes region, suggesting that the intensity of interaction may indicate how powerful and influential "outside" elements were perceived among some prehistoric communities (Helms 1993).

PERSPECTIVES IN SYMBOLIC ARCHAEOLOGY

In a 1998 article, John Robb reviewed the study of symbols in archaeology in an attempt to determine where archaeology stood on the subject. He synthesized a number of sources in which archaeologists had explored this concept and made progress in understanding how it works in the greater study of prehistoric cultures. Robb (1998:332) categorized the research on symbolism into three different perspectives: symbols as tokens, symbols as girders, and symbols as tesserae.

The first perspective, "symbols as tokens," refers to how they represent meanings and are manifested materially. These tokens are considered to possess a primary purpose, as objects that transmit information (Robb 1998:332). Symbolic tokens are described as being "badge-like," meaning these symbols provided leaders with authority needed to perpetuate their status in a hierarchical system (Robb 1998:340). The information transmitted through symbols is commonly interpreted as being used by elites for the purpose of legitimization and prestige

(Cohen 1979; DeMarrais et al. 1996; Firth 1973; Turner 1975). In other words, elites or leaders used symbols that identified them with a greater power or religious system with the intention of gaining followers who would offer tribute in the form of goods or services.

The perspective "symbols as girders" refers to the use of symbols by people to structure their mental and social world (Robb 1998:333). They are a means of graphic expression of a system of belief or social reality. Girders aid in organizing social relationships and are often material representations of religion. Robb (1998:335) describes this perspective as being a very structural approach, in which he states, "humans orient themselves in the world, think, and act through learned, culturally specific structures that recur wherever they organize themselves and their material productions." The organization of one's existence and reality can be materially manifested as symbols, acting as girders that support and perpetuate cultural traditions.

The last point of view, "symbols as tesserae," is described as the treatment of symbols as fragments of a mosaic, that when assembled, create meaning for the people experiencing them (Robb 1998:338). This view is inherent in the poststructuralist critique and suggests that the meaning of symbols does not inherently exist within people or the objects themselves, instead it is manifest only in the moment in which "people apprehend [symbols] and assemble them into meaningful formations" (Robb 1998:337-338). An example of this may be the moment in which a person combines various objects, like corn and fire, during a ceremony or ritual in an area set off as sacred space. During that event, the combination of the corn with other ritual symbols likely generates a different meaning than when the corn is consumed as part of daily subsistence. Robb (1998:338) clarifies that due to the fact that this perspective relies on the experience in which a symbol's meaning is created, it requires in-depth contextual analysis that is often conducted on the microscale.

I used these categories as interpretive

models for the outcomes of my analysis. I suspect that if elites used foreign iconographic symbols as tokens of power, their distribution will be exclusive to those who held some sort of authority over others within that society. On the other hand, if these symbols were more widely distributed among all members of a society, they may represent a common ideology or worldview, and therefore may have acted as existential girders. There is also the possibility in which symbols are a combination of several types. For example, elites or leaders may use symbols that are part of a wide-spread ideology in an elaborated or special way. They may incorporate these symbols into public rituals or ceremonies in a way that is distinct from common symbolic expression possibly found on pottery or clothing.

Salado and Casas Grandes Sociopolitical Organization and Social Hierarchy

The Salado and Casas Grandes traditions were related to contemporaneous societies that were regional neighbors and that grew and thrived in the SW/NW from around A.D. 1200 to 1450 (Figure I.4.1). Their pottery exhibited common iconography including some that may have derived from Mesoamerica, which suggests that people practicing these traditions also likely shared similar ideologies that worked to structure their worlds.

VanPool et al. (2006) first compared the Salado and Casas Grandes regions in a preliminary study and suggested that differences in sociopolitical organization, such as settlement hierarchies, should be considered as evidence supporting the idea that people in these regions participated in different religious systems (VanPool et al. 2006:242-246). They also emphasized differences in iconography between these two regions as representing a schism in ideological continuity.

While VanPool et al. (2006) focused on differences in religious institutions, I examine differences in the integration of foreign iconographic symbols and their relationship to sociopolitical organization. I selected the Salado and Casas Grandes regions for this study because they involved noticeably different systems of organization where people were using similar systems of iconography, including iconographic symbols that likely derived from Mesoamerica. Salado sites were architecturally and hierarchically diverse, and this system could be described as one of dispersed regional centers (Searcy 2010:5). Some Salado sites located in the Tonto Basin and in the San Pedro Valley of central and southeastern Arizona demonstrate a type of community organized around platform mounds that likely facilitated a moderate level of centralized political and ceremonial authority (Clark 2001; Rice 1998, 2000; Simon and Jacobs 2000). For the most part, people associated with the Salado tradition who inhabited southeastern Arizona and southwestern New Mexico lived in smaller, less-centralized communities with less social hierarchy. These patterns of community organization suggest that the Salado region was made up of a series of autonomous, middle-level polities, no one of which was dominant.

Some archaeologists have considered platform mounds that were built shortly before and during the Salado horizon (A.D. 1200-1450) to be Mesoamerican in origin (Haury 1976:346-347). The construction of platform mounds as public ritual staging grounds and eventually as elite residences in the SW/NW reflects similar uses of platform mounds and pyramids in Mesoamerica (see Rice 1998:235 for a discussion on the evolving function of platform mounds among the Salado). While these architectural features may have resulted from interaction with Mesoamerican peoples, it is more likely that they evolved from local architectural traditions. The construction of such large communal architecture suggests communities with some type of hierarchical social structure, although there are differing views on the nature and scale of this hierarchy (Craig et al. 1998; Rice 1998)

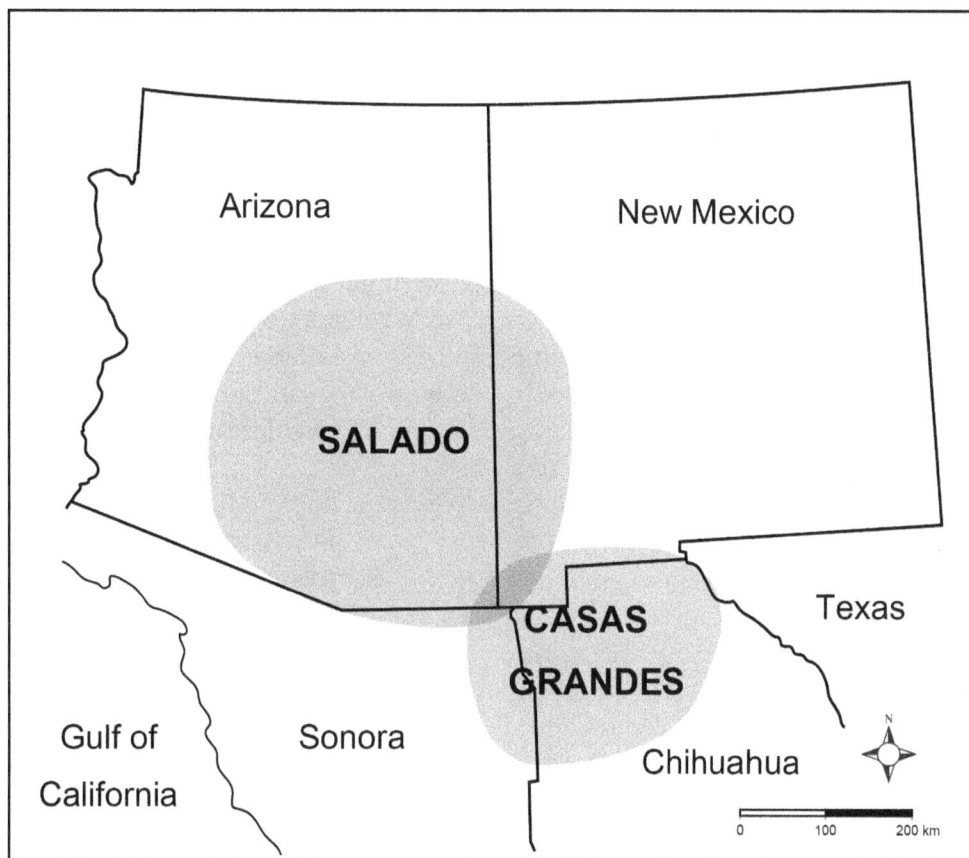

Figure I.4.1. Map of the Salado and Casas Grandes traditions.

Some of the sites included in my study are found in the Tonto Basin located in east-central Arizona. For this area, the thirteenth century brought dramatic change in architecture, social organization, and an influx of immigrants to communities in the basin (Clark 2001; Lyons 2003a). As part of the Roosevelt Platform Mound Study conducted in this region, archaeologists determined that communities organized around platform mounds represent asymmetry in power between elites and non-elites and marked some level of ranked social organization (cf. Clark 2001; Rice 2000; Simon and Jacobs 2000). Simon and Jacobs (2000:210-212) propose that those inhabiting non-elite residential sites would have been motivated by elites occupying platform mounds to aid in the construction of this type of architecture and to contribute to and participate in rituals performed at these ceremonial centers.

Data from the comparisons of burials and access to resources for people living on the mounds and in mound compound structures actually suggest little social differentiation in comparison to those living off the mounds. Although those living on the mounds may have been closely linked with religious rituals, their status as elites is not considered to be administrative (Rice 1998:237). Rice suggested that these "elite members of the community" were more ceremonial specialists rather than elites who enjoyed "heightened economic privileges or responsibilities."

Several contemporary Salado sites in southeastern Arizona and southwestern New Mexico were also included in this study and provide a useful contrast to those located in the Tonto Basin. They were not as centrally organized as their northwestern neighbors, who developed communities centered on platform mounds. Although platform mound sites have been identified in the San Pedro Valley of southeastern Arizona, most sites recognized in this and surrounding areas exhibit little support for the idea that they were hierarchically organized as evidenced by the lack of monumental architecture and the homogeneous distribution of resources.

The Casas Grandes region, on the other hand, had an obvious center at the site of Paquimé in northern Mexico, which had no peers. Its role as a major polity for smaller surrounding communities is evidenced by its massive size and the large quantities of exotics and public ritual features. Whalen and Minnis (2001:205) have characterized the late prehistoric societies of the Casas Grandes region as achieving an "intermediate level of complexity." Paquimé reached its pinnacle of development in the 1300s, and it towered over surrounding communities with multi-storied compounds and monumental architecture, including ballcourts and mounds (Whalen and Minnis 2009:148).

In addition to this large center are hundreds of satellite sites where people participated in the ritual and political culture of Paquimé. Whalen and Minnis (2009:278) have interpreted Paquimé's political situation as one "in which the central place projects its authority outward through a complex, negotiated set of relationships in fragmented political contexts." Their data show that inhabitants of sites in close proximity to Paquimé were likely controlled more closely than those farther out. Whalen and Minnis (2001, 2009) developed a model for how this area was structured based on large-scale surveys and several excavations, combined with the earlier work of Di Peso (1974) at Casas Grandes. Their model suggests that the site of Paquimé likely served as the central authority over surrounding communities of an Inner Zone located within about 30 kilometers of this primary center.

Farther out, Middle Zone sites on the periphery were more scattered and simpler than those of Inner Zone sites, lacking core features such as ball courts and large ovens (Whalen and Minnis 2001:175-176). Whalen and Minnis (2001:172) proposed that those who inhabited sites outside of the Inner Zone participated in a "low level of system organization." These communities could be characterized as having less intercommunity organization compared to those in the Inner Zone. Although this was the case, Whalen and Minnis suggested that there was still a strong relationship between the two zones because of the similarities in ceramic assemblages and architectural features.

SUMMARY OF REGIONAL SOCIOPOLITICAL ORGANIZATION

To summarize briefly, one of the ways these two cultural areas are similar is that they include communities with characteristics that suggest local elites or religious leaders held some type of power or authority. In addition, many communities in both regions do not exhibit highly-structured, centralized social hierarchies. The Casas Grandes region is characterized by one large elite center (Paquimé) surrounded by smaller villages inhabited by people who likely contributed to the building, maintenance, and religious functions associated with this large, central community. In contrast, the Salado region has been called a "regional phenomenon" commonly identified by the appearance of Salado Polychrome pottery (Dean 2000). Salado sociopolitical organization varied from site to site and one of the main contrasts is between communities with platform mounds, suggesting distinctions between elites and non-elites, and those lacking this type of monumental architecture, indicating a less centralized and less hierarchical social system.

Although sociopolitical organization differed between these regions (dispersed regional centers versus one primary center), they both included communities that were central places associated with some centralized authority and/or participated in a higher level of social hierarchy. They also involved smaller communities that were less centrally organized and more egalitarian in their social structure. In order to compare both regions, I labeled sites as either more or less hierarchical. To clarify, I do not mean to suggest that all hierarchical communities are also central places, but in this comparison of the Casas Grandes and Salado regions, I found that centrality and hierarchy are characteristics that appear to coexist. Although I am reluctant in placing sites into categories, I have used the labels "more hierarchical" and "less hierarchical," as general identifiers for sites specific to the two regions analyzed in this study. In addition, the qualifiers "more" and "less" are used to imply that most societies involve some sort of social hierarchy, but that they vary in intensity and scale.

To reiterate, there is no doubt that some level of hierarchy within communities in the SW/NW existed, but how we describe it should directly correlate to the scale presented to us by the archaeological data. I argue that hierarchical communities exist in many terms along a sliding scale. At one extreme, major hierarchical systems would likely involve ruling elites who controlled resources and possessed the ability to sway the masses to follow their direction in building monumental architecture, entering battle, or paying tribute. I would describe the large empires built by the Maya and Aztec as operating at this level of hierarchy. At the other end of the scale lie more egalitarian communities, often organized along lines of kinship. Small groups of people, usually living in smaller structures and subsisting with enough surpluses to support the group, organized themselves in less hierarchical communities. This is not to say that hierarchy in these smaller groups did not exist, but status was likely ascribed according to gender (matrilineal or patrilineal), age, or lineage. Members of the community recognized distinct social and political positions. Emerging leaders also have the potential to achieve status in order to gain authoritative power over the group, thus categorically sliding them closer towards the hierarchical extreme of the scale.

No group should be considered statically resigned to one position on this scale, nor should it be assumed that movement along this scale is unilineal or that it occurs slowly over time. An increase in hierarchical complexity can occur as the result of massive population increase, perhaps deriving from migration, and hierarchy can also transform quickly, over one or two generations or even in a single shift in power following warfare or civil unrest.

The consequences that result from a community organizing themselves in a way that involves hierarchical leadership should be recognizable in several aspects of their society. This especially includes privileged access to food, arable land, trade goods, and other resources. In addition, disparity between elite leaders and commoners can be identified through the analysis of burial treatments and differences in residential and ritual architecture. I plan to show that the use of foreign symbols and ideology can also provide evidence that furthers our interpretations of prehistoric sociopolitical organization and social hierarchy.

In order to make a comparison of the use of iconography in the Salado and Casas Grandes regions, I examined whole pots from sites within each region (Table I.4.1). The locations of these sites included in this iconographical study are found on Figure I.4.2. Three platform mound sites in the Tonto Basin located northeast of present-day Phoenix represent *more hierarchical* communities that practiced a sociopolitical organization that was more centralized and hierarchical within the Salado tradition. I analyzed 164 vessels from these platform mound sites. Another 152 whole vessels were also examined from seven Salado sites located in southeastern Arizona and southwestern New Mexico. These *less hierarchical* communities appear to lack centralization and political authority that shaped social organization. For northern Chihuahua, 212 vessels were analyzed from *more hierarchical* sites, including Paquimé and five other sites or areas (those within 30 km, i.e., the Inner Zone)

Table I.4.1. Summary of Sites		
Salado Sites	Site Number	Number of Vessels
*Clines Terrace Platform Mound	AZ U:4:33 (ASM)	107
*Schoolhouse Point Platform Mound	AZ U:8:24 (ASM)	19
*VIV	—	38
Curtis	AZ CC:2:3 (ASM)	5
Dinwiddie	—	24
Kuykendall	AZ FF:2:2 (ASM)	91
Nine Mile	—	20
Slaughter Ranch	AZ FF:11:21 (ASM)	3
Webb	AZ FF:6:4 (ASM)	2
Ormand Village	LA 5793	7

Chihuahuan Sites	Site Number	Number of Vessels
*Paquime	CH D:9:1 (ASM)	38
*Rancho Corralitos	CH D:5 (ASM)	123
*Colonia Enrique Vicinity	CH D:5 (ASM)	6
*Colonia Enrique Site	CH D:5:8 (ASM)	35
*CH E:5:9	CH D:5:9 (ASM)	1
*Galeana Vicinity	CH D:14:5 (ASM)	9
CH A:16:2	NM EE:16:2 (ASM)	69
CH B:13:1	CH A:13:1 (ASM)	26
Janos Vicinity	CH C:4 (ASM)	6
Babicora Basin	CH H:9:11 (ASM)	7
Sitio de Tres Alamos	CH C:3:1 (ASM)	1
Joyce Well	LA 11823; Site 29HISAR63-16	2
Total		639

*More hierarchical

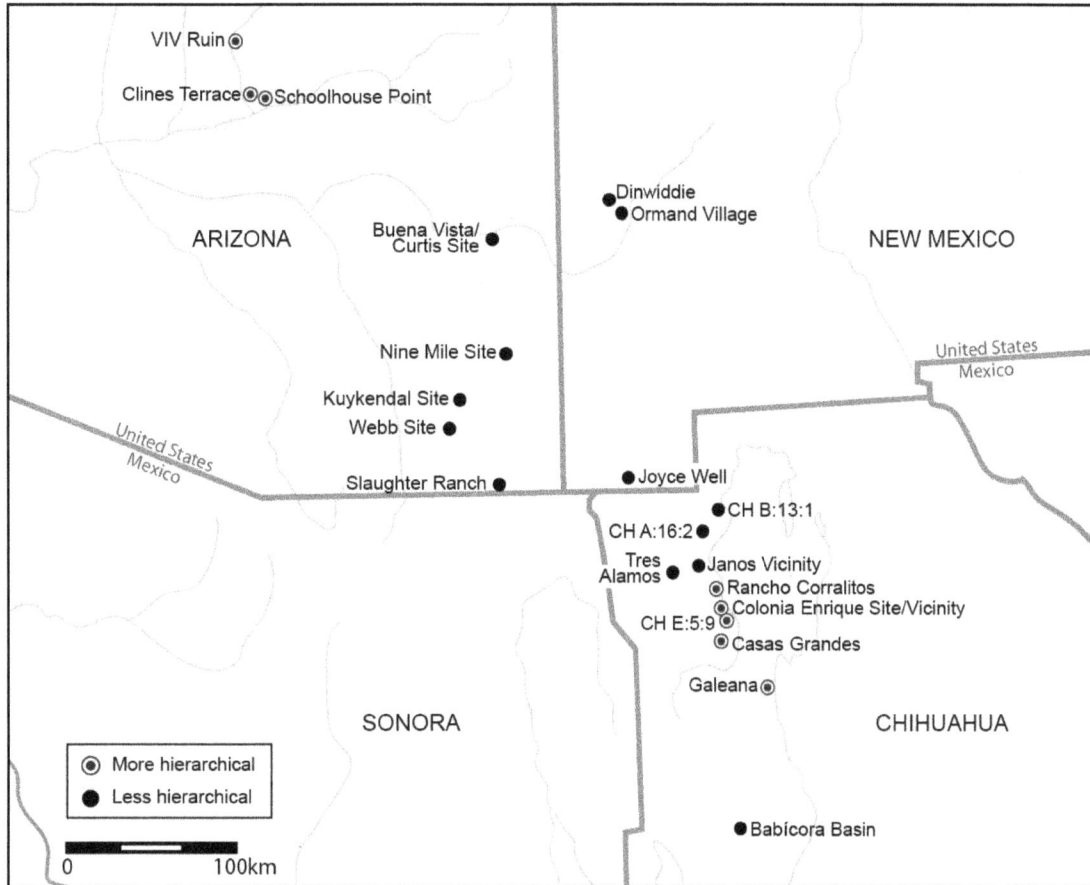

Figure I.4.2. Sites included in this study.

closely surrounding this ceremonial/political center. Finally, I analyzed 111 pots from six *less hierarchical* sites located outside the Inner Zone, those that likely were not fully integrated with Paquimé and sites found within the Inner Zone.

MESOAMERICAN ICONOGRAPHY IN THE SW/NW

Before beginning the iconographical analysis of Mesoamerican iconography, it was important to identify which symbols archaeologists have recognized as Mesoamerican in the SW/NW. This abbreviated review includes references to the original author(s) with some description, but more details explaining their interpretations and my own critiques and comments on these declarations can be found in the original study

(Searcy 2010). I conclude with a summary of the Mesoamerican iconography that was identified in the analysis stage of this research.

Plumed/Horned Serpents: One of the most predominant Mesoamerican symbols identified in the SW/NW is the depiction of a plumed or horned serpent. The depiction of this creature has been found among a number of SW/NW traditions, including Casas Grandes, Salado, Ancestral Puebloan, and Mimbres (Di Peso 1974; Riley 2005; Schaafsma 1998, 2001; VanPool 2003; VanPool and VanPool 2007). They have also been documented in many forms including a serpent with feathers along its body, a serpent with a simple forward pointing horn or feather, and more abstract designs of only a head with an appendage.

In prehistoric Mexican traditions such as those at Teotihuacán and Monte Albán, the plumed serpent was a representation of the god Quetzalcoatl (Adams 2005:241). For the Casas Grandes tradition, Di Peso (1974:549) also associated depictions of this symbol with the Mesoamerican deity Quetzalcoatl and describes this god as "a fertility spirit who concerned himself with life-giving water." Di Peso suggested that people at Casas Grandes worshipped Quetzalcoatl as both the Wind God (Ehécatl) and as a creator (Di Peso 1974:548).

In the Casas Grandes region, the plumed/horned serpent was most common on Ramos Polychrome pottery. In addition to pottery, there exists architecture at Paquimé that attests to the importance of this symbol. The Mound of the Serpent is a 113.3 meter-long platform mound that is shaped like a horned serpent (Di Peso 1974:5:478). It runs along the western side of an associated room block in which a horned serpent was carved into the wall of a possible kiva. VanPool and VanPool (2007:30) consider the location of this design in this kiva structure an indication of the "ritual importance" of the plumed/horned serpent. A plumed serpent was also carved in a piece of caliche that Di Peso (1974:5:477-478) considered to be the west stone eye of the serpent mound.

In Crown's (1994) study of pottery designs found on Salado ceramics, she noted that serpent imagery was the most abundant, appearing on 315 of her 779 vessel sample (Crown 1994:146). Within this category, serpents with a horn or plume make up half of the 14 different identified serpent styles. These plumed serpents were recorded in a number of alternate forms. Although she was skeptical about Mesoamerican origins in the late A.D. 1200s for the introduction of this motif into the Southwest, Crown (1994:222) reiterated that she did not "question the many parallels in the imagery and beliefs between the Southwestern Cult and Mesoamerican religion."

Macaws: Macaw imagery has been found on several pottery types in the SW/NW, including Mimbres, Casas Grandes, and Salado types. Macaws are significant Mesoamerican icons

for the fact that scarlet macaws were likely transported from the lowland tropical forests of central and southern Mexico to the arid desert regions of the SW/NW (Somerville et al. 2009; Wyckoff 2009).

Macaw/Plumed-horned Serpent Combinations: In the analysis of Ramos Polychrome from Paquimé, Fenner (Di Peso 1974:6, 99) identified both the P-motif and half/whole spade as the macaw. She commented that this macaw design was "noted often enough to be considered a hallmark of this type." Although they were not found on all the whole Ramos Polychrome vessels excavated from Paquimé, spades and P-motifs, considered to represent macaws by Di Peso (1974:6:283), were noted to be the most numerous of the zoomorphic and anthropomorphic motifs identified on this pottery type.

Some archaeologists (Crown 1994:165-166; Schaafsma 1998:40; VanPool and VanPool 2007:114-115) have suggested that the half and whole spade motifs found on Ramos Polychrome pottery, represent both the macaw and plumed/horned serpent. VanPool and VanPool (2007:114-115) stated that "the implied ambiguity of plumed/horned serpents and macaws is such that some motifs of this style are clearly horned serpents, some are clearly macaws, and others were probably intended to be read as both horned/plumed serpents and macaws." Schaafsma (1998:40) noted that the combination of macaw and horned serpent traits "may suggest a ritual affinity between them."

In addition to the spade motif, the P-motif appears to be an abstract form of the spade motif. The curving line may depict the plume of the serpent or the beak of the macaw. As stated above, Di Peso (1974) originally identified this motif as a macaw, but I argue that it represents both the macaw and plumed/horned serpent.

Tlaloc, The Storm God: Another often mentioned similarity between the SW/NW and Mesoamerica is the symbolic representation of the Storm God. In the Maya region, he was referred to as *Chak* and as *Tlaloc* in central

Mexico among the Aztecs. This god was related to rain, mist, clouds and water (Riley 2005:10). His main characteristics in Mesoamerica include large round eyes, a large swirling or hooked nose, and fangs (Di Peso 1974:567). The Mesoamerican Storm God has been suggested to appear on rock art near Casas Grandes and El Paso, on Mimbres pottery, and in the imagery of the Anasazi (Ancestral Puebloan) Kachina cult (Di Peso 1974:566; Riley 2005:140-141; Schaafsma 1999:171-172).

Schaafsma (1999) has found correlations between the depictions of Tlaloc in Mesoamerica and on rock art across the SW/NW, and Di Peso (1974:565) also identified a copper crotal or bell as depicting Tlaloc, recognized by what he calls "its great round eyes and demoniacal teeth."

Knife-wings: Kelley (1964) originally compared the knife-wing motif on Mimbres pottery to depictions found in Mexico at Chichén Itzá in the Yucatan and in central Mexican codices. Among other things, Kelley noted that the knife-wing was connected to death and war in both Mesoamerican and U.S. Southwest contexts. Thompson (2000) revisited this correlation, but he focused on the knife-wing motif on Mimbres ceramics. Thompson (2000:147) proposed that knife-wing motifs depicted on artifacts associated with the Mimbres are "early examples from a cultural continuum extending into Mesoamerica," and he also mentioned that this was over a considerable amount of time.

Phalluses: Di Peso suggested that the phallus was a form of Mesoamerican symbolism at Casas Grandes. These were found as carved stone objects and on effigy vessels at Paquimé (Di Peso 1974:558), and in rare instances associated with imagery on Classic Mimbres pottery. At Paquimé, Di Peso (1974:557) considered these to be associated with Xiuhtecutli, the Lord of Fire among people of central Mexico. He stated that this was a "basic theme in various harvest dances that featured male participants who wore exaggerated penises and, in the midst of a display of filth, enacted certain fertility rites" (Di Peso 1974:558).

It is also interesting to note that people who participated in the Chalchihuites cultural tradition and who inhabited portions of present-day Durango and Zacatecas, Mexico, also carved similar stone phalluses (Bridget Zavala, personal communication 2010). Several scholars have noted the connection of Paquimé to the Chalchihuites and Aztatlán tradition, and this connection has also been evidenced by other characteristic features such as I-shaped ball courts and platform mounds (Foster 1986; Lister and Howard 1955; VanPool et al. 2008).

Death Masks: Another Mesoamerican symbolic influence proposed by Di Peso (1974:560-561) was the death mask figure that "featured closed eyes, an open mouth (sometimes with a protruding tongue), and occasionally wearing a feather nose ornament." This was thought to have been related to the Mesoamerican representation of the Toltec *Xipe Tótec*, a god of springtime and the regeneration of nature. The Toltec would offer gifts of flayed human skin to this god, and participants in the ritual sacrifice would drape these offerings over their bodies in similitude of *Xipe Tótec*.

Di Peso (1974:561) considered depictions on Casas Grandes pottery similar to depictions of *Xipe Tótec* found in the Borgia Codex and mentioned that this "cult" also was represented by "trophy heads, vestiges of cannibalism, and ceremonial drinking as ordained by the goddess of the maguey plant (*Mayáhuel*), who was a vital part of the *Xipe* pantheon of vegetation gods."

Twins or Pairs: In Thompson's (1999) study of Mimbres Black-on-white pottery iconography, he compared imagery depicting Mimbres cosmology to that of the sixteenth century Kiche' Maya historical record, the *Popol Vuh*. He found that paired images appeared on more than 200 Mimbres bowls (12 percent of those with Mimbres figurative motifs) (Thompson 1999:125-126). Of these, Thompson (1999:125) noted that 53 of the bowls included paired anthropomorphs, and he interpreted these pairs to represent the Pueblo War twins as well as the Hero Twins of ancient Mayan mythology (Thompson 1999:113).

VanPool and VanPool (2007:38) also noted duality in the form of opposing pairs on Medio period (A.D. 1200-1450) pottery designs at Paquimé. These include "scrolls, triangles with hooks, and various forms of a step element," as well as "macaw or horned-serpent motifs, circles, and P-shaped designs." They suggest that this focus on duality during the Medio period is indicative of the cosmology of Casas Grandes, specifically reflecting the association with an "upper world and underworld centered around the middle world of the here-and-now, a view that is consistent with the emphasis on the axis mundi as a center spot uniting these worlds" (VanPool and VanPool 2007:41-42).

The Flower World: Jane Hill introduced the concept of a "Flower World" resulting from her examination of verbal art through song of SW/ NW and Mesoamerican ethnographic groups. The Flower World is a spirit land where the dead go, and it is represented by a number of symbols (Hays-Gilpin and Hill 1999, 2000). These include flowers, colorful birds, butterflies, and rainbows. Hays-Gilpin and Hill (1999:16) stated that "in Mesoamerica, as in the Southwest, flowers occur in wall paintings and ritual regalia. Most notable are the depictions of flowery paradises, including multiple representations of flowering trees, birds, butterflies, many symbols of water, and images of divinities found at Teotihuacán."

Hays-Gilpin and Hill (1999:3) also suggest that Flower World imagery may have "intensified during periods of heightened economic stress and social tension." They found it among the Hohokam, Mimbres, Anasazi, Teotihuacán, and possibly Casas Grandes traditions. Crown (1994) also identified flowers and butterflies on Salado pottery, and suggested that they were associated with the Southwestern Cult that she proposes arose with the appearance of the Salado tradition.

Mathiowetz (2008) has also identified iconographical and ethnohistorical similarities between the Flower World complex of Mesoamerica and the Sun Youth in the U.S. Southwest. In particular, he noted similarities between Xochipilli, the central Mexican deity linked to the sun and the Flower World complex, and Payatamu, the Sun Youth of Puebloan mythology.

SUMMARY OF MESOAMERICAN ICONOGRAPHY

As reviewed in the description of iconography above, plumed/horned serpents, macaws, macaw/ serpent combinations, Tlaloc imagery, knife-wing motifs, phalluses, death masks, twins, and Flower World imagery have all been considered to have origins in Mesoamerica. While several of these symbols have been identified on Salado and Chihuahuan Polychrome pottery, there are a few that were not recognized on the vessels in this study. While Tlaloc imagery is abundant as rock art, it has only been identified in the SW/ NW on Mimbres pottery (Rice 2010; Schaafsma 1999). I did not identify any design elements or motifs that reflect Tlaloc imagery on the polychrome traditions of the Salado and Casas Grandes regions. In addition, Di Peso (1974:560-561) suggested that death mask iconography in the form of human effigy faces with closed eyes and open mouths was evidence of a link between the SW/NW and Mesoamerica. While similarities do exist, I am not convinced that these facial features are connected to the Toltec deity *Xipe Tótec*, and therefore I did not record these types of characteristics as being Mesoamerican iconography.

Those that were included in the iconographical analysis include plumed/horned serpents, macaws, macaw/serpent combinations, knife-wing motifs, phalluses, twins/pairs, and Flower World imagery (Figure I.4.3). These are considered Mesoamerican following the interpretations described above, and the inclusion of these symbols in this study follows a preliminary analysis that I conducted to determine

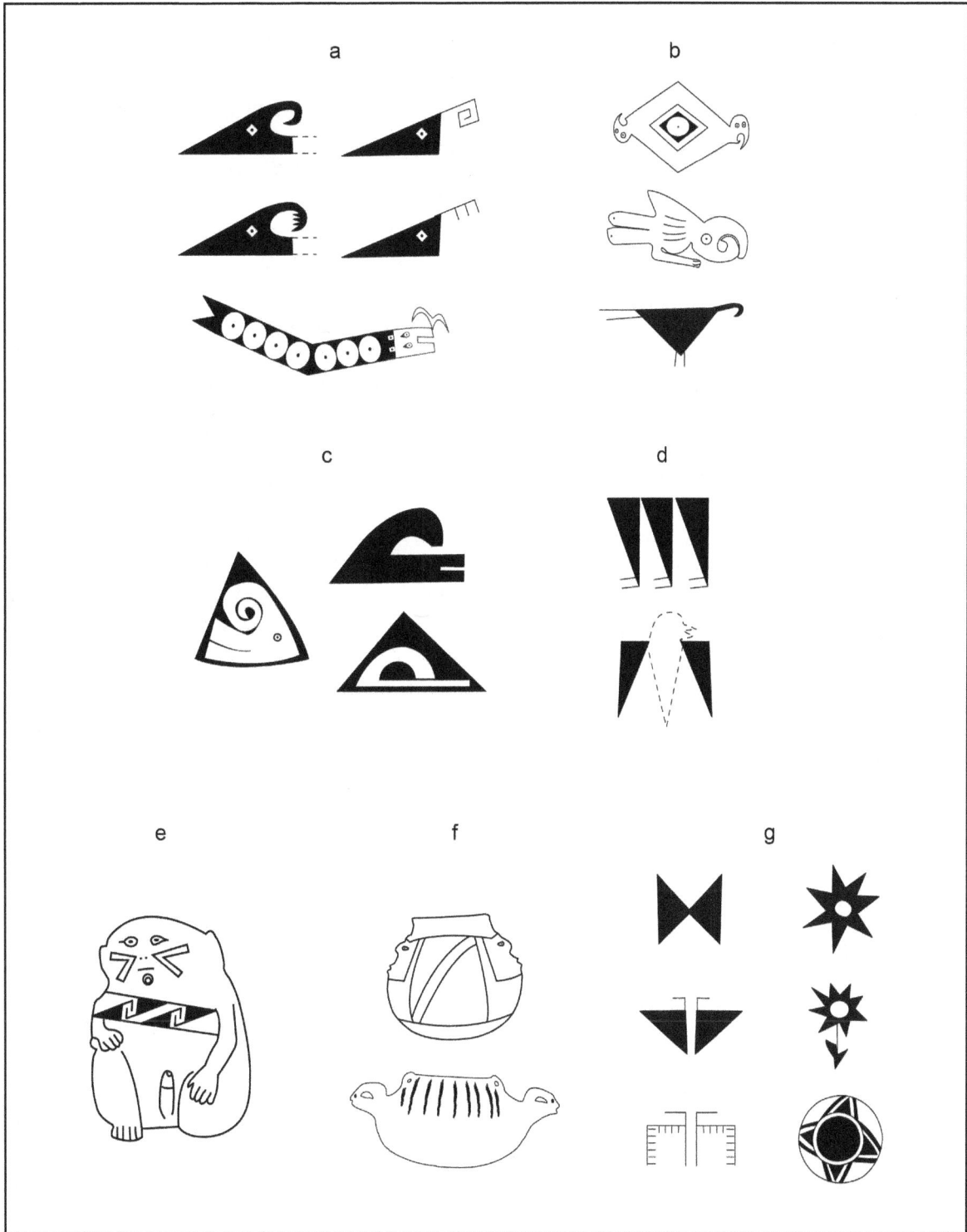

Figure I.4.3. Spade motif which may be the horned/plumed serpent, macaw, or a combination of the two from a) Mimbres (from Di Peso 1974, vol. 2:553 Figure 335-2), b) Salado (from Crown 1994:133, Figure 9.1), and c) Casas Grandes pottery (from Di Peso et al. 1974, vol. 6:272, Figure 290-6-55), d) Mimbres (from Di Peso et al. 1974, vol. 6:100 Figure 69-6-4), e) Casas Grandes Pottery, f) Salado, and g) Casas Grandes pottery.

which traits would be recorded during the full iconographical analysis. For pottery from the Casas Grandes and Salado regions, plumed/horned serpents typically appear as heads only, which are triangular in shape with some type of appendage that represent the plume or horn, and one or two eyes. This is following Crown's criteria (1994:135) in her study of Salado iconography. Macaws appear in different forms, such as whole bodies or as heads only, and are considered Mesoamerican for the fact that these images represent animals that were physically transported from regions in Mesoamerica. In relation to macaw and plumed/horned serpent imagery, I recorded spade and P-motifs as abstract combinations of these Mesoamerican-derived symbols. Knife-wing and phallus iconography is rare on Salado and Casas Grandes pottery, but I identify them as Mesoamerican following the interpretations of Kelley (1964), Thompson (2000), and Di Peso (1974). I would also agree that the depiction of twins/pairs in the SW/NW may be connected to Mesoamerican mythology. Although possibly a result of artistic convention, duality appears to be a theme for several of the motifs examined in this study. Finally, I found that images such as flowers, butterflies, and birds were also depicted, and as others have suggested (Hays-Gilpin and Hill 1999, 2000; Mathiowetz 2008), these motifs may be related to the Flower World complex that may have originated in Mesoamerica.

Distribution of Mesoamerican Iconography among Salado and Casas Grandes Sites

The purpose of this research was to determine how people of Salado and Casas Grandes traditions incorporated aspects of Mesoamerica into their cultures and how it may relate to sociopolitical organization. For the comparison of motifs between the Salado and Casas Grandes regions, I examined frequencies for each of the 10 Mesoamerican motif types. In order to examine

differences between more and less hierarchical sites found in each region, I recorded the presence/absence of each motif category.

There are almost twice as many vessels from sites categorized as more hierarchical in the Casas Grandes region, and due to these differences in sample size, I calculated and compared the frequency percentage of each motif category. I also calculated the Brainerd-Robinson coefficient (*BR*) for each motif category, which measures the similarity of percentages between samples. A *BR* coefficient of 200 suggests that the samples are exactly alike; in contrast, a *BR* of zero indicates absolute difference (Cowgill 1990:513). The lowest *BR* coefficients show which motifs differed the most between more and less hierarchical sites.

Table I.4.2 shows the frequencies of Mesoamerican symbols/motifs among more and less hierarchical Salado and Casas Grandes sites. The frequencies indicate that the majority of the motifs are equally distributed among both more and less hierarchical sites within each area. The Brainerd-Robinson coefficients support this observation for both the Salado and Chihuahuan traditions, with no *BR* coefficient being less than 181.6. Generally speaking, this indicates that there was very little difference in the distribution of symbols on pottery at more and less hierarchical sites.

Although the Brainerd-Robinson coefficient can produce information regarding general differences between samples, significance testing provides data associated with the strength of these differences. I used Fisher's Exact Test to calculate a p-value by comparing the presence and absence of each motif category. P-values equal to or less than 0.05 are considered to be significantly different. As shown on Table I.4.2, plumed/horned serpents were the only motif frequency that was significantly different between more and less hierarchical Salado sites and they also had the lowest *BR* coefficient (< *BR* 190). Plumed/horned serpents were more common at more hierarchical Salado sites, but only by 9 percent.

Motif frequencies at Chihuahuan sites produced different results. Twins/pairs, P-motifs, and spades had *BR* coefficients of less than 190. Of these, the only motifs depicted more often on vessels at less hierarchical sites in the Casas Grandes region were the plumed/horned serpents and birds. All other motifs occurred more often at Paquimé and at other more hierarchical sites, although only slightly more often than at less hierarchical sites. Significance testing of frequencies in the Casas Grandes region shows that twins/pairs and plumed/horned serpents were the only motifs that occurred at significantly different rates (p < .05).

In sum, the differences in motif frequencies between more and less hierarchical sites in both the Salado and Chihuahuan regions are minor as defined by significance testing, but a general comparison of the frequencies of the two traditions shows some interesting trends. First, the frequencies of motifs at Salado sites show that there are seven motifs that are more common at less hierarchical sites, and three occur at a higher rate at more hierarchical sites. In contrast, only two of the 10 motifs at Chihuahuan sites were present more often at less hierarchical sites while eight had higher frequencies at more hierarchical sites.

For Chihuahuan sites, I found that there was a trend toward higher frequencies of Mesoamerican symbols at sites within the Inner Zone (Figure I.4.4). These motifs have an occurrence rate of 53 percent at Inner Zone sites and 35 percent for communities outside of the core zone. The only Mesoamerican motif that occurs more often at sites outside of the Inner Zone is the plumed/horned serpent, but this is only represented by three occurrences. In addition, if spade and P-motifs are considered abstract forms of either the macaw, plumed/horned serpent, or both, then not only is the frequency of macaws and plumed/horned serpents much higher in the Casas Grandes region, but they also occur more often at Inner Zone sites.

On average, Salado vessels rarely depict what others have considered Mesoamerican symbols. The combined frequency of occurrence of Mesoamerican symbols at more hierarchical sites is 32 percent, and less hierarchical is 32 percent as well. The percentages show that these motifs are equally frequent at all of the Salado sites (Figure I.4.4). The largest difference in motif frequency for Mesoamerican symbols among Salado sites is that associated with plumed/horned serpents, which occur more frequently at more hierarchical sites. This is also the only Mesoamerican motif that was found to be significantly different (p = 0.017) in the comparison between more and less hierarchical sites. Twins/pairs occur at a slightly higher frequency at more hierarchical sites, but this is based on only four occurrences, and their frequencies are not significantly different (p = 0.6).

Finally, spade and P-motifs are only found at less hierarchical Salado sites, but this is due to the fact that they were found on Chihuahuan vessels at Slaughter Ranch, which is the southernmost Salado site that lies on the northern Casas Grandes periphery. Slaughter Ranch was likely engaged in trade with communities in northern Chihuahua due to evidence of trade items, including several Chihuahuan Polychrome vessels. Mills and Mills (1971:23-24) also noted that approximately half of the painted pottery found at Slaughter Ranch was Salado, while the other half was Chihuahuan.

In summary, the results of the iconographical analysis showed that while there were not overwhelming significant differences in the distribution of iconography among more and less hierarchical sites, some patterns still indicate differences between the Salado and Casas Grandes regions. Importantly, I found that Mesoamerican symbols occurred at a higher rate at more hierarchical Casas Grandes sites, although they also occurred frequently at less hierarchical sites, whereas these symbols were similarly distributed among Salado sites of varying social hierarchy.

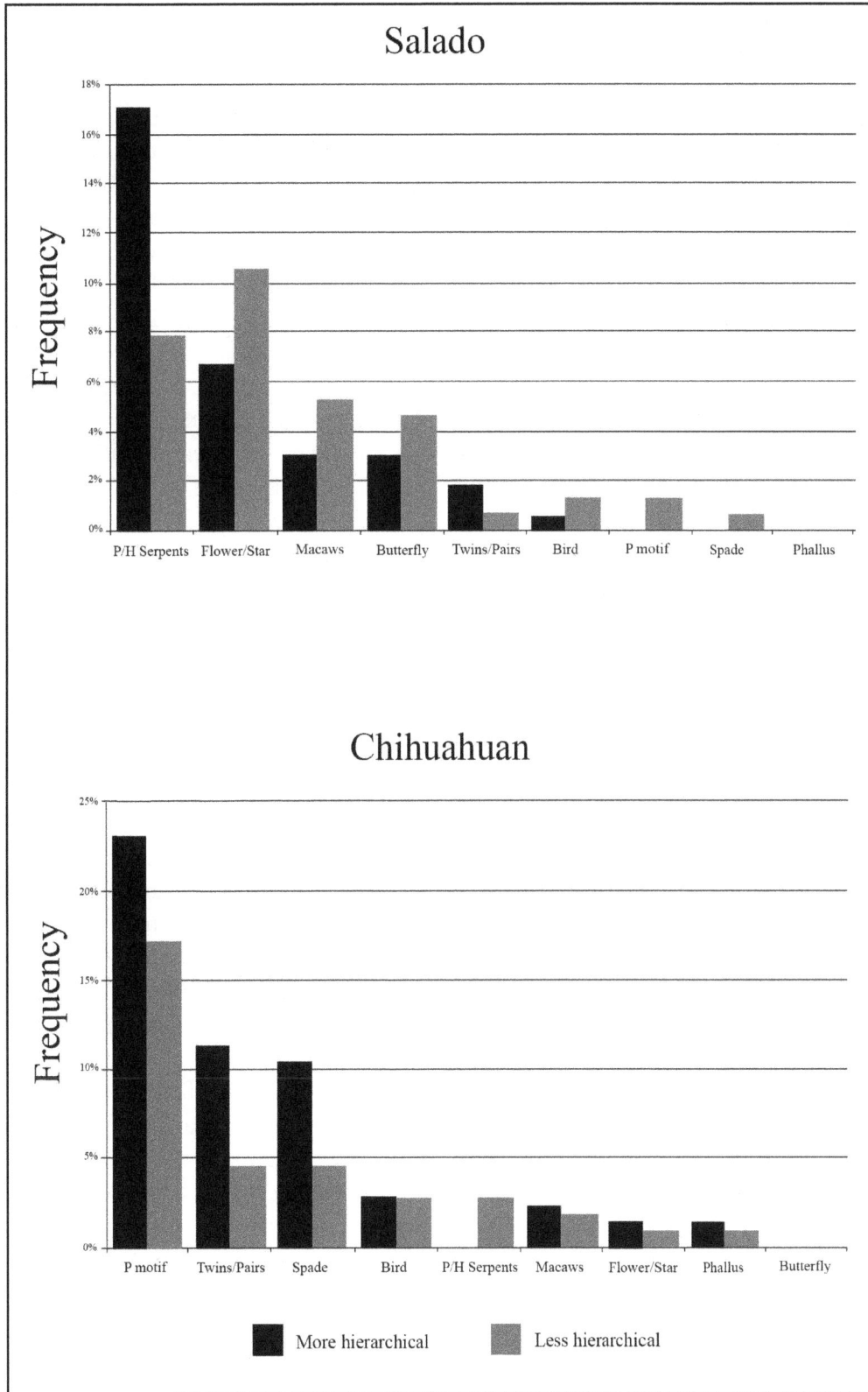

Figure I.4.4. Comparison of frequency of Mesoamerican motifs between more and less hierarchical sites among the Salado and Chihuahuan traditions.

OTHER MESOAMERICAN INTERACTION MARKERS

As stated above, several other Mesoamerican interaction markers have been identified in the SW/NW, and I look at four that are considered key identifiers of long-distance interaction with the Mesoamerican world: ballcourts, macaws, copper bells, and shell. Three of the most numerous foreign trade items found in the SW/NW that derive from Mesoamerica are macaws, shell, and copper bells. These artifacts have been traced to the coastal regions of southeastern (macaws), northwestern (shell) and western (copper bells) Mexico, and their patterns of distribution at both Salado and Chihuahuan sites provide evidence for how these goods were being used.

Distribution patterns associated with these four interaction markers also suggest that more direct interaction between Casas Grandes and Mesoamerican communities solidify the notion that symbols such as macaws and plumed/horned serpents were considered to be linked to a foreign source. In addition, this information indicates that less direct interaction occurred between Salado and Mesoamerican communities, and in this case may suggest that Mesoamerican symbols could have derived from previous local traditions who had adopted these symbols at an earlier period of time.

Ballcourts. Haury (1976:346-347) notes that between A.D. 500 and 1200, ballcourts "stand preeminently" as markers of a time when "the Hohokam received the most massive infusions out of the south." He goes on to suggest that ballcourts and other architectural forms "are only the tangible evidence for a complex of ideas, activities, and behavior patterns associated with them," and they "may have been the main 'vehicles' on which lesser and perhaps unrelated ideas and things rode in."

Ballcourts were constructed and used *en masse* across the Hohokam landscape between A.D. 750-1000, but they were falling out of use by the thirteenth century, with the last being built around 1250 (Cordell 1997:337; Doyel 1991:255; Wilcox 1991). Ballcourts were typically oval-shaped depressions with berms built up on the sides, and it is presumed that a form of the Mesoamerican ballgame was played on them (Scarborough and Wilcox 1991; Wilcox 1991). While Abbott, Smith and Gallaga (2007) and Wilcox (1991) have documented their importance in regional exchange and ritual among the Hohokam, Salado sites in general are not associated with this architectural feature. The only record that I could find of a ballcourt at a Salado site was at Buena Vista/Curtis Site on the Gila River just east of Safford, Arizona (Neuzil 2008:18; Wilcox 1991:112), and the ballcourts may or may not have been associated with the Salado occupation of this site.

Lekson (2008:171) has suggested that the discontinuation of ballcourts and the surge in platform mound construction in the Hohokam region in the thirteenth century A.D. is one indication of a shift in the "Hohokam canon." This time also marks the appearance of the Salado phenomenon evidenced by the wide-spread production of Salado Polychrome pottery. I would further suggest that the abandonment of ballcourts and the increase in platform mound construction may indicate a shift away from "outside" sources of interaction and a focus on the building and strengthening of local cultural traditions. The lack of ballcourts at Salado sites may suggest that not only had this tradition fallen out of favor, but that interaction with Mesoamerica had also faded.

In the Casas Grandes region, ballcourts are present not only at Paquimé, but also at sites within close proximity (< 30 km) of this central site (Harmon 2005, 2006; Whalen and Minnis 2001, 2003, 2009). There are three courts at Paquimé, two of which are the classic I-shaped court found in Mesoamerica. Although other ballcourts at sites outside of Paquimé were not all constructed in the I- or T-shape, Whalen and Minnis (2003:327) only identified them at sites in the core zone, those that were more integrated into the Casas Grandes political and social system (i.e., those I have labeled more hierarchical). Harmon (2005, 2006:192) also suggests that ballcourts in the Casas Grandes region represent a strong link to those in Mesoamerica, which would include similar I-shaped and open-ended ballcourts at La Quemada in Zacatecas and the La Ferrería Site in Durango to the south (Kelley 1991:88).

Macaws: Macaw remains have been found in both the Salado and Casas Grandes regions. They have also been identified at other contemporaneous SW/NW sites, including Kinishba, Grasshopper, Point of Pines, Turkey Creek, Reeve Ruin, and Freeman Ranch (Di Peso 1974:8, 273; Hargrave 1970:43-48; McKusick 1982:92), but the number found at these sites combined are less than were discovered at Paquimé alone.

The excavations at Paquimé resulted in 503 macaws, and of these many were likely sacrificed as part of ritual tradition (Di Peso 1974:554-555; Di Peso 1974:8, 272). Macaw breeding pens as well as the remains of birds in many growth stages also provide evidence of aviculture. At sites in the core zone within 30 kilometers of Paquimé, Whalen and Minnis (2000:176) identified circular stones that were perforated in the center, considered to be macaw pen doors. Although the practice of macaw aviculture occurred at sites outside of Paquimé, this evidence of aviculture indicate that the distribution of this activity was found to be restricted to more hierarchical sites. These patterns suggest that the possession and distribution of macaws were controlled by elites at the core sites, including Paquimé and its nearest neighbors.

Copper Bells: Copper bells have been found in the SW/NW at several Hohokam sites, and the largest known quantities were discovered at Gatlin (n = 55) and Snaketown (n = 28) (Haury 1976:278; Vargas 1995, 2001:202). They have also been found at Salado sites, although in lesser

quantity. Gila Pueblo, for example, had the most copper bells of any site after A.D. 1250 with 40 bells (Vargas 2001:203). Other contemporary sites where copper bells have also been found include Grasshopper Pueblo and Kinishba (Vargas 2001:203). Interestingly, Cline Terrace Mound and Schoolhouse Point Mound, two of the Salado platform mound sites included in this study, do not have evidence of any copper bells (cf. Jacobs and Rice 1997; Lindauer 1996). This may indicate that copper bell trade to this area slowed after A.D. 1250, or that it shifted to Casas Grandes.

Excavations at Paquimé resulted in 115 copper bells, the largest quantity and widest variety ever found in the SW/NW (Vargas 2001:203). Using technological and stylistic analysis, Vargas was also able to trace all but one type of bell to the copper manufacturing tradition of West Mexico, suggesting that most of the copper items at Paquimé were originally manufactured in Mesoamerica. In addition, Vargas (2001:203) investigated the distribution of copper bell types across the SW/NW and found that few bells were found at sites thought to have received copper items from Paquimé, leading to her interpretation that Paquimé was more of a consumer than a trading post for exotic goods. Whalen and Minnis (2009:249-250) report that only one copper bell was found at Site 204, a site located within 30 km of Paquimé, and they also reference Sayles (1936:58-59, Plate XIX) who reported the discovery of only two bells and a few items of copper jewelry at the Ramos site, which is also located within the core zone of Casas Grandes.

Shell: Another abundant foreign trade item at sites in both the Salado and Chihuahuan regions was shell. Evidence from Paquimé suggests that it was the principal receiver of marine shell items from west coast regions in Mexico with millions of pieces being found at this primary center (Di Peso 1974:6:401). As with copper bells, shell artifacts brought to the Casas Grandes region were concentrated at Paquimé. Whalen and Minnis (2009:238) carried out excavations at sites within 30 km of Paquimé and these resulted in fewer than 200 pieces of shell. Although the paucity of data from sites outside the Inner Zone prevents us from comparing shell distribution beyond the core zone in Casas Grandes, there is likely a limited amount of this artifact type possibly linked to restricted control by those at Paquimé.

Turning to Salado sites, shell was widespread in this region and has been found at several sites including VIV, Kuykendall, Slaughter Ranch, Cline Terrace Mound, and Schoolhouse Point Mound. Shell items include beads, tinklers, pendants, bracelets, and even trumpets. In her analysis of shell exchange across the SW/NW, Bradley (1999:219) noted that Salado sites in southern Arizona and southwestern New Mexico showed relatively little variety in the types of shell artifacts. There were many more beads than any other shell item.

The detailed shell artifact inventories from Cline Terrace and Schoolhouse Point Mounds provide interesting patterns related to the intrasite distribution of shell within these two Salado platform mound communities (Bradley and Rice 1996; Jacobs and Rice 1997). At Schoolhouse Point, 2,572 shell artifacts were recovered, the majority of which were beads. While 42 percent of the artifacts derived from freshwater contexts, the majority were marine shell that was probably transported from the Gulf of California into the Tonto Basin. Included in this category were four large trumpets that have been associated with communal rituals that were likely the focus of activity at this mound site (Bradley and Rice 1996:595). At Cline Terrace, 612 shell items were found, the majority of which were marine (83 percent) and for the most part were finished ornaments (Bradley and Rice 1997:458). Furthermore, Jacobs and Rice (1997:581) noted that rooms constructed at the top of the platform did not contain more

scarce resources (such as shell) than those at ground-level, leading them to suggest that this community represented a ranked segmentary society. They describe these types of societies as those in which "hierarchical organizations can be founded largely on ideological principles, and distinctions within the hierarchy need not be reflected in sumptuary items" (Jacobs and Rice 1997:581).

DISCUSSION

Patterns of ballcourt, macaw, copper bell, and shell distribution provide further evidence concerning the intensity of interaction with Mesoamerica and their roles in each tradition. For Salado sites, the lack of ballcourts and the likely adoption of platform mound construction from people participating in the Hohokam tradition suggest that interaction between Salado communities and Mesoamerica may have been less intense than that with Casas Grandes. The adoption of I- and T-shaped ballcourts indicates more direct contact with Mesoamerica for those in the Casas Grandes region, and the restricted construction of these features at sites in the core zone of Paquimé suggests that leaders used their connection to and knowledge of the these foreign entities to increase their influence over those participating in the Casas Grandes ritual system.

Macaws, shell, and copper bells are present in both Salado and Casas Grandes regions, but the numbers of these artifacts at Casas Grandes dwarf those found in the rest of the SW/NW. This evidence suggests that the intensity of interaction between Casas Grandes and Mesoamerica was much stronger. The fact that these exotic artifacts were also primarily found at the central site of Paquimé suggests that local leaders may have used them as symbolic tokens that served to legitimize their authority. As has been suggested by Jacobs and Rice (1997:581), the general distribution of resources among Salado communities of varying social hierarchy also correlates well with the results of the iconographical analysis and provides further evidence that people in these communities likely did not emphasize their association with Mesoamerica as a foreign source of power or authority.

CONCLUSIONS

The iconographical analysis conducted in this study shows that the differential distributions of Mesoamerican symbols provide another line of evidence in clarifying our understanding of the putative nature of sociopolitical organization among late prehistoric societies in the SW/NW. Foreign symbols can represent a link to the outside world and in some cases were used as tokens of power and authority (Helms 1993; Robb 1998). In other situations, their association with Mesoamerica may have been lost as symbols were locally reproduced and passed from one generation to another. In these cases, foreign symbols may have been integrated into local ideologies, became part of the worldview associated with these local traditions, and were seen as symbolic girders that organized relationships within society.

Data from the Casas Grandes region support the idea that these foreign symbols acted as tokens of authority or power at the site of Paquimé and at other more hierarchical sites, where emerging elites and ritual specialists likely legitimized their control by demonstrating their links to Mesoamerica. Although these symbols were expressed more frequently and elaborately at more hierarchical sites in the Casas Grandes region, they were also present on pottery at less hierarchical communities on the periphery where they likely served as ideological girders connected to a unified system of belief or worldview. The Salado sample also provided evidence of a system in which symbols on pottery were distributed widely among people of differing positions of status. In this region, these also may have served as symbolic girders that likely represented a reorganized, local religious canon that served to link distant participating groups. While the differences between elites and commoners were minimal at Salado sites, people who did have influential authority (i.e., those who lived on or were tied to the performance of ceremonies at platform mounds) maintained ritual prominence and seemingly supported an ideology of inclusion rather than exclusion.

I also examined the distribution of other Mesoamerican interaction markers which support the results of the iconographical analysis. The Casas Grandes sociopolitical organization was focused on an elite network of communities where emerging elites likely used exotic goods and rituals, such as the Mesoamerican ballgame, as markers of authority. The smaller amounts of macaws, shell, copper bells and the absence of ballcourts at Salado sites may indicate that interaction with Mesoamerica was less intense (or the relationships were variable), and the equal distribution of resources among all echelons of Salado society suggest that these foreign goods and symbols were not generally utilized as tokens of authority.

This study has shown that elements of Mesoamerican culture were probably integrated differently into existing sociopolitical systems. The broader implications of this research include contributions to the discussion of long-distance relationships within prehistoric societies by focusing on the local integration of foreign cultural elements. In addition to studies concerning the exchange of commodities between communities, I have shown how examining iconographical systems can contribute to our understanding of these distant relationships.

The Lost Century
El siglo perdido

Part II, Chapter 1
The Hohokam-Upper Piman Continuum Revisited

Patrick D. Lyons, J. Brett Hill, and Jeffery J. Clark

ABSTRACT

Three models have traditionally dominated archaeological thinking regarding the relationship between Piman-speaking groups in Arizona (the Akimel O'odham and Tohono O'odham) and the Hohokam archaeological culture. The dominant viewpoint among archaeologists in the U.S. Southwest is that Piman-speakers are the direct biological and cultural descendants of the Hohokam. The second is that Upper Piman descent can be traced to non-Hohokam populations indigenous to southern Arizona. The third perspective is that Piman-speakers recently moved into Arizona, from northern México, into what was essentially a vacant niche. However, apart from the work of Charles Di Peso, the question of Upper Piman origins has generally been a by-product of other research projects and has largely been pursued on the northern side of the international border. In this chapter, we reexamine the three dominant models as well as a reconstruction we refer to as the Late Arrival and Absorption model, a version of which was first presented more than 30 years ago by W. Bruce Masse. This model is consistent with the archaeological record, tribal oral tradition, and historical documents. A key focus of our approach to illuminating Hohokam-Upper Piman relationships is understanding the demographic dynamics of the 150 years preceding the "lost century," A.D. 1450-1540. In this larger context, we argue that one-to-one relationships between living peoples and cultural historical units used by archaeologists should be the exception rather than the rule and that cultural-historical trajectories are best conceived as "braided river channels."

RESUMEN

Tradicionalmente, tres modelos han dominado el pensamiento arqueológico en cuanto a la relación entre los grupos hablantes de Pima (los Akimel O'odham y Tohono O'odham) y la cultura arqueológica Hohokam. El primer punto de vista entre los arqueólogos del Suroeste de Estados Unidos es que los hablantes de Pima son descendientes directos biológicos y culturales de los Hohokam. El segundo es que descienden de poblaciones indígenas no-Hohokam del sur de Arizona. La tercera perspectiva es que los hablantes de Pima recientemente se mudó a Arizona, desde el norte de México, en lo que era esencialmente un nicho vacante. Sin embargo, además del trabajo de Charles Di Peso, la pregunta sobre el origen de los Pimas sólo ha sido un sub-producto de los proyectos de investigación, y generalmente sólo se considera desde el norte de la frontera internacional. En este capítulo, reexaminar los tres modelos dominantes, así como una reconstrucción que nos referimos como el modelo "La Llegada Tardía y La Absorción", una versión de la que se presentó por primera vez hace más de 30 años por W. Bruce Masse. Este modelo es compatible con los datos recogidos de la tradición oral tribal, los documentos históricos, y el registro arqueológico. El objetivo principal de nuestro enfoque

Patrick D. Lyons Arizona State Museum and School of Anthropology, University of Arizona, and Archaeology Southwest
J. Brett Hill Department of Sociology and Anthropology, Hendrix College, and Archaeology Southwest
Jeffery J. Clark Archaeology Southwest

para entender la relación Hohokam-Pima es el entendimiento de la dinámica demográfica de los 150 años anteriores al "siglo perdido", 1450-1540 d.C. En este contexto más amplio, sostenemos que uno-a-uno entre los pueblos vivos y unidades culturales-históricas utilizados por los arqueólogos deben ser la excepción y no la regla, y que las trayectorias culturales-históricos son mejor concebidos como "canales de ríos trenzados".

The nature of the relationship between the Hohokam archaeological culture and the historic period Piman-speaking groups of the U.S. Southwest and northwest México has been of interest to archaeologists since the late 1800s (e.g., Bandelier 1884:80-85). In this chapter, we review the three dominant models of this relationship and contrast them with one introduced by W. Bruce Masse (1981; see also Seymour 2011a:7-8, 93, 299), which we refer to as the Late Arrival and Absorption model. We then examine evidence from the archaeological record and tribal oral tradition and address inferences recently drawn from the accounts of the de Niza and Coronado expeditions (e.g., Brasher 2007, 2009; Seymour 2009a). Among archaeological data, we emphasize the results of our recent research on demographic trends in the southern U.S. Southwest during the 150 years preceding the "lost century" of A.D. 1450-1540 (Hill et al. 2004; Lyons et al. 2011). We conclude that the available evidence is consistent with Masse's reconstruction of links between the Hohokam and Piman-speaking groups, and that such connections are best conceived and communicated in non-cladistic terms, using a "braided river channel" model of cultural relationships.

MODELS OF HOHOKAM-UPPER PIMAN CONTINUITY AND DISCONTINUITY

The title of this chapter is a reference to Paul Ezell's (1963) concept of a "Pima-Hohokam continuum," expanded to explicitly include, along with the Akimel O'odham (formerly referred to as Pima), other Piman-speakers: the Tohono O'odham (formerly known as Papago), and the Sobaipuri, the Piman-speakers who inhabited the San Pedro

Valley and part of the Santa Cruz Valley at Spanish contact. Here, all three are collectively referred to as O'odham or Upper Pimans.

As noted by Bernard Fontana and his colleagues (1962:85, 93), "the problem of Papago [Tohono O'odham]-Hohokam relationship is vastly complicated . . . In fact, there have been few problems in regional archaeology that have inspired so much speculation based on so little substantive evidence." These observations apply to the ancestry of all Piman-speaking groups in Arizona. It is important to note, however, that the question of Upper Piman origins, apart from Charles Di Peso's work, has generally represented an "incidental by-product of other research interests" (Ezell 1963:61).

Susan Brew and Bruce Huckell (1987:172) succinctly encapsulate the three dominant schools of thought on this issue:

> The first holds that the Pima [Akimel O'odham] and Papago [Tohono O'odham] are the descendants of the Hohokam . . . , the second suggests that the Pimans are the descendants of non-Hohokam populations long indigenous to southern Arizona . . . , and the third proposes that the Pimans are relatively recent immigrants into southern Arizona not genetically related to the Hohokam or other prehistoric groups known from southern Arizona. With the first two views, the Upper Pimans are seen as the product of in situ cultural evolution, while with the third they are viewed as new arrivals, moving into what may have been an essentially unoccupied area.

The first described and dominant viewpoint is "traditional" among U.S. Southwest archaeologists (e.g., Doyel 1981, 1989; Gilpin and Phillips 1999:32; Gladwin 1937, 1957:344-345; Haury 1945:211-212, 1950:542-543; 1976:357); the second is associated with Di Peso (1953, 1956, 1958, 1979, 1980, 1981; also see Hayden 1970; McGuire 1991), initially offered during the 1950s; and the third began to appear in the literature in the 1970s (Fontana 1976:45-46; Fritz 1977, 1989; Rea 1997:6-8). In each of these models, the Sobaipuri are often the focus of attention because they were contacted earlier than the other Piman-speakers of the region (arguably much earlier; see Seymour 2009a, 2011a), and because the vast majority of the available data from protohistoric and early Historic period Upper Piman archaeological sites has been recovered from the San Pedro and Santa Cruz valleys.

The Direct Descent Model

As early as the late 1800s, anthropologists explicitly assumed (Bandelier 1884:80-85; McGee 1895:371-373) a direct link between groups now identified as Hohokam and the Piman-speakers of the region. Later researchers specifically pointed to aspects of Upper Piman oral tradition and broad similarities in Hohokam and Upper Piman material culture as evidence (Fewkes 1912:153-155; Gladwin and Gladwin 1929:129-131). Harold Gladwin (1937:99, 121, 1957:344-345) eventually argued that the Tohono and Akimel O'odham were the direct descendants of the Hohokam and that the Mogollon and Salado were the ancestors of the Sobaipuri.

Emil Haury (1945:211-212), in his report on the Hemenway Expedition materials, was probably the most thorough in his discussion of Hohokam-Upper Piman similarities, suggesting that, "the Pima mirror the culture of the Hohokam in so many respects that no matter how enthusiastically one tries to prove otherwise, they still remain, logically, the descendants of the Hohokam." Haury pointed specifically to similarities in domestic architecture (pre-Classic Hohokam and historic Upper Pimans), rancheria spatial organization, the use of canal

irrigation, and pottery produced via the paddle-and-anvil technique. He offered the case of late prehispanic pitstructures cut into an underlying compound at Casa Grande as evidence of a return to rancherias before the arrival of the Spaniards. Like earlier writers (e.g., Fewkes 1912:154-155; Gladwin and Gladwin 1929:130), he was troubled by the apparent absence of cremation among modern Piman-speakers. Russell (1908:194), however, reported that Akimel O'odham warriors were sometimes cremated and suggested that this practice might have been adopted from neighboring, Yuman-speaking groups (see also Underhill 1939:190).

Haury's (1980; see also McGuire 1982; Reid 2008) later Papagueria Project, which was designed to produce integrated research from the four anthropological subdisciplines, had as one of its foci the nature of the relationship between the Hohokam and the Tohono O'odham. The plan had been to pursue this question by excavating the early historic site of Batki (AZ Z:16:6[ASM]), on the Tohono O'odham reservation. Permission was initially granted and then quickly retracted, however. Nonetheless, based on the results of other permitted excavations, including those at Ventana Cave (AZ Z:12:5[ASM]), Haury (1950:542-543) concluded that "a continuum can be postulated." He added shared physical traits and varieties of corn to the list of links between the two groups, as well as aspects of basketry technology and the probable use of the horizontal loom. Haury (1976:357) later extended the list of parallels, including dancing on mounds and the enclosure of ritual areas with palisades.

Many other discussions of Hohokam-Upper Piman relationships have addressed the question in this manner, listing shared traits and attempting to explain the changes in material culture and the loss of population evident between the late Classic period and Spanish contact (Doyel 1981, 1989; Ezell 1963; Fontana et al. 1962; Loendorf 2012; Loendorf et al. 2013; Wells 2006). J. W. McGee (1895:371-373; also see Gladwin 1937, 1957) hypothesized that some Piman-speakers were driven to marginal areas and to residentially mobile subsistence strategies by Apache raiding. Others have posited that climate change, floods, and environmental degradation were causal factors in transforming the late Classic period Hohokam into the early Historic period O'odham (e.g., Doyel 1981:76-77, 1989:142-144). Over the last two decades, there has been much discussion of declining health during the Classic period (e.g., Abbott 2003:213-215). Some have even championed the idea that European diseases arrived in the U.S. Southwest before face-to-face contact with Spaniards (e.g., Dobyns 1989; Ezell 1963; Upham 1986; cf. Reff 1987, 1989).

Whatever cause is attributed, population decline is a key fact to be addressed in any model. Ezell (1963:65), in the context of a review of arguments regarding a Hohokam-Upper Piman continuum, suggested that, "the diminution of a population below a critical point leaves too few personnel to carry on the culture, and the more complex the system, the more marked the changes." At first glance, this observation seems to support – or at least allow room for – the notion of direct continuity, but it is also consistent with the O'otam model and the Late Arrival and Absorption model discussed below.

The O'otam Model

Di Peso (1953, 1956, 1958, 1979, 1980, 1981) argued for the existence of an O'otam or "Desert Mogollon" culture, indigenous to southern Arizona, portions of southwestern New Mexico, and parts of northern México, manifest in the San Pedro Valley and surrounding areas in the form of the Dragoon Complex, the Babocomari Tradition, the San Simon Branch, and the remains of other local groups who made red-on-brown painted pottery (as opposed to Hohokam red-on-buff painted ceramics). He traced the origin of O'otam groups to the area's Archaic period inhabitants. Di Peso asserted that southern Arizona was colonized by the Hohokam (to whom he attributed a Mesoamerican origin) during the Colonial period (now dated circa A.D. 750-950), and that puebloan immigrants established themselves in the region during the Civano phase of the Classic period (now dated circa A.D. 1300-1450). He also posited that the Sobaipuri were the descendants of the indigenous O'otam and puebloan immigrants, and that the Sobaipuri drove most of the Hohokam out of Arizona, absorbing small remnant groups (Di Peso 1956:264-265, 1958:163).

Many elements of Di Peso's O'otam model have been borne out by more recent work. Currently available evidence suggests that the early farming villages of the southern Southwest were broadly similar and exhibited many traits associated with the Mogollon archaeological culture (Wallace et al. 1995; Whittlesey 1995). Furthermore, the Hohokam archaeological culture or tradition is now viewed as representing something unique, as compared to other local traditions; a phenomenon that developed very rapidly and relatively late in the Ceramic period sequence (Wallace et al. 1995; contra Haury 1976). Although most researchers today believe that the Hohokam tradition developed in the Phoenix Basin, the notion that Mesoamerica was the source of the ideology expressed through Hohokam material culture remains popular (e.g., McGuire and Villalpando C. 2007; Wallace et al. 1995). Also, evidence of puebloan immigrants in central and southern Arizona during the late Classic period is now known to be robust (e.g., Clark 2001; Lyons 2003a; Neuzil 2008; Woodson 1999).

Di Peso's model (1953, 1956, 1979, 1980) linking the prehispanic O'otam and the protohistoric Sobaipuri is based on three premises: (1) he was successful in locating protohistoric sites, early Historic period sites, and sites whose occupations spanned the transition (such as Quiburi, Gaybanipitea, San Salvador de Baicatcan, San Joaquin de Baosuca, and San Cayetano del Tumacácori); (2) he correctly correlated these sites with settlements referred to in Spanish documents; and (3) he demonstrated continuity between Classic period and Sobaipuri artifacts and architecture. More recent research, however, has cast significant doubt on all three of these hypotheses (e.g., Fritz 1989; Gerald 1968; Lyons 2004a; Masse 1981; Phillips 1992; Seymour 1989, 2007a, 2011a).

Presenting a model quite similar to Di Peso's, Julian Hayden (1970) suggested that: (1) the Uto-Aztecan dialect chain, which linked indigenous Piman-speakers in Arizona with linguistic relatives in México, made it possible for a group of immigrants from the south to bring Hohokam culture to the Phoenix Basin; (2) another group of linguistic relatives, present in southeastern Arizona before the Hohokam – the Sobaipuri – later drove out the Hohokam, or at least their leaders, leaving the Salt River Valley empty; and (3) remnant Hohokam groups were incorporated into the Akimel and Tohono O'odham, where their descendants are members of the Red Ant and Buzzard moieties, respectively.

Like Di Peso's reconstruction, Hayden's assumes a long-term Sobaipuri presence in Arizona and he similarly holds them responsible for the Hohokam collapse. Hayden (1970:91), however, noted that

> far too little is known…of Hohokam-Pima-Papago archaeology between A.D. 1400 and the Spanish entry to warrant further discussion other than in the manner of Ezell (1963:61-66), who examined trait lists and intercultural relationships to suggest a Hohokam-Pima culture continuum.

The Replacement Model

Ellsworth Huntington (1911, 1914:48) was among the earliest scholars to express skepticism regarding a Hohokam-Upper Piman continuum, but this perspective seems to be an outgrowth of his fierce environmental determinism, i.e., that most cultural similarities can be attributed directly or indirectly to the effects of climate, and also an apparent distaste, on his part, for what would later be called ethnographic analogy and the direct historical approach. Others have approached this issue from the perspective of the abundant and obvious differences between the material culture and customs of Classic period groups in southern Arizona and the historically and archaeologically documented Piman-speakers of the same region (e.g., Fontana 1976:45-46; Fritz 1989; Hadley and Sheridan 1995:8-11). Others add that, since earliest European contact, Piman speakers have often either denied a relationship to, or true knowledge of, the identity of the ancient peoples who built the now ruined sites found in southern Arizona (e.g., Rea 1997:6-8). There are also dental (Turner 1987; Turner and Irish 1989) and linguistic data (Hale and Harris 1979; but see Shaul and Hill 1998) that seem to suggest population replacement.

Though many researchers consider wholesale population replacement a real possibility, the most completely developed argument has been offered by Gordon Fritz (1977, 1989; see also Seymour's [2011a:81-95] critique). Fritz focuses on three key issues: (1) the lack of absolute dates, ceramic indicators, and clear documentary evidence of a post-1450 but pre-1680s occupation of southern Arizona; (2) the differences between late Classic period and Sobaipuri material culture and the similarity of Sobaipuri material culture to some complexes in northern Mexico; and (3) possible ecological clues pertaining to the apparent gap between the prehispanic and early Historic period occupations of the region, including a huge accumulation of bighorn sheep horn-cores at an early Historic Upper Piman village along the Gila reported by Manje in 1697. He concludes that southern Arizona must have been a vacant niche from the mid-A.D. 1400s to some time between 1540 and the 1680s, when the Historic-period Piman-speakers of the region entered the area. A key data point related to the issue of clear ceramic indicators is a vessel, recovered from a burial at Bac, that was originally identified as a specimen of an unnamed Jeddito Yellow Ware type (from the Hopi Mesas) dating to the late 1600s (Ayres 1970). This vessel, ASM Catalog No. A-36,192, has since been reclassified as an early specimen of Matsaki Polychrome, a Zuni type made between

A.D. 1400 and 1680. Additional vessels of this type (also most likely produced between A.D. 1400 and 1500, based on stylistic and technological criteria) have recently been recovered as a result of cultural resource management projects within the San Xavier District of the Tohono O'odham Reservation.

The Late Arrival and Absorption Model

This model combines aspects of the O'otam and Replacement models, in that Sobaipuri are cast as relative newcomers to Arizona, arriving after the Hohokam collapse (i.e., the historic Upper Pimans did not cause the collapse of the Hohokam regional system), and the absorption of small, remnant late prehispanic groups by the Sobaipuri is posited. Masse (1981), using much of the same data employed by Fritz in his version of the replacement model, has presented the clearest discussion of this perspective. He points out the myriad differences between Sobaipuri material culture and that of the late Classic period, hypothesizing that the former may have originated in northern México. He specifically calls attention to parallels in domestic architecture, pottery, and projectile points (cf. Seymour 2011a:79-94).

Masse (1981:47) concludes that "the historic Upper Pimans are (in part) recent immigrants (post A.D. 1450) to southern Arizona," but that the Hohokam, having "gone through a period of significant population decline...had become so socially fragmented that they were easily assimilated into the mainstream of Upper Piman culture." He attributes the northern movement of the Sobaipuri during the early historic period to hostile Spanish incursions into northern México, including raids for the purpose of capturing slaves.

A late arrival from the south by the majority of the Upper Pimans of Arizona is also consistent with their settlement pattern as observed during the early Historic period; population was concentrated in the middle Santa Cruz and the San Pedro valleys, with very limited occupation of the Gila valley and no apparent use of the Salt (Doelle 1981). One

could argue that as population expanded, these groups were pushing farther northward through time.

RECENT RESEARCH ON THE LATE PREHISPANIC AND PROTOHISTORIC SOUTHERN U.S. SOUTHWEST

Regardless of which model of Hohokam-Upper Piman relationships a researcher espouses, the collapse of the Hohokam regional system must be acknowledged (see, e.g., Seymour 2009a:404, 2011a:7, 17, 80, 93, 141, 240, 294, 296-297). Different conceptions of the Hohokam collapse have implications for these models, and though most scholars have posited some sort of catastrophic event or short-term process at the end of the Hohokam sequence (e.g., Ezell 1963; Gregory 1991), others hypothesize a more gradual decline (e.g., Abbott 2003).

Our reconstruction of the Hohokam collapse is based on a macro-regional population study employing the Coalescent Communities Database, fieldwork in the lower San Pedro River Valley, and work with existing museum collections (Clark and Lyons 2012; Hill et al. 2004, 2010; Lyons et al. 2011). We and our colleagues have inferred gradual population decline precipitated by social and economic coalescence in the southern U.S. Southwest, including the Hohokam region. In short, we suggest that an influx of immigrants from the north, beginning in the late A.D. 1200s, led local groups to abandon dispersed, extensive settlement and subsistence strategies, resulting in increased competition, conflict, aggregation, and economic intensification.

These changes, which occurred in the context of severe environmental degradation in key areas, diminished diet breadth and negatively impacted health, causing a shift from long-term population growth to decline. We conclude that over approximately 150 years, gradual demographic decline (between 1 percent and 2 percent per year) resulted in small remnant groups unable to maintain viable communities. These groups were ultimately unable to continue identifiable Hohokam cultural traditions and consequently disappeared from the archaeological record of southern Arizona circa A.D. 1450, through migration and/or a shift in lifestyle that rendered them archaeologically invisible. Below we discuss the key elements of this reconstruction before exploring its implications for the Hohokam-Upper Piman continuum.

Immigrants from the North, Coalescence, and Population Decline

A suite of material markers, including perforated utility ware plates, Maverick Mountain Series painted pottery, kivas, and entryboxes, has been used to identify dozens of Kayenta immigrant enclaves in central and southern Arizona (Di Peso 1958; Haury 1958; Lyons 2003a; Lyons and Lindsay 2006; Neuzil 2008; Woodson 1999). These are visible in nearly every major settlement cluster occupied between A.D. 1250 and 1450 in the eastern half of Arizona, bounded on the north by the Little Colorado River Valley, and on the south by the U.S./Mexico border.

More importantly, the quality of this evidence has improved as archaeological theory and method have continued to develop (Clark 2001; Neuzil 2008). Recent research indicates that northern immigrants experienced different opportunities for and constraints upon the expression of identity in different portions of the Hohokam region – depending upon local socioeconomics and demography – and that in some places, a blending of local and exotic traditions is evident late in the sequence (Lyons and Clark 2008; Lyons et al. 2008). Some evidence suggests that dispersed immigrant enclaves were linked to each other in a network and maintained a shared identity like historic populations in diaspora (Clark et al. 2013; Lyons and Clark 2012; Lyons et al. 2011; Mills et al. 2013).

Recently compiled demographic data and newly developed theoretical models suggest that, on a regional scale, population declined and contracted spatially throughout the late Classic period in the southern Southwest, even in the face of immigration from the north, with remnant populations coalescing in areas allowing easy access to other groups (Hill et al. 2004; Wilcox et al. 2003). Based in part on recent refinements to Roosevelt Red Ware typology and chronology (Lyons 2013), the latest prehispanic population refugia in southern Arizona and southwestern New Mexico include a few dozen sites in portions of the Agua Fria drainage, in parts of the lower Salt River valley, in the Santa Cruz flats, along the Gila River from the San Simon confluence to its headwaters, and in the Sulphur Springs Valley.

At the local level, we can now model the gradual depopulation of individual river valleys such as the San Pedro and the lower Salt. In the case of the San Pedro, we can see settlement contracting down-river to the confluences with Aravaipa Creek and the Gila, apparently with complete depopulation by A.D. 1425 or shortly thereafter (Clark and Lyons 2012). In the lower Salt, we infer that environmental degradation making agriculture more precarious in areas adjacent to core settlements, at the headgates of irrigation canal systems, reached a critical level at about the same time that population began to coalescence in the outskirts. We posit that many of those who joined outlier settlements were immigrants from the Kayenta region to the north, people born of Kayenta immigrant parents, and people of mixed parentage. Our model holds that groups from the core area were, over time, thrust into competition and conflict with groups on the outskirts, with depopulation the ultimate outcome (Lyons et al. 2011).

Some of those who left central and southern Arizona during the 1400s appear to have relocated to northeastern Arizona and northwestern New Mexico, establishing themselves on the Hopi Mesas and on lands now encompassed by the Zuni reservation. This inference is based in part on the recovery of shell trumpets, like those found at Hohokam platform mound villages, from late prehispanic sites in the mountains and on the southern edge of the Colorado Plateau (Lyons 2003b; Mills and Ferguson 2008). Such objects are still used today by both the Hopi and the Zuni in ceremonies that involve the plumed or horned water serpent. In addition, cremated human remains interred in late Roosevelt Red Ware vessels have been recovered from late prehispanic and protohistoric deposits at Zuni (Kintigh 2000; Smith et al. 1966). A specific method of "vessel-killing" also links Zuni ancestors who cremated their dead to the ancient inhabitants of the Point of Pines region (Robinson 1958; Robinson and Sprague 1965).

Recent research by Matthew Peeples (this volume) has produced biodistance data that suggest some of the immigrants who inhabited the protohistoric Zuni towns were descended from groups who had first migrated from the Kayenta region in the late 1200s and had lived in central and southern Arizona during the 1300s. Below, we briefly examine corroborating evidence expressed in O'odham, Hopi, and Zuni oral traditions.

Tribal Oral Traditions

At a very basic level, O'odham creation accounts are about migration and cultural hybridization (cf. Loendorf 2012:118). Though O'odham oral accounts of events preceding the coming of the Spaniards seem clear on the point that the O'odham are related to the Hohokam, they are equally clear in communicating that the Hohokam existed in the past and were in some sense a different people. This corpus of texts represents a vivid, emic account of change in which multiple populations of varying ethnic backgrounds merged and divided over a span of centuries, with small remnant groups in southern Arizona assimilated by emergent groups (Bahr 1971; Bahr et al. 1994).

Thus, O'odham ancestors are to be found among both the locals (small remnant groups) and the emergent groups (the Sobaipuri). The emergent groups are said to have originated in the south and to have moved westward from the San Pedro,

settling mainly on the Gila and only lightly on the Salt. One benefit of the Late Arrival and Absorption model and the O'otam model, compared to the Direct Descent and Replacement models, is that the former accommodate an apparent contradiction in Upper Piman oral accounts regarding Hohokam-O'odham relationships: that the O'odham are both the same and different from the Hohokam. Indeed, in some oral accounts, the O'odham are specifically described as a mixture of Hohokam groups and Piman-speakers who entered the region from the southeast (Bahr et al. 1994:1-2, 257; Underhill 1946:13).

Hopi oral tradition frequently mentions clans that originated in or migrated through what is now southern Arizona (Ferguson 2003; Ferguson and Lomaomvaya 1999; Lyons 2003a). Relevant Hopi accounts are told from the opposite perspective of O'odham accounts, as if they record the lives of late prehispanic people who fled southern Arizona (Teague 1993). Likewise, there are Zuni oral texts that refer to groups who left to reside in a land to the south, of "everlasting summer" (Cushing 1896, 1920).

In summary, where previous researchers have wrestled with what appeared to be a catastrophic collapse of the Hohokam system, we infer a gradual process of decline that included some movement of population out of the region, northward and perhaps southward, and the likely persistence of small remnant groups with faint archaeological signatures. There is, however, an abrupt discontinuity in architecture and artifacts evident between the A.D. 1400s and Spanish contact. Early Historic period houses and domestic features, ceremonial architecture, site layout, settlement pattern, ceramics, groundstone, ornaments, and burial location differ dramatically from what is characteristic of the late prehispanic period. This discontinuity may be related to demographic processes in that remnant groups may have been too small to maintain cultural transmission (Eisenberg 1991; Ezell 1963; Shennan 2000). Alternatively, it could be a reflection of the absorption of small remnant groups by new arrivals. Because the nature of Sobaipuri archaeology is so critical to the question of Hohokam-Upper Piman connections, and since a considerable amount of research has recently been reported, below we review what is currently known about Upper Piman material culture in Arizona.

THE ARCHAEOLOGY OF THE SOBAIPURI

What comes after the Hohokam in the archaeological record of southern Arizona is a complex associated with Upper Pimans. This complex was first identified by Di Peso (1953) as material traces of the Sobaipuri. Despite debates about the geographical ranges and specific ethnic identities of different protohistoric Piman-speaking groups, archaeologists working in southern Arizona have come to recognize distinctive architecture and artifacts attributable to the Sobaipuri of the San Pedro and Santa Cruz valleys. The similarities among the remains of structures, ceramic vessels, and projectile points at Di Peso's Gaybanipitea (AZ EE:8:5[AF]; AZ EE:8:15[ASM]; Pitaitutgam, see Seymour 1989) Alder Wash Ruin (AZ BB:6:9[ASM]), England Ranch Ruin (AZ DD:8:129[ASM]), the Tinaja Canyon site (AZ DD:8:128[ASM]), and three sites in the Santa Rita Mountains (Huckell 1984), have led Fritz (1977, 1989), Masse (1981), and Seymour (1989, 1993a, 1993b, 1997, 2003, 2011a; also see Doyel 1977) to identify the following diagnostic traits (cf. Ravesloot and Whittlesey 1987; Seymour 2002, 2009b): (1) rancherías comprised by elliptical houses marked by upright cobble foundations; (2) Whetstone Plain or pottery very similar to Whetstone Plain; and (3) a distinctive type of triangular projectile point characterized by a deep, concave basal notch and serrated edges (Brew and Huckell 1987:166-171, Figure 2a-d).

Seymour (2002, 2004, 2008, 2009b, 2011a:65, 76, 78) has argued, however, that only a subset of the points assumed to be diagnostic of Upper Pimans indeed are. She refers to these as Huachuca

points (Seymour 2011a:Figure 4.1, 90-94) and distinguishes them from other protohistoric stone arrow tips. According to Seymour, similar points found on and near Sobaipuri sites, along with other distinctive lithic tools, are part of a widespread tradition (occurring as far east at Texas) associated with residentially mobile protohistoric groups such as the Jano, Jocome, Manso, and Suma. She refers to this tradition as the Canutillo Complex and hypothesizes that the presence of such objects at Upper Piman sites may reflect coresidence by O'odham and members of one or more of these mobile groups. In addition, or perhaps alternatively, she posits that these may be a marker of a process of ethnogenesis by which, for example, the Upper Pimans of the San Pedro mixed with mobile groups to become the Sobaipuri, as this is suggested by the available historical documents (Seymour 2007b, 2008). However, she concludes that, in some cases, Canutillo Complex points are found at O'odham sites as a result of attacks by mobile groups.

Other characteristics of Upper Piman habitation sites include sparse artifact assemblages compared to Classic period and pre-Classic habitation sites, and the occasional presence of trace amounts of red ware and/or red-on-brown pottery (Doyel 1977). Although small numbers of Upper Piman artifacts have occasionally been recovered from the surfaces of late prehispanic sites, to the best of our knowledge, no one has yet found in situ late prehispanic material culture at an Upper Piman site. Indeed, the temporally diagnostic, non-Upper Piman (or non-Canutillo Complex) material culture at most Sobaipuri sites is Spanish in origin.

In a flurry of recent publications (including nearly twenty over the last seven years), Seymour has presented a number of arguments that focus attention on issues at the heart of understanding Hohokam-Upper Piman connections:

• protohistoric groups were present in southern Arizona by A.D. 1400, and there was widespread occupation of the Santa Cruz and San Pedro valleys in the 1400s and 1500s (Seymour 2007b, 2007c, 2008, 2009a, 2009b, 2009c, 2010a, 2010b, 2011a);

• despite a "substantial break" from earlier traditions (Seymour 2010a:240) described as "a cultural, material, and organizational disjunction" (Seymour 2009a:404), there was not an occupational hiatus between the Hohokam or Salado and these protohistoric groups, and there was no late prehispanic population collapse (Seymour 2007c, 2008, 2009a, 2009b, 2009c, 2010a, 2010b, 2011a);

• the Sobaipuri (Cayetano Complex), Apaches (Cerro Rojo Complex), and non-Athabascan/non-Piman mobile groups such as the Manso, Suma, Jano, and Jocome (Canutillo Complex) were encountered by Fray Marcos de Niza, in 1539, and some were met by the Coronado Expedition, in 1540 (Seymour 2002, 2007c, 2009a, 2009b, 2011a);

• as discussed above, the Sobaipuri may represent a blending of sedentary and mobile protohistoric groups (Seymour 2007b, 2008, 2009b); and

• the Sobaipuri replaced, are a modified form of, or – most likely – absorbed the Hohokam (Seymour 2007c, 2009c, 2010a, 2010b, 2011a).

Discussion

According to Seymour (2011a:222),

> Now that chronometric results are available, the temporal depth of the Sobaipuri presence in southern Arizona is clear. Direct (luminescence) dates on O'odham pottery, corroborated with radiocarbon results, establish an O'odham presence in the 1400s and early 1500s at several sites including Pitaitutgam,

Sonoita Creek site, AZ EE:4:32, AZ EE:4:36 in Locus A, and the Sharples site where O'odham ceramics were dated.

Seymour's claim of widespread occupation of the Santa Cruz and the San Pedro during the 1500s may be accurate, given her reconstruction of Fray Marcos de Niza's route, which we discuss below. However, extending this inference back into the 1400s, we believe, is problematic.

Of the five sites listed above, three are located in the San Pedro Valley: Pitaitutgam, AZ EE:4:32(ASM), and AZ EE:4:36(ASM). The other two, the Sharples site (AZ DD:8:44[ASM]) and the Sonoita Creek site (AZ EE:9:153[ASM]) are located in the Santa Cruz Valley. Seymour's (2011a:Table 9.2) compilation of Sobaipuri chronometric dates indicates that the earliest that any of the San Pedro Valley sites could have been occupied is A.D. 1488, given an optically stimulated luminescence (OSL) date from AZ EE:4:32 of A.D. 1523 + 35 (A.D. 1488-1558). The earliest date she reports for nearby AZ EE:4:36, which also produced glass beads from the 1500s (Seymour 2011a:4), is A.D. 1563 + 30 (A.D. 1533-1593, OSL). Pitaitutgam (which also yielded objects of Spanish origin) is even later, with its earliest date at A.D. 1594 + 30 (A.D. 1564-1624, OSL).

Dates from the Sharples site, in the Santa Cruz Valley, do not represent strong evidence of a pre-1500 Sobaipuri occupation either. Seymour (2009b, 2010b, 2011a) characterizes it as a multicomponent site with stratified prehispanic, Canutillo Complex (protohistoric), and Apache occupations. The earliest pottery she identifies as O'odham-made is dated A.D. 1524 + 40 (A.D. 1484-1564, OSL) and A.D. 1524 + 60 (A.D. 1464-1584, OSL), and she indicates it likely made its way to the site as a result of trade with, or raiding of, nearby O'odham settlements (Seymour 2009b:433, 2011a:Table 9.2). A careful reading of one of Seymour's (2010b:171-172, Table 1) papers and a comparison of data in that paper with information in her recent book (Seymour

2011a:Table 9.2), however, suggests that even the identification of one of these sherds as O'odham-made is in doubt.

Indeed, in the same article, on the same page, a single sherd (OSL:X2069; dated 1524 + 60) is identified as both "early O'odham pottery" and "currently untyped...[but]...seem[ingly] ... derived from the Sonoran brownware tradition" (Seymour 2010b:172). Even more confusing, Seymour (2010b:172) indicates that the sample of five dated sherds from the Sharples site includes "two sherds that are clearly early O'odham and three previously undescribed Terminal Prehistoric plainwares that could have originated with any number of groups," yet three of the five dated sherds listed in Table 1 (in the same article) are identified as Whetstone Plain, including sample OSL:X2069 (also see Seymour 2011a:Table 9.2). Finally, from the Sonoita Creek site, also in the Santa Cruz Valley, Seymour (2011a: Table 9.2) reports two OSL dates from the same feature: A.D. 1474 + 50 (A.D. 1424-1524) and A.D. 1484 + 50 (A.D. 1434-1534).

In summary, Seymour has dated three sites in the San Pedro Valley to as early as A.D. 1488, A.D. 1533, and A.D. 1564, respectively. In the Santa Cruz Valley, she has dated one site to as early as A.D. 1464 and another to as early as A.D. 1424. We submit that one site in the San Pedro Valley with a date possibly in the late 1400s and one site in the Santa Cruz Valley with a date possibly in the early 1400s does not constitute "varied and abundant evidence point[ing] to people being present in southern Arizona from at least AD 1400 forward, with no perceivable break with their predecessors or ancestors" (Seymour 2011a:44). Nor does it support Seymour's (2011a:299) claim that Upper Pimans absorbed remnant Hohokam populations after having "likely arrived in the 1300s or early 1400s."

Furthermore, Seymour's assertion that there is no evidence of a late prehispanic population crash is simply untenable (see e.g., Abbott 2003; Dean et al. 1994; Hill et al. 2004; Mills et al. 2013). This can be shown through counts of sites

or rooms, patterns in absolute dates, and the near absence in southern Arizona of pottery types known to date between A.D. 1400 and 1630. As discussed above, another point that undermines the idea of substantial temporal overlap is the lack of credible evidence of interchange between late prehispanic and protohistoric groups (i.e., a lack of *in situ* late Classic period material culture on Sobaipuri sites).

Despite our differences, Seymour's prolific output has highlighted the importance of understanding the faint traces of protohistoric groups and the great potential of the documentary record as a source of hypotheses and corroborating evidence. In addition, she can perhaps be credited with producing the first absolute dates that place protohistoric groups in southern Arizona before the arrival of de Niza in 1539 – though we await more details and more dates. Her most important recent contribution, however, may be her inferences regarding the de Niza and Coronado routes relative to the locations of protohistoric groups in the San Pedro Valley.

THE *ENTRADA*: CLUES FROM THE DOCUMENTARY AND ARCHAEOLOGICAL RECORDS

Those who have delved into the literature on the first Spaniards to enter the U.S. Southwest know that the documents associated with the expeditions of Fray Marcos de Niza and Francisco Vázquez de Coronado represent critical pieces of evidence in any attempt to understand the relationships among ancient groups and present-day American Indians. It is also a contentious literature, with entrenched positions on the de Niza and Coronado routes and other key issues (Reff 1997; Sánchez 1997). Unfortunately, much of the work that archaeologists have done to reconstruct these pathways has involved the use of flawed translations and incorrect assumptions (Flint and Flint 2005:1-15; Seymour 2009a, 2011b).

Fortunately, Richard Flint and Shirley Cushing Flint (2005) have published new annotated translations of the documents and consensus is settling on a corridor that includes the San Pedro Valley (Flint and Flint 2011). In addition, recent research by Nugent Brasher (2007, 2009, 2010, 2011a, 2011b, 2013) and Deni Seymour (2009a) has produced exciting results. There is now a credible association between an Arizona ruin and a place name important in the Coronado expedition reports – Chichilticale – an anchor point for more precisely interpolating the routes between Culiacán and Zuni taken by de Niza, Díaz, and Coronado, and more importantly, the locations of groups of native peoples encountered along the way.

Brasher's (2007, 2009, 2010) work at the Kuykendall site (AZ FF:2:2[ASM]; see also Mills and Mills 1969a, 1969b) has turned up iron crossbow boltheads, a lance-tip, a Spanish coin from the early 1500s, 16th century nails, and shot produced from Spanish lead, as well as evidence of a campsite which he interprets as traces of the Coronado expedition. Tarascan copper bells, possibly brought to the site by natives from México, were also found.

Previously identified Chichilticale candidates abound, including Casa Grande Ruins (Simpson 1871); the cliff dwellings at Tonto National Monument (Undreiner 1947); more than a dozen contenders in the upper Aravaipa drainage and the northern Sulphur Springs Valley (Bandelier 1892:407-409; Bolton 1964; Duffen and Hartmann 1997; Hartmann and Lee 2003; Haury 1984; Sauer 1932); and sites on the Salt River arm of Roosevelt Lake (Schroeder 1955) and in the Upper Gila River Valley near Cliff, New Mexico (Riley 1985). These have been championed by different authors based on interpretations of locations indicated in Spanish documents, elements of the landscape, and gross chronological information associated with prominent sites in an area meeting the first two criteria. The assumption has been that Chichilticale must have been occupied late in the prehispanic period due to the visibility of its architecture. In some cases, researchers have also put considerable effort into finding areas with reddish soil, as the ruin at Chichilticale is described as having walls made of red earth.

The decorated pottery assemblages at the latest-occupied sites in Southeastern Arizona, where most had believed Chichilticale would be found, are dominated by Roosevelt Red Ware. Therefore, Gila Polychrome and Tonto Polychrome became the key chronological indicators in the search for the Red House. There were two problems, however. First, many sites in the region have yielded these types. Second, the dates associated with these types, as they were originally defined, do not allow researchers to distinguish between sites occupied until just after A.D. 1350 and those inhabited until 1450.

Tracking the distribution of newly defined Roosevelt Red Ware types (Lyons 2004b, 2013; Lyons and Neuzil 2006; Neuzil and Lyons 2006) helps to narrow the field considerably, and focuses attention on the area investigated by Brasher. Based on work with survey collections from southeastern Arizona and southwestern New Mexico, analysis of excavated collections from these areas, and Anna Neuzil's (2008) study of ruins in the Safford Basin, Aravaipa Creek, and the Sulphur Springs Valley, a small number of sites stand out as the latest occupied, having yielded specimens of one or more of the latest types in the Roosevelt Red Ware sequence (Dinwiddie Polychrome, ca. 1390-1450; Cliff White-on-red, ca. 1390-1450; Phoenix Polychrome, ca. 1375-1450; and Nine Mile Polychrome, ca. 1375-1450). These include the Curtis site (AZ CC:2:3[ASM]), Fort Grant Pueblo (AZ CC:5:1 and AZ CC:5:8[ASM]), the Nine Mile site (AZ CC:15:1[AF]), and the Kuykendall site. Ceramic evidence of a terminal prehispanic occupation at the Kuykendall site strengthens Brasher's inference that the ruin at which he found a Coronado-era campsite is indeed the Red House referred to in the documentary record.

Seymour's (2009a) placement of de Niza's turn to the northeast, toward Zuni – leaving the San Pedro Valley in the area around Benson – and her arguments regarding Coronado's route make sense, especially in light of Brasher's identification of the Kuykendall site as Chichilticale. Thus, Coronado left the San Pedro too far south to have encountered Sobaipuris, whereas de Niza, who traveled farther north before leaving the valley, met people who must have been Sobaipuris. This would have been in 1539, more than 100 years after the San Pedro was depopulated by groups who archaeologists refer to as Hohokam and/or Salado.

SUMMARY AND CONCLUSION

Four models of the relationship between Piman-speaking groups in Arizona and the Hohokam archaeological culture have been reviewed. We assert that the Late Arrival and Absorption model – which combines aspects of the O'otam and Replacement models – best accommodates the available data, even in light of Seymour's recent chronometric contributions and her arguments regarding the de Niza and Coronado routes. The distinction between our version of the Late Arrival and Absorption model and Masse's (1981) is that we accept a Sobaipuri presence a some point before the de Niza expedition, rather than positing an arrival closer to the time of Kino.

We conclude by discussing the utility of thinking and communicating about cultural relationships using a "braided river channel" model. Following T. J. Ferguson (2004:32; see also Moore 1994, 2001), we argue that cultural-historical trajectories are best conceived as braided river channels, having resulted in "the development of small, diverging populations subjected to a constant flow of people across the fuzzy boundaries of ethnic groups or polities." Thus, one-to-one relationships between living peoples – such as the O'odham – and cultural historical units used by archaeologists – such as the Hohokam – should be the exception rather than the rule.

Trees, Nets, and Rivers

Anthropologists have often used one of three images to convey relationships among social groups: trees, nets, and braided river channels (Bellwood 1996; Dewar 1995; Ferguson 2004; Moore 1994; Terrell 2001). This is important to

consider, because the way we model phenomena shapes the ways in which we study them. Cladistic models, which employ the tree metaphor, reflect the notion that human social groups are discrete, easily-defined entities. In this framework, each group can be traced to a single common ancestor through a series of hierarchical relationships. New groups evolve as distinct ethnic limbs, which split off from the main trunk.

U.S. Southwest archaeologists during the 1930s and 1940s developed an explicitly arboreal model, parsing archaeological cultures into roots, stems, and branches (Colton 1939; Gladwin and Gladwin 1934). Strict adherence to this perspective is easily attacked as essentialist, in that it treats cultural identities and cultural transmission as if they were limited in the same ways as biological units of analysis and the process of genetic transmission (Terrell 2001:5; Lyons and Clark 2008).

The opposite approach is to view all social groups as interconnected and to compare their linkages to a net, a lattice, or a reticulated graph. This perspective emphasizes diffusion and hybridization and is also consistent with the notion that ethnic groups are very fluid. A corollary, however, of the extreme version of this perspective is that reconstruction of ancestor-descendant relationships is impossible (Dewar 1995:305).

A "middle road" favored by many, and one with a long history in American anthropology, is the "tree of human culture" (Kroeber 1948:Figure 18, 259-261), "banyan tree" (Linton 1955:v) or "braided river channel" (Moore 1994) model, which represents an attempt to combine the best of the cladistic approach and the reticulated graph approach. As Alfred Kroeber (1948:260) put it:

> the course of organic evolution can be portrayed properly as a tree of life, as Darwin called it, with trunk, limbs, branches, and twigs. The course of development of human culture cannot be so described, even metaphorically. There is a constant branching-out, but the branches grow

together again, wholly or partially, all the time. Culture diverges, but it syncretizes and anastomoses too …. The tree of culture… is a ramification of such coalescences, assimilations, or acculturations.

Adelin Linton's (1955:v) imagery is similar:

The [tree of culture]…refers not to the familiar evolutionary tree with a single trunk and spreading branches, but to the banyan tree of the tropics. The branches of the banyan tree cross and fuse and send down adventitious roots which turn into supporting trunks. Although the banyan tree spreads and grows until it becomes a miniature jungle, it remains a single plant and its various branches are traceable to the parent trunk. So cultural evolution, in spite of diffusion and borrowing and divergent development, can be traced to its prehistoric origins.

Kroeber's and Linton's statements reflect the fact that similar material culture traits and customs can exist in different places as a result of multiple processes, including diffusion and migration. Some have suggested that different processes and different aspects of social identity are more amenable to a particular type of model – cladistic or reticulate – than others (Bellwood 1996; Dewar 1995). This notion is consistent with our approach to tracking ancient social groups in that we do not treat all types of material culture, or aspects thereof, as equally useful in tracking social identity (Carr 1995a, 1955b; Clark 2001). Thus, the premises that underlie the braided river channel model are that: (1) ethnic groups are not necessarily fixed and unchanging, but membership is not infinitely variable, malleable, or negotiable; (2) ethnic groups are products of history (time, place, and process); and (3) cultural differences

do not necessarily correspond with ethnic group boundaries, but cultural differences are the raw materials from which such boundaries are constructed (see Jenkins 1997:13-14, 40, 47-58, 64). In summary, despite the fact that ethnic groups are somewhat flexible and different social processes can cause people to flow across fuzzy boundaries, strands of continuity can be traced.

In the late prehispanic era and the protohistoric period, we see migrations and mixing of populations; cycles of settlement contraction (coalescence); gradual regional demographic decline; the eventual depopulation of large areas of the southern U.S. Southwest, with some groups moving to still-occupied parts of the northern Southwest, such as the Hopi and Zuni areas, and to northern México; and a later influx, into parts of Arizona traditionally occupied by Piman-speakers, of people from northern México who absorbed small remnant populations descended from the region's Classic period inhabitants (Hill et al. 2004; Lyons et al. 2011).

A braided channel model of Upper Piman-Hohokam relationships best communicates what we see as a complicated history of cultural blending with strands of probable continuity, such as language and some religious practices (Figure II.1.1). In the future, we hope to build on the exciting work by Brasher and Seymour discussed here, refining the chronology of early Upper Piman archaeology and improving our ability to identify the traces of small remnant groups that bridge the "lost century" in southern Arizona. Finally, we agree with Seymour's (2011a:80) suggestion that the most rigorous way to address the question of the geographical origin of Sobaipuri material culture – and to demonstrate migration into Arizona – would be to generate archaeological data from sites in northern Sonora, complementing inferences about Upper Piman architecture, artifacts, and settlement pattern derived from the documentary record.

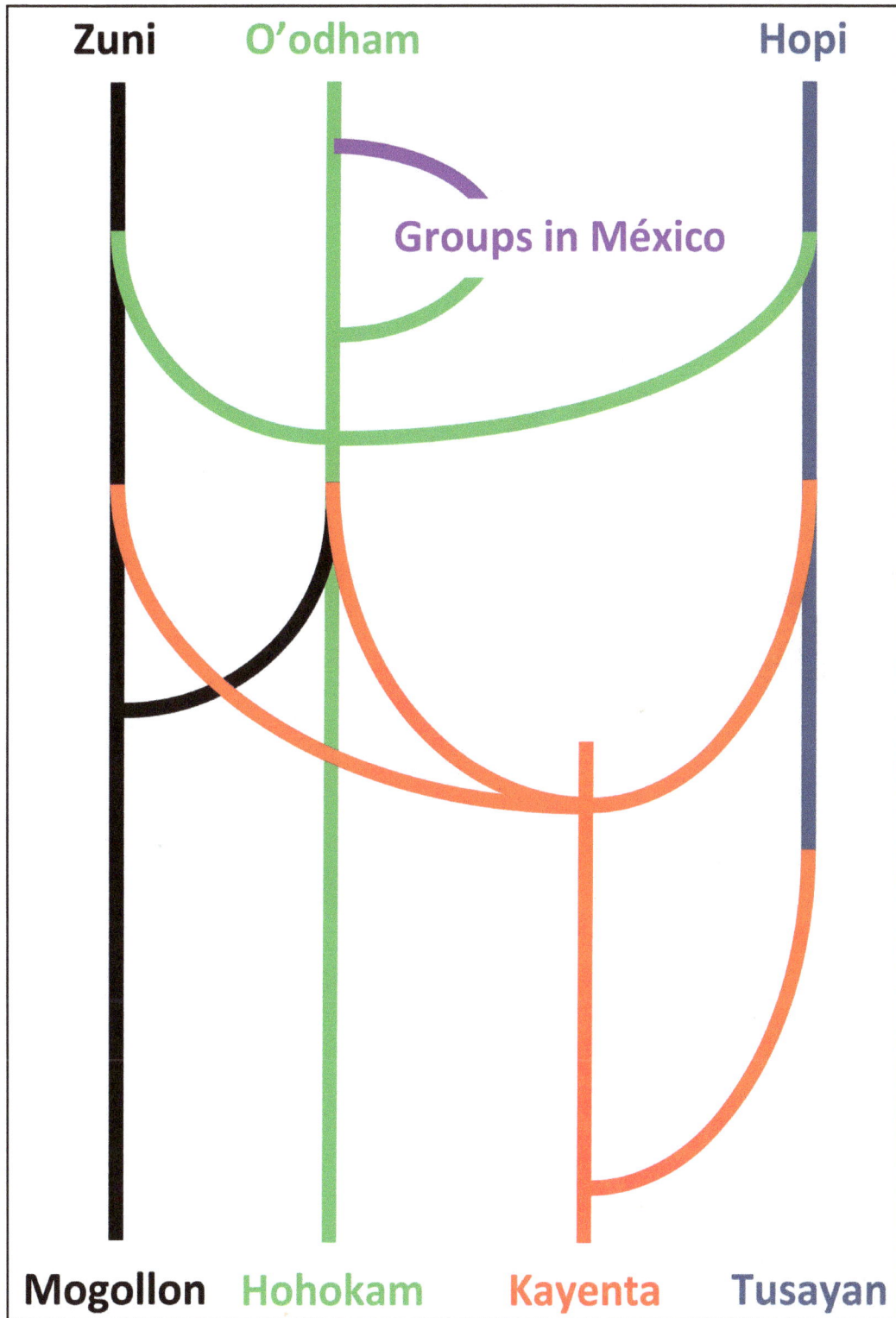

Figure II.1.1. A "braided river channel" model of connections among the Mogollon, Hohokam, Kayenta (Anasazi), and Tusayan (Anasazi) archaeological cultures and the present-day Zuni, O'odham, and Hopi. This model depicts a late arrival of the O'odham in the U.S. Southwest and their absorption of small remnant groups of Hohokam.

Part II, Chapter 2
Population History of the Zuni Region Across the Protohistoric Transition: Migration, Gene Flow, and Social Transformation

Matthew A. Peeples

ABSTRACT

The construction of the protohistoric Zuni towns in the late 14th and early 15th centuries was marked by major changes in settlement, architecture, ceramic design/technology, and burial practices that suggest that the Zuni region was a destination for populations from some of the areas to the south that were largely depopulated between 1450 and 1540 A.D. In this chapter, I explore the population history of the Zuni region from a biodistance perspective. Using methods for quantitative comparison of skeletal morphometric variation, I assess genetic evidence for immigration across the protohistoric transition. Further, I compare skeletal variation in the Zuni region with a number of other areas across the Southwest in order to identify potential regional scale patterns of gene flow related to population movement. This biogeographical perspective is particularly important because long distance population movement has frequently been implicated in many of the changes associated with the establishment of the protohistoric Zuni towns. The results presented here suggest that the protohistoric transition at Zuni involved substantial immigration, potentially from several sources across the Southwest, but that there was also a large local population. The history of population movement suggested by this analysis has further implications for considerations of many widespread changes occurring across the Southwest during the so-called "lost century."

RESUMEN

La construcción de la protohistoria de los pueblos Zuni de finales del siglo XIV y principios del XV fue marcada por cambios fundamentales en el patrón de asentamiento, la arquitectura, los diseños y tecnología cerámica, así como las prácticas de enterramiento, lo cual sugiere que la región Zuni fue un destino para poblaciones que emigraron de territorios del sur, que estuvieron básicamente deshabitados entre 1450-1540 d.C. En este capítulo exploro la historia poblacional de la región Zuni desde una perspectiva biodistante. Usando métodos para comparaciones cuantitativas de la variación morfométrica osteológica, evalúo la evidencia genética de migración en la transición protohistórica. De manera adicional comparo la variación esquelética en la región Zuni con otras áreas del Suroeste, con la finalidad de identificar patrones potenciales a escala regional de flujos genéticos relacionados con movimientos de población. La perspectiva biogeográfica es particularmente importante debido a que los movimientos de población han estado implicados frecuentemente en muchos de los cambios que se han asociado con el establecimiento de los pueblos Zuni protohistóricos. Los resultados aquí presentados sugieren que la transición protohistórica en Zuni incluyó migraciones importantes, potencialmente de varias fuentes en el Suroeste, pero que también existió una gran población local. La historia de los movimeintos de población sugerida por este análisis tiene además otras implicaciones en las consideraciones de la dispersión de muchos cambios que ocurrieron en el Suroeste durante el llamado "siglo perdido".

Matthew A. Peeples Archaeology Southwest

The protohistoric period in the Southwest (ca. A.D. 1450 to 1540) has frequently been depicted as a "lost century" because the pace and scale of demographic decline and cultural change occurring at this time make it particularly difficult to link archaeological remains to the historic ethnolinguistic groups documented at contact. This century was not really "lost," per se, in the historic Pueblo communities of Arizona and New Mexico, as there is extensive evidence of continuous occupation from the prehistoric period up to contact and beyond in several locations (see chapters in Adams and Duff 2004). At the same time, due in part to traditional disciplinary distinctions between archaeology and history, substantially less archaeological work has been focused on the protohistoric period than on earlier eras (see Wilcox and Masse 1981). Thus, even in many of the areas with good evidence of continuous occupation across the transition from prehistory to history, the "lost century" represents a hinge point in our knowledge of settlement, population movement, and culture change.

Currently available data suggest that the protohistoric transition in the Zuni region (referring to the period from ca. A.D. 1400 to 1450) is marked by a major shift in settlement as most areas that were intensively occupied during the 14th century and earlier were depopulated and nine protohistoric towns were established along the Zuni River and its major tributaries (Figure II.2.1; Huntley and Kintigh 2004; Kintigh 1985). This shift in settlement location coincided with apparently rapid changes in ceramic production (Mills 2007; Schachner 2006), agricultural technologies (Kintigh 1985), and burial practices (Howell 1994; Kintigh 2000; Smith et al. 1966) that cannot be easily explained in light of the Zuni region alone. As early as the late 19th century, archaeologists attributed many of these changes to the arrival of immigrants from regions across the Southwest that were experiencing population decline during the mid-15th century and earlier (e.g., Cushing 1890; Spier 1917:305, 1918:337-

338). Despite early interest in this period, the specific processes involved in this apparent immigration are still poorly understood.

In this chapter, I explore the population history of the Zuni region from a biodistance perspective. Specifically, using methods for quantitative comparison of skeletal morphometric variation, I assess genetic evidence for immigration across the protohistoric transition. Further, I compare skeletal variation in the Zuni region with a number of other areas across the Southwest in order to identify potential regional scale patterns of gene flow related to population movement. This biogeographical perspective is particularly important because long distance population movement has frequently been implicated in many of the changes associated with the establishment of the protohistoric Zuni towns. The results presented here suggest that the protohistoric transition at Zuni involved substantial immigration, potentially from several sources across the Southwest, but that there was also a large local population. The history of population movement suggested by this analysis has further implications for considerations of many widespread changes occurring across the Southwest during the so called "lost century."

THE PROTOHISTORIC TRANSITION AT ZUNI

The establishment of the protohistoric towns at Zuni is extremely difficult to date, in no small part due to the rapidity of the changes in settlement and material culture occurring at this time.

Major projects focused on the protohistoric/ historic period in the Zuni region include excavations by the Hendricks-Hodge expedition at Hawikku between 1917 and 1923 (Smith et al. 1966) and excavations at Kechiba:wa conducted by the University Museum of Cambridge in 1923 (Kintigh 2000). More recently, excavations have been conducted at the historic Zuni mission in the contemporary Zuni Middle Village (Halona:wa)

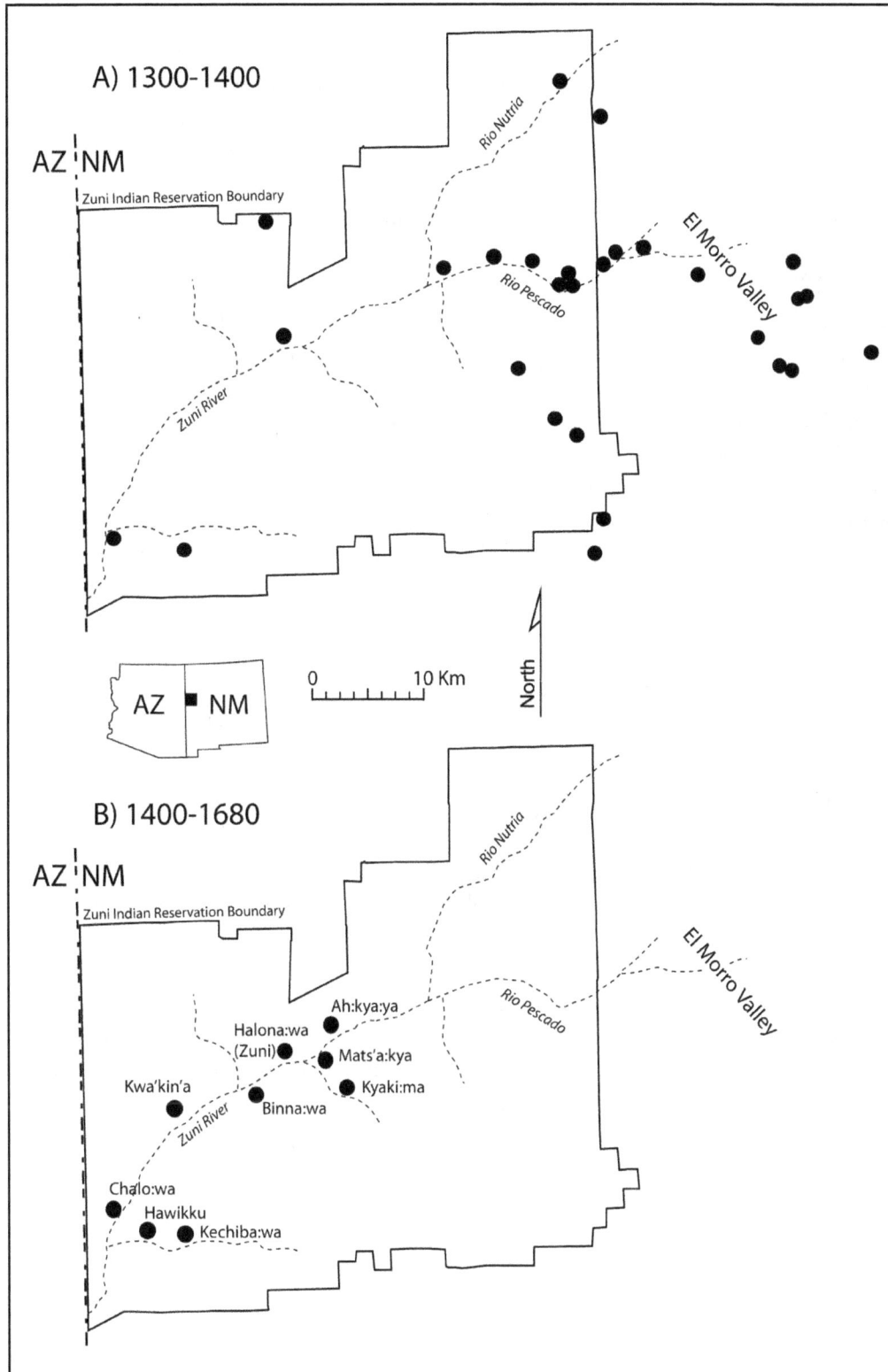

Figure II.2.1. Major sites in the Zuni region in the A) Pueblo IV and B) Protohistoric periods. Based on Huntley and Kintigh 2004 Figures 7.5, 7.7, and 7.8.

by the National Park Service (Caywood 1967). Between 1997 and 2001, the Zuni Cultural Resource Enterprise carried out an extensive house renovation and reconstruction project at the Zuni Middle Village that has provided a great deal of data relating to the protohistoric period. These projects have been supplemented by smaller surface collections and excavations (see Kintigh 1985:7-9). Although there are few absolute dates, the best available information suggest that the protohistoric towns were likely first occupied around the beginning of the 15th century (ca. A.D. 1400-1450; see Kintigh 1985; Smith et al. 1966), although there is also evidence of substantial 14th century occupation in at least one Zuni town (Halona:wa; see Scholnick 2003). The establishment of the large towns during the protohistoric transition represented a major change in the organization of architectural space. Prior to the protohistoric period, large villages in the Zuni region consisted of planned, nucleated pueblos, most of which were constructed in a limited number of rectangular, oval, or composite shapes (Kintigh 1985). The protohistoric towns, however, consisted of massed clusters of accretionally constructed room blocks, informally arranged around one or more irregular plaza spaces (Huntley and Kintigh 2004). This transition in site layout coincided with a shift in settlement location to the lower reaches of the Zuni River and its major tributaries. This shift in location was also likely also associated with a transition from run-off based agriculture to an agricultural system characterized by substantially greater reliance on stream and spring-fed irrigation (Kintigh 1985:103-109).

In addition to changes in settlement organization and location, the protohistoric transition in the Zuni region was marked by wide spread changes in ceramic design and technology. Breaking with a long sequence of ceramic technological and stylistic developments culminating in the production of Zuni Glaze Ware pottery by the late 13th century, potters in the Zuni region at around A.D. 1400 began producing matte-painted pottery known as Matsaki Buff Ware (Schachner 2006; Smith et al. 1966).

The shift from assemblages dominated by Zuni Glaze Ware to assemblages dominated by Matsaki Buff Ware was apparently rapid (see Scholnick 2003; Smith et al. 1966), though Zuni Glaze Wares may have still been produced along side Matsaki Buff Ware for some time. Matsaki Buff Ware has strong stylistic ties to pottery produced in other parts of the Southwest, in particular Sikyatki Polychrome within Jeddito Yellow Ware (see Mills 1995, 2007; Smith et al. 1966:329-330). The production of Matsaki Buff Ware represented a major shift in the technology related to firing and painting ceramics that also coincided with changes in culinary wares (Thomas and Mills 2003; Mills 1995, 2007).

The protohistoric transition at Zuni also saw new patterns of inter-regional interaction. For example, the protohistoric towns in the Zuni region show a drastic increase in the frequencies of non-local ceramic wares including Roosevelt Red Ware and small quantities of Jeddito Yellow Ware pottery. Prior to the establishment of the protohistoric towns, the Zuni River valley was characterized by extremely small frequencies of non-local ceramics (see Duff 2002). Available evidence suggests that the infiltration of these non-local wares into the Zuni region likely occurred somewhat before the earliest production of Matsaki Buff Ware pottery (Schachner 2006:134-135). The processes leading to the increased frequencies of non-local pottery may have differed among the protohistoric towns, but several researchers have linked this change to the arrival of migrant populations (see Kintigh 2000; Mills 2007; Smith et al. 1966).

Another major change associated with the protohistoric transition at relates to burial practices. Excavated burials from the protohistoric towns of Hawikku and Kechiba:wa include substantial numbers of cremations (ca. 1/3 of all burials; Kintigh 2000; Smith et al. 1966). The practice of cremation has not been noted in the Zuni region prior to the protohistoric transition (see Kintigh 2000; Schachner 2006:135). In addition to this, the practice of "killing" vessels appears to have become much more common in the Zuni region after the establishment of the protohistoric towns, particularly on vessels associated with cremations (Smith et al. 1966). Similar practices are known in several areas across the Southwest that were experiencing rapid population decline around the beginning of the protohistoric period including the Lower Salt River valley (Mitchell and Brunson-Hadley 2001:table 4.1), the Point of Pines region (Robinson and Sprague 1965), the Upper Gila (Lekson 2000:280-281), and the Safford area in Southeastern Arizona (Lekson 2000; Mills and Mills 1978). Interestingly, excavated cremations and inhumations in the Zuni region appear to be concentrated in groups (Smith et al. 1966) that have been interpreted as discrete cemeteries used by social units with different burial practices (Howell and Kintigh 1996; Kintigh 2000).

Explanations for the Changes Marking the Protohistoric Transition

The earliest attempt to explain the changes seen across the Zuni region was, arguably, the first formal archaeological expedition in the Southwest. The Hemenway Southwestern Expedition, beginning in 1886 under field director Frank Hamilton Cushing, was explicitly focused on combining insights from archaeology, history, ethnology and biological anthropology to determine where the historic Zuni people originated (Brunson 1989; Cushing 1890). In order to do this, Cushing initiated excavations at several Classic Period Hohokam sites in the Phoenix Basin including large scale excavations at the site of Los Muertos (Brunson 1989: Table II.2.1). Based on a consideration of the architectural remains, burial practices, pottery, and his own knowledge of Zuni culture, Cushing

argued that the occupants of the Salt River Valley near Phoenix were "unquestionably" direct ancestors to the contemporary Zuni people (Cushing 1890:162; see also Brunson 1989:37-44). This interpretation subsequently sparked a great deal of research into the question of Zuni ancestry, including the Hendricks-Hodge expedition to Hawikku (Smith et al. 1966).

In the decades following Cushing's pioneering study, a number of researchers have offered additional interpretations relating to the changes seen across the protohistoric transition at Zuni. Based primarily on general similarities in burial practices and ceramics with patterns seen at the protohistoric Zuni towns, researchers have posited influxes of population into the Zuni region from several sources including the Mogollon Highlands (Rinaldo 1964), the Little Colorado, (Martin and Rinaldo 1960:288; Spier 1918:341-345), the Upper Gila (Reed 1955; Rinaldo 1959:284-285), southern Arizona (Smith et al. 1966), and Paquimé (Di Peso 1974:760). Individual researchers have disagreed, however, as to the degree to which such population movements may have represented the addition of a small number of new arrivals or a total population replacement.

More recently, Kintigh has provided additional insights into the nature of the protohistoric transition at Zuni. Using methods and analyses developed by Howell (1994; Howell and Kintigh 1996), Kintigh (2000) compared burial practices and accompaniments at two protohistoric Zuni towns; Hawikku and Kechiba:wa. In this study, he found village level differences in burial orientation, treatment, as well as the ceramic wares accompanying burials and argued that some of these differences may have been based on ethnic distinctions within and between the protohistoric Zuni towns. He further argues that these ethnic differences may have risen from either the diverse origins of the founding populations of these towns or the uneven migration of new arrivals into

Table II.2.1. Craniometric Data Included in This Study

Sample	Major Sites/Areas	N	Source*
Chaco Canyon	Pueblo Bonito, Pueblo del Arroyo, small sites	54	AH, EKR, MS, NJA
Globe, AZ	Togetzoge	10	MS
Grants-Acoma Area	East of the Zuni Mountains	13	EKR
Grasshopper	Grasshopper Pueblo	43	JS
Hopi	Hopi Mesas, Homolovi	8	AH
Kayenta	Black Mesa, Tsegi Canyon	39	DM, EKR
Lower Salt	Los Muertos, Las Acequias	117	AH, PM
Mesa Verde	Mesa Verde NP	45	KB
Pottery Mound	Pottery Mound	17	MS
Puerco of the West	Petrified Forest, Kin Tiel	46	AH
SE Utah	Grand Gulch area	61	AH
Sinagua Area	Chaves Pass, Wupatki, Elden	51	AH, B&S
Zuni PII/III	Village of the Great Kivas, Whitewater	26	MS, TDS
Zuni PIV	Atsinna, Heshotauthla, Pueblo de los Muertos	29	CT, LS, MS
Zuni Proto/Historic	Hawikku	111	AH, MS
Zuni Historic	Halona:wa Mission	26	EKR

* AH=Aleš Hrdlička, B&S=Shara Bailey and Kimberly Spurr, CT=Christy Turner, DM=Debra Martin, EKR=Erik K. Reed, JS=Jeffrey Shipman, KB=Kevin Bennett, LS=Linda Smith, MS=Michael Schillaci, NJA=Nancy J. Akins, PM=Penny Minturn, TDS=T.D. Stewart

certain Zuni villages. In other words, the protohistoric transition at Zuni likely involved immigration, possibly from many locations, and pre-migration social distinctions may have structured social interaction within and between protohistoric villages for at least several generations. Importantly, Kintigh (2000:112) notes that it is also possible that some of the diversity among the protohistoric Zuni towns may relate to pre-existing distinctions between earlier Zuni settlements (see also Gregory and Wilcox 2007) and not necessarily long distance migrants.

Thomas, Mills, (Thomas and Mills 2003; Mills 2007) and Schachner (2006) have recently made similar arguments based largely on ceramic evidence. In general, these authors argue that some level of immigration across the protohistoric transition is likely. While agreeing with Kintigh (2000) that distinctions may have been maintained between migrants and the pre-existing local population in burial practices, these researchers suggest that the development of Matsaki Buff Ware technology and design may have related more to the integration of diverse populations than the maintenance of social differences (see Schachner 2006:140). The technology of Zuni Buff Ware production would have been new to migrants and locals alike and may have served to cement burgeoning social identities developing in the wake of the arrival of immigrants (Schachner 2006; Thomas and Mills 2003:10-13). Further, ceramic design styles found on Zuni Buff Ware were shared across much of the Western Pueblo world and may have related to an even broader scale of social identification developing at this time (Mills 2007:233).

As this brief overview suggests, many past researchers relying on several different lines of evidence, have argued that the protohistoric transition at Zuni was characterized by some degree of immigration. The potential sources for migrants as well as the potential proportions of locals vs. new arrivals have, however, differed dramatically between these studies.

The analyses presented below are specifically directed at addressing some of the differences among these interpretations. Consideration of biological evidence for the nature and degree of population movement is particularly important because social interactions developing across the Southwest at this time were likely influenced by the diverse origins of individuals and groups involved.

USING HUMAN SKELETAL MORPHOLOGY TO TRACK POPULATION MOVEMENT

For more than a century, variation in human skeletal morphology has been used by biological anthropologists and archaeologists to reconstruct genetic relationships among individuals and populations at various scales. The methods and theoretical basis for such studies have changed dramatically over the decades as have the questions to which such data have been applied (see Buikstra et al. 1990; Konigsberg 2006; Rakita 2006; Stojanowski and Schillaci 2006 for historical overviews). Rather than focusing on typological or racial characterizations (e.g., Hrdlička 1931; Seltzer 1944), recent studies of biological relationships based on skeletal variation have ranged from considerations of migration and gene flow (Ortman 2012; Schillaci 2003; Schillaci, Irish and Wood 2009; Steadman 2001) to kinship patterns (Corruccini and Shimada 2002; Howell and Kintigh 1996; Stojanowski 2005; Strouhal 1992) and post-marital residence (Schillaci and Stojanowski 2002, 2003).

A great majority of recent biodistance studies have focused on variation in the craniofacial skeleton including analyses of both non-metric and metric traits. Studies of archaeological and contemporary populations have shown that, although selective pressures and environment play a role in skeletal variation, there is also a substantial genetic component (compare

Konigsberg and Ousley 1995; Relethford 2004; Relethford and Lees 1982; Roseman and Weaver 2004). Phenotypic variation has been demonstrated to be proportional to genetic variation (Relethford and Blangero 1990; Williams-Blangero and Blangero 1989). Further, when environmental and climatic differences are reasonably small, such as in the range of areas occupied by agricultural populations across the U.S. Southwest, a higher relative proportion of total variation is attributable to gene flow and genetic drift between populations (see Schillaci et al. 2001:135-136; Schillaci 2003:226). This suggests that craniofacial measurements provide a reasonable proxy for genetic relationships among populations within this context, which can be used to study patterns of gene flow through time and across space.

An additional advantage of using craniofacial measurements to explore genetic relationships is that many measurements based on standardized cranial landmarks have been regularly recorded in the U.S. Southwest for nearly a century. Biodistance studies using both metric and non-metric data have been widely applied across the region creating an ever growing database of cranial measurements and trait frequencies (e.g., Akins 1986; Corruccini 1972; El-Najjar 1978; Minturn 2006; Ortman 2009, 2012; Schillaci 2003; Schillaci and Stojanowski 2002, 2003, 2005; Schillaci et al. 2001; Turner 1993). Although there are potential issues with using multi-observer datasets (Utermohle et al. 1983), measurements by different analysts on the same crania have been demonstrated to be highly correlated (Ortman 2009:169-171, 2012:97-100). Thus, by compiling these datasets, a number of important questions regarding genetic diversity across the U.S. Southwest can be addressed using existing data.

Following a brief discussion of the data and methods used here, I present two related biodistance analyses. First, I present a comparison of prehistoric and protohistoric population samples from the Zuni region directed at determining whether or not there is evidence for phenotypic changes that could be interpreted as the result of gene flow. If substantial immigration characterized the protohistoric transition, I would expect to find significant phenotypic differences between populations in the Zuni region before and after this transition. Second, I present a broader biogeographical analysis of the craniometric data across the Southwest. This analysis consists of a quantitative comparison of the cranial measurements from individuals from a number of sub-regions that are potential sources of population into the Zuni region across the protohistoric transition. I expect that the protohistoric Zuni sample will be more phenotypically similar to regional populations that were sources of immigrants, and therefore gene flow, across the protohistoric transition.

The Dataset and Data Pretreatment

For the current study, I have compiled existing data for 11 commonly recorded craniofacial measurements on nearly 700 individuals from a number of sub-regions west of the continental divide as well as in additional locations with other evidence of connections to the Zuni region (Figure II.2.2; Tables II.2.1-II.2.2).

Orbital breadth was not included in the R-matrix analysis as it was measured based on different landmarks by several analysts. Measurements of orbital breadth made from dacryon to ectoconchion were, however, included in the EM estimation procedure because they were correlated with other measurements (see also Ortman 2009:171-176). Measurements were selected based on the frequency with which they were recorded, a demonstrated lack of age dependency, and a high degree of inter-observer consistency based on a small portion of the sample analyzed by multiple individuals. Additionally, the selected measurements all come from the cranial base or anterior face and thus, are

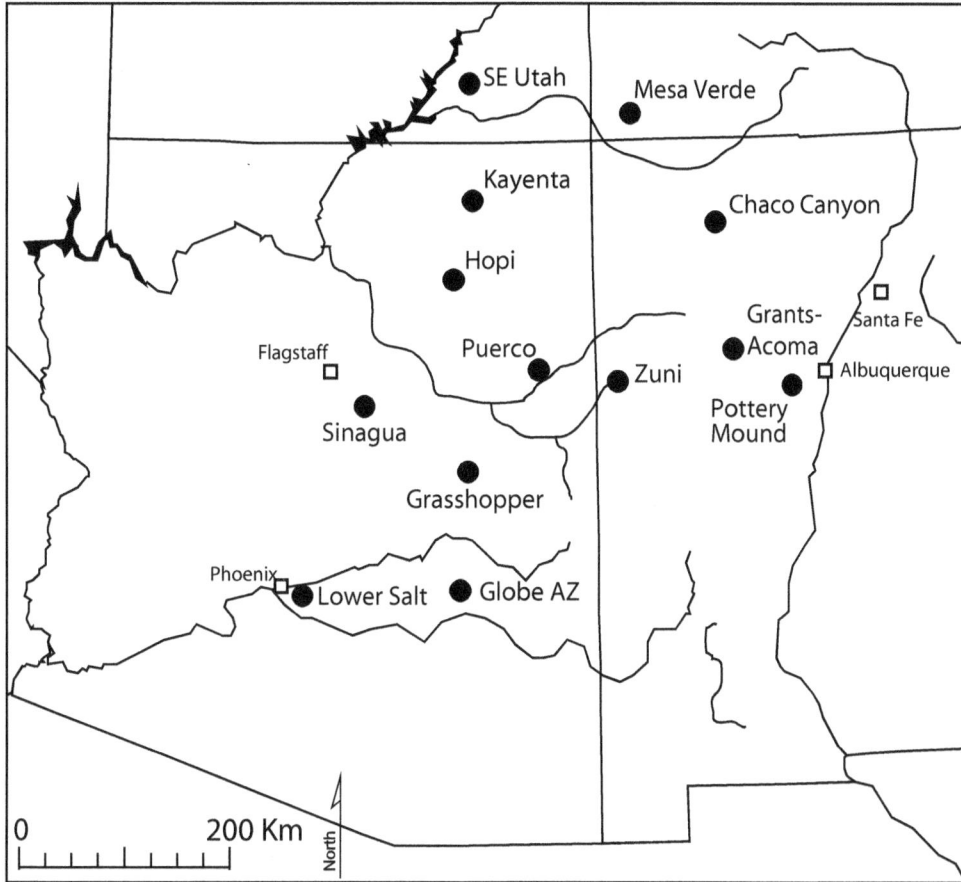

Figure II.2.2. Approximate locations of the sub-regional samples for the R-matrix analysis.

Table II.2.2. Craniometric Variables Used in This Analysis		
Measurement Name	Abbreviation	Measurement Landmarks‡
Basion-Alveolar Length	BAL	ba-alv
Cranial Base Length	CBL	ba-n
Bizygomatic Breadth	ZYB	zy-zy
Maxillo-Alveolar Breadth	MAB	ecm-ecm
Maxillo-Alveolar Length	MAL	pr-alv
Minimum Frontal Breadth	WFB	ft-ft
Nasal Breadth	NLB	al-al
Nasal Height	NLH	n-ns
Mean Orbital Breadth	OBB*	dk-ek
Mean Orbital Height	OBH	⊥ dk-ek
Nasion-Alveolar Height	NAH	n-alv

‡ Measurement landmark descriptions can be found in Buikstra and Ubelaker (1994).
* Mean orbital breadth is used to calculate missing data but is not included in the R-matrix analysis due to inconsistencies in measurement (see preceding text).

less influenced by the practice of cradle-boarding than measurements including the cranial vault (see Droessler 1981:110-116; Kohn et al. 1995).

This sample includes nearly 200 individuals from sites in the greater Zuni region divided into four temporal units; Pueblo II/III (ca. A.D. 1000-1275), Pueblo IV (ca. A.D. 1275-1400), a protohistoric/historic sample from Hawikku (ca. 1400-1680), and a later sample from excavations at the historic mission at Halona:wa (ca. A.D. 1700).

Data pretreatment procedures followed currently standard procedures for the analysis of craniometric data. All samples for which at least four of the 12 measurements were available were subjected to the expectation-maximization procedure that estimates missing data through iterative comparisons of covariance matrices from available dimensions (see Ortman 2009:171-176; Stojanowski 2004:320). Additionally, measurements were pooled by sex and Z-score standardized to control for the effects of sexual dimorphism (Ortman 2009:176-177, 2012:100-105; Schillaci et al. 2001:138).

Multivariate Analysis of Skeletal Variation

The data described above were subjected to two levels of analysis. First, data from the different temporal units in the Zuni region were compared using Kruskal-Wallis tests following procedures described in detail below. This analysis was directed at determining whether or not there were statistically significant differences in cranial measurements between populations in the Zuni region by time period. Second, data from all sub-regions were used to create a genetic relationship matrix (R-matrix). R-matrix analysis provides a measure of genetic distance among populations and also provides parameters that help to estimate population level heterogeneity and the degree of gene flow into a population from external sources (Relethford and Blangero 1990; Relethford and Lees 1982; Relethford et

al. 1997). This method of analysis is commonly used in contemporary biodistance studies (e.g., Ortman 2012; Schillaci, Irish and Wood 2009; Steadman 2001; Stojanowski 2005). R-matrix calculations were performed using the RMET 5.0 software written by Relethford and available online (http://*konig.la.utk.edu/relethsoft.html*).

The specifics of R-matrix analysis for phenotypic data are described in detail elsewhere (Relethford et al. 1997) and will not be covered in detail here. An R-matrix of phenotypic data is essentially a matrix of relative distances among populations based on the variance and covariance of all of the included traits and weighted by relative population size (Relethford et al. 1997:459-463).

The calculation of a scaled R-matrix requires relative estimates of effective population sizes to account for the effects genetic drift in small regional samples. Population estimates from Ortman (2009:table 5.5) were used for regions that overlapped with that study. Rough relative population estimates for other regions were based on regional summaries in Adler (1996), Adams and Duff (2004), and Kintigh (1985). The results presented here are robust to a wide range of estimated effective population sizes. Globe, AZ = 1500, Grants/Acoma = 2500, Grasshopper = 1500, Lower Salt/Las Acequias = 3500, Kayenta = 3500, Puerco = 1500, Pottery Mound = 800, Sinagua = 1500, Hawikku/Halona:wa = 1000.

The R-matrix also allows for the calculation of a measure of genetic variability (or heterogeneity) known as F_{st}, which is defined as the mean distance between all populations and the regional centroid.

The calculation of an R-matrix and F_{st} based on phenotypic data requires an estimate of the average heritability of the included traits. The heritability of a suite of traits can rarely be directly estimated with much precision, but previous studies have shown that the relationships defined through R-matrix analyses are very robust to a range of heritability values (Relethford and

Blangero 1990). In order to place the results in the context of other regional studies of genetic diversity, a heritability of one is assumed, which is defined as the matrix of minimum genetic distances (Williams-Blangero and Blangero 1989). Using minimum genetic distances allows for values of F_{st} obtained in this study to be directly compared with other regional studies of genetic heterogeneity (see Konigsberg and Ousley 1995; Steadman 2001:66-67; Williams-Blangero and Blangero 1989:6).

One final useful parameter that can also be obtained from the R-matrix is the expected within-group heterogeneity for each individual population. The expected variance E is calculated as $E[v_i] = v_w (1 - r_{ii}) / 1 - F_{st}$, where v_i is the expected variance for a population i, v_w is the mean within-group variance for all variables, r_{ii} is the distance between population i and the regional centroid. F_{st} is the region wide measure of heterogeneity described above (Relethford et al. 1997). The expected variance can be subtracted from the actual observed phenotypic variance across all variables to calculate the residual variance (referred to as a Relethford-Blangero residual; see Relethford and Blangero 1990). A population with a positive Relethford-Blangero residual variance experienced greater than average gene flow from external sources and a population with a negative residual variance experienced less than average gene flow. External sources, in this context, refer simply the genetic signatures of any population not included in the R-matrix analysis.

GENETIC EVIDENCE FOR IMMIGRATION ACROSS THE PROTOHISTORIC TRANSITION

Before turning to a regional consideration of gene flow across the Southwest, it is first important to determine whether or not there is evidence for major phenotypic changes within the Zuni region across the transition from the prehistoric to the protohistoric period that may

relate to gene flow. To do this, I compare the standardized craniofacial measurements from the Zuni region, separated by time period, using the non-parametric Kruskal-Wallis test. The Kruskal-Wallis (K-W) test compares variables based on the rank order of observations and can be used to identify statically significant differences between pre-defined groups. In this analysis, K-W statistics and probabilities were calculated for each of the 10 variables to be included in the R-matrix analysis in two pairwise comparisons; 1) Pueblo II/III and Pueblo IV Zuni samples and 2) all prehistoric samples combined (Pueblo II/III and Pueblo IV) against the protohistoric/historic sample from Hawikku. In order to simplify this presentation, the historic sample from Halona:wa was not included in K-W tests presented here. Comparisons including Halona:wa produce comparable results. I expect that comparisons among populations that have substantial phenotypic differences will result in statistically significant differences for a relatively high proportion of the tested variables.

As Table II.2.3 shows, K-W tests for comparisons of variables among the two prehistoric samples from the Zuni region revealed statistically significant differences for only one out of 10 variables at the 0.15 level, suggesting that the cranial measurements are similar for population samples in both time periods. Comparisons between all prehistoric samples and protohistoric/historic Hawikku, however, revealed statistically significant differences for seven out of 10 variables at the 0.15 level.

This suggests that there are substantial phenotypic differences between these samples derived from sites occupied on either side of the protohistoric transition. In order to further evaluate this result, Relethford-Blangero residual variances were calculated for each of the three Zuni samples included above. As Table II.2.4 illustrates, Hawikku has a relatively high residual variance compared to the prehistoric Zuni samples. The high positive residual suggests

Table II.2.3. Kruskal-Wallis Tests for All Variables Included in the R-matrix analysis.
Statistically Significant Differences (0.15 level) are Indicated by an Asterix

Measurement	PII/III - PIV		PII/PIII & PIV - Hawikku	
	K-W Statistic	Probability	K-W Statistic	Probability
BAL	354	0.698	3869	0.005*
CBL	318	0.320	2896	0.052*
ZYB	365	0.833	3144	0.099*
MAB	363	0.813	3164	0.146*
MAL	316	0.304	2796	0.779
WFB	394	0.781	3340	0.973
NLB	355	0.711	2241	0.005*
NLH	299	0.186	3477	0.145*
OBH	340	0.533	2285	0.008*
UFH	267	0.062*	3390	0.247

Table II.2.4. Relethford-Blangero Analysis of Zuni Craniometric Data

Sample	Distance to Regional Centroid	Observed Phenotypic Variance	Expected Phenotypic Variance	Relethford-Blangero Residual
Zuni PII/III	0.011181	0.988	0.842	0.147
Zuni PIV	0.006694	0.645	0.842	-0.197
Hawikku	0.074352	1.082	0.783	0.299

greater than average gene flow from sources not included in comparisons among the Zuni samples. This suggests the gene flow from outside of the Zuni region across the protohistoric transition.

It is difficult to directly consider the relative genetic contribution of new arrivals and migrants in protohistoric/historic Hawikku, but the population level heterogeneity measure F_{st}, calculated from an R-matrix including only the Zuni sub-region, can help to interpret relative changes in diversity through time. F_{st} values are influenced by a number of factors including the length of time that a set of samples represent as well as the size of the area over which samples were derived (see Stojanowski 2004). In general,

however, comparisons between time periods that result in higher values of F_{st} are more heterogeneous (Relethford and Blangero 1990).

Table II.2.5 shows values of F_{st} for comparisons between the prehistoric samples and between the prehistoric samples and the protohistoric/historic sample from Hawikku. Comparisons including Hawikku are more heterogeneous than the comparison among the prehistoric Zuni samples alone. F_{st} values for all comparisons are, however, fairly typical of regional scale heterogeneity levels from other studies worldwide.

Steadman (2001: Table II.2.3) provides F_{st} values for a number of populations from the Late

Table II.2.5. Values of F_{st} for Comparisons By Time Period Based on Zuni Craniometric Data

Comparison	F_{st}	Time Span Represented
Zuni PII/III - Zuni PIV	0.00971	~ 450 years
Zuni PIV - Hawikku	0.01515	~ 300 years
Zuni PII/III & PIV - Hawikku	0.01397	~ 600 years

Woodland and Mississippian regions as well as several comparative regions of similar a spatial extent to the Zuni region. The average value of F_{st} for similarly sized regional samples in Steadman's study is $F_{st} = 0.018$, which is higher than any of the values reported here. The average value of $F_{st} = 0.018$ was obtained by averaging the first 13 populations presented in Steadman (2001:table 3) as these populations were derived from similar spatial scales to the Zuni samples included in this study.

From this, I argue that the levels of heterogeneity seen in the comparisons among the Zuni samples suggests that, although extra local gene flow likely did account for a portion of the genetic diversity at the protohistoric village of Hawikku, there was also a substantial genetic relationship with earlier populations from the Zuni region.

POTENTIAL SOURCES OF NEW ARRIVALS

The next step in this analysis is to place the evidence for new arrivals in the Zuni region across the protohistoric transition in a broader regional context. In order to do this, an R-matrix was calculated including 12 sub-regional samples from areas that include many potential sources of new arrivals into the Zuni region as well as the four samples from the Zuni region described in the previous section.

This regional comparison is not an attempt to directly model patterns of gene flow among the individuals included in this analysis, as not all individuals were alive at the same time and thus, could not have directly exchanged genes. Instead, sub-regional populations are treated as samples of lineages which can be used to define estimates of the phenotypic variability present within a population across several generations. Like the Zuni region described above, each of these sub-regional populations may vary due to differential patterns of gene flow through time or across space (e.g., Schillaci 2003), but robust patterns of directed gene flow should still be identifiable (Ortman 2012:94-96).

In order to summarize the complex relationships among the sub-regional populations included here, the genetic distances calculated from the R-matrix were subjected to principal coordinates analysis (Figure II.2.3). The relative distances between points in this principal coordinates plot represent the relative phenotypic similarities among sub-regional populations. I have circled a few groups of sub-regional populations in order to highlight particularly interesting relationships in terms of the goals of this analysis. These groups are simply meant to facilitate discussion of the patterns in these data and do not necessarily relate to discrete biological lineages. Interestingly, sub-regional populations with strong phenotypic similarities tend to come from spatially proximate regions with a few exceptions, including the protohistoric Zuni samples.

The prehistoric Zuni samples show relatively high phenotypic similarities between the two time periods represented as well as with Chaco Canyon, the Sinagua, and Lower Salt sub-regional samples. The protohistoric/historic sample from Hawikku is relatively distant from both of the prehistoric Zuni samples, as would be expected given the results of the Kruskal-Wallis tests presented above. The Hawikku sample shows the strongest similarities with sub-regional populations including the Hopi, Southeast Utah, and Kayenta sub-regions. These are all areas typically associated with Uto-Aztecan groups. The historic sample from the Halona:wa mission is closer to the regional centroid and also shows strong relationships with several sub-regional populations from east and central Arizona including Grasshopper, the Globe area, and the Puerco of the West.

Although the relationships noted here do not rule out other areas as potential sources of genes, this analysis suggests that the strongest genetic signature for new arrivals across the protohistoric transition at Hawikku is associated with Uto-Aztecan groups. Further, although other temporal factors may be at work as well, Hawikku and Halona:wa may have experienced somewhat different patterns of gene flow.

MIGRATION, GENE FLOW, AND THE PROTOHISTORIC TRANSITION AT ZUNI

In general, the results of the biodistance analyses presented here support several aspects of the traditional archaeological interpretation of the protohistoric transition at Zuni. This transition likely included a degree of immigration but, importantly, a large local population was also involved. Beyond this, the apparent differences in the closest genetic relationships between Hawikku and Halona:wa suggests the possibility that individuals with diverse genetic origins may have unevenly migrated into certain Zuni towns. Such differences in origins may relate to the village level differences in burial practices,

and perhaps ethnic distinctions, previously noted by Kintigh (2000), though this possibility could best be evaluated with data from additional Zuni towns. For example, numerous inhumations were excavated by the University Museum of Cambridge at Kechiba:wa in 1923 (see Lahr and Bowman 1992), but craniometric measurements have not been recorded. This skeletal sample could provide an additional avenue to explore differences among protohistoric Zuni towns.

In order to further evaluate the specific external genetic relationships suggested by the analyses presented above, it is necessary to consider these results in relation to other available lines of evidence. The protohistoric and historic Zuni samples from Hawikku and Halona:wa show close genetic relationships with several population samples from east and central Arizona as well as several Uto-Aztecan population samples from the northern Southwest. Several of these areas have previously been posited as likely sources of immigrants based on other archaeological data, but there is one major issue with these results that requires additional explanation.

Specifically, the Uto-Aztecan population samples from the northern Southwest (Kayenta, SE Utah, and Hopi) showing close relationships to the Zuni village of Hawikku come from areas that, with the exception of the Hopi Mesas, were largely depopulated a century or more before the protohistoric transition at Zuni (see Hill et al. 2004: Figure II.2.3). Further, the Hopi Mesas were another major *destination* of migrating populations at this time (Adams et al. 2004) and not likely a primary source of new arrivals to Zuni. What then do the strong relationships between protohistoric Hawikku and northern Uto-Aztecan groups suggest?

Additional lines of archaeological evidence suggest that the apparent discontinuity between the genetic relationships suggested by this analysis and the timing of immigration into the Zuni region may be due, in part, to earlier

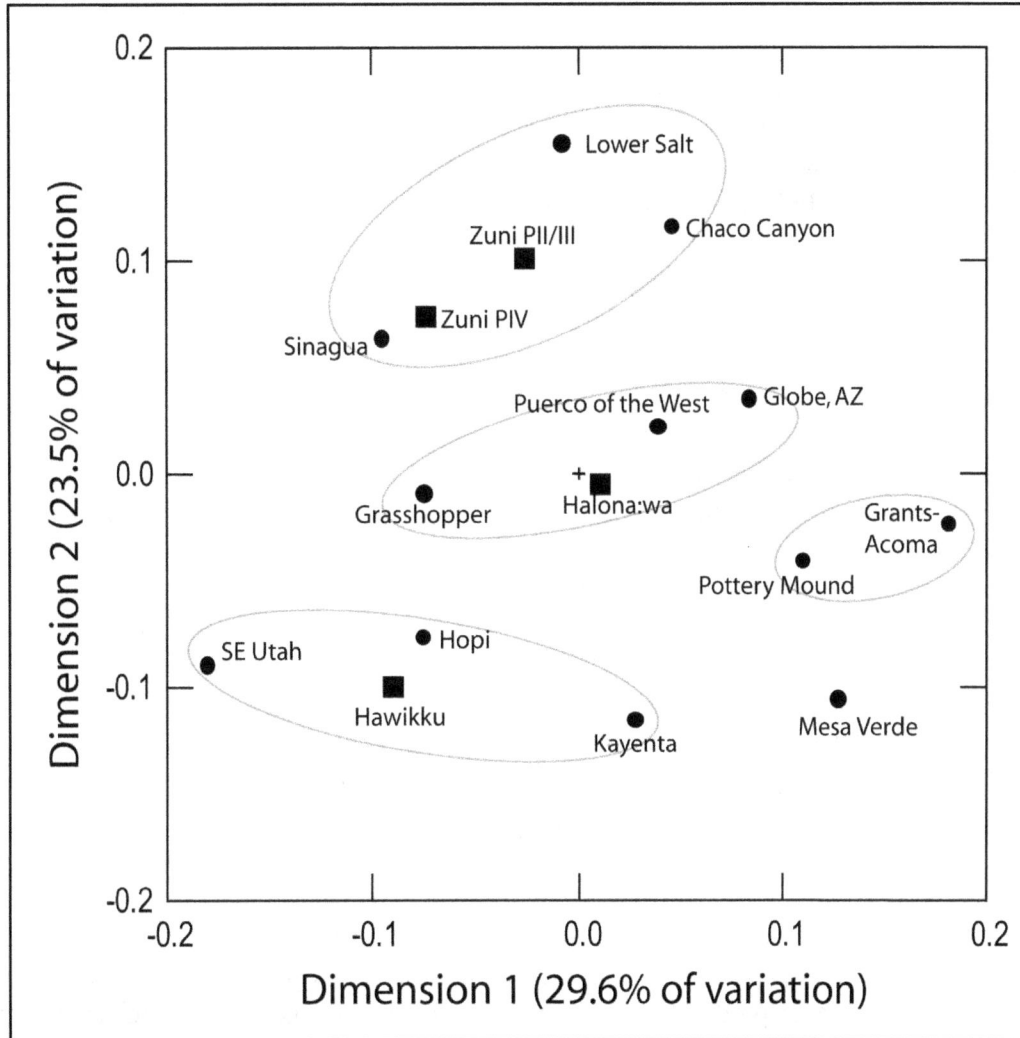

Figure II.2.3. Principal coordinates analysis of the R-matrix for all craniometric data. The circled points represent groups of sub-regions that highlight potential genetic relationships relevant to this discussion.

periods of population movement across the Southwest. Specifically, Lyons (2003; see also Haury 1958) has recently argued, based on numerous similarities in material culture styles and technologies, for a late 13th and early 14th century migration by populations from the Kayenta region of northeastern Arizona into most of the major drainages across southern Arizona, southwestern New Mexico, and perhaps south into Mexico. Further, building on earlier work by Crown (1994), Lyons (2003) links the origin and spread of Roosevelt Red Ware pottery to migrant populations from the Kayenta region. An ever-

growing body of research suggests that a similar suite of changes are seen in the destination areas of migrant populations from the Kayenta area in the 14th century including evidence for the production of Roosevelt Red Ware pottery and dramatically increased frequencies of obsidian (see Clark et al. 2012; Huntley et al. 2010).

Interestingly, several of the areas with strong evidence of Kayenta migrant populations in the 14th century were characterized by a form of cremation burial similar to that seen in the Zuni villages after the protohistoric transition (see Lekson 2000; Mills and Mills 1978). Although cremated individuals cannot be directly included in a biodistance study such as this, several areas were characterized by a combination of inhumation and cremation similar to that seen at the protohistoric Zuni towns.

Although this possibility needs to be further evaluated using craniometric data from the southern Southwest and northern Mexico, recent arguments linking populations in the southern Southwest areas to migrations from the Kayenta region could be combined with the results of this study to argue that some of the new arrivals at Zuni in the protohistoric region may have been the descendants of individuals who had migrated south more than a century earlier. Like many of the areas with strong evidence of Kayenta migrant populations in the 14th century, the protohistoric period at Zuni is characterized by a dramatic increase in the frequency of Roosevelt Red Ware pottery from virtually 0 percent during the Pueblo IV period to over 20 percent of the mortuary pottery assemblage at protohistoric Kechiba:wa (Kintigh 2000: Figure 6.8; Schachner 2006; Smith et al.1966). Compositional analysis of a small sample from the Zuni region suggest that some of the Roosevelt Red Ware found in the Zuni region may have been produced there (see Crown 1994; Duff 2002:155-156).

In addition to this, available data suggest that the protohistoric towns in the Zuni region are characterized by dramatically higher frequencies of obsidian than earlier villages in the region (see Howell 2003). Obsidian makes up over 18 percent of the total lithic assemblage from excavations at the protohistoric/historic town of Halona:wa from the Zuni Middle Village Project. A majority of the obsidian at Halona:wa has been sourced to the Mount Taylor area, but numerous other sources are present and more distant sources increase in frequency through time. Obsidian is extremely rare in earlier sites across the Zuni region, however, and usually accounts for less than 0.5 percent of the total lithic assemblage.

It should also be noted, however, that the genetic relationships suggested by the analyses presented here could also relate to gene flow from a more general Uto-Aztecan population, possibly including the descendants of earlier residents of the southern Southwest. There is intriguing linguistic evidence of connections between the Zuni and Piman languages (Uto-Aztecan language) that suggests a period of contact between speakers of these languages (Hill 2007; Shaul and Hill 1998). In addition to this, the Coronado expedition in 1540 included guides who spoke a Piman language and reported having traveled to Zuni to work in agricultural fields (Hodge 1937). This suggests well established interactions between Zuni and residents of southeastern Arizona at the time of contact. An earlier period of interaction including substantial gene flow between speakers of Zuni and southern Uto-Aztecan populations (possibly including other ancestors of Piman speaking groups) could potentially account for some of the genetic diversity noted in this study. This possibility could be further evaluated if an adequate sample of craniometric data from the southern Southwest, especially in southeastern Arizona, the Upper Gila, and the Mogollon Highlands, could be integrated with other lines of archaeological and linguistic evidence.

As this brief synthesis of the archaeological and biological evidence for population movement across the protohistoric transition suggests, many of the changes seen in the Zuni region at this time were spurred by an even longer history of population movement across the Southwest. The protohistoric Zuni towns were established by a diverse group of individuals (biologically, and likely culturally and linguistically as well) including people with origins in a number of locations. Many of the changes in material culture, settlement, and technologies that mark the protohistoric period in the Zuni region were likely responses to the changing social environment as local Zuni populations and migrants came together and created new social institutions and identities. Thus, the Zuni that Coronado encountered in 1540 was the culmination of over two centuries of population movement, reorganization, and social transformation (see Mills 2008).

CONCLUSIONS

The results of the analyses presented here suggest several interesting possibilities regarding the population history of the Zuni region, and the Southwest in general. Although interpretations of similarity in skeletal morphometric variation alone are not adequate for reconstructing complex patterns of population movement, such studies are useful in that they provide a source of testable relationships which can be used to further evaluate other lines of evidence for population movement (e.g., Schillaci et al. 2001). However, this characterization of genetic diversity in the Zuni region is not the same as a reconstruction of the origins or spread of Zuni culture or of the Zuni language. The next necessary step will be to integrate the kinds of analyses presented here with other lines of evidence to provide a more complete picture of how local Cibola populations and migrants came together to form the historic ethnolinguistic group known as Zuni (e.g., Ortman 2012).

Finally, it is important to note that Zuni oral traditions relating to the origins of the contemporary A:shiwi (Zuni) people further support many aspects of the population history presented here. Zuni traditional knowledge relating to the establishment of the Zuni towns includes descriptions of diverse migration pathways that converge along the Zuni River (Ferguson 2007; see also Mills 2008). The apparent increase in genetic diversity across the protohistoric transition suggested by the analyses presented here, potentially including the arrival of people from many portions of the Southwest, is consistent with these Zuni migration traditions. This diversity is not, however, consistent with many previous archaeological models based on notions of the Pueblos as homogenous cultural groups (see discussion in Dongoske et al. 1997). Together, these archaeological and biological lines of evidence emphasize the fact that populations throughout the Southwest were and are more diverse than archaeological cultural group definitions often suggest.

Acknowledgments I am indebted to several individuals who provided data and guidance over the course of this project. I would especially like to thank Scott Ortman, Michael Schillaci, and Chris Stojanowski for numerous conversations that were instrumental in developing many of the ideas presented here. I am also grateful to the generous researchers who made their craniometric data available to me including Nancy Akins, Debra Martin, Penny Minturn, Scott Ortman, and Michael Schillaci. Keith Kintigh, Michael Schillaci, and Greg Schachner all provided useful comments on various versions of this chapter.

Part II, Chapter 3

New Light on the Francisco Vásquez de Coronado Expedition of 1540-1542

Matthew F. Schmader

ABSTRACT

The lost century of 1450 to 1540 ended with several important transborder events. The final part of Cabeza de Vaca's route across northern México generated renewed interest in finding new lands. In response, a small exploratory party accompanying Fray Marcos de Niza sent in 1539 by Antonio de Mendoza ventured as far north as Zuñi pueblo. The de Niza exploration set the stage for a full-scale expedition led by Francisco Vázquez de Coronado, which left Compostela, Nayarit in February 1540 with more than 2,000 men and 5,000 head of livestock. It eventually covered a distance of about 4,000 miles over a period of 2 ½ years before its return to México. This was one of the largest and farthest-ranging expeditions to have ever been sent from New Spain. Although the hoped-for riches and "another México" were not realized, Coronado's venture was notable for its small loss of life and gains in geographic knowledge. The sociopolitical context and organizational details of the expedition will be detailed, especially its impacts on native peoples. New information about Coronado's time in the Río Grande valley will be emphasized, focusing on recent discoveries, remote sensing, and artifactual assemblage found at a major site near Albuquerque, New Mexico. The integration of remote sensing with architectural information and expeditionary artifact assemblages has produced a major advance in understanding the dynamics and effects of the first contacts between outsiders and the native peoples of the American southwest.

RESUMEN

El siglo perdido entre 1450 y 1540 d.C. terminó con varios eventos importantes transfronterizos. La última porción de la ruta de Cabeza de Vaca en la parte norte de México generó un nuevo interés en la tierra nueva. En respuesta, Antonio de Mendoza comisionó en 1539 a Marcos de Niza junto con un pequeño grupo exploratorio que se aventuraron en el lejano norte hasta el pueblo de Zuni. La expedición de Niza plantó el escenario para una expedición de gran escala lidereada por Francisco Vázquez de Coronado, quien partió de Compostela, Nayarit, en febrero de 1540 con más de 2,000 hombres y 5,000 cabezas de ganado. Eventualmente, la expedición cubrió una distancia de aproximadamente 4,000 millas durante un periodo de dos años y medio, antes de que regresaran a la Nueva Galicia. Esta expedición representa una de las más largas y de más largo alcance comisionada desde la Nueva España. Aunque la esperanza del hallazgo de "otro México" y muchas riquezas no se cumplieron, la aventura de Coronado fue notable por las pocas vidas perdidas y el conocimiento geográfico adquirido. En esta ponencia se puntualiza el contexto sociopolítico y los detalles organizativos de la expedición, poniendo especial énfasis en el impacto a las poblaciones nativas. Será discutida nueva información sobre el tiempo que pasó Coronado en el valle del Río Grande, enfocándose en los descubrimientos recientes, las revelaciones de las técnicas de prospección remota y el conjunto artefactual encontrado en uno de los sitios más grandes cerca de Albuquerque, Nuevo México.

Matthew F. Schmader Open Space Division, City of Albuquerque

Introduction

The so-called "lost century" of A.D. 1450 to 1540 ended with several transformative transborder events. One of the most pivotal of these events was the organization and launching of the famous early exploration of the American Southwest led by captain general don Francisco Vázquez de Coronado from 1540 to 1542. This paper will describe the sociopolitical context of that exploration and will detail recent discoveries made in the vicinity of Albuquerque, New Mexico that have changed our understanding of the expedition.

The first non-natives known to have entered the American Southwest were the fabled survivors of the ill-fated Pánfilo de Narváez expedition. Narváez had been given a royal commission to explore *la Florída* in 1528, but the venture ended in utter disaster with most of his men drowning at sea in handmade boats. A handful of men washed up on the gulf coast of Texas near Galveston Bay. The last of them, Alvár Nuñez Cabeza de Vaca (the expedition's treasurer), Andres Dorantes, Alonso del Castillo Maldonado, and the black slave Esteban undertook an arduous and incredible seven year-long trek of some 2,000 miles across present-day southern Texas, northern Mexico and the southwestern United States. They were ultimately found by a slave scouting party under Diego de Alcaráz not far from the Pacific coast and escorted to Culiacán and then to México City (Goodwin 2008).

In the mid-1530s, the political environment in New Spain was fertile ground for seeking riches and expanding horizons. Hernán Cortés had vanquished the Aztec empire nearly two decades earlier. The Pizarro brothers' conquest of Peru took place little more than 10 years after Cortes. In the wake of those events, the Spanish crown had opened up fronts in *la Florída* and was poised to sweep northward from Nueva España into the unknown lands of the continental interior.

At the time, there was considerable geographic uncertainty as to the size of unexplored oceans or continents and the distance to Asia. Voyages of discovery sailing west from Europe expected to find the islands of Antillia, the lands of Sipango and Cathay, or the shores of India (Flint 2008). Mythical places such as Anian, Tolm, Marata, and Totonteac awaited (Figure II.3.1). The route to the orient seemed to be to the north or northwest of New Spain. Cabeza de Vaca's odyssey raised new questions about the size of the continent and how far north it extended. Vaca's *Relacion* of his experiences spurred further Spanish interest in exploring the *tierra adentro* – lands of the interior (Sánchez 1988).

Events following Cabaeza de Vaca's return to Mexico unfolded rapidly. Viceroy Antonio de Mendoza was charged with ensuring the interests of the Spanish crown, but there were powerful competitors vying for the chance to lead the next great sanctioned expedition. A long-running feud flared up between Mendoza and Cortés, who had spent the years after his conquest of the Aztecs finding pearls along the Pacific coast while in search of a jumping off point to the west and the Orient. Both men claimed the privilege to further explore the north by the right of having discovered new lands – a dispute ultimately won by Mendoza in front of the of the Indies (Flint 2008).

Slave trader Nuño Beltran de Guzmán was the first governor of a province called Nueva Galicia (see Figure II.3.1). He based his claim by virtue of his former governance and exploration of Nueva Galicia but also lost that case before the Council of the Indies. Hernando de Soto, a veteran of the Peruvian campaigns, had been made governor of Cuba and tried to expand his royal license to explore *la Florída* further into the western interior. But his 1539-1542 exploration of the southeastern United States was an utter failure and de Soto did not survive.

The greatest challenge to Mendoza may have been from Pedro de Alvarado, lieutenant of the Cortes campaign, governor *adelantado* of Guatemala, and bearer of a royal decree for exclusive rights to explore the Pacific (Flint 2008). He and Mendoza had negotiated an agreement to coordinate explorations of *la tierra nueva*, but then

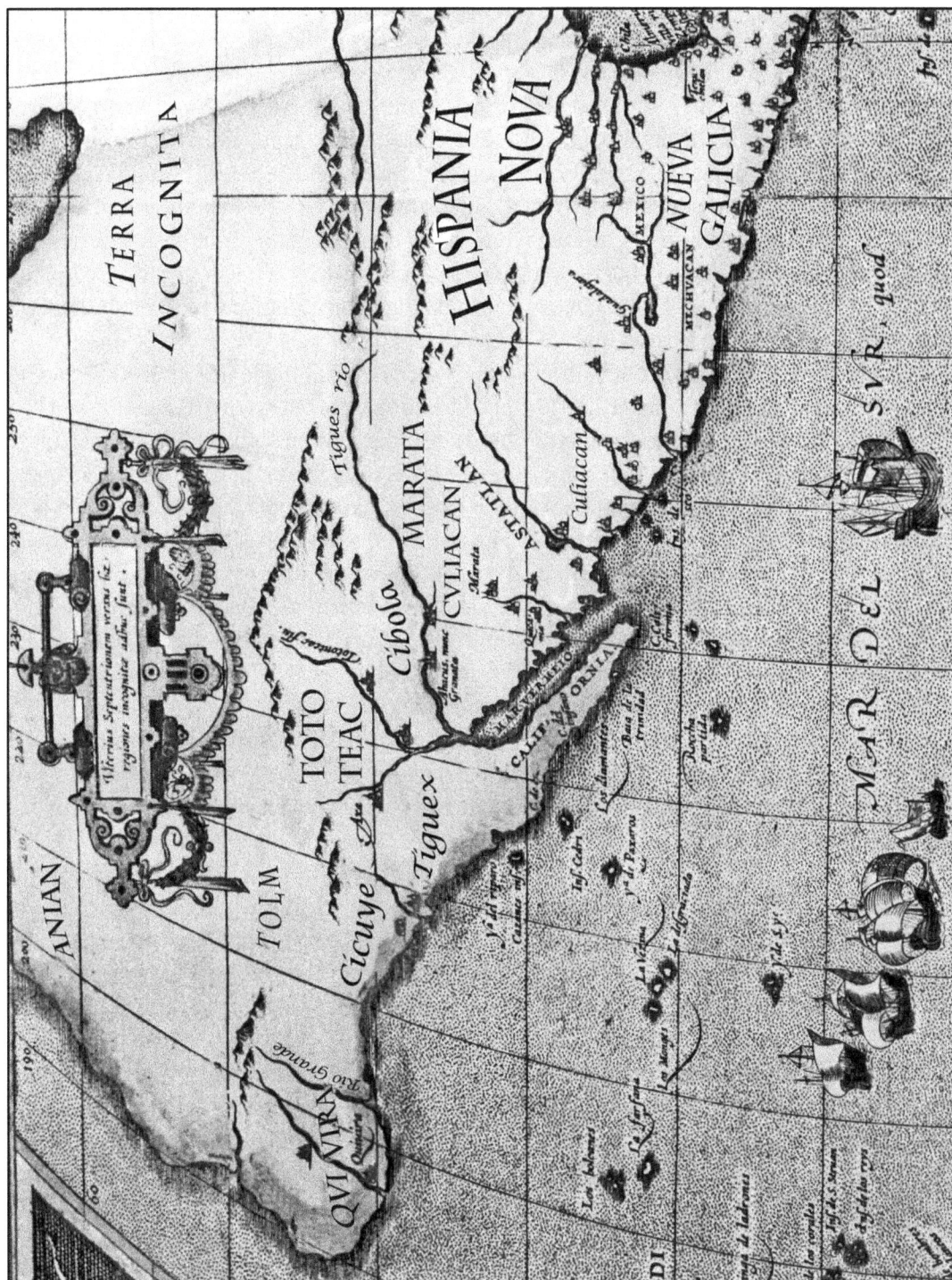

Figure II.3.1. Map of Hispania Nova ("New Spain") showing place names mentioned in the text. Map by M. Schmader (2013) as modified from the original Americae Sive Novi Orbis by Abraham Ortelius (1570).

the Mixtón uprising occurred in Nueva Galicia. Alvarado was crushed to death in 1541 when his horse rolled over him following the decisive battle of Nochistlán (Flint 2008).

Mendoza was also concerned that a northern foray not be dominated by military force, nor by treasure-seeking greed. Increasingly influenced by the writings of cleric Bartolomé de las Casas, Mendoza had to heed the warnings of King Carlos V to avoid unwanted atrocities against native people. He laid his trust, then, not in a seasoned man of war nor in political expedience, but rather at the feet of the church. He selected Fray Marcos de Niza, at the urging of powerful Bishop Juan de Zumárraga, to conduct a small-scale scouting trip to determine what may lie to the north (Flint 2008).

De Niza was no stranger to these matters, having been with Francisco Pizarro during some of the Peruvian campaign and later brought back from service in Guatemala by Bishop Zumárraga in 1537. Mendoza had also hoped to recruit Cabeza de Vaca or Andres Dorantes to guide the small force but that plan did not materialize, as both men were en route to Spain. The only available veteran in México turned out to be Esteban, the black slave of Dorantes who evidently earned his freedom through extraordinary talents with language, communication with native groups, and for his widespread reputation as a healer and shaman (Goodwin 2008).

By the end of 1538, Fray Marcos was handed Viceroy Mendoza's commission by the newly selected successor to Guzmán as governor of Nueva Galicia, don Francisco Vázquez de Coronado (Sánchez 1988). A small group consisting of de Niza, Esteban, Fray Onorato, and native allies set out from Culiacán in March, 1539. Travelling in a generally due north direction, they crossed the present day United States – México border possibly near the San Pedro River valley (Figure II.3.2).

Esteban perhaps hoped to stake his own first claim on riches that might lay ahead, or to secure his freedom forever (Goodwin 2008). Leading an advance party, he was instructed to send back

crosses to inform de Niza of the size of settlements found ahead. Soon a very large cross was sent back, suggesting a great city may be not far off. Esteban, in fact, had become the first non-native person ever to see the villages of Zuñi. Esteban's next moves were costly, as recounted by the terror-struck runners who reported back to de Niza. He overplayed his shamanic powers and he and most of the party had been killed, sending the rest fleeing south. De Niza gathered himself and the remaining contingent and cautiously covered the 100 or so miles toward Zuñi, but may never gotten close enough for a detailed look or description (Goodwin 2008).

When de Niza made it back to Culiacán he had little to salvage but his own reputation and had the death of Esteban on his hands. With few choices left, he likely exaggerated his findings to Mendoza. The land he had explored was called Cíbola (see Figure II.3.1), a name possibly coined by Esteban himself (Goodwin 2008). Niza described Cíbola as the finest settlement of any seen in the region, built of stone, and "larger than the city of México." Further, de Niza related, he had been told of even grander cities beyond.

Mendoza had heard the information he needed and moved ahead with plans for a major expedition, which he decided should be led by his 29 year-old protégé, Vázquez de Coronado. By the time approval from the king arrived, Coronado was already preparing to lead the undertaking. Excitement ran through the province and men, induced by the prospects of another México, rushed to join the expedition. However, as was the emerging practice of the day, the enterprise had to be privately funded and would not be underwritten by the Spanish royal crown (S.C. Flint 2003).

For his share, Vázquez de Coronado staked a goodly portion of his wife Beatriz Estrada's estate. Mendoza contributed even more heavily, and most of the leaders and captains paid well for the privilege (S.C. Flint 2003). Arms, personal gear, and horses were supplied by the men themselves. The estimated cost of the expedition was about 574,000 silver pesos, worth about $20,000,000 in

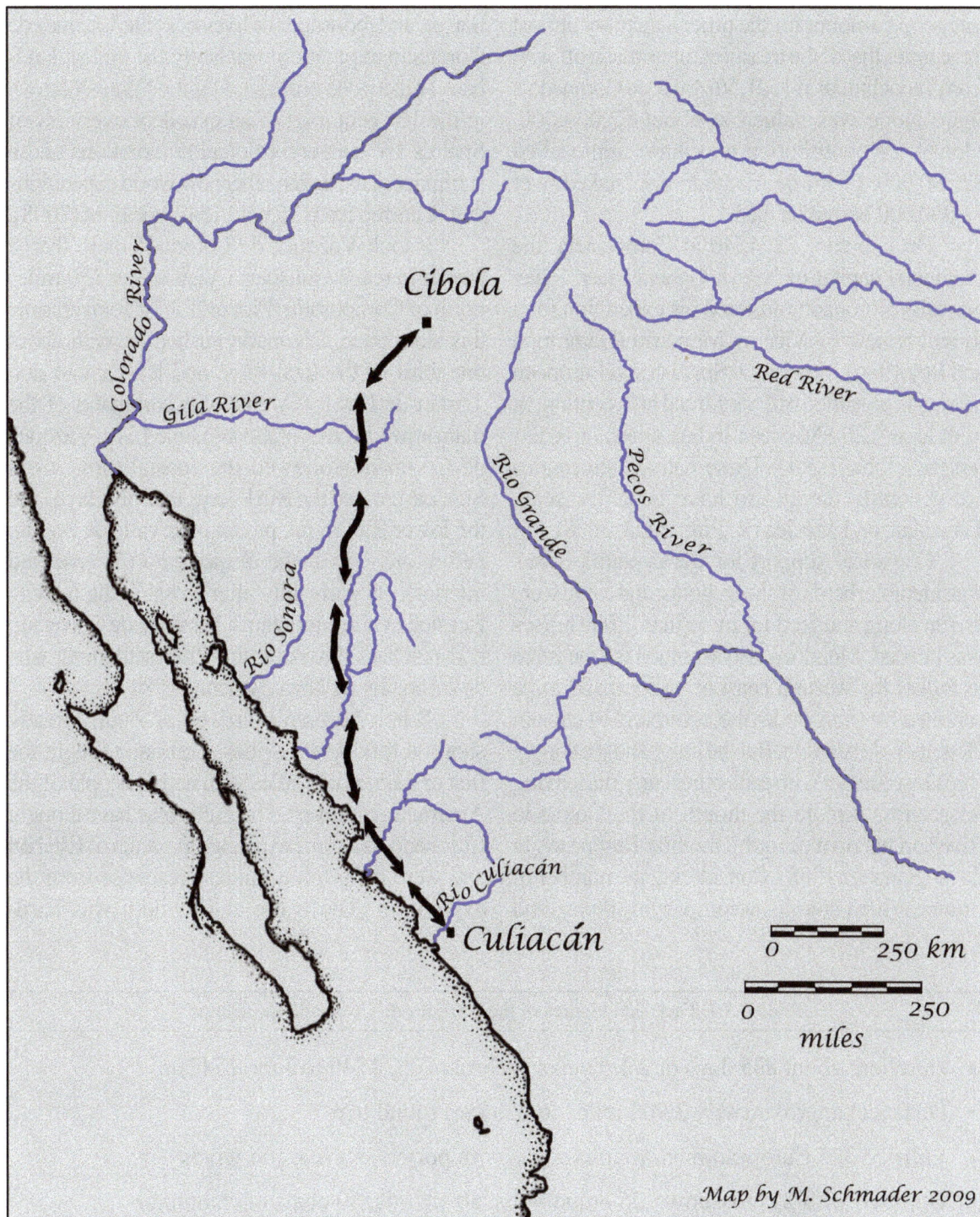

Figure II.3.2. Route of the expedition led by Fray Marcos de Niza (1539).

today's value of silver (Table II.3.1). This was a staggering amount for the time: a quantity almost three times that of the treasure Cortes made off with from Tenochtitlán in 1521. Vázquez de Coronado's share alone was valued at about $2,000,000. Mendoza's contribution may have approached $2,500,000. Pedro de Alvarado also staked over $2,000,000 before he died.

On February 22, 1540 at Compostela, the provincial capital of Nueva Galicia (near Tepic, Nayarit), Coronado mustered his expedition for a formal review by Viceroy Mendoza (Hammond and Rey 1940). Nearly 300 Spanish and European men at arms started off, reinforced by a contingent of at least 1,200 Mexican Indian allies, or *indios amigos* (Table II.3.1). These native mercenaries are generally thought to have been Tarascan, Tlaxcalan, and México (R. Flint 2003, 2008).

Logistical support for the expedition was considerable: herds of sheep, goats, and cattle were driven along and feed for more than 1,000 horses was needed. Mendoza also arranged for the force to follow the western coast of Mexico and to be supplied by ships under the command of captain Hernando de Alarcón. But the army and the supply ships lost contact with each other early on, leaving Alarcón to explore the mouth of the Colorado River on his own accord – the first Europeans to do so (Sánchez 1988). Considering the number of European men-at-arms, accompanying porters and

slaves, the hundreds of native Méxican soldiers, horses, and thousands of livestock, the Vázquez de Coronado expedition was likely the largest land-based enterprise organized by the Spanish crown in the 16th century. For an excellent overview of Spain's 16th century colonial explorations and a summary of the dozen other new world expeditions that occurred from 1539 to 1542, see Flint (2008).

It took Vázquez de Coronado more than a month to reach Culiacán, a distance of 350 miles north of Compostela (Figure II.3.3). To overcome this slow pace, Coronado pushed on with about one-third of the total force and left captain don Tristán de Luna y Arellano in command of the main army. From April to late June 1540, Vázquez de Coronado followed the coastal trail across Sinaloa, crossed the Río Fuerte, the Río Mayo, and the lower Río Yaqui, passing the Valle de Sonora before arriving at the *despoblado* (or unsettled interior). By early July after crossing the heavily forested White Mountains, Vázquez de Coronado had reached Hawikku, the Zuñi settlement first described by de Niza (Sánchez 1988).

When he finally arrived at Zuñi, already short on food and supplies, Coronado fought the first of a series of battles with native people of the American southwest. The Zuñis may have thought Coronado had come to avenge the death of Esteban and were met with a military response from the expedition. The battle at Hawikku was hard-

---

Table II.3.1. Facts and Figures of the Vázquez de Coronado Expedition

- Duration: about 845 days or 2 1/3 years (February 23, 1540 to June 1542)
- Distance: approximately 3,900 miles (6,250 km) round trip
- Enlisted 375 European men-at-arms along with porters, slaves, and wives
- Outfitted with 21 crossbows, 25 arquebuses, 60 swords, 50 coats of chainmail
- Supported by an estimated 1,200 to 2,000 or more Mexican indios amigos
- Utilized 544 saddle horses and more than 600 pack horses
- Brought an estimated 5,000 to 10,000 head of livestock (sheep, cattle, pigs)
- Cost $574,000+ sixteenth Century silver pesos (about $20,000,000 USD in silver value)

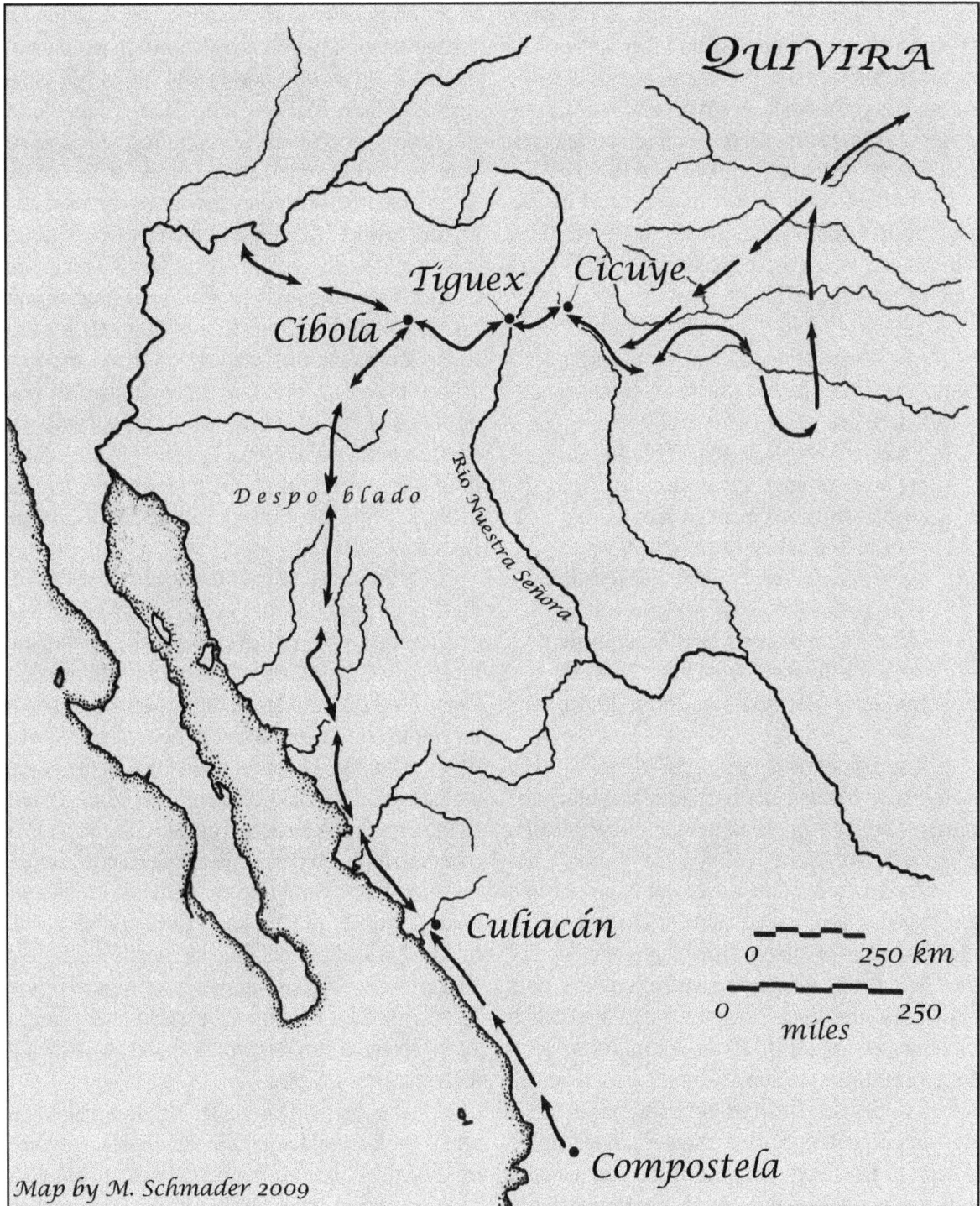

Figure II.3.3. Route of the expedition led by Francisco Vázquez de Coronado (1540-1542).

fought but decisive despite Coronado receiving several wounds (Hammond and Rey 1940). The expedition rested and reprovisioned during the summer months while an advance scouting party under Captain Hernando de Alvarado pushed east past Acoma pueblo (Hammond and Rey 1940).

By September 1540, Alvarado had led the first group of non-natives to see the present day Rio Grande, which they named the Rio de Nuestra Señora (see Figure II.3.3):

The Nuestra Señora river flows through a broad valley planted with fields of maize. There are some cottonwood groves. There are twelve pueblos. The houses are made of mud, two stories high. The people seem good, more given to farming than to war. They have provisions of maize, beans, melons, and chickens in great abundance. They dress in cotton, cattle [buffalo] skins, and coats made with the feathers from the chickens [turkeys] (Hammond and Rey 1940).

The region was thereafter called the *Provincia de Tiguex*, situated north of and including the present-day city of Albuquerque, New Mexico (Figure II.3.4).

Alvarado continued eastward through the Galisteo Basin and to the pueblo of Cicuye (present day Pecos pueblo) before arriving at the edge of the Great Plains. There, he heard of possible gold and riches even further east towards a land called Quivira (see Figure II.3.3). By then it was late in the year and time to return to Tiguex to join Captain Diego López de Cárdenas, who had begun to set up winter quarters outside a major village called Alcanfor. Coronado arrived in the Rio Grande valley slightly later by way of a more southerly route (Sánchez 1988). By the time the entire force had reassembled, the especially harsh winter of 1540 had set in and the group was woefully unprepared. Cold and hunger forced them to take over Alcanfor.

Demands for food and clothing, the imprisonment of native guides, and assaults on pueblo women worsened relations. In retaliation, pueblo people stole horses and killed Méxican guards. These frictions erupted into a battle at the nearby pueblo of Arenal, after which more than 100 pueblo men were burned at the stake. The remaining puebloan resistance consolidated at "the strongest" pueblo, called Moho, three to four leagues away from Alcanfor. Vázquez de Coronado personally led at least one initial assault on Moho, but it took a siege of 50 to 80 days to finally overcome the village (Hammond and Rey 1940). Dozens more native people died in that prolonged series of skirmishes. Coronado was not able to control the worsening tensions that occurred during the winter of 1540-1541, and permanent damage to Spanish-Native relations had been done (Schmader 2012a).

By the spring of 1541 Coronado hurriedly left the Tiguex province for Pecos, also called Cicuye or Cicuique. Spurred ever eastward by stories, trickery, and hopes of fortune, the expedition soon found itself on the edge of the Great Plains. There they noted its vastness, many tribes, and massive herds of buffalo. Continuing on through the Texas panhandle, Coronado decided to send nearly all of the expedition back to Tiguex while he and 35 others rode on, possibly as far as Kansas before realizing there would be no Quivira or cities of gold. Vázquez de Coronado came within a few hundred miles of meeting Hernando de Soto's westernmost point. Remarkably, starting out over 2,000 miles apart, the two expeditionary forces nearly spanned the entire continent before retracing their respective routes.

Vázquez de Coronado was compelled to return for a second winter in the Tiguex province in 1541-1542 before doubling back to México. The *salida* was an inglorious conclusion marred by dropouts and infighting. Coronado's return to Culiacán was not marked by triumph. He did deliver his force with few casualties, although he never fully recovered from a fall off his horse and died at the age of 44 some twelve years later in 1554 (Bolton 1949).

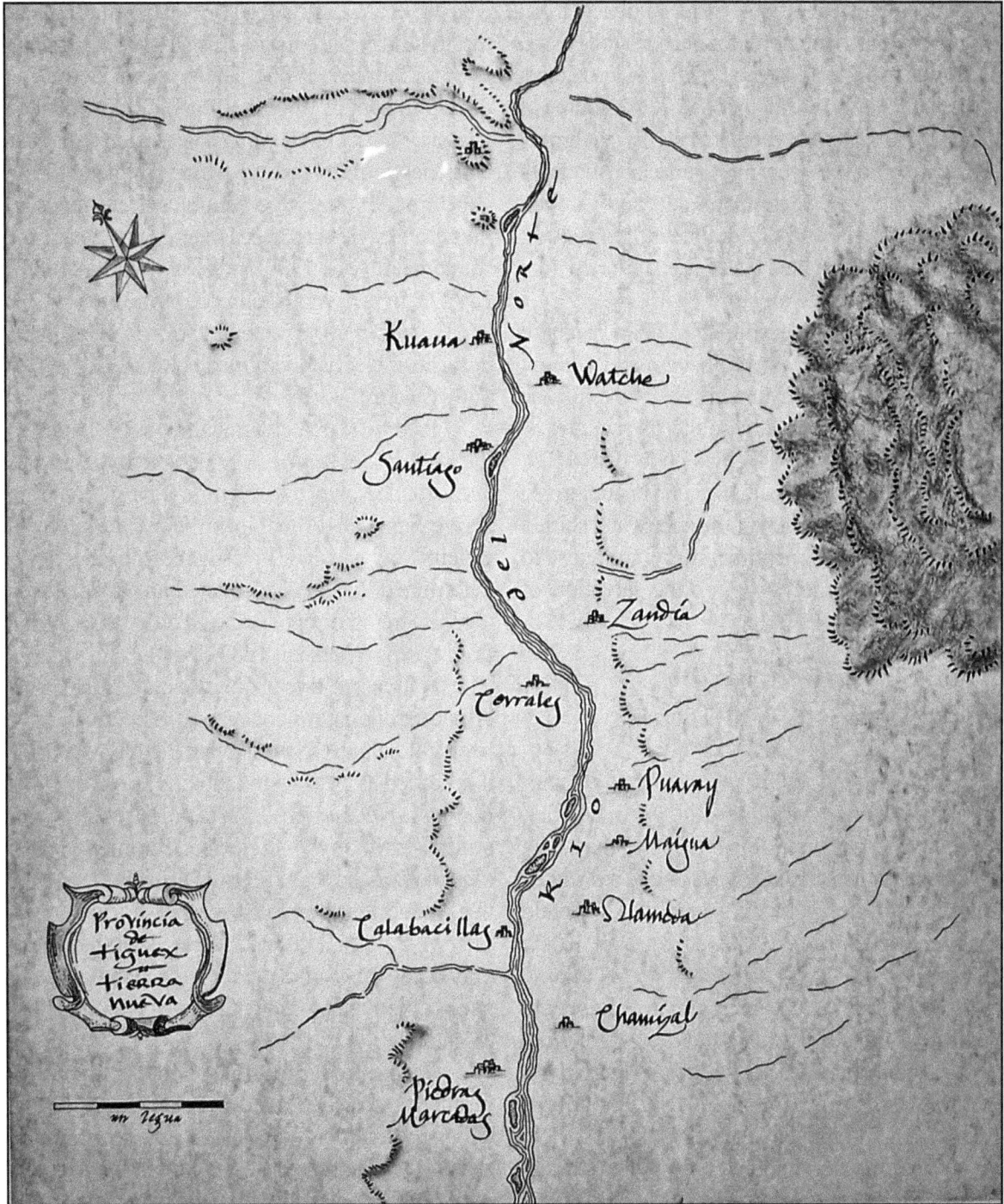

Figure II.3.4. Map of the central Río Grande valley or "Tiguex Province" of Vázquez de Coronado, showing most of the known occupied villages (modern map by M. Schmader 2010, using present-day place names for sites).

No major initiatives were launched from Nueva España to the north for decades following, partly due to the lackluster outcome of Coronado's venture. Not only did another México or source of riches fail to materialize, but investors went broke, charges of atrocities were made, and legal inquiries were held. Vázquez de Coronado and Captain López de Cárdenas both defended themselves; Coronado was acquitted but Cárdenas served time in prison (Hammond and Rey 1940).

A major turning point had been reached: no further explorations would be made without strict controls under royal contract. The influence of the Church was codified in the "New Laws of the Indies," enacted by King Felipe II in 1573. The New Laws specifically forbade unauthorized acts to be taken against native peoples and shifted the emphasis away from military conquest to "pacification" largely through the salvation of souls.

PIEDRAS MARCADAS PUEBLO

Recent investigations by the author at a major pueblo site near Albuquerque, New Mexico have yielded important materials that may well change our understanding of events and associated material culture of the Vazquez de Coronado expedition (Schmader 2008a, 2008b, 2009, 2011, 2012b).

The site is called Piedras Marcadas pueblo ("village of the marked rocks") due to its proximity to large concentrations of images in Petroglyph National Monument (Figure II.3.5). Piedras Marcadas is designated as site number LA 290 in the New Mexico Laboratory of Anthropology ("LA") system, a low number reflecting the fact that it was first recorded before 1930 (Fisher 1931). The site's size and importance gained the early attention of local scholars who attempted to place it in the context of 16th century explorations of the middle Rio Grande valley (Meacham 1926; Vivian 1932).

Estimated dates of occupation for Piedras

Marcadas are from circa A.D. 1200 until at least the first European contacts in 1540-1541 (Marshall 1986; Schmader 1986). The span of occupation covers the entire Ancestral Pueblo, "Río Grande Classic," or Pueblo IV period as used in the Pecos classification devised by Alfred Kidder (1932). Río Grande glazeware ceramics were made in numerous styles and types over a 300+ year time frame from A.D. 1300 until well into the 1600s. LA 290, in fact, was designated as the type site for Río Grande Glaze E pottery type of Tiguex Glaze-polychrome, which was made circa A.D. 1500 to 1600 (Mera 1933:8).

Piedras Marcadas is regarded as the largest of the known Contact-period pueblos in the middle Río Grande Valley for a 50 mile-long stretch from above San Felipe Pueblo to below the town of Belen, New Mexico. Investigations in the 1980s determined that the site covered an area of seven to nine acres and contained well over 1000 ground floor rooms (Marshall 1987, 1988).

Native American involvement in City of Albuquerque site management objectives have been influential. Observing that Piedras Marcadas is regarded as an ancestral village, they asked that non-invasive research take place and that no broad-scale excavations be conducted. Commenting that other nearby sites have been extensively excavated, they requested out of respect that at least one of their villages be left intact. At present, the site is only accessed by guided tours several times a year and is otherwise closed with the exception of field research.

Commitments to the pueblo community resulted in a research program developed by the City of Albuquerque which focuses on remote sensing and noninvasive techniques (Schmader 2008a, 2009). Much of the field work done in the 1990s centered on analyzing surface artifacts, mapping topography, and identifying adobe walls periodically visible at certain times of the year. In 2000, the City of Albuquerque secured funding to initiate a remote sensing program for site interpretation and to better inform resource and visitor management. Initially, several techniques

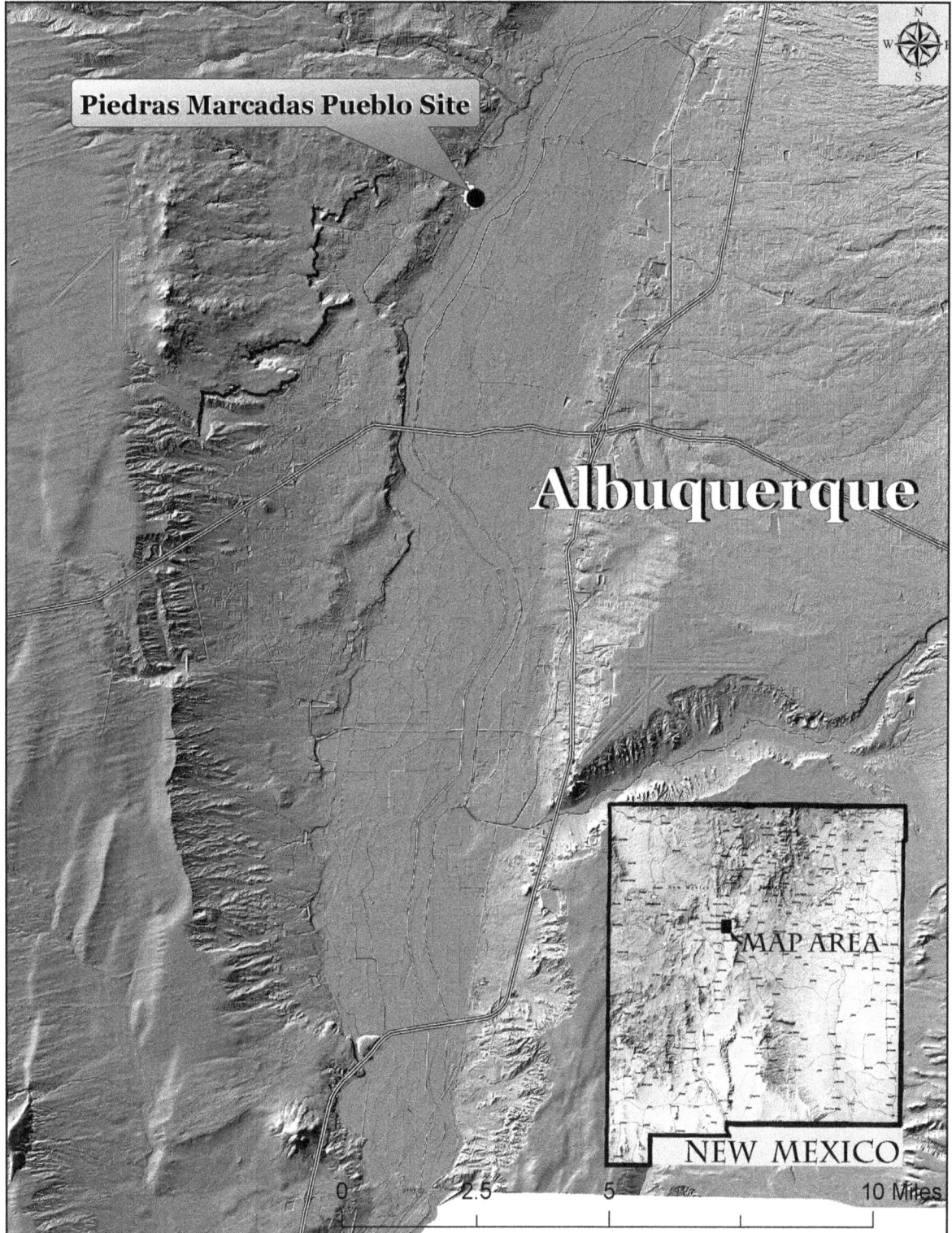

Figure II.3.5. Map of the Albuquerque metropolitan area showing location of Piedras Marcadas pueblo.

such as electrical resistivity, archaeomagnetics, and ground penetrating radar were used to locate adobe walls and other features (Markussen 2006).

Electrical resistivity was selected as the most effective technique when compared to magnetometer and ground-penetrating radar. Electrical resistivity is a technique which measures the strength and speed of currents between two probes inserted into the ground surface at regular intervals. When done over a broad area, the variance in data is analyzed and a map can be made with outputs not unlike taking a below-ground "X-ray" at a depth equal to the spacing of the probes.

The majority of the electrical resistivity work was done at a depth of 50 cm, and produced remarkable results. An area in excess of 8,000 square meters (nearly two acres) was investigated in 2005 and 2006, which resulted in identification of several hundred adobe wall signatures in the middle portion or central roomblock of the site (Markussen et al. 2007). Along with the resistivity surveys, a permanent 20 m x 20 m grid control was set across the site. None of the remote sensing was done with an expectation of finding contact-period or Coronado expeditionary material.

In early 2007, several surface metal artifacts were recovered following the clearing of shrubbery to conduct the electrical resistivity surveys (Schmader 2008a, 2011). Most notable among these artifacts was a bent but complete wrought iron "facet headed" nail (Figure II.3.6a). The artifacts were consistent with known 16th century materials such as those found at the sites of Santiago pueblo (Vierra 1989) and at Hawikku in Zuñi (Damp 2005).

The presence of 16th century metal artifacts fit with the datable surface ceramics at the site, which implied a continuous occupation from before A.D. 1300 until the end of the 1500s. These occupation dates had been first put forward by Mera (1940) and confirmed by others (Marshall 1986, 1987; Schmader 1986). It had also been suggested by several researchers over the decades that Piedras Marcadas was likely one of the dozen Tiguex

pueblos (see Figure II.3.4) encountered by the Vázquez de Coronado expedition (e.g., Marshall 1986, 1988; Schmader 1986, 2008a; Vierra 1989; Vierra and Hordes 1997; Vivian 1932).

With evidence from a few surface artifacts, efforts turned to recovering more metal items that might be linked to the Coronado expedition. A 20 m x 20 m study unit was selected in April 2007 for intensive metal detection survey within a plaza area surrounded by adobe rooms as determined by electrical resistivity survey. Artifacts located by metal detectors are excavated and their exact locations are mapped in place. The average depth of 16th century metal artifacts in 5 cm to 10 cm below present gropund surface. Due to the small amount of soil disturbance needed to find each item, recovery is not considered to be broad-scale excavation. Rather quickly, the metal artifact assemblage increased as dozens of items including chainmail (Figure II.3.6b), lead balls (Figure II.3.6c), copper crossbow boltheads (Figure II.3.6d and e), and a broken dagger tip (Figure II.3.6f) were found.

During a six-year period from 2007 through 2012, a total of thirteen 20 m x 20 m grid units have been thoroughly investigated by metal detection survey. The investigation area covers a total of 5,200 square meters (just over one acre in total area). Within the intensively surveyed units, over 1,000 metal artifacts classified as 16th century or non-modern have been recovered based on their form, material, and deterioration (Schmader 2012b).

SITE STRUCTURE

Piedras Marcadas pueblo represents an excellent laboratory setting to combine various remote sensing techniques in order to produce a broad-scale picture of site structure. Electrical resistivity surveys (Markussen et al. 2007) have identified the adobe wall outlines of several hundred rooms in the central part of the site. These rooms were built around open plaza areas similar to the architecture

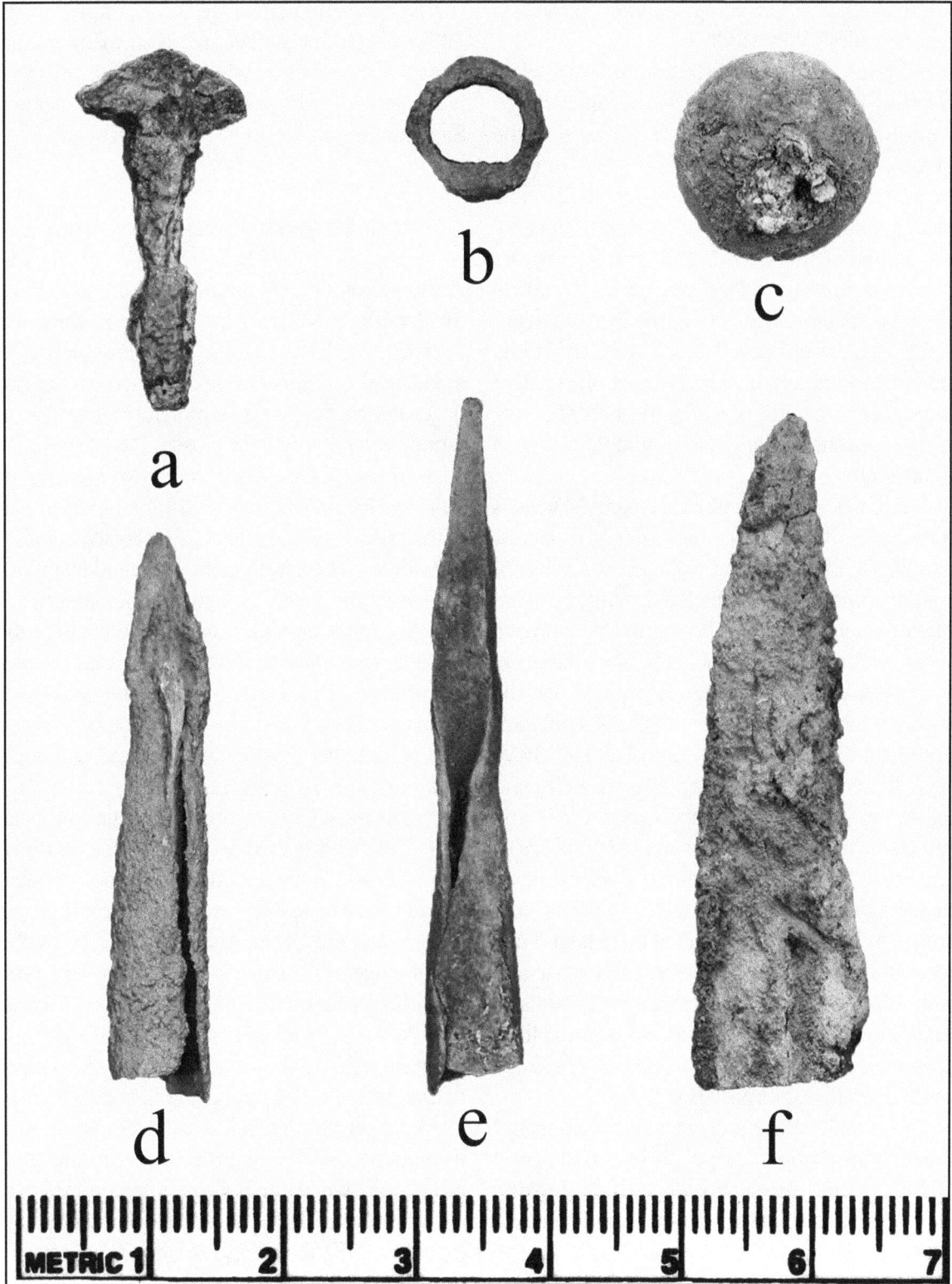

Figure II.3.6. Sixteenth century metal artifacts recovered from Piedras Marcadas pueblo: a, facet-headed wrought iron nail; b, iron chainmail link; c, lead ball for arquebus or musket; d, copper crossbow arrow tip or bolthead; e, copper crossbow arrow tip or bolthead; f, broken steel dagger tip.

found by excavations at nearby sites in the Rio Grande valley (Vierra 1989).

Metal artifact distributions identified at Piedras Marcadas pueblo are within an enclosed central plaza area and include portions of the encompassing architecture and areas outside the central roomblock (Schmader 2012). The investigated area represents a fraction of the total site and what has been found thus far appears to have a relatively high degree of structural integrity. As described above, the average depth of 16th century artifacts is 5 cm to 10 cm below modern ground surface. This indicates the relative degree of site integrity and the potential for relating subsurface artifacts to remotely sensed architecture.

Activities that took place at Piedras Marcadas pueblo were the result of high-energy situations resulting in the common breakage and/or loss of numerous metal artifacts, including many personal items. Simply stated, the site was the location of a major conflict or battle(s) fought between members of the Vázquez de Coronado expedition and the pueblo's inhabitants. Some crossbow boltheads were bent or shattered and some lead balls have been flattened from impact. Bronze bells and copper sheet have been ripped apart. Nails and nail shafts have been broken and many pieces of iron are in fragmentary condition. Personal items such as clothing fasteners, buckles, or aglets were broken or lost. Importantly, all of these items have been found in association with each other and with reference to the known location of walls as determined by remote sensing. All of these lines of evidence point to the high likelihood of a single battle or multiple skirmishes at the site.

The material consequences of a high-energy situation involving many people in a short period of time would produce high artifact density, high loss rates of personal items, and frequent breakage (Schmader and Sánchez 2009). The site of Hawikku at Zuni, where Coronado fought his earlier first battle, has a similar but smaller 16th century metal assemblage (Damp 2005). Battle-related assemblages contrast with other site types such as encampments (see for example, Vierra 1989) which many have involved many people over a longer period but without the resultant breakage or loss of personal gear (Schmader and Sánchez 2009).

ARTIFACT ASSEMBLAGE AND INVENTORY

Arthur Aiton (1939) summarized the *alarde*, or muster roll, of Vázquez de Coronado's forces on February 22, 1540 as follows: 21 crossbows, 25 arquebuses, 13 daggers, five dozen swords, several dozen lances, five suits of armor, four suits of horse armor, several pairs of cuirasses, 38 helmets, 38 coats of mail, 12 jackets of mail, two breeches of mail, two leggings of mail, two mail shirts, one pair of mail sleeves, two gauntlets, four corselets and 20 kneepieces. These weaponry types and quantities carried by the 375 or so Spanish men-at-arms of the expedition provide a general context for the artifacts recovered at Piedras Marcadas pueblo. There were also at least 554 saddle horses, 600 or more pack horses or mules (Flint 2008:63), related tack and saddlery, packs and baggage, and horse shoes or mule shoes and hundreds of iron nails.

The most recognizabe diagnostic European artifact of the early to mid-1500s was the crossbow bolthead (see Figure II.3.6d and e). Crossbows had already been in use for centuries across Europe, Eurasia and the Orient. Crossbows of the period had a range of hundreds of yards and were used very effectively in the Spanish conquests of Mexico and Peru (1519 to 1532). The stout crossbow arrow, or bolt, was commonly tipped with a piece of triangular metal. Crossbow boltheads fashioned from copper are distinctive to those *entradas* in the southwestern United States originating from New Spain, while iron boltheads are found almost exclusively in the southeastern United States (Rhodes 1997). Use of the crossbow was in steady decline by the latter part of the 1500s and so they are a sensitive time marker for the decades up to and including Vázquez de Coronado's expedition. The "Coronado expedition appears to have been the last *entrada* to use crossbows as weapons" in the southwest (Hordes 1989:218).

Mid-sixteenth century weaponry of the terminal medieval period was left behind for more advanced innovations like the musket or *arquebus*. Mention of the crossbow, particularly prominent in the accounts of conquests of the 1520s to 1540s, was basically nonexistent by the 1570s (Rhodes 1997). Distances then started to be reckoned by the length of an *arquebus* shot instead of a crossbow shot. It is important that the 40 year-long hiatus in the American southwest between the 1540-1542 Coronado entrada and the next, 1581-1582 *entrada* of Chamuscado-Rodriguez, spans exactly the time that the crossbow was phased out in favor of the *arquebus* (Schmader and Sánchez 2009). This was not the case in the southeast, where expeditions occurred in the 1560s, even during the period that the crossbow was being phased out (Hudson 1990). In any event, it is generally agreed that one of the most diagnostic artifacts of the first half of the 16th century was the crossbow bolthead, and that copper ones in particular should be considered a specific diagnostic of the Coronado exploration of the American southwest (Flint 1997:48).

The inventory of likely 16th century metal artifacts found from 2007 through 2012 at Piedras Marcadas pueblo includes 21 whole or nearly complete copper crossbow boltheads (none are made of iron). Ten additional pieces of heavy copper sheet or torn fragments represent probable or possible parts of boltheads such as sheared off shafts or ferrules. A total of 32 round, partly flattened, or completely flattened lead balls have been recovered, of varying sizes ranging from 6 mm to 15 mm in diameter (roughly .24 to .59 caliber).

An additional 63 pieces of other heavy copper and/or copper alloy sheet have been recovered from Piedras Marcadas pueblo, some of which have cut or torn edges. The exact reason for the frequency of heavy copper sheet pieces is not known, as they likely derived from several sources such as broken personal items, implements, and usable scrap. Rhodes (1997:43) discusses Kidder's

recovery of similar copper sheet fragments at Pecos, some of which were apparent early-stage attempts at making boltheads on the spot. Probable evidence for expedient bolthead manufacture from copper sheet has been found at Piedras Marcadas pueblo (Thibodeau et al. 2012).

Eighty items recovered recovered from Piedras Marcadas pueblo are considered to be personal gear or attire such as buckles (Figure II.3.7a), aglets (Figure II.3.7b), needles (Figure II.3.7c), clothing fasteners, strap ends, belt loops, scabbard tips, or chainmail (see Figure II.3.6b). This category includes 13 whole or partial aglets or lace tags used on the ends of leather or cloth cords to tie clothing. The plain, small aglets as shown in Figure II.3.7b are diagnostic of the early 16th century, as aglets became longer and more ornate in the latter part of the century (Andersen 1979). Seven whole or broken buckles, belt loops or strap ends and 13 probable clothes fasteners have also been found at Piedras Marcadas.

An additional 57 pieces of thin copper alloy sheet have been found at Piedras Marcadas pueblo, 25 of which are analyzed as probable bell fragments. It is notable that all bell pieces are fragmentary and some are badly torn; only one still has an intact, folded or square-crimped seam. Copper alloy bells are diagnostic of the time period and are called *cascabeles* when associated with horse gear, as distinct from trade items (Flint 1992). While trade bells remained in use for centuries, the *cascabel* or "Clarksdale" type appears to have be uniquely distinctive to the mid-1500s (Deagan 2002:145-146)

The more ubiquitous wrought iron "facet headed" nail (see Figure II.3.6a) is primarily thought to be a horse shoe or mule shoe nail, although various other uses have been suggested by researchers (e.g., Vierra 1989). Some nails are quite large and suggest that the horses or mules and the shoes being used were proportionately large. It is possible that 16th century facet-headed nails may have been intended to be multi-functional, having the ability to serve as either horse shoe nails or as wood fasteners depending on necessity. The facet-

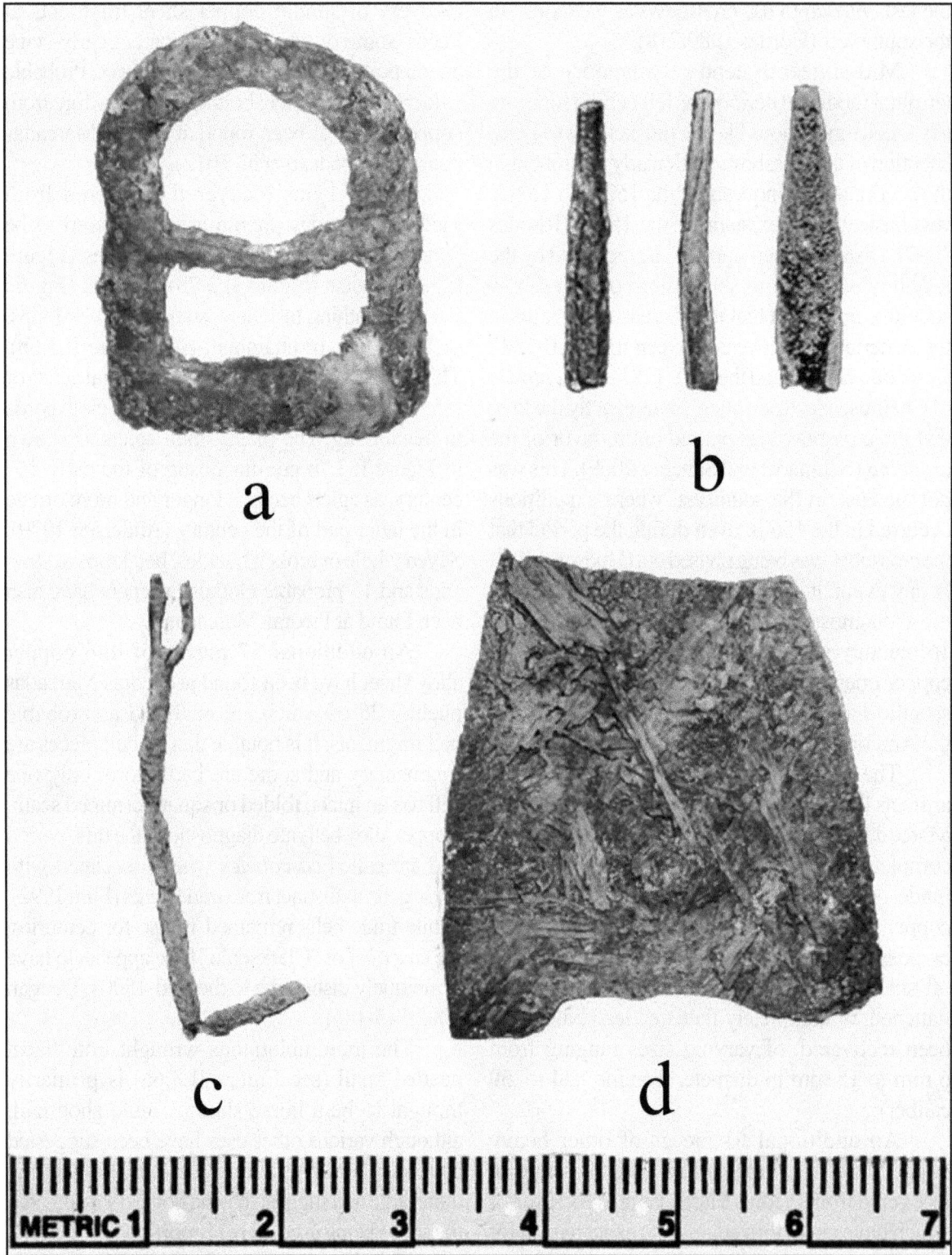

Figure II.3.7. Sixteenth century metal artifacts recovered from Piedras Marcadas pueblo: a, copper alloy belt buckle; b, copper clothing lace tags or aglets; c, copper needle; d, copper plate covered with straw impressions, probable piece of body armor.

headed nail is also considered to be diagnostic of the mid-16th century (Mathers and Haecker 2011). Fifty-one facet-headed nails in more than 50 percent complete condition have been recovered at Piedras Marcadas; another 59 faceted nail heads have also been found.

Numerous other non-faceted iron nails (41) and other nail head types (73) have been identified at Piedras Marcadas pueblo. Some are smaller tack types of nails while others have a distinct L-shaped head similar to those found at sites in the southeastern U.S. Nail shaft and nail tip fragments (including curved shoeing clenches) are more wide-spread, as 134 have been found so far at the site. Another equally abundant artifact category is non-descript fragmentary iron (190 pieces). The reasons for this degree of iron fragmentation are not fully understood. One hypothesis being considered is that, as standard ammunition became scarce, scrap iron was collected or possibly deliberately cut up for use as a type of shrapnel to augment lead shot. More intensive examination of size, shape and micro-wear analysis may suggest other causes for the fragmentation.

Among the 115 wire items found at Piedras Marcadas are three whole or mostly complete chain mail links (see Figure II.3.6b) and 13 additional chain mail fragments. Other larger pieces of diagnostic iron include several broken links of chain and at least three large pieces which may be horse shoe fragments. No large obviously diagnostic horse shoe pieces have been identified, however.

PIEDRAS MARCADAS ASSEMBLAGE AS A REFERENCE SITE

An important aspect of the site assemblage at Piedras Marcadas pueblo is that almost all metal artifacts appear to be either modern (i.e., 20th century) or likely 16th century in age. Most expeditionary and colonial sites in the Rio Grande valley have a mixture of 17th, 18th, and 19th century materials. But at Piedras Marcadas the

occupational sequence has a relatively clean break between earlier 16th century and clearly modern 20th century material.

The quantity, density, diversity, and distribution of identifiable 16th century metal artifacts firmly establishes the importance of Piedras Marcadas pueblo among other known Vázquez de Coronado expeditionary sites. With over 1,000 identified probable 16th century items in a one-acre investigation area, the average density is about 100 artifacts per 20 m x 20 m grid. The diversity of these objects is demonstrated by the consistent representation of numerous artifact categories such as personal items, weaponry, and functional items such as horse shoe nails or hardware.

The artifact diversity and association of directly related items from Piedras Marcadas pueblo considerably expands the archaeological inventories of previously documented major Vázquez de Coronado expeditionary sites. While some of the better known artifact types – crossbow boltheads, lead balls, facet-headed nails, copper alloy bells, chainmail, aglets, awls or needles – are described for one or more other Coronado sites (compare Blakeslee 1997; Damp 2005), other items are apparently unique. Their combined and associated presence as an entire assemblage at Piedras Marcadas, therefore, adds measurably to the whole of the Vázquez de Coronado expeditionary inventory. Unique items, or those found in relative abundance at Piedras Marcadas but rarely or never found elsewhere include:

The broken tip of a steel dagger or dirk (see Figure II.3.6f);

Several decorative copper alloy buckles, belt loops, strap ends, or scabbard tips (for example, see Figure II.3.7a);

A piece of thick copper sheet covered on both sides with organic residues, which possibly had been sewn into a cotton vest stuffed with straw for body armor (Figure II.3.7d);

A copper arrow point, smaller and distinctive from those made for crossbows. An 11 cm long copper awl, a probable sandal making or repair tool (Figure II.3.7d)

In general, the overall assemblage of items from Piedras Marcadas has a relatively high percentage of copper-based items. Nearly one-fourth (218 of 1,024) of the artifacts are copper or copper alloy; when the lead items are added, one-third of the assemblage is non-ferrous (334 of 1,024).

Non-Metal Artifacts

It is important to emphasize that three-fourths of the Vázquez de Coronado contingent was not European but rather were Mexican Indian allies (Flint 1997:47, 2008, 2009). It is estimated that there were at least 1,200 and possibly 2,000 or more *indios amigos* in addition to the 375 Europeans in the ranks of the expedition. The European men-at-arms had a modest assortment of Old World weapons, along with defensive gear such as vests, helmets, and coats of mail. However, nearly all of the soldiers also had native weapons listed in their possessions: the term "native weapons" or "native arms" appears for 256 of the individuals listed in the *alarde* (muster roll).

Mexican Indian allies were likely not outfitted with any Old World weapons, but rather used indigenous arms-of-the-field (or *armas de la tierra*) such as the obsidian-edged wooden warclubs called *macahuitls* or *macanas* (Flint 1992:136-137). Other weapons like sharpened wooden pikes may have been carried but would not be found archaeologically. Thus, *macahuitl* debris may be one of the only durable indicators of the native Mexican contingent of allies (Flint 1997:53).

Research on the surface obsidian debris at Piedras Marcadas is ongoing, as it is a complex question to address. In particular, more intensive analysis of attributes such as platform type, cross-sectional profile, flake scars, and edge wear needs to be done along with dimensional attributes such as width, thickness, and width:thickness ratio. Surface obsidian density in other 'non-plaza' areas of Piedras Marcadas needs to be compared to that found in the central plaza area. Morphological characteristics of surface obsidian from the central plaza area need to be compared to other nearby excavated sites. Preliminary obsidian sourcing studies need to be expanded. Finally, comparison of obsidian morphology to that found at other known Coronado expedition sites such as Hawikku or Santiago Pueblo needs to be carried out in order to advance this line of research.

Surface artifact mapping has also resulted in the recent identification of at least a dozen slingstones (Schmader 2012a, 2012b) at the site. Slingstones are frequently described as being about the size and shape of an egg (York and York 2011), but larger ones may weigh as much as a half kilogram. Slingstones are formally shaped in various parts of the world where indigenous warfare technology was highly developed, such as Hawai'i and other Pacific islands. Some of those slingstones are pointed on both ends, for example.

The probable slingstones found at Piedras Marcadas are slightly ground on the ends of an otherwise natural cobble, while other examples are completely ground around the circumference of the rock. The possibility exists that throwing rocks and rocks formally shaped to be hurled by a sling are both present at the site. These two types may represent actual native-against-native fighting that could have occurred at the site. If so, these artifacts may be by-products of fighting between indigenous Mexican *indios amigos* soldiers and pueblo peoples trying to defend their village at Piedras Marcadas. As the Coronado expeditionary chronicler Pedro de Castañeda de Nájera stated about the first attack on the pueblo of Moho, "the enemy had been getting ready for many days and had so many stones to hurl on our men that they stretched many on the ground" (Hammond and Rey 1940:228). Slingstones do not appear to have been described at any other Contact-period site in the American southwest.

IDENTIFYING PIEDRAS MARCADAS PUEBLO

Much investigation in the middle Rio Grande valley has centered around identifying the location of Alcanfor, the main headquarters for the Coronado expedition in the winter of 1540-1541. That effort has been concentrated mostly at sites such as Kuaua (LA 187) and Santiago pueblo (LA 326), and later at the discovered location of an expeditionary campsite west of Santiago pueblo (Vierra 1989). Gordon Vivian (1932:67) appears to have been the first researcher to suggest that Alcanfor was located at Santiago Pueblo.

It was Vierra's (1989) work at the nearby Coronado campsite of LA 54147 that may have established Santiago pueblo's probable identity. With that body of work, the consensus among researchers today is that Santiago pueblo was indeed the most likely location of Alcanfor (Barrett 1997:199, 2002:27-28; Flint 2011; Schmader 2011). But there has been less agreement about other major named expeditionary site locations in the Tiguex province such as Arenal, Moho, and Alameda (Flint 2011; Mathers 2011; Schmader 2011).

If Santiago pueblo was indeed Alcanfor, as an emerging consensus of scholars now believe, then the expeditionary location called by several names including "Moho" or "Pueblo del Cerco" was either three to four leagues north of Santiago pueblo, or the same distance south:

> After he [López de Cárdenas] had remained there for a few days, information reached the general [Coronado] to the effect that in a pueblo in the province of Tiguex – located three or four leagues from Alcanfor – where the said general and Spaniards

were quartered – the Indians of that pueblo, and those from the other pueblos that had been abandoned, were entrenched in the said pueblo, the name of which he does not remember (López de Cárdenas, in Hammond and Rey 1940:358-359).

Expeditionary chronicler Pedro Castañeda de Nájera called the same pueblo "Tiguex" (Hammond and Rey 1940:227), while Vázquez de Coronado himself called it "Moho" or "Mohi" (Hammond and Rey 1940:333).

The site of Moho, or Pueblo del Cerco ("village of the siege"), was described in several documents as the "strongest" of the villages in the provincia. Whether this refers to size or where the head chief resided is not completely clear, but certainly size and construction point to Moho being among the most formidable of all the villages.

> When the rest [of the Tiguex people] had seen this they abandoned their pueblos, except for two. One [was] the strongest of them all, at which the expedition spent two months (*Relación del Suceso*, in Flint and Flint 2005:500).

Moho became synonymous with the name Tiguex as well (Castañeda de Nájera in Hammond and Rey 1940:227) and was the last stronghold where the aged pueblo head chief Xauian ("Juan Aleman") assembled his people for a final stand-off with Francisco Vázquez de Coronado.

Piedras Marcadas is the largest of all the adobe pueblos built along the Rio Grande in Vázquez de Coronado's "provincia de Tiguex" (Schmader 2011). It is fully two to three times the size of the next largest villages in the vicinity in terms of areal extent (Marshall 1988:24). Total room counts are somewhat more ambiguous: Vierra (1987) states that Kuaua had about 1,000 rooms while Marshall (1988) says that Piedras Marcadas contained an estimated 1,500 rooms. Barrett (2002:27) confirms that Piedras Marcadas was the largest pueblo in the province.

Piedras Marcadas pueblo was clearly the site of a major engagement or conflict. With as many or more crossbow boltheads, lead shot, and personal objects as have been found at any Contact-period site, plus items such as chainmail, dagger tip, fragmentary iron, and possible body armor this conclusion is inescapable. It is either the location of a documented conflict, of which there are several in the chronicles, or it was not described in the documents (Richard Flint, personal communication 2009). At present, it seems most plausible that Piedras Marcadas was not only a described site, but was one which figured prominently in the events that unfolded in the winters of 1540 to 1542 and in subsequent testimonies. Besides the site contents, the physical features of the place and the geographic relationship to other sites will play a role in trying to determine if Piedras Marcadas pueblo can be positively linked to the expedition's documents. The discussions in Schmader (2011), Flint (2011), and Mathers (2011) are the most current thinking on the topic.

CONCLUSIONS

This paper has described the social and political contexts for what was arguably the most important *entrada* to have occurred in the greater transborder Mexican-American Southwest during the 16th century. It has also detailed the site structural context and related artifact assemblage of a major site discovery from the famed exploration of 1540-1542 led by captain general don Francisco Vázquez de Coronado. The outcome of the expedition permanently changed both Spain's orientation and knowledge of *la tierra nueva* and the social structure of all native populations encountered.

The failure of the Vázquez de Coronado expedition to find new civilizations or sources of wealth and trade was a combination of unrealistic expectations and of poor execution. There never were passages to the Orient, new civilizations, grand cities, or riches "*un poco mas alla*" (Sánchez 1988). The personal economic losses of those who invested in the enterprise lasted the rest of their lives, while the sociopolitical ramifications of the failed expedition persisted for over 40 years. It would not be until 1582 that another exploration of Nuevo México would be sanctioned by the Spanish crown.

The primary failures in execution derived from institutionalized ways of dealing with new peoples and the ingrained usage of force when confronted. To that extent, the Vázquez de Coronado expedition fit into a persistently hostile pattern that pervaded 16th century Spanish approaches to colonizing the New World. The first encounters between native peoples and outsiders in the transborder region and greater southwest are a case in point. Several major battles fought by Vázquez de Coronado resulted in the deaths of hundreds of pueblo people and insurmountable distrust (Schmader 2012a). Nuevo México in particular would never escape the focus of the Spanish crown even when interests shifted from economics and exploration to colonization and the salvation of souls.

Vázquez de Coronado showed little pragmatism in confronting many of the provocative actions of his force and his captains. He personally led several of the key attacks on native villages pueblos such as Hawikku and Moho. Despite these shortcomings, the expedition was notable for its low number of casualties. Perhaps 90 percent of the European men-at-arms returned; the survival rate of the *indios amigos* is not known. In comparison, Coronado's exploration may be distinguished from some of the catastrophic failures of other 16th century expeditions such as those led by Pánfilo de Narváez, Hernando de Soto, or Gonzalo Pizarro, who lost many hundreds of their own men. Coronado was not unaffected: he never fully recovered after falling from his horse on the way back to Mexico, and died at the age of 44 in 1554.

The Vázquez de Coronado expedition derives its fame not only from the scope of its failure but also from its timing and sheer size. It was the first major expedition launched from

New Spain into the present-day United States. It was nearly contemporary with the parallel effort in *la Florida* led by de Soto, who began less than a year earlier from Cuba. Coronado's exploration covered significant territory – nearly 4,000 miles – and resulted in major gains in geographic knowledge. The routes to sources of oriental trade goods such as spices, silk, or porcelain were not found, nor were the mythical and elusive places of Sipango, Cathay, India, or Quivira discovered. The expedition was notable for the "discovery" of important real world places. Along the way, the exploration had the first non-native people to have seen the lower Colorado River, the Grand Canyon, the western pueblos, the Río Grande and its pueblos, eastern pueblos, the Great Plains, and many, many tribes.

The 1540-1542 exploration led by Vázquez de Coronado lasted far longer, covered greater distances, had more people, and many more animals than other expeditions of the period. The enterprise was larger by any measure than almost any other 16th century Spanish exploration (Schmader 2011). Despite its size, remarkably little in the way of physical evidence has been found. Coronado's expedition also had the most varied of site types, including encampments, battles, sieges, travel camps, and advance parties. Given these parameters, sites from the Vázquez de Coronado exploration should be the most prevalent, most visible, and most variable of any expedition in the archaeological record (Schmader and Sánchez 2009). Nonetheless, major Coronado expeditionary sites are very few in number. New methods and better recognition criteria for these sites and their associated diagnostics have developed in the past quarter-century but especially in the last several years and are now beginning to yield new information (Schmader 2011).

Discoveries which radically change or add to our knowledge of the places, events, and material correlates of the famous Vázquez de Coronado expedition occur only a few times in a generation. The discovery of the Jimmy Owens site in Texas (Blakeslee 1997; Blakeslee and Blaine 2003)

as a major locality on the journey to Quivira is one example. Another is Vierra's (1989; Vierra and Hordes 1997) work at the Coronado *entrada* campsite outside of Santiago Pueblo in the mid-1980s. Damp's more recent (2005) investigations at Hawikku has identified the expedition's battle at Zuñi. The recent discoveries at Piedras Marcadas pueblo reported here ranks among these in importance.

Research and discoveries at Piedras Marcadas pueblo could have a lasting effect on the study of the first Spanish explorations in the American southwest. When coupled with what has been found at Zuñi Pueblo, Santiago pueblo, and in the Texas panhandle, plus several other sites along the expeditionary route, major break-throughs in our understanding of the expedition and its activities are at hand. It should be noted, however, that with new discoveries come new challenges for interpretation, site protection, limits to site access, artifact conservation, and above all, opportunities for renewed dialogue with the Native American and Hispanic communities.

Significant aspects of the Piedras Marcadas pueblo investigation are that evidence and data collection have been methodically deliberate, and that non-invasive techniques and remote sensing have been integrated. This is a necessity given the few remaining places and the often elusive kinds of material left behind from the time period. Only now is better information being pieced together on the locations, organization, tactics and logistics, materiel, and a more complete assemblage of the Vázquez de Coronado expedition. Chief among these efforts is the recent discovery of significant numbers and variety of artifacts directly related to the expedition's time spent in the Tiguex province at Piedras Marcadas pueblo. Its assemblage may represent a reference or type site for many expeditionary materials. The relationship between the site's adobe architecture and 16th century metal distribution can also present a case example for non-invasive archaeological studies.

Previously, there had been only one major proven pueblo site in the Rio Grande valley definitively associated with the Coronado expedition, which was Santiago pueblo (Vierra 1989). Given those circumstances, efforts to research and identify other villages related to the Vázquez de Coronado expedition rotated around a fixed point. With Piedras Marcadas pueblo and with the large quantity of recently found material, there now appears to be not so much a fixed point as there is a fixed line that defines the Tiguex pueblos and presents a possibility of better identifying other site locations.

Piedras Marcadas will hopefully form a basis for the future study and understanding not only of the Francisco Vázquez de Coronado expedition but also for knowledge about the 16th century Spanish exploration of the greater transborder region. After being known to scholars for more than 80 years, the site has been awakened in a dramatic way that should permanently change the equation for future studies of the Francisco Vázquez de Coronado expedition.

Part II, Chapter 4

Continuidad Cultural en la Periferia Sur del Noroeste/Suroeste: El Periodo Protohistórico en el Sur de Sonora y el Norte de Sinaloa

John Carpenter y Guadalupe Sánchez

RESUMEN

Investigaciones recientes por parte del Proyecto Arqueológico Norte de Sinaloa (INAH-CONACYT), sugieren que durante el "siglo perdido" se observa una continuidad cultural en la frontera sureña del Noroeste/Suroeste; aunque se registra un colapso abrupto de la red de intercambio de larga distancia, existe una continuidad de las tradiciones culturales señalado en las tradiciones cerámicas mayores entre las tradiciones de Huatabampo y Serrana (Río Sonora) del periodo Prehispánico tardío y el periodo Histórico temprano en el extremo sur de Sonora y el norte de Sinaloa. Proponemos que estas tradiciones forman parte de una extensa tradición cerámica Cahita que seguramente representa a los ancestros de los numerosos grupos de hablantes de la lengua Cahita documentados por los españoles en el siglo XVI (Ahome, Guasave, Ocoroni, Sinaloa, Tehueco, Zuaque, entre otros) y que actualmente comprenden la comunidad Yoreme (Mayo).

ABSTRACT

Recent research by the Proyecto Arqueológico Norte de Sinaloa (INAH) suggests that in the southern frontier of the Northwest/Southwest during the "Lost Century" that, although an abrupt collapse of the long-distance exchange network is observed, there exists a continuity among cultural traditions and principal ceramic traditions between the Huatabampo and Serrana (Río Sonora) traditions of the late prehistoric period and the early historic period in southernmost Sonora and northern Sinaloa. We propose that these traditions are part of a widespread Cahitan ceramic tradition. We further suggest that the descendants of many of the numerous groups of Cahita speakers documented by the Spaniards in the 16th century (Ahome, Guasave, Ocoroni, Sinaloa, Tehueco, Zuaque, etc.) today comprise part of the contemporary Yoreme (Mayo) community.

INTRODUCCIÓN

La antigua provincia española de Cinaloa abarcó la zona de la planicie costera y los paisajes de la serrana entre el río Sinaloa y el río Mayo, incorporando las llamadas "tierras Cahitas" (Figura II.4.1); término que delimitó el contraste de estos territorios con la extensión septentrional de las sociedades mesoamericanas que constituyeron la provincia de Culiacán (Carpenter 1996). La información etnohistórica indica que esta zona estuvo

John Carpenter Centro INAH Sonora
Guadalupe Sánchez Centro INAH Sonora

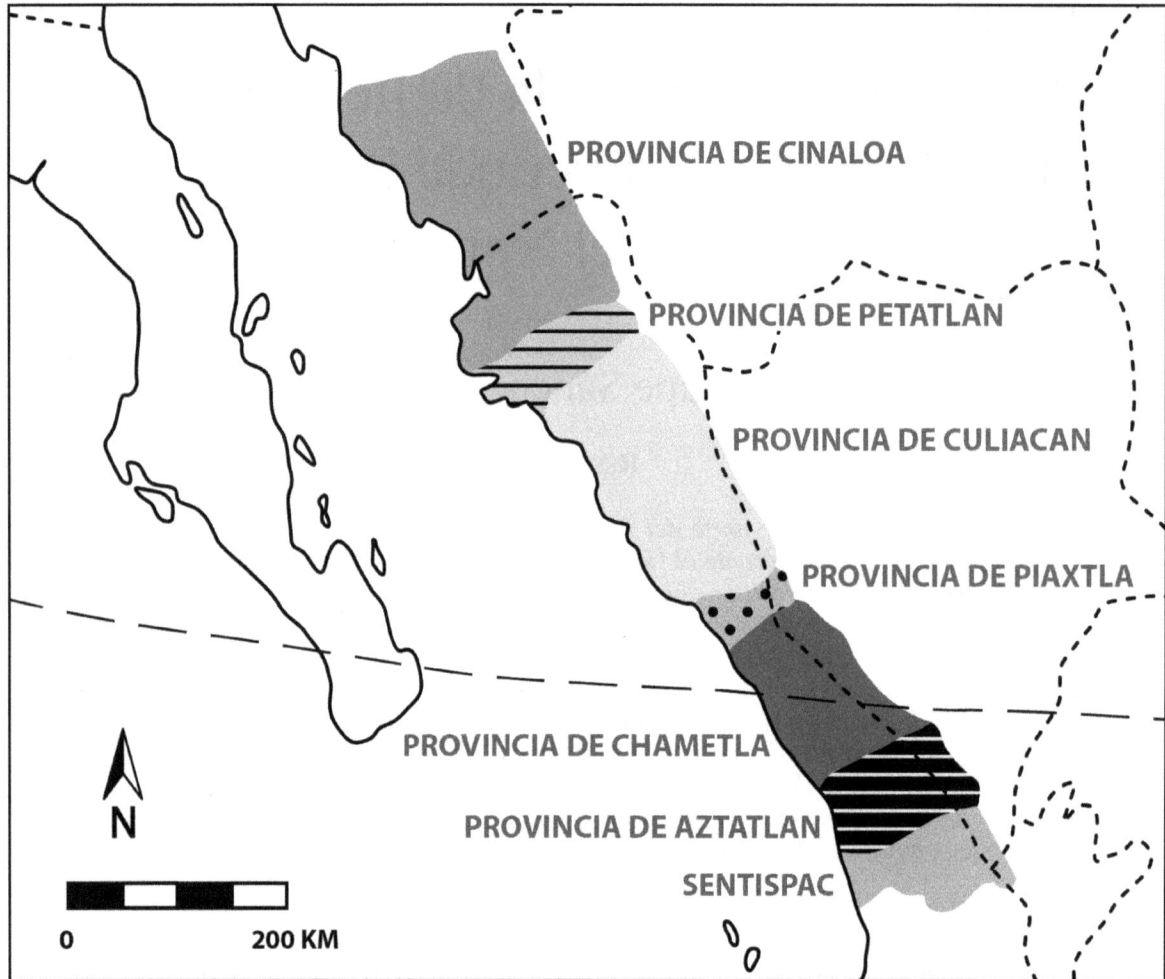

Figura II.4.1. Provincias Históricas de la Planicie Costera.

densamente poblada, con rancherías continuas ubicadas en los márgenes de los ríos principales entre la sierra y el mar, donde las poblaciones de agricultores sembraban maíz, fríjol, calabaza y algodón (cf. Obregón 1988).

Los datos etnohistóricos y arqueológicos revelan que estos grupos participaron en redes de intercambio a larga distancia que conectaba el Occidente de México con las comunidades sedentarias del Noroeste/Suroeste (Carpenter y Sánchez 2008). Vasijas y objetos Aztatlantecos han sido encontrados en contextos funerarios en el sitio de Guasave (El Ombligo), en el río Sinaloa y en Mochicahui, en el valle del río Fuerte. Vasijas cerámicas polícromas, malacates, sellos cilíndricos, cascabeles de cobre y fragmentos de navajas prismáticas de obsidiana – seguramente procedente de la región de Aztatlán – son algunos de los elementos que han sido reportados. En conjunto algunos tepalcates de Arevechi Rojo sobre Café y Babícora polícromo encontrados en el sitio de La Viuda/Rincón de Buyubampo parecen mostrar la interacción entre las regiones que existió en estas tierras (Carpenter y Sánchez 2007). Nuestros recientes estudios señalan que la producción de ornamentos de concha fue una actividad común en varias de las comunidades Cahitas durante el periodo prehispánico tardío y posiblemente uno de los productos intercambiados con las regiones circundantes.

LA CONQUISTA ESPAÑOLA DE LA PLANICIE COSTERA

La historia del contacto español y la conquista de la costa noroccidental de México fueron particularmente sangrientas y trágicas si se considera el nivel de violencia perpetrado por los conquistadores. Ninguna otra región de México fue tan rápida y completamente diezmada como la planicie costera de Nayarit y el sur de Sinaloa. Como consecuencia, estos ásperos eventos, nos dejaron con menos información de los grupos indígenas de esta región de la que suelen tener las fuentes documentales (Figura II.4.1). Como lamentaban los geógrafos Carl Sauer y Donald Brand (1932:41), si la entrada española al noroeste de México hubiera sido pospuesta por solo una generación, el precipitoso impulso de destrucción total se hubiera reemplazado por el incentivo de explotación y probablemente tendríamos muchos más relatos históricos valiosos de la vida indígena de la región.

Los pocos pobladores que sobrevivieron la violenta conquista española fueron diezmados y casi exterminados por las enfermedades contagiosas que traían los europeos y para las cuales los grupos indígenas no tenían defensas inmunológicas, sufriendo así un segundo exterminio (Crosby 1972; Dobyns 1966, 1976, 1983; Reff 1991). Aunque en la actualidad se sigue debatiendo la severidad del impacto epidemiológico (Hinton 1959:12; Hu-deHart 1981:51; Pennington 1963:24), no cabe duda que las enfermedades infecciosas contribuyeron a la devastación de las poblaciones indígenas de las Américas y provocaron rápidos y profundos cambios culturales.

Reff (1991) documenta numerosas epidemias que sufrieron las poblaciones indígenas del noroeste de México, incluyendo viruela, escarlatina, tifoidea, sarampión, malaria e influenza. Estas enfermedades ocasionaron la aniquilación de algunos grupos indígenas y

jugaron un papel importante en el proceso de reducción poblacional en virtualmente todos los grupos. Las cifras de mortandad para el México noroccidental podrían haber alcanzado el 50 por ciento dentro de la primera década de contacto y 90 por ciento en los siguientes 60 años (Reff 1991:194); lo anterior como consecuencia de la acumulación de eventos epidémicos de las diversas enfermedades infecciosas, modificando profundamente todos los aspectos de la estable vida indígena.

Podemos describir el periodo inicial del post-contacto como una época de exploración y conquista, resultando en la fundación de algunas villas españolas que duraban muy poco tiempo por los continuos conflictos entre los españoles y la población indígena; la inestabilidad de este periodo en la región se observa en el mínimo impacto tecnológico y económico que dejó este contacto esporádico. Aunque se aprecia un reacomodo de la población a posiciones más defensivas, no se observan influencias importantes en las dimensiones económicas, ideológicas o culturales hasta la llegada de la Compañía de Jesús, quienes establecieron 29 misiones en la región entre los años de 1591 y 1620, dando por resultado el sincretismo socio-cultural entre los españoles y los grupos indígenas que se refleja durante el periodo protohistórico e Histórico (1591-1900 d.C.).

En contraste con otras trayectorias culturales en el Noroeste/Suroeste, parece que las tradiciones prehispánicas del norte de Sinaloa/sur de Sonora resistieron las intrusiones españolas, cuyas poblaciones, aunque bastante reducidas por las enfermedades, sobrevivieron sin ningún cataclismo, solamente moviendo sus asentamientos a posiciones más estratégicas.

El entierro más lujoso–en cuanto a ofrendas que lo acompañaban–documentado en el montículo funerario de El Ombligo, en Guasave, Sinaloa, tiene una fecha calibrada de radiocarbono de 1410, lo cual sugiere que este cementerio seguía en uso en el siglo XV (Carpenter 1996). Dos entierros históricos en urnas funerarias del estilo Tahue, documentados por Isabel Kelly en la región de Culiacán, uno con un impacto de bala en la frente, indican la continuidad cultural entre la tradición arqueológica de Aztatlán y los Tahue (Hulse 1945).

Durante los últimos cinco años hemos tenido la oportunidad de investigar sitios arqueológicos en la región más norteña de Sinaloa en el valle del río Fuerte y río Ocoroni, que demuestran una larga ocupación que sobrepasa los periodos prehispánico-protohistórico e histórico (Figura II.4.2). Aunque lo estudios continúan en proceso y hasta la fecha no contamos con fechamientos absolutos, aquí presentamos algunos de los resultados con base en el análisis del patrón de asentamiento y los análisis de los materiales cerámicos y de otros artefactos, encontrados durante las investigaciones.

Los sitios de La Viuda y Rincón de Buyubampo en territorio de los Sinaloas

Los sitios de La Viuda y Rincón de Buyubampo se encuentran ubicados en el municipio de Choix, Sinaloa, a unos cinco kilómetros de la frontera sonorense en el valle del río Janalacahui, tributario del rio Fuerte, dentro del núcleo del territorio de los Sinaloa del siglo XVI. Según las fuentes históricas, los pueblos de los Sinaloa empezaban aproximadamente seis leguas arriba de la fortaleza de Montesclaros (hoy en día El Fuerte) establecida por Hurdaide (Pérez de Ribas 1944 I:342). En 1533, había 20 o 25 pueblos con entre 100 y 300 casas de petate (Segunda Relación Anónima 1955:167). Los españoles estuvieron tan sorprendidos y asustados con la presencia de unos 20,000 guerreros armados con arco y flecha, que se olvidaron de tomar esclavos y trataron de firmar la paz lo más pronto posible con los *caciques*

de los pueblos de los Sinaloas (Segunda Relación Anónima 1955:168). Treinta años después, Obregón (1988:77) describió el pueblo de Ciguini de los Cinaro (Sinaloa), con sus fortificaciones de madera a manera de "torreones." En Tepulco, el pueblo más grande de los Sinaloas, la expedición de Ibarra encontró a 1,000 guerreros divididos en cuatro escuadrones, todos con escudos, lanzas, arcos, flechas y macanas, adornados con muchos plumajes multicolores de guacamayas y pájaros del mar, con conchas y piedras de colores colgadas como cinturones, pulseras y tobilleras que hacían un ruido fuerte al marchar y estaban vestidos sólo con faldas de algodón (Obregón 1988:77-78). A lo largo del territorio de los Sinaloa, observó extensos campos del cultivo en todo el rededor del valle del río Fuerte, con abundancia de maíz, fríjol, calabaza y algodón (Obregón 1988:79).

Rincón de Buyubampo es un sitio arqueológico que fue descubierto en 2005, durante un recorrido sistemático de la zona; los restos de ocupación humana estaban tan bien enterrados por depósitos de los últimos siglos, que los pobladores del pueblo de Buyubampo, localizado a menos de un kilómetro del sitio, no sabían de su existencia, por lo que se encontró con una preservación extraordinaria. Rincón de Buyubampo es un sitio habitacional que se localiza en y alrededor de pequeño cerrito al sur del arroyo Janalacahui, que tiene una extensión de aproximadamente 12,000 km². Las investigaciones preliminares sugieren que la ocupación prehispánica consistió de aproximadamente 10 a 15 unidades habitacionales o complejos residenciales, con varios elementos arquitectónicos entre los que figuran terrazas, casas con cuartos contiguos y casas de un solo cuarto y graneros o bodegas (Figura II.4.3) (Carpenter y Sánchez 2007, 2008).

Se intervinieron en total tres unidades habitacionales aunque ninguna se excavó

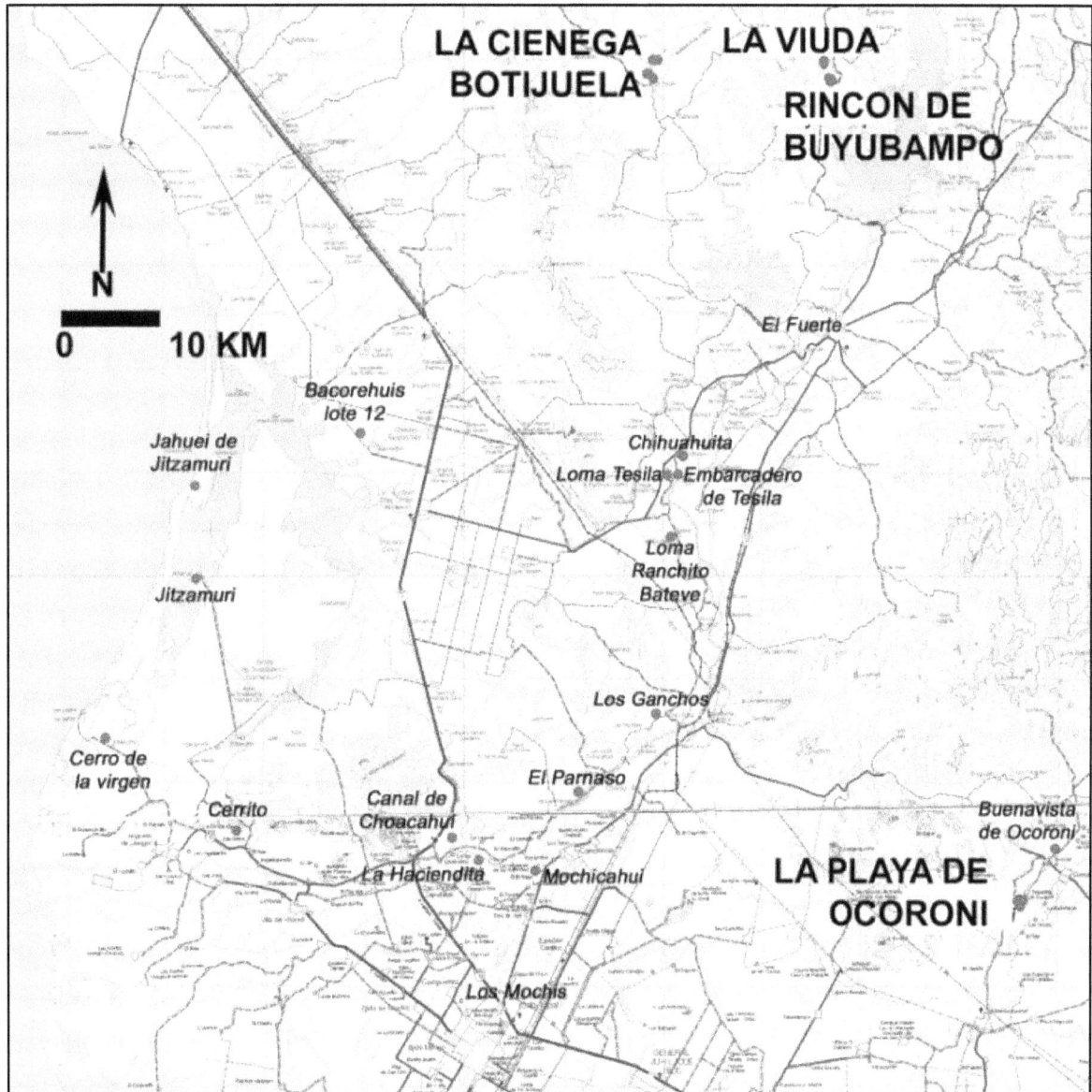

Figura II.4.2. Localización de los sitios mencionados.

por completo. La unidad habitacional dos se localiza en la parte baja del cerro y está constituida por una casa grande formada por tres cuartos contiguos, dos de 10 x 8 metros y uno de 10 x 4 metros (Figura II.4.3). Los muros de los cuartos en la casa grande tienen cimientos de piedra laja careada, con un grosor de 50-60 cm; en los pisos de los cuartos se encontraron hornillas en forma de "U" o "doble U", a veces con manos y metates usadas en actividades de molienda asociadas.

Se encontraron numerosos hoyos de postes con los postes de madera todavía preservada; la mayoría de la madera es de amapa (*Tabebuia chrysantha*), la mejor madera para hacer postes en la zona. Parece ser que fueron utilizados para soportar los techos de estos cuartos de enormes dimensiones, los cuales requirieron para sostener el techo dos o tres hiladas de postes de hasta 50 cm en diámetro. Los hoyos para los postes fueron excavados en la roca madre hasta 50 cm o más de profundidad. Los

Figura II.4.3. Las estructuras habitacionales de Buyubampo y La Viuda.

techos fueron construidos con vigas cubiertas por terrado. La ocupación principal del sitio puede colocarse en los periodos Prehispánico tardío y Protohistórico, es decir entre 1300 y 1800 d.C. (Carpenter et al. 2006).

El sitio de La Viuda se localiza aproximadamente 900 metros al norte de Buyubampo sobre la planicie aluvial del río Janalacahui, el sitio está compuesto por estructuras habitacionales y probablemente otros elementos arqueológicos que desafortunadamente fueron destruidos por la erosión, consecuencia de los cambios que experimentó el cauce del río por la construcción de la presa del Maune-Miguel Alemán, en la década de los años cincuenta del siglo pasado. Las excavaciones realizadas en los sitios demuestran una ocupación continua de aproximadamente 1000 años. En el sitio se observa una amplia ocupación que comenzó alrededor de 800 d.C. y continuó hasta el siglo XV.

El componente más temprano se localiza cerca del arroyo Janalacahui, los elementos culturales están casi completamente destruidos por la erosión aunque se pudieron hacer algunos pozos estratigráficos; los lugareños hablan de un lugar en donde se erosionaban varios entierros humanos hace unos 10 años que llaman "Los Muertos", del cual no queda nada en la actualidad. La parte del sitio en terreno más alto está cerca del camino que comunica El Fuerte, Sinaloa, con Álamos, Sonora. En esta zona se pudieron excavar por lo menos dos estructuras. La estructura 2 excavada en 2008 es una estructura con tres cuartos contiguos y parece constituir un componente temprano de La Viuda, con una temporalidad tentativa entre 700 y 1200/1300 d.C., representada por los tipos cerámicos Batacosa, Huatabampo y Guasave, lo que parece indicar que la dirección de las interacciones eran de la costa a la serrana (Carpenter et al. 2008) (Figura II.4.3). La estructura 1 fue excavada en 2005,

representa una de las unidades habitacionales más tardías del sitio de La Viuda y parecen ser precursoras de las unidades habitacionales encontradas en Rincón de Buyubampo, tal es el caso de la estructura 1 donde los materiales más abundantes – aparte de la cerámica local – son cerámicas protohistóricas representadas por los tipos San Miguel/Papachi y Cuchujaqui; sin embargo dentro de los adobes de la estructura se encuentran comúnmente cerámicas Huatabampo Rojo y Guasave Rojo sobre Bayo. Abajo del piso de la ocupación principal de la estructura, también se encontraron cerámicas Huatabampo, Guasave y cerámica Batacosa, testimonio de una ocupación más temprana que la de la estructura (Carpenter et al. 2006) (Figura II.4.3).

Con base en las variaciones de tipos cerámicos y el cambio tecnológico en la producción de ornamentos de concha podemos proponer que la población que se encontraba en el sitio de La Viuda en la víspera del periodo protohistórico, cambió su patrón de asentamiento de las tierras bajas en el arroyo a una posición mucho más vigilante en el cerrito de Rincón de Buyubampo, donde se podía observar quien entraba y salía del valle. La distribución cerámica en estos contextos tardíos, aun sin fechas absolutas, sugiere la posibilidad de que el tipo Guasave Rojo sobre Bayo siguió siendo producido hasta el siglo XVI y que la vajilla San Miguel comenzó a producirse en el siglo XVI; la extensa distribución espacial de los tipos San Miguel desde la costa hasta la sierra parece indicar que son cerámicas domésticas burdas que se comenzaron a fabricar en las misiones jesuitas utilizando el estiércol de vaca (Figura II.4.4).

La producción de ornamentos de concha se reduce significativamente en la ocupación de Rincón de Buyubampo, además de que existe un cambio en la utilización de especies y la elaboración de ornamentos específicos como son los brazaletes de concha que casi

Figura II.4.4. Tipos cerámicos San Miguel en el piso de la estructura 2 de Rincón de Buyubampo.

desaparecen en Rincón de Buyubampo. Los brazaletes de concha representan una mercancía importante en las actividades de intercambio de productos. Una de las consecuencias de la presencia española en la región es el rompimiento de las interacciones entre regiones que detiene el intercambio regional y pan-regional y los ornamentos de concha se convierten en mercancías relegadas y de poca importancia. El estudio preliminar de los artefactos de concha revela que en la estructura 1 de La Viuda la producción de ornamentos de concha como brazaletes, cuentas, figurillas de animalitos y pendientes son muy comunes; sin embargo en la estructura 2 de Buyubampo la variedad de ornamentos se reduce, y especialmente los brazaletes que casi desaparecen por completo, mientras que

el uso del bivalvo *Pecten* sp. es más abundante en la elaboración de pendientes y parecería que la producción doméstica para usos locales se vuelve mucho más común.

Dada la escasa cantidad de materiales españoles encontrados en Rincón de Buyubampo se puede proponer que la interacción con la red comercial española durante los primeros 150 o 200 años de la conquista era mínima y está representada por algunos objetos de metal como clavos, botones, algunos fragmentos de mayólicas tempranas (Figura II.4.5) de principios del siglo XVIII y algunas porcelanas chinas del siglo XVII y XVIII.

Un hallazgo inusual en la estructura 2, fueron tres sellos de plomo modificados en medallones (Figura II.4.6), que indican la ocupación del sitio hasta la primera mitad del

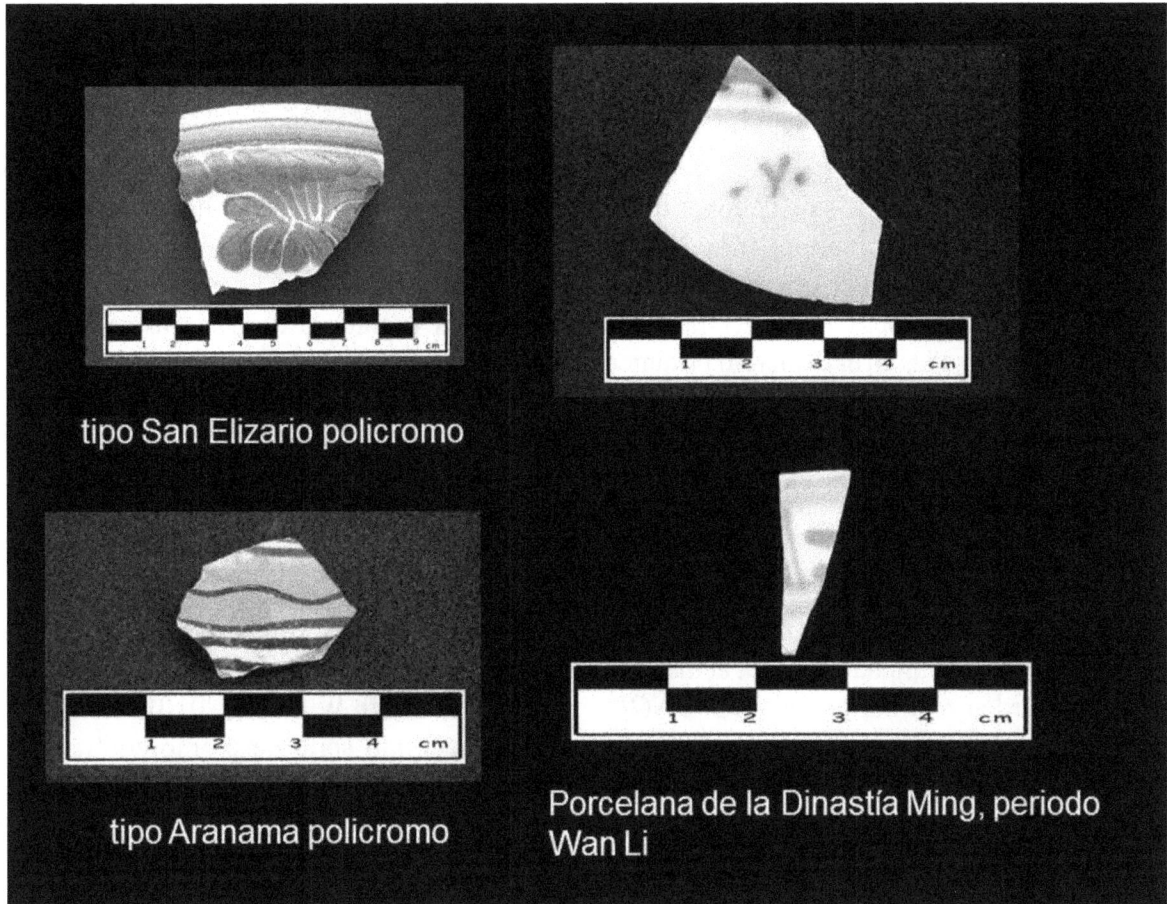

tipo San Elizario policromo

tipo Aranama policromo

Porcelana de la Dinastía Ming, periodo Wan Li

Figura II.4.5. Mayólicas y porcelanas del sitio de Rincón de Buyubampo.

Figura II.4.6. Sellos de plomo recuperados abajo del piso de ocupación en la Estructura 3.

siglo XVIII. Los tres objetos son de interés especial por el lugar donde se encontraron, su morfología y por su procedencia (Figura II.4.7).

Esos objetos fueron encontrados en distintos lugares debajo del piso en el mismo cuarto 3, sugiriendo que los medallones quizá fueron escondidos de manera intencional. Curiosamente, todos son de origen británico y representan sellos de ropa o bolsas (comparable a etiquetas) utilizadas en el comercio británico para distinguir la calidad de la mercancía que se estaba vendiendo. El primer sello (Figura II.4.6a) fabricado principalmente de plomo y con residuos de oro, parece indicar que originalmente presentó una leve chapa de oro. Presenta el escudo de armas de Inglaterra con la frase "*DIEU ET MON DROIT*" (Dios y mi derecho) de la monarquía británica actual y el dicho del orden real del garter "*HONI SOIT QUI MAL Y PENSE*" (vergüenza a él quien piensa mal de ello), una asociación aristocrática

establecida en 1348, con membrecía otorgada solamente por el rey o la reina. El león a la izquierda simboliza Inglaterra, mientras que el unicornio al lado derecho representa Escocia; en el cuadrante superior derecho del escudo interior se ven tres flores de lis, en referencia a Francia y en el cuadrante inferior izquierdo el arpa, icono de Irlanda. Este escudo de armas aparece en Inglaterra desde la ascensión de Jorge I en 1714 hasta el Acto de Unión entre Gran Bretaña e Irlanda en 1801 (comunicación personal de Hugh Willmott, 2010; footguards. tripod.com). Este tipo de sellos de ropa fueron parte de un sistema de identificación y de control de calidad. Se utilizaron en Inglaterra y el resto de Europa entre los siglos XV al XIX, pero también se encuentran fuera de Europa como etiquetas de telas (comunicación personal de Hugh Willmott, 2010).

El segundo sello de plomo contiene la inscripción del número "4" incorporando una

Figura II.4.7. Fotografía de los sellos de plomo.

cruz y abajo las letras "SB" y una pequeña estrella adentro de un corazón (Figura II.4.6b). Este sello tiene un anillo para colgarse que seguramente fue una modificación a la pieza original. Este sello parece ser una etiqueta o una marca de un comerciante o un productor particular; por su parecido a sellos similares parece ser del siglo XVII-XVIII.

El último sello (Figura II.4.6c) también es de plomo, con un motivo de escudo compuesto de tres leones acostados y un león parado. Además, en su parte inferior presenta un mapa del continente americano, mostrando a México en el espacio central, completado con las líneas de latitud y longitud y las letras "MAR DEL ZUR" indicando el océano Pacifico y "MAR DEL N" identificando el océano Atlántico y/o el mar Caribe, con una representación de una ballena arriba a la derecha del mapa. También se observan las letras "SS & FC" en el contorno de la pieza, perteneciente al South Sea and Fisheries Co. (Hezel Forsyth, comunicación personal 2010); esta compañía fue la encargada de las operaciones comerciales de la corona inglesa en América y a finales del siglo XVII expandieron el negocio para comercializar aceite de ballena.

Vajillas foráneas del siglo XVII-XVIII se pueden ver en pocas cantidades en la estructura 2 de Rincón de Buyubampo. Los tipos encontrados son mayólica Abó policromo elaborada en Puebla de los Ángeles (México) entre 1650-1750, mayólica Puebla azul sobre blanco elaborada en Puebla de Alcocer (España) entre 1675-1800 y mayólica Huejotzingo azul sobre blanco, elaborada en Puebla de los Ángeles entre 1750-1800. También se encontró porcelana de la Dinastía Ming del periodo Wan-Li, que aproximadamente inicia 1575 y termina en 1623, porcelana China Imari elaborada en China del 1700-1780, porcelana Dinastía Ch Ing polícroma con decoración sobre el vidriado, elaborada en China entre 1700 y 1750. La cerámica foránea más abundante es la mayólica Puebla azul sobre blanco con 35 tiestos; el resto de las cerámicas mayólicas y las porcelanas están representados por solo uno o dos tiestos pequeños (Carpenter et al. 2006). La escasez de tipos foráneos es otro indicador de la mínima interacción que esta zona tuvo con la red de intercambio español.

En suma, los estudios de la ocupación arqueológica del valle del arroyo Janalacahui indican que este valle comenzó a ser ocupado intensamente desde 800 años d.C. Las casas excavadas en Rincón de Buyubampo y la estructura 2 de La Viuda, revelaron que bajo los pisos de ocupación protohistórica existieron ocupaciones más tempranas representadas por los tipos cerámicos de Cuchujaqui, Batacosa y Guasave. Durante el siglo XV-XVI el patrón de asentamiento se modificó y la población se movió a una posición más defensiva encima del cerrito de Buyubampo, desde donde se puede vigilar el valle, y aparentemente existe un rompimiento del sistema de intercambio prehispánico regional. La ocupación continuó hasta por lo menos mediados del siglo XVIII sin muchas modificaciones aparentes y sin que se vea la influencia de un dominio foráneo, o la integración a las redes comerciales españolas.

LOS SITIOS DE LA BOTIJUELA Y LA CIÉNEGA

Se localizan en la cuenca del arroyo Carrizal, afluente tributaria del río Cuchujaqui/Álamos, en el municipio de Álamos, Sonora. Representa una de las zonas más bajas de esta pequeña cuenca donde se formaba una ciénaga, que seguramente fue parte del territorio Tehueco. Los sitios de La Botijuela y La Ciénega revelan una ocupación continua que comenzó en el siglo XV y continuó hasta mediados del siglo XIX. Los dos sitios presentan una tradición cerámica con filiación a la tradición serrana tardía.

Según las fuentes históricas, los Tehueco

ocupaban tres pueblos en un territorio que empezaba a unas cuatro leguas río arriba desde el último pueblo Zuaque, y se extendía por el río Fuerte a lo largo de siete leguas (Pérez de Ribas 1944 I:310-311). Pérez de Ribas observó que los hombres tenían tres o más consortes, organizaban muchos bailes y consumían muchas bebidas alcohólicas, a más que daban muchos regalos de algodón (Pérez de Ribas 1944 I:311). Según Pérez de Ribas (1944 I:278), los Tehueco pudieron desplegar hasta 15,000 arqueros durante las batallas. De los relatos de Antonio Ruiz (Nakayama 1974:17), se puede conjeturar que el territorio Tehueco se extendía desde el actual pueblo de Tehueco en el margen derecho del río Fuerte hacia el norte en todo el valle del río Alamos/ Cuchujaqui hasta por lo menos el pueblo de Basiroa, localizado en Sonora 50 km al norte del actual pueblo de Tehueco sobre el río Álamos; los Tehuecos controlaban tanto el cruce del río Fuerte como la ruta hacia el norte por el Río Álamos. Basiroa el pueblo más norteño de los Tehuecos, funcionó como refugio indígena durante los recurrentes conflictos entre Tehuecos y españoles, ya que constituía una ciudad amurallada con torres que resultaba impenetrable.

Limitadas intervenciones arqueológicas realizadas en La Botijuela demostraron que este sitio contiene por lo menos una estructura de cimientos de cantos rodados con cuartos contiguos ubicados alrededor de un patio central (Figura II.4.8). Los materiales incluyen tipos cerámicos tardíos de la tradición Serrana entre los que figura el tipo Cuchujaqui, aunque los tipos cerámicos protohistóricos son los más abundantes; evidencias de la producción de ornamentos de concha y huesos de ganado equino y bovino se observan en los contextos excavados. Aparentemente el sitio de La Botijuela fue parcialmente inundado y abandonado, ya que se encuentra en tierras bajas donde se formaba una ciénega y el

poblado fue reubicado en tierras más altas aproximadamente un kilómetro al este en el sitio de La Ciénega, arriba de una lomita. En el sitio de La Ciénega (Figura II.4.9) se observan evidencias de una ocupación en unidades domésticas dispersas del siglo XVII que permanecieron hasta aproximadamente 1850 d.C. Existe evidencia de que en el sitio se manufacturaron grandes ollas del tipo cerámico San Miguel, que seguramente se utilizaron en algún proceso que implicaba la cocción en gran volumen y existe una cantidad limitada de tipos cerámicos foráneos. Cabe mencionar que en la actualidad la ciénega está seca y el actual poblado de La Ciénega, representado por cinco casas, se encuentra ubicado 600 metros al oeste del sitio protohistórico de La Ciénega en la zona más baja.

La continuidad cultural es particularmente evidente en las tradiciones cerámicas, principalmente a través de la serie San Miguel; tipos históricos derivados de las tradiciones prehispánicas locales como Cuchujaqui Rojo junto con algunos tepalcates de Guasave Rojo sobre Bayo fueron encontrados en el sitio de La Botijuela. Los ornamentos de concha que también nos sirven de indicadores para los cambios en esta época, revelan que en La Botijuela se continuaron elaborando ornamentos de concha, siendo los pendientes pintados del bivalvo *Pecten* sp. los ornamentos más numerosos. En el sitio de La Ciénega no se recuperaron ornamentos de concha, lo que parece indicar que para el siglo XVIII ya existía un rompimiento de la interacción prehispánica indígena y las conchas dejaron de ser una mercancía importante.

EL SITIO LA PLAYA DE OCORONI, SINALOA

En los documentos históricos los Ocoroni son ilustrados como principales enemigos de los Guasave y los Nio y estaban ubicados a 12

Figura II.4.8. Unidad habitacional con patio central en el sitio de La Botijuela, Sonora.

Figura II.4.9. Unidades habitacionales del sitio La Ciénega, Sonora.

leguas al norte de Petatlán, al lado del arroyo Ocoroni, tributario del río Sinaloa (Obregón 1988:73). El pueblo principal conocido como Ocoroni, consistía de 400 casas y fue gobernado por una cacica, conocida como Luisa (Obregón 1988:74). Según Obregón, Luisa era una Tahue nacida en el valle de Culiacán, quien después de haber sido capturada cinco veces por diversos grupos, eventualmente se convirtió en la esposa del cacique de los Ocoroni y fue reconocida como la líder *de facto* (1988:74; Nakayama 1974:45-49). La cacica Luisa fue la traductora en la expedición de Ibarra a la región de Paquimé de ida y vuelta (Nakayama 1974:45-49). Durante la década de 1580, Ruiz (Nakayama 1974:59-60) relata los continuos conflictos entre españoles y Ocoronis, que resultaron en la conformación de una milicia bajo el comando de Gonzalo Martínez, quien subsecuentemente fue asesinado y canibalizado ritualmente por su tremendo valor en la batalla. La población combinada que vivía en los valles de los ríos Ocoroni y Sinaloa es estimada en 15,000 habitantes (Sauer 1932, 1935:5).

La Playa de Ocoroni es un poblado en el valle del río Ocoroni, afluente del río Sinaloa, localizado a unos 50 km al noroeste de Guasave y cuarenta kilómetros al oeste de San Blas. Integrantes del proyecto Norte de Sinaloa realizaron un reconocimiento regional en la zona y encontraron en esta comunidad cuatro montículos artificiales, con dimensiones de 40 a 50 metros de diámetro y medio metro de altura. Aunque no se realizaron excavaciones en los montículos, éstos parecen representar tanto elementos constructivos como posiblemente montículos funerarios. La recolecciones de superficie controladas realizadas en y alrededor de los montículos, indican que están afiliados a la ocupación Guasave con una cantidad considerable de cerámicas Guasave decoradas, junto con algunos tipos de la Sierra en bajas cantidades, Guasave Liso y Guasave Rojo sobre Bayo principalmente,

algunas cerámicas Batacosa, tipos San Miguel y algunos tepalcates del tipo San Felipe y Santiago, considerado de producción regional y asociado al establecimiento de las misiones jesuitas en la región.

En la actualidad los montículos son incorporados en los rituales Yoreme de Ocoroni; por ejemplo, durante Semana Santa los danzantes pasan de un montículo al otro durante la ceremonia y cabe mencionar que las hornillas ceremoniales que se usan actualmente, son iguales a las encontradas en el sitio Rincón de Buyubampo, aunque están puestas en pretiles. La Playa de Ocoroni es un sitio que tiene una continuidad cultural que empezó por lo menos en el siglo VIII y perdura hasta la fecha; estos grupos Ocoroni sobrevivieron a la conquista, a las enfermedades y a los sangrientos enfrentamientos con los españoles y posteriormente se adaptaron a la vida misional en su territorio ancestral. El Fuerte, Sinaloa, en la actualidad es también un importante centro ceremonial Yoreme.

INTEGRACIÓN CULTURAL Y PERMANENCIA EN LA REGIÓN CAHITA DEL NORTE DURANTE EL SIGLO PERDIDO

Los Cahitas forman un continuo lingüístico que se extendió desde el río Piaxtla hasta la Opatería en el noroeste de Sonora (y tal vez, Paquimé). Los grupos Cahitas han sido identificados como un elemento integral en la red de intercambio entre el Occidente de México y el Noroeste/Suroeste (Carpenter 1994, 2008; Carpenter y Vicente 2008, 2009) y parecen haber tenido fuertes lazos económicos y sociales a través de su territorio. El abrupto rompimiento en la red de intercambio de larga distancia que ocurrió durante la época de contactos militares esporádicos, un poco antes del periodo de la llegada de los Jesuitas, podría asociarse a las sangrientas masacres perpetradas por

Beltrán Nuño de Guzmán en las provincias de Sentispac, Aztatlán, Chametla, Piaxtla y Culiacán. Sin embargo, aunque se rompe la red de intercambio de larga distancia, las relaciones económicas y sociales regionales permanecen intactas hasta los siglos XVII-XVIII.

Los registros arqueológicos recientemente investigados están en sintonía con los relatos de los primeros españoles sobre la región Cahita del norte. Era un territorio muy poblado, con sociedades agricultoras que se extendían en los valles de los ríos y afluentes tributarios que caracterizan la región. El siglo perdido en esta zona se caracteriza por pequeñas transformaciones culturales observadas en el patrón de asentamiento hacia localidades más defensivas dentro del territorio y la ruptura de algunos mecanismos de interacción regional. Sin embargo, el orden social y económico Cahita continúa sin cambios aparentes. Entre los factores que contribuyeron a la continuidad y permanencia de las poblaciones durante el siglo perdido en la región Cahita, se puede destacar el paisaje rivereño sinaloense con sus ambientes estables para la producción agrícola.

Los ornamentos de concha y el algodón, entre otros productos, seguramente repre-sentaban mercancías que formaban parte de la red de intercambio de larga distancia. Los datos arqueológicos indican que la producción de ornamentos de concha termina de manera abrupta en los primeros años después de la permanencia de la ocupación española. En varios de los sitios, la única distinción entre los componentes prehispánicos tardíos y los de los primeros años post-contacto español, es la presencia/ausencia de concha en los sitios, ya que las técnicas constructivas, los elementos arquitectónicos y las tradiciones cerámicas se preservan.

Con base en nuestras investigaciones en el norte de Sinaloa y el sur de Sonora, podemos proponer que los grupos Cahita que poblaron la planicie costera y la zona serrana constituyeron un continuo cultural que funcionó como un corredor de ideas y mercancías donde los diferentes grupos Cahita, tanto de la costa como de la serrana, funcionaron como nodos en el sistema de integración e interacción cultural regional y pan-regional. Hoy en día, los descendientes de los varios grupos Cahita identificados por los españoles en el siglo XVI, como los Ahome, Zuaque, Guasave, Ocoroni, Tehueco, Sinaloa, etc., conforman la comunidad Yoreme (Mayo).

Archaeology and Society
Arqueología y Sociedad

Part III, Introducción
Arqueologías Mexicana y Norteamericana: Entre la obligación moral y los shovel bums

César Villalobos

INTRODUCCIÓN

La relación que mantienen México y Estados Unidos ha sido una portentosa fuente de inspiración y debate. Las relaciones diplomáticas de estos dos países muestran una asimetría geo-política por su llamada pertenencia a los mundos del subdesarrollo y al desarrollo económico, respectivamente. Además de compartir una frontera lineal de 3,326 kilómetros, las interacciones cotidianas se vuelven necesariamente obligadas y la propia inercia las convierte en relaciones omnipresentes en diversos sectores de la sociedad. Las arqueologías de ambos países son parte de este complejo sistema de intercambios y encuentros. En el presente texto expondré los elementos centrales que caracterizan a las arqueologías practicadas en ambos países. Por un lado, la actitud nacionalista de la arqueología mexicana le ha conferido una función casi exclusiva en la construcción de la identidad. Ello contrasta sin duda con el dinamismo de la arqueología norteamericana en donde múltiples transformaciones en su devenir muestran su proclividad a satisfacer intereses de diversos grupos. Más allá de estas diferencias formales, también muestro que a lo largo del siglo se pueden observar particulares formas de interacción retroalimentación.

ARQUEOLOGÍA EN MÉXICO Y ESTADOS UNIDOS

En México la arqueología se ha utilizado como una forma de integrar el pasado prehispánico al proyecto de nación. La arqueología fue usada como una de las formas para fortalecer la identidad a través de la herencia prehispánica. Esto ha tenido como resultado que la arqueología en México sea practicada bajo un esquema gubernamental en donde el estado nacional por medio del Instituto Nacional de Antropología e Historia (INAH) creado en 1939, administre y supervise todos los aspectos relacionados con el patrimonio arqueológico (Olivé 2003 [1988]).

El arqueólogo es formado bajo los preceptos de servir a la nación debido a que la arqueología es una prerrogativa del estado. La formación de sus estudiantes se centró originalmente en el estudio de las culturas mesoamericanas dando posterior cabida a otras regiones del país. Para su regulación se aplica la Ley Federal Sobre Monumentos y Zonas Arqueológicos, Artísticos e Históricos publicada a principios de 1970 (INAH 1972), pero que proviene en esencia de una ley publicada originalmente en 1934 (Olivé 1980:41-42). Independientemente el tipo de propiedad de tierra se aplica la ley de 1972. El Consejo de Arqueología es un órgano centralizado del INAH que emite permisos y evalúa los reportes arqueológicos emitiendo su aprobación o rechazo y en su caso la continuidad o suspensión de los trabajos arqueológicos (García-Bárcena 2007:14). Todo ello hace que la arqueología mexicana se defina como una practica nacionalista (Trigger 1984:359).

Por su parte la arqueología en Estados Unidos se utilizó como una forma del reconocimiento de "la otredad". La arqueología norteamericana

César Villalobos Durham University

forma a sus estudiantes con una visión teórica sobre las diferencias culturales desde una perspectiva global (Newell 1999). En el modelo norteamericano el control de la arqueología radica en diversas instituciones y existe la arqueología comercial o privada. No hay un modelo único sino una combinación de circunstancias acerca de qué tipo de legislación se aplica, no obstante algunas generalidades existen. En los Estados Unidos el estatus de la propiedad de la tierra y el grado de participación de gobierno determinan el tipo de legislación que se aplicará (Anyon and Ferguson 1996:915). Las leyes federales aplican para proyectos que se llevan a cabo en tierras ya sea federales o tribales, en caso de que el proyecto sea financiado por el gobierno. Proyectos con financiamiento privado ejecutados en tierras privadas no necesitan seguir el protocolo de leyes federales en lo relacionado los recursos culturales a menos que les sea solicitado un permiso federal (Watkins 2003:276). Las tribus indígenas son reconocidas por el Gobierno de Estados Unidos como naciones dependientes internas que tienen ciertos poderes soberanos. La soberanía indígena implica que toda investigación arqueológica llevada a cabo en tierra indígena requiere la aprobación del gobierno indígena, y que la tribu retiene los derechos de propiedad de todo el material cultural encontrado en sus tierras (ibídem). La arqueología norteamericana, además de imperialista de hecho, ha sido considerada antinacionalista (Trigger 1984:366).

Habiendo iniciando esta comparación me gustaría retomar el camino trazado precisamente por Trigger, es decir, que la arqueología mexicana es nacionalista y la norteamericana imperialista (Trigger 1984). Con ello pretendo vislumbrar los mecanismos de interacción que se dan entre ambas prácticas. La caracterización de la arqueología desde la perspectiva de Trigger provocó críticas entre las que se encuentran por ejemplo Michel Tierney, quien argumenta que la propuesta de Trigger sufría de una inadecuada elaboración de los términos esenciales e invitaba a los arqueólogos a tener una mejor compresión

de los términos antes de utilizarla en su propio trabajo (Tierney 1996:12).

Posteriormente Philip Kohl mencionaba que pese a que los estados nacionales fomentaban un arqueología nacional, no toda esa arqueología es usada por la ideología nacionalista, lo que dejaba entrever que no toda la arqueología nacional es utilizada de la misma manera (Kohl 1998:226). Recientemente Díaz-Andréu ha mencionado que aun en las arqueologías nacionalistas puede verse una práctica de colonialismo interno (Díaz-Andreu 2007:100). El mismo Trigger se había percatado de que su clasificación no estaba libre de problemas y que estas arqueologías no eran monolíticas y podían entremezclarse de acuerdo a diferentes momentos en la conformación de los modernos países (Trigger 1984:355), pese a lo anterior me interesa utilizar estos conceptos en su acepción más general, sin entrar en las variantes que cada uno de ellos implica.

LA ARQUEOLOGÍA MEXICANA PATRIOTERA HASTA EL AGRESIVISMO

Por medio de una gruesa caparazón nacionalista, la arqueología mexicana hace frente al permanente embate de la arqueología imperial norteamericana, usándola cuando la necesita y cerrándole las fronteras cuando se siente amenazada. Los mecanismos de interacción son en efecto complicados. Uno de estos mecanismos ha sido la formación de arqueólogos mexicanos en las universidades norteamericanas. Los arqueólogos mexicanos han recibido influencia intelectual y entrenamiento directamente por medio de su participación como estudiantes en las universidades norteamericanas. Ello a la larga, ha propiciado que la incorporación de las ideas en boga en Estados Unidos, sean integradas parcial o completamente a sus respectivos proyectos de investigación en suelo mexicano y/o a la enseñanza en las universidades mexicanas sin detrimento del nacionalismo de la arqueología mexicana.

En la sección que sigue por medio de la comparación de dos facetas en la obra de Manuel Gamio pretendo demostrar que, por un lado que la arqueología mexicana ha recibido un impulso considerable por medio de la incorporación de técnicas y conocimientos producidos en Estados Unidos. Y que por otro lado, también en Gamio puede ser encontrada otra faceta interesantísima que demuestra precisamente lo contrario, es decir que una vez superada su etapa internacionalista, se repliega al interior de las fronteras nacionales generando la idea nacionalista que acompañará a la arqueología mexicana hasta bien entrado el siglo XXI.

Manuel Gamio fue el primer arqueólogo mexicano que se reconoce formalmente entrenado en las universidades norteamericanas y de ahí, una lista bastante robusta podría ser mencionada hasta la actualidad. Gamio sintetiza esta compleja y contradictoria forma de ser de la arqueología mexicana. En su época temprana adopta el pensamiento intelectual en boga en la Universidad de Columbia, su internacionalismo lo lleva a conducir la llamada primera excavación estratigráfica en México y a participar en el primer intento de academizar la arqueología en México a través de la creación de la Escuela Internacional de Arqueología y Etnología Americanas (EIAEA) (Boas 1915). Veamos la excavación primero y posteriormente aclararé a que me refiero con lo de contradictoria y compleja.

El método estratigráfico habia sido desarrollado por la geología europea y fue paultinamente incorporado a la arqueología mediterránea y europea hacia 1860. Sin embargo este método no fue incorporado en tales fechas. La *revolución* estratigráfica empieza a ser desarrollada casi paralelamente en dos áreas, en Mesoamerica por Manuel Gamio y en el Suroeste Norteamericano por N. C. Nelson, ambos jovenes arqueólogos que habian sido entrenados en las universidades norteamericanas, el primero por Franz Boas y el segundo por Alfred Kroeber, quien a su vez habia sido alumno de Boas (Willey and Sabloff 1980:84). La importancia de este

trabao incial de Gamio fue además de introducir un nuevo método en la arqueología mexicana, el establecer una secuencia arqueológica para el Valle de México (Gamio 1920, 1924).

A pesar de que esta excavación de Gamio ha sido celebrada como una gloria de la arqueología nacional, poco a poco se va desmitificando su imagen idilica de padre fundador, y la importancia de su figura cobra una relevancia historica más realista de acuerdo al contexto social en el que elaboró su trabajo (Rutsch 2001:85). Es sabido que la idea intelectual de la excavación estratigráfica en gran medida, proviene de la Universidad de Columbia, y más claramente de la figura de Franz Boas a quien le interesaba refinar la suección cultural en el Valle de México (Gamio 1920:129; Matos Moctezuma 1983:5). La fortuna de haber tendio la primera excavacion estratigráfica en Aztapotzalco, es de alguna manera producto del avance intelectual de la arqueología en las instituciones norteamericanas y del contexto circunstancial que le tocó participar. Obviamente sin Gamio nada hubiera sido posible como sucedió y eso es un mérito insoslayable. Un buen ejemplo de esta desmitificación que pone al relieve e influencia de otros arqueólogos antes y despues de la excavación en Azcapotzalco, es el análsis que presenta Daniel Schávelzon (Schávelzon 1999) quien demuestra que precisamente Gamio fue parte de un contexto social mayor, y que si bien fue el artifice de la institucionalizacion del método estratigráfico en México, mucho le debe al ambiente intelectual norteamericano en el cual hizo su trabajo, del cual se nutrió y el cual aplicó al campo de la arqueología mexicana

Posteriormente el trabajo de Gamio contrasta con el internacionalismo de la EIAEA y de su excavación estratigráfica. Aquí es donde encuentro el motivo de la contradicción que mencioné arriba. Gamio literalmente se repliega al interior de las fronteras nacionales y propone lo que hasta en la actualidad es el paradigma de la arqueología posrevolucionaria mexicana. En 1916 publica *Forjando Patria*, que con el subtítulo pro-nacionalismo, le da sentido a las subsecuentes generaciones de estudiantes de antropología. Las ideas de *Forjando Patria* han gozado de robusta salud en el contexto oficial mexicano hasta bien entrada la década de 1970, cuando las propuestas del indigenismo oficial empezaron a ser severamente cuestionadas por los antropólogos mexicanos, sin embargo este modelo aún se mantiene en pie (Gamio 1916).

Forjando Patria fue el bastión más importante e influyente en la creación de la conciencia nacional a través de la arqueología. En este libro Gamio intenta remover impulsos nacionalistas e ideas gestadoras de Patria (Gamio 1916:VII). Los argumentos esenciales de la propuesta de Gamio, pueden verse de forma casi poética a partir de la anécdota maravillosa de su almuerzo en Mérida. Vale la pena relatarla: cuando alguna vez almorzaba en Mérida Gamio pidió una cerveza, ¿nacional o extranjera? le preguntó el mozo. Éste pidió entonces una extranjera imaginando, o mejor dicho saboreando supongo, que le traerían una cerveza alemana o norteamericana. Su sorpresa fue mayúscula cuando le trajeron una cerveza Dos Equis de Orizaba.

Alterado le llama la atención al mozo argumentando que había solicitado una cerveza extranjera. El mozo sorprendido le responde que la Dos Equis era la única cerveza extranjera que tenían, pero que sí quería le podría traer una nacional, es decir una cerveza yucateca. Gamio relata que con su orgullo metropolitano herido, le aclara al mozo una serie de consideraciones geográficas y políticas acerca de la relación que Mérida guardaba respecto a la Ciudad de México. El mozo a su vez le replica una serie de apreciaciones – que Gamio oculta – acerca del por qué en Mérida la cerveza de Orizaba era considerada extranjera. Gamio desaprueba los conceptos del mozo y confiesa al lector que ese incidente le hace ver lo que es un *"nacionalista en extremo y a veces patriotero hasta el agresivismo"* (Gamio 1916:17-18).

Esta anécdota me sirve para ilustrar que en efecto, aparte del gusto por la cerveza en todas sus modalidades, ya sean extranjeras o yucatecas, el modelo del arqueólogo mexicano emanado de la figura de Gamio, está aún presente en la actualidad, siendo ciertamente en muchos casos nacionalista en extremo y patriotero hasta el agresivismo. Este modelo de la arqueología nacional que raya en lo monopólico por parte del estado nacional, ha creado una legislación que aplica para todo el país, en todas las circunstancias. Ello contrasta con el modelo norteamericano, como a continuación detallo.

LA ARQUEOLOGÍA EN LOS ESTADOS UNIDOS

Un análisis o siquiera un resumen de la arqueología norteamericana es altamente complejo. La promulgación de legislaciones al paso del siglo, sus transformaciones y modificaciones, la posibilidad de obtener recursos financieros, ya sea por parte del gobierno o de patrocinadores privados, la hacen ser extremadamente dinámica a la luz de su propio devenir. Sumado a ello partir de la década de 1970 los indígenas norteamericanos ganaron derechos sobre el manejo de los sitios arqueológicos.

Las leyes federales más importantes relacionadas con el manejo del patrimonio arqueológico son el *National Historic Preservation Act, Archaeological Resources Protection Act, Native American Graves Protection and Repatriation Act, American Indian Religious Freedom Act, and the National Environmental Policy Act* (Anyon and Ferguson 1996:915). Asimismo la mayoría de los Estados tienen leyes para proteger los restos humanos sin importar la propiedad de la tierra. Virtualmente todas las investigaciones arqueológicas realizadas en tierras federales o tribales requieren la consulta de las comunidades indígenas, sin embargo, yacimientos arqueológicos en propiedad privada son tratados como propiedad privada (Ferguson 1996:66). Hacia el inicio del sigo XXI se considera que existían a los menos 36 programas en los cuales las comunidades indígenas estaban activamente involucradas con el objetivo de influenciar la investigación arqueológica en sus territorios. Adicionalmente a los programas de las tribus indígenas otras dependencias del gobierno (el *United States Department of Agriculture Forest Service*) llevan a cabo programas de capacitación de indígenas en el trabajo arqueológico (Watkins 2003:279).

La soberanía indígena significa que toda la investigación arqueológica llevada a cabo en reservaciones indígenas requieren la aprobación del gobierno indígena, y que la tribu retiene los derechos de propiedad de todo el material cultural encontrado en sus tierras (Watkins 2003:276). Así mismo las comunidades indígenas pueden emplear arqueólogos o antropólogos para realizar investigación (Anyon and Ferguson 1996:913). Sin embargo, la promulgación de leyes y el manejo de los sitios no necesariamente se ha hecho desde la perspectiva de los valores indígenas sino desde la perspectiva occidental. Los sitios son considerados por su carga de información y no por los valores inmateriales asociados a las culturas indígenas, como por ejemplo su relación con la tierra, la relación con los ancestros, la cultura y tradiciones, los sitios representan fuerzas vivas. Sea como sea es interesante por ejemplo observar la evolución de la estructura de los programas de manejo cultural con los Zuni, quienes desde 1975 diseñaron un programa para la conservación de los sitios arqueológicos, el cual ha sido enriquecido y modificado desde que fue planteado (Anyon and Ferguson 1996:914-916).

Este desarrollo trajo aparejado la emergencia de lo que se ha denominado *Cultural Resource Managment* (CRM). El CRM agrupa a lo que se ha llamado arqueología de contrato, pública o de rescate (Green and Doershuk 1998:122). Se ha argumentado que el CRM emergió principalmente a partir de la promulgación del *Archaeological and Historic Preservation Act* de 1974 pero también por el *National Environmental Policy Act (1969)*. Es a partir de mediados de la

década de 1970 cuando el modelo de CRM toma forma como se conoce actualmente, mientras que hacia la década de 1980 proliferó el sector privado de consultorías (ibid:124).

El CRM se enfoca en la identificación, evaluación y manejo de sitios que son amenazados por el desarrollo. El CRM incluye lucrativas y no lucrativas empresas, agencias gubernamentales, universidades, comunidades indígenas y consultarías privadas por lo que en este último apartado es también considerado un negocio. La arqueología en Estados Unidos es básicamente orientada como CRM, lo cual significa que la mayoría de los arqueólogos están empleados en puestos no-académicos, y aún, dentro de la academia una parte significativa se gana la vida a partir del CRM (ibid:121). La *Shovel Bums*, un sitio web que aglutina a los arqueólogos de contrato en Estados Unidos, por ejemplo, tiene registrados 14,000 miembros quienes trabajan en CRM (http://*www.shovelbums. org/*). Similarmente en otras partes del mundo el CRM agrupan una cantidad bastante grande de arqueólogos, en el Reino Unido, por ejemplo, se calcula que trabajan 5,000 arqueólogos en CRM, ya sea en arqueología de contrato o relacionada al patrimonio arqueológico (Kristiansen 2009:644).

Este modelo crea que en la actualidad los arqueólogos puedan ser empleados en los museos, curadurías, en la enseñanza, en la arqueología de contrato o poseer su propia consultoría privada. Un arqueólogo puede también trabajar para compañías de arqueología de contrato, algunas de ellas como he señalado lucrativas y otras no. Además de las universidades, museos, fundaciones y firmas privadas, existen un buen número de agencias gubernamentales Estatales y Federales que contratan a sus propios arqueólogos para la realización de análisis de impacto ambiental que las obras de infraestructura puedan ocasionar sobre los restos arqueológicos, como por ejemplo el *U.S. Bureau of Land Management, la U.S. Army Corps of Engineers,* el *U.S. Forest Service,* el *U.S. National Park Service,* y otras agencias estatales.

¿DIFERENCIAS O SIMILITUDES?

Nuestra historia compartida ha sido ciertamente una lucha de contrarios y el análisis de nuestras historias, más que reconciliarnos, nos hace parecer cada vez más diferentes. En este contexto, las arqueologías mexicana y norteamericana son parte de este fenómeno cultural en el que nos acercamos y nos alejamos con la misma fuerza reciproca. En la actualidad ha quedado demostrado que la arqueología, además de su valor académico, también es un poderoso instrumento político y económico. Esto es cierto no solo para los gobiernos, sino igualmente para empresarios, grupos indígenas, comunidades locales y aún para saqueadores y traficantes de antigüedades (Skeates 2000). Esta diversidad vista en nuestras arqueologías hace emerger una serie de contradicciones y acuerdos que tácitamente nos mantienen unidos pero juegan la suerte de un tabú, no los mencionamos pero los reproducimos y nos regocijamos por su existencia, y como en cualquier tabú, la tensión de la transgresión esta siempre presente y mantiene viva la incertidumbre.

Ignacio Bernal tiempo atrás había mencionado que mientras que para los extranjeros la arqueología practicada en México era una cuestión de ejercicio intelectual, para los mexicanos era parte de su pasado, por tanto de su propia vida (Bernal 1979:12). Esta aseveración me permite formular dos postulados, que como sana provocación he de enumerar esperando posteriormente justificar y explicar su pronunciamiento. Debido a que en el presente texto se pretende comparar el saber disciplinario en dos países, más allá de los límites de la excavación y del dominio de la cucharilla, me atrevo a traspasar la arqueología al terreno de la sociedad, y proponer dos tabúes, uno de cada lado de la frontera.

Primero, como parte de nuestra identidad y formación académica los arqueólogos mexicanos estaremos reacios a asumir abiertamente que sin las aportaciones norteamericanas realizadas en siglo XX, estaríamos rezagados teórica y metodológicamente (recordemos, es un tabú), y que esas contribuciones, más allá del contenido académico, han servido en gran medida para la comprensión de la historia cultural en diferentes regiones del actual México. De hecho, en algunas áreas son los norteamericanos quienes han propuesto las historias culturales originales, que posteriormente han sido re-interpretadas por los arqueólogos locales. Así mismo protegidos, y a veces, más bien replegados en el caparazón nacionalista hemos dejado escapar el complejo análisis de las múltiples legislaciones y problemas de aplicabilidad, los vicios y virtudes del modelo norteamericano.

Segundo, también resguardados en sus propios tabúes, los norteamericanos no han terminado por comprender que antes de sus aportaciones en el siglo XX, la arqueología mexicana tenía ya una historia bastante larga que la sustentaba como una de las prácticas arqueológicas de más arraigo en el mundo, y que en la actualidad hay una producción masiva de investigación publicada en español que poco se conoce y se cita en sus trabajos. Además, no han terminado de comprender que la arqueología en México es una obligación moral, y que los mexicanos están profundamente orgullosos del pasado prehispánico. Sumado a ello, lo que los norteamericanos critican tácitamente, y casi en secreto, como absurda burocracia del INAH, es en realidad la gruesa caparazón nacionalista en contra del intervencionismo extranjero, que a la vez protege los bienes más preciados de la nación y que es la esencia de la identidad y ahí por ende, encontraran también la esencia del rechazo a la comercialización de la arqueología, tan normal del otro lado del río Grande (¡no sabía que yo mismo podría ser patriotero hasta el agresivismo!).

Estas dos perspectivas de análisis – que más jocosamente llamo tabúes – se enumeran desde la generalización aludiendo a trabajos vistos en su contexto de producción mayor. Asumo que existen múltiples diferencias individuales, que deberían por fuerza ser tratadas en otro apartado. Con el ánimo generalizador de este análisis no aspiro a agotar las particularidades y diferencias de cada arqueólogo o arqueóloga en ambos países. Con estos tabúes en mano, que a primera instancia parecieran desproporcionados y tendenciosos, intentaré analizar en un contexto mayor, que estas posiciones responden a las necesidades de la arqueología en sus contextos de producción.

Es bien sabido que el flujo "normal" en arqueólogos ha sido de Norte a Sur; es decir, los arqueólogos mexicanos tradicionalmente no han incursionado en la arqueología norteamericana. Se ha mencionado que hay tres aspectos fundamentales por los que no ha ocurrido: 1) la arqueología mexicana es más interesante, 2) no existen universidades privadas o fuentes de financiamiento para realizar tales investigaciones y 3) no hay suficientes arqueólogos para las propias necesidades de México. Estos argumentos que parecerían haber sido elaborados por quien esto suscribe, fueron originalmente publicados por Donald Brand a finales de la década de 1940 (Brand 1948:69). Este proceder en realidad no es privativo de la arqueología mexicana sino de las arqueologías nacionalistas en general; o sea, replegarse al interior de sus fronteras nacionales, con arqueólogos nacionales, o nacionalizados y trabajando en instituciones nacionales, valga la redundancia.

El hecho de que los arqueólogos mexicanos no hayan cruzado la frontera para realizar proyectos de investigación, los ha convertido en férreos críticos de lo que hacen sus contrapartes norteamericanos en suelo nacional, además de estar mejor preparados por el manejo del inglés acerca de lo que se escribe del otro lado de la frontera. En este sentido, Peter Jiménez ha señalado que uno de los apartados éticos en que los arqueólogos norteamericanos han fallado es tanto su falta de lectura y referencia de trabajos en español, como la entrega de sus informes y publicaciones al INAH (Jiménez 2007:34). Menciona que esta ha sido una constante –

negativa – por parte de un buen número de arqueólogos norteamericanos al cruzar a México, *vienen, excavan y se van.* En algunos casos sin entregar los informes de las actividades realizadas al Consejo de Arqueología.

En este sentido doy completa razón a Jiménez, sin embargo, siendo justos con la objetividad, nuestra arqueología mexicana también ha jugado esa suerte de colonialismo interno. Una buena cantidad de proyectos arqueológicos nacionales, si no es que la mayoría, *vienen, excavan y se van.* En algunos casos también sin entregar su informe al Consejo de Arqueología. Y lo que es aún peor, sin provocar mayor influencia en las comunidades de los alrededores, especialmente si se trata de comunidades indígenas, donde cualquier información extra podría tomarse como un intento de darles poder sobre los restos arqueológicos, y eso es casi considerado como un atentado a la nación.

Cada una con su cada tabú, en este sentido ambas arqueologías han sido coloniales a su manera.

Sin abundar mucho en este aspecto, sólo agregaría que el concepto de Mesoamérica ha materializado esa suerte de colonialismo interno en México. Ignacio Rodríguez ha enumerado una buena cantidad de argumentos para considerar que Mesoamérica fue por mucho tiempo el valor predominante para asignar recursos y apoyo institucional, todo lo que estuviera fuera de ella, carecía de valor en términos políticos, presupuestales y aún académicos (Rodríguez 2000). No me negarán los colegas con ello, que la política económica del concepto Mesoamérica y su colonialismo implícito ha sido la prueba más evidente de que en esencia, también nos parecemos a los vecinos del norte. Y mejor que no nos toquen esa canción, porque si algunas áreas se convirtieron en marginales desde la óptica centralista Mesoamericana fueron las áreas sin pirámides, especialmente en el norte de México. Nelly Robles refuerza esta crítica a la práctica neo-colonial de la arqueología mexicana cuando afirma que en general los proyectos sometidos al Consejo de Arqueología para su evaluación, ya sean nacionales o extranjeros, virtualmente ignoran el contexto social, tratando los sitios arqueológicos como si estuvieran en un vacío abstracto respecto a las realidades sociales (Robles 2007:30).

En otro sentido algunos datos son interesantes para percatarse de que el modelo nacionalista determina la velocidad, impacto y modos de investigar. El INAH cuenta con alrededor de 350 arqueólogos de tiempo completo (Martínez 2007:17). Mientras que en 2004 se calculaba que alrededor de 626 proyectos fueron realizados en México, el 77 por ciento correspondió a proyectos del INAH, 10 por ciento a otras instituciones mexicanas y 13 por ciento a proyectos extranjeros (García-Bárcena 2007:15). Esto es diametralmente opuesto a las cifras de Estado Unidos. El Departamento del Interior reporta que en 2008 se efectuaron 103,000 estudios de campo en las que se incluyen 518 excavaciones realizadas únicamente por agencias federales (Altschul y Ferguson, este volumen). Estos números no incluyen una considerable cantidad de proyectos realizados por agencias privadas y estatales. Como se mencionó arriba existe un *web page* con 14,000 miembros registrados presumiblemente trabajando en CRM.

Sin duda México debe abrir el camino para la inclusión de más arqueólogos, propuesta que en la actual condición de legislación monopólica es difícil de conseguir. Sumado a esta carencia de arqueólogos, se tiene que los foros de discusión y aplicación de leyes más actuales e inclusivas, permiten que por presiones de carácter político sucedan casos como el del show de luz y sonido en Teotihuacan, o la compra reciente por el gobierno del estado de Yucatán de los terrenos en donde se encuentra Chichén Itzá. Estas acciones muestran que las decisiones unilaterales del monopolio del gobierno y de ciertos grupos de elite en torno al manejo de recursos arqueológicos, fincadas en su interrelación de una legislación, son una vieja práctica que debe ser erradicada.

Si bien el estado nacional mexicano engendró a la arqueología en el modelo del Indigenismo como una forma de fortalecer la identidad, es bien sabido que después de la crisis económica de los ochenta del siglo pasado y posteriormente al alzamiento zapatista de 1994, el viejo modelo del mestizaje, con todos los aspectos positivos que entrañó, ha sido severamente cuestionado por diversos grupos sociales, antropólogos, intelectuales y más aún por los propios grupos indígenas. El modelo absoluto de control estatal de la arqueología ha mostrado debilidad para responder cabalmente a la adecuada protección, salvaguarda e investigación de los recursos arqueológicos en México (Gómez 2006).

Por otro lado y en lo que se refiere al segundo tabú mencionado, o sea, a la práctica imperialista de la arqueología, mi argumento se sustenta en que gran parte de arqueología norteamericana en México ha sido realizada desde una perspectiva imperialista y colonialista, claro que con sus notables excepciones, y sin detrimento de las aportaciones particulares que muchos de los colegas que están leyendo este trabajo en español han realizado. Para ilustrar este punto mencionaré que a mediados de la década de 1990 hubo una seria preocupación de los arqueólogos norteamericanos por la creación de un código de ética que coadyuvara a regular la práctica arqueológica debido al cada vez más apabullante crecimiento del CRM. El resultado titulado *Ethical Principles of Archaeological Practice* fue publicado originalmente por la *Society for American Archaeology* en 1996 (Lynott 1997). Esta preocupación anglosajona contrasta con la contraparte mexicana.

Corriendo el año de 1968 Alfonso Caso publicó, lo que a mi parecer es el primer código de ética en la arqueología mexicana (Caso 1968), que en conjunto con la legislación publicada desde 1934 han regido éticamente a la arqueología en México. En ella Alfonso Caso realiza una arenga a los jóvenes arqueólogos mexicanos invitándolos tomar seriamente el ejercicio profesional de la arqueología. Caso advierte que no se debe olvidar la obligación de publicar y divulgar, pero sobre todo se debe asumir la responsabilidad que como científicos se tiene con la nación. Dicha publicación incluye básicamente los principios éticos que la arqueología anglosajona ha destacado como importantes en el mencionado código de ética. Lo que quiero destacar con ello, es que los arqueólogos mexicanos han presentado ideas que de alguna manera fueron re-inventadas por los arqueólogos norteamericanos; sin embargo, al estar publicadas únicamente en español, poco conocimiento se tuvo, y se tiene de ellas en la literatura en inglés. Repito, que este pequeño detalle ilustra que una mirada post-colonial podría ser una de las formas en que la arqueología norteamericana se podría nutrir de su contraparte mexicana y de otras tradiciones locales.

Por otro lado, y para cerrar este apartado de los tabúes, apuntaría que más que las múltiples diferencias que han sido mencionadas, por fortuna o mala fortuna, compartimos a lo menos una serie de elementos comunes: 1) la preocupación por la formación de los recursos humanos, 2) la elaboración y calidad de los reportes provocados por la arqueología de Salvamento o CRM, 3) la importancia de lograr un balance entre el patrimonio y la preservación con las necesidades del desarrollo contemporáneo y 4) la necesidad de incluir en nuestras agendas discusiones acerca de saqueo y tráfico ilegal de objetos arqueológicos (Sebastian 2007:13). Adicionalmente ha sido mencionado acertadamente que uno de los problemas transnacionales que compartimos en arqueología se refiere al empleo marginal y a la pobreza institucionalizada del número creciente de arqueólogos (Patterson 1999:169), quienes a falta de capacidad institucional desertan de la arqueología o maquilan información en el formato de los CRM sin orientación precisa, lo que deviene en una falta de claridad intelectual sobre los objetivos de la arqueología. Otro punto problemático compartido, y como ha sido mencionado en este texto, se refiere a los reclamos, cada vez mayores, que otras

comunidades y grupos dicen tener para el manejo legítimo de los recursos arqueológicos, sean grupos de empresarios, políticos, indígenas, mestizos y los propios arqueólogos.

Lo más importante es reconocer que la arqueología responde a un contexto social, y que su función, integración, desarrollo y usufructo debe estar relacionado con el marco social, político y cultural que le da existencia. De nada nos servirá emular los sistemas norteamericanos, por ejemplo de financiamiento privado (que en cierta medida ya han aparecido en la arqueología mexicana), o a los norteamericanos de nada les interesará establecen relaciones de afinidad con el pasado prehispánico cuando en realidad su pasado biológico y cultural en América es mucho más reciente.

CONCLUSIONES

Despojando a nuestras arqueologías de su coraza imperial o nacional, si analizamos su aspecto científico y ético, hay que mencionar tanto los aportes fundamentales de la arqueología norteamericana a la mexicana así como las aportaciones críticas que la arqueología nacionalista mexicana ha hecho a la norteamericana. Simplemente basta pensar en los diversos proyectos de larga duración conducidos por norteamericanos o instituciones norteamericanas en México para darse cuenta de la influencia que en ambas direcciones se ha tenido en la interpretación y aportaciones metodológicas. ¿Donde estaría la Cuenca de México sin Sanders, el valle de Puebla sin MacNeish, Casas Grandes sin Di Peso, Teotihuacan sin la retícula de Millon, el Occidente sin Isabel Kelly o Chichén Itzá sin la Carnegie Institution? ¿Qué hubiera sido de la Escuela Internacional de Arqueología y Etnología Americana sin la influencia de Franz Boas? Por otro lado hay que resaltar el aspecto positivo de la arqueología en México: ¡ayudó a construir y aglutinar la identidad de un país bastante lastimado con intervenciones extranjeras y conflictos internos después de su independencia! Y eso no es poca cosa. La arqueología en México es usada por su aportación científica pero también es una herramienta moral; como diría Ignacio Bernal, es creadora de símbolos de identidad y probablemente será el último reducto que nos distinga en la globalización voraz y del intervencionismo.

Randall McGuire parafrasea al músico inglés de canciones de protesta Billy Bragg cuando éste menciona que es tristemente obvio que las injusticias en el mundo – el racismo y fascismo, específicamente – no se acabarán por el simple hecho de escribir canciones de protesta. McGuire en la misma dirección menciona que es penosamente obvio que haciendo arqueología tampoco se derribarán tales ideologías; no obstante señala que la sensación de imposibilidad de ese cambio no debe detener a los arqueólogos en intentar hacerlo (McGuire 2008:234).

Sumándome a la protesta de Bragg y McGuire, finalizaré este texto mencionando que para transformar al mundo se requiere de un cambio en la forma en que los sujetos viven y piensan la historia. El sociólogo Vincent de Gaulejac menciona que los sujetos no pueden cambiar la historia en la medida en que lo acontecido ya aconteció, pero que estos sujetos pueden cambiar la forma en que la historia actúa en ellos o ellas (de Gaulejac 2002:31). Nuestras historias paralelas y disímbolas nos quedan como un monolito inaccesible, lejano, etéreo y eterno, pero las acciones de lo que excavamos, interpretamos y escribimos día a día es la única forma en que los arqueólogos podemos incidir sobre algo que a la postre se convertirá en historia. Ahí, es donde algún día los arqueólogos del futuro interpretarán si este coloquio de arqueología transnacional, que contribuyó desde su propia especificidad en algo a dirimir nuestras diferencias y aprovechar nuestras similitudes.

Part III, Chapter 1

Conservación del Patrimonio y Transformación de la Sociedad en las Cordilleras Centrales de la Península de Baja California, México

María de la Luz Gutiérrez M.

RESUMEN

La sierra de San Francisco es una región cultural que se encuentra inscrita en la lista de Patrimonio Mundial de la UNESCO desde 1993. La razón de esta inscripción se basó en los excepcionales sitios de arte rupestre que aquí se concentran, principalmente los del estilo denominado "Gran Mural". El arte rupestre es tan solo uno de los elementos que conforman este ancestral paisaje de naturaleza extraordinaria. Desde 1994 los recursos culturales de esta sierra han sido administrados por un Plan de Manejo que fue elaborado con el consenso de sus habitantes y de todos los sectores involucrados con el patrimonio. En la ponencia se describirá brevemente como ha sido este proceso de gestión y se analizará la estrategia a partir de dos aspectos fundamentales e indisociables: el éxito en la conservación del patrimonio y el fracaso en los intentos para preservar la identidad cultural de los serranos. La pobreza extrema de la región y el interés del gobierno del estado por masificar el turismo hacia los sitios rupestres, han generado un profundo cambio social, influenciado negativamente a las comunidades no solo de la sierra de San Francisco, sino de toda la región donde se expresa esta tradición de pintura rupestre monumental.

ABSTRACT

The Sierra de San Francisco is a cultural region that was placed on the UNSECO's World Heritage List in 1993. The purpose of the listing was to recognize the exceptional rock art sites in the area, including many in the "Great Mural" style. The rock art is just one of the elements that make up this amazing ancestral landscape. Since 1994 the cultural resources of this area have been administered through the cooperation of the local residents and relevant governmental agencies under a formal Management Plan. This paper describes the management plan and explores two important consequences of its implementation: the successful conservation of the cultural patrimony and the failure to preserve the cultural identity of the serranos people. The extreme poverty of the region and the state government's interest in expanding tourism to the rock art sites have generated significant social changes, negatively affecting the communities, not only in the Sierra de San Francisco, but of the entire region, where the amazing pictographs occur.

María de la Luz Gutiérrez M. Centro INAH – Baja California Sur

Introducción

La investigación y valoración del arte rupestre en México ha sido un proceso lento y complejo. Actualmente sigue siendo uno de los materiales arqueológicos menos estudiados del país y, por consiguiente, su importancia como patrimonio cultural es poco reconocida. Esta situación es paradójica en virtud de que esta manifestación es muy abundante y distintiva, sobre todo hacia el norte del país, región que por circunstancias geográficas y climáticas ha permitido la buena conservación y visibilidad de numerosos sitios con arte rupestre.

Afortunadamente el panorama está cambiando. En la década de 1980 se inician proyectos de investigación que lo abordan de manera consistente y sistemática. El incremento en el inventario de sitios rupestres demuestra este interés, aunque todavía es insuficiente. La península de Baja California es una región que ejemplifica muy bien este cambio de actitud. Localizada en el noroeste de México, permaneció casi inexplorada hasta muy avanzado el siglo XX. Su condición casi insular mantuvo a los pueblos nativos relativamente aislados de las influencias continentales, permitiendo el desarrollo de excepcionales complejos culturales. Y, precisamente, uno de los rasgos más sobresalientes de la prehistoria peninsular es que estos pueblos promovieron, en algunas regiones, la producción masiva de arte rupestre desde tiempos muy remotos. Actualmente el inventario de sitios rupestres peninsulares representa el 43 por ciento del total nacional.

La región de la península que quizás presenta más profusión de esta manifestación cultural es la que ocupan las cordilleras centrales. Con mucha frecuencia, sus paisajes se encuentran matizados por el arte rupestre y su abundancia y complejidad es, en ocasiones, abrumadora. En ciertas regiones es omnipresente, se observa en cañadas y mesas, en filos y portezuelos, en tinajas y malpaíses.

Los filos son pasajes estrechos que dividen las partes más elevadas de los arroyos, es decir, donde nacen, los cuales se denominan localmente testeras. Los portezuelos son pasajes naturales bajos entre cañadas. Las tinajas son oquedades naturales excavadas en la roca madre por erosión eólica y pluvial, aquí se concentra el agua de lluvia y fueron esenciales para determinar los movimientos estacionales de los indígenas. Estas tinajas debieron haber detentado un profundo simbolismo para estos pueblos y en muchas de ellas se concentran petroglifos de motivos acuáticos y terrestres. Los "malpaíses" son derrames de lava que se encuentran fracturados en miles de bloques. Algunos de estos fueron ideales para la realización de petroglifos.

Marca, rubrica, se integra al paisaje con notable persistencia, lo inscribe simbólicamente y le otorga un significado cultural mostrándonos con claridad el fluido movimiento de los pueblos que lo crearon, testigos y protagonistas del partir y el retornar (Conkey 1984:264-267; Gutiérrez Martínez y Hyland 2002:30) En este sentido, uno de los principales valores de esta región es el propio paisaje, entendido como el extenso espacio en el que, a través del arte rupestre, fueron fijados los pensamientos y las memorias de sus antiguos moradores.

Adicionalmente, estas montañas fueron el escenario de otro extraordinario suceso prehistórico: el desarrollo de la tradición rupestre de los Grandes Murales. Para describir estas pinturas rupestres, Harry Crosby acuñó el término Gran Mural (Crosby 1972) el cual ganó una amplia aceptación. El área de distribución de este estilo incluye las sierras de San Borja, San Juan, San Francisco y Guadalupe. Hasta el momento las sierras mas investigadas son las de San Francisco y Guadalupe en las cuales se han registrado cerca de 1,150 sitios rupestres, incluyendo sitios pintados, grabados, mixtos y geoglifos (Esquivel 1995; García-Uranga 1986; Gutiérrez 1992; Gutiérrez Martínez y García-Uranga 1990; Gutiérrez Martínez 2003) (Figura III.1.1).

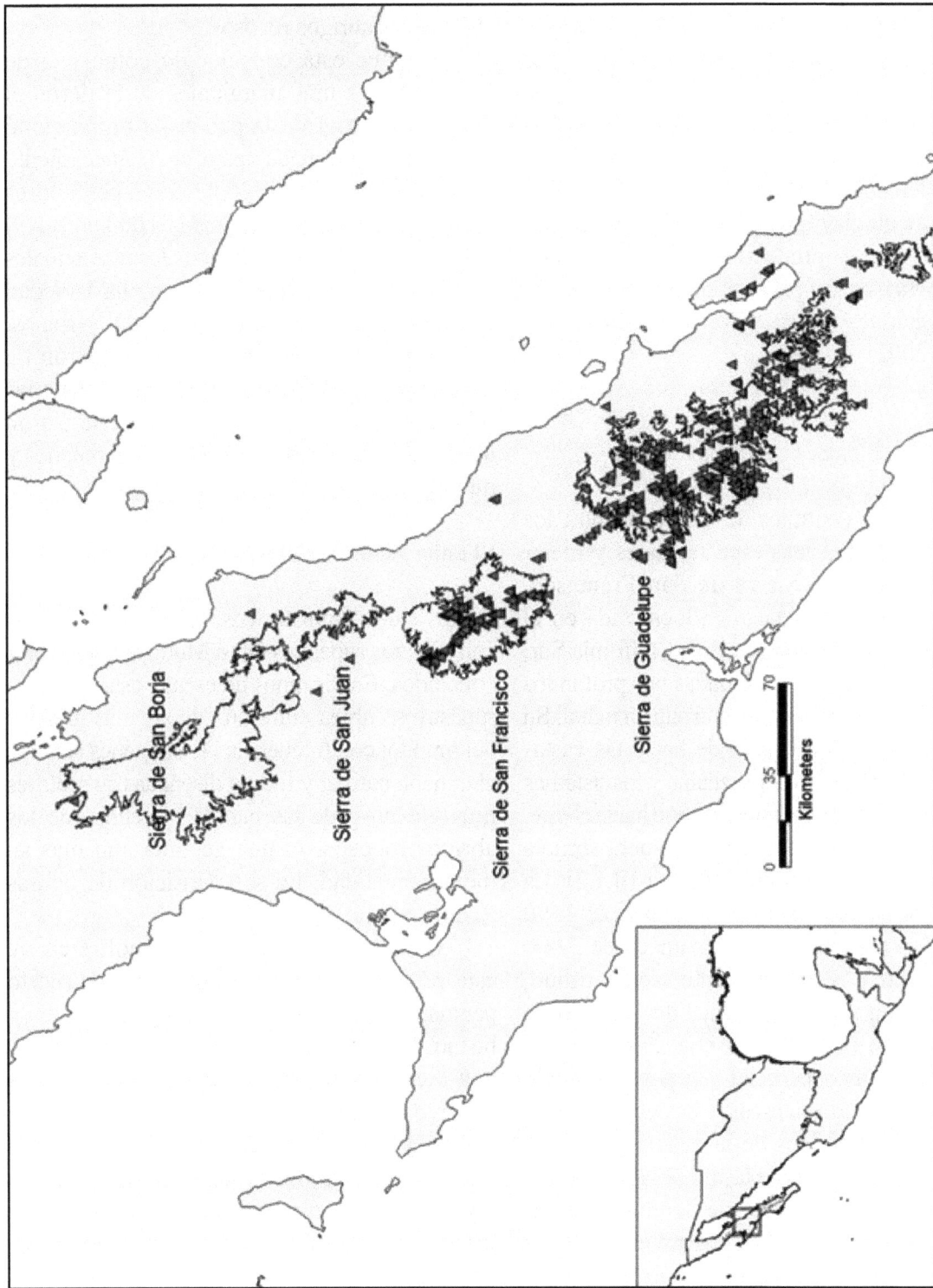

Figura III.1.1. Las Cordilleras Centrales de la península de Baja California. Los triángulos rojos indican los sitios con arte rupestre localizados hasta el momento.

Por tratarse de un tema de estudio excepcional, a partir de 1980 el Instituto Nacional de Antropología e Historia (INAH) inició en la región una investigación arqueológica de largo plazo. En 1997 concluyó la primera fase de dicha investigación, la cual tuvo como escenario la Sierra de San Francisco y amplios sectores aledaños. Este proceso contribuyó indudablemente a resolver asuntos y prioridades de la arqueología regional, posibilitó un análisis más enfocado y productivo del arte rupestre y sentó las bases para el planteamiento de investigaciones futuras (Gutiérrez Martínez y Hyland 2002)

LA SIERRA DE SAN FRANCISCO

De las sierras centrales, la que concentra los sitios Gran Mural más espectaculares y mejor conservados es la Sierra de San Francisco, pequeña cordillera volcánica localizada en el extremo norte del estado de Baja California Sur; presenta altas mesas seccionadas por profundos cañones que se extienden en un patrón radial. Su vertiente occidental desciende hacia las vastas planicies del Desierto del Vizcaíno y los sistemas lagunares del Pacífico, mientras que hacia el este, las montañas se encuentran de manera abrupta con el Golfo de California (Figura III.1.2). La sierra alcanza una elevación máxima de 1590 m.s.n.m. y tiene un área aproximada de 3,600 km², su clima es generalmente seco y cálido, recibiendo en promedio menos de 100 mm de precipitación por año. En consecuencia, las fuentes de agua superficial son pocas, estando bastante confinadas a escasos arroyos perennes y tinajas. En términos de la vegetación, en la sierra ocurren algunas de las más espectaculares comunidades del Desierto de Sonora, mientras que hábitats riparios relativamente frondosos se encuentran a lo largo de los arroyos mejor irrigados. Sus cauces principales son: San Pablo, San Pedro, San Gregorio, San Gregorito, Cuesta Blanca, Los Monos, Santa Marta, Palmarito, El Parral, El Infierno, La Ascensión y El Batequi; estos arroyos y sus afluentes contienen abundantes abrigos rocosos.

Aunque esta considerado como uno de los ambientes más marginales de la tierra, el Desierto Central de la península proporcionó condiciones adecuadas para el establecimiento de grupos cazadores-recolectores-pescadores desde el Pleistoceno terminal (10,000 años AP) hasta el arribo de los misioneros Jesuitas a finales del siglo XVII. Utilizando la amplia variedad de ambientes costeros, de planicie y serranos, los indígenas siguieron un intenso patrón de movilidad en la búsqueda de alimento, materias primas y agua. Como resultado de este patrón los sitios arqueológicos en el área son muchos y muy diversos.

El estilo pictórico Gran Mural

De los sitios prehistóricos, los abrigos rocosos con pinturas rupestres Gran Mural son los mejor conocidos. En términos de escala, esta tradición rupestre se ubica entre una de las más grandes del mundo; con frecuencia las imágenes rebasan el tamaño natural y fueron diseñadas en sectores muy elevados de las paredes y techos de los abrigos rocosos, lo que acentúa aún mas su monumentalidad. La sobreposición de figuras es muy común.

Gracias a la naturaleza geológica de esta región y al clima seco del semidesierto peninsular, su estado de conservación es muy bueno, encontrándose a veces enormes paneles con cientos y aun miles de figuras pintadas en vivos colores. El estilo es esencialmente realista y esta dominado por figuras humanas y animales, terrestres y acuáticas diseñadas en rojo y negro, y esporádicamente en blanco y amarillo (Figura III.1.3). Abundan también los sitios con petroglifos, muchos de los cuales concentran miles de figuras individuales; éstos se localizan hacia las mesas intermontanas y las

Figura III.1.2. La sierra de San Francisco presenta altas mesas seccionadas por profundos cañones, Desde aquí una vista de su vertiente occidental; se alcanzan a ver los sistemas lagunares del Pacífico y los picachos de la Sierra de Santa Clara.

Figura III.1.3. Panel este de Cueva Pintada, Arroyo de San Pablo, Sierra de San Francisco. En el estilo Gran Mural predominan las figuras humanas y animales diseñadas especialmente en rojo y negro.

planicies aledañas a la sierra. El arte rupestre es tan solo uno de los elementos que conforman este extraordinario y ancestral paisaje. La inscripción de la Sierra de San Francisco en la lista de Patrimonio Mundial se basó en los excepcionales sitios Gran Mural que aquí se concentran.

Las primeras referencias de los Grandes Murales se encuentran en los registros de los Jesuitas del siglo XVIII (Barco 1988). La era moderna en la investigación se inicia en los finales del siglo XIX cuando en 1894 Leon Diguet, un químico industrial que trabajaba en la mina de cobre El Boleo, en Santa Rosalía, realizó exploraciones en las sierras de San Francisco y de Guadalupe. Subsecuentemente publicó descripciones de varios de estos sitios (Diguet 1895).

La impresión de los Jesuitas que en algún momento visitaron sitios Gran Mural fue que las pinturas eran "viejas". Los reportes de los Jesuitas Joseph Mariano Rothea y Francisco Escalante se encuentran en Barco (1988:221-212). Esta opinión se basó no solo en la valoración de las características físicas de la imaginería, sino, de manera más definitiva, en las respuestas que obtuvieron de sus informantes cuando les preguntaron acerca de las pinturas. Los grupos Cochimís locales negaron tener conocimiento acerca de la imaginería y de sus orígenes, atribuyendo su autoría a una antigua y desaparecida raza de gigantes que habían provenido del norte.

Los mitos relatan que seres gigantescos fueron reportados ampliamente en Baja California (Barco 1988:209-213) y coinciden con las leyendas europeas de las Amazonas de California. Es interesante notar que los Seri, cruzando el Golfo en Sonora también tuvieron mitos relacionados con gigantes y tenían la costumbre de atribuir sitios arqueológicos Seri y aún recientes atributos culturales a una antigua raza de gigantes (ver discusión en Bowen 1976:103-107).

Dada la política Jesuita de erradicar la religión nativa, la veracidad de tales respuestas esta abierta a un serio cuestionamiento.

Valoración del significado de la Sierra

Como hemos visto, el principal valor reconocido en estas montañas es su excepcional arte rupestre, pero para que el significado de esta expresión cultural sea conservado, existen otros valores que necesitan ser preservados. Sus valores históricos incluyen los sitios prehistóricos, pero también los restos de evidencia del periodo misional y la supervivencia de las tradiciones culturales serranas cuyas raíces se remontan a eventos históricos del siglo XVIII. Existen muy fuertes valores estéticos, no solo en su espectacular arte rupestre, sino también en la belleza del paisaje y en la vegetación de los cañones y mesas. Sus valores científicos entran en el campo de acción de la investigación de su biodiversidad y alto grado de endemismo de especies de flora y fauna, así como en el estudio y conservación de los sitios de arte rupestre. Finalmente, la Sierra tiene un fuerte valor social en el papel que su cultura juega en la conservación de los vínculos tradicionales entre las comunidades serranas y los sudcalifornianos y mexicanos en general, en contribuir para la apreciación de la verdadera historia de Baja California desde la prehistoria, a través del periodo misional hasta el presente. El "misterio" del origen de las pinturas ha sido por mucho tiempo un importante valor simbólico; este es ahora menguado con el avance de la investigación arqueológica, no obstante, para muchos, permanecerá como un valor perdurable (Gutiérrez et al. 1996)

La política general para la administración de estos recursos, destaca la preservación de aquellos valores que juntos le dan significado a la Sierra, mientras que al mismo tiempo la conservación se constituya en una fuente de beneficio económico. El desarrollo de la zona debe ser sustentable y compatible con la preservación de sus valores educativos, históricos y ambientales, permitiendo que de esta manera sean usados y disfrutados por las generaciones presentes y futuras.

Gestión del Patrimonio Cultural

Antecedentes

El proceso de evangelización que inició en la península a finales del siglo XVII provocó la total desaparición de los antiguos pobladores de estas tierras, artífices del arte rupestre de la región. Los actuales habitantes de la sierra de San Francisco descienden de empleados misionales hispánicos que se establecieron en San Ignacio hace más de 150 años o bien de administradores y mineros de la Compañía Francesa El Boleo, la cual extrajo el cobre de la región desde finales del siglo XIX. Durante años estas poblaciones se mantuvieron casi completamente aisladas al interior de las montañas.

Antes de 1970, los serranos subsistían de la cría de ganado caprino y vacuno y la producción de queso, la densidad de población era baja y en general el área carecía de vías de comunicación. Estas condiciones permitieron que el paisaje y los sitios arqueológicos se mantuvieran en equilibrio y así, durante años, sólo los residentes de la sierra tuvieron conocimiento de la existencia de estas pinturas rupestres monumentales. Sin embargo, a raíz de las expediciones de Erle Stanley Gardner (1962) y Harry Crosby (1997) y la divulgación que se hizo de las mismas (Hambleton 1979), la situación dio un vuelco, el número de visitantes a la sierra se incrementó considerablemente, generándose un mosaico de problemas.

Los visitantes empezaron a contratar a los serranos como guías y a rentar las bestias de monta y carga necesarias para las expediciones. Esto generó una fuente de ingresos alternativa, pero indudablemente fue un factor que detonó severas transformaciones en la idiosincrasia de estas personas. En 1990 los habitantes de la sierra

no rebasaban los 250, para el 2008, la población se incrementó a 482 personas; esto nos habla de los cambios demográficos que ha experimentado la región a raíz de la apertura de caminos y la introducción de nuevas ideas.

Santa Marta y San Francisco de la Sierra

Antes de 1984, el turismo que visitaba estas montañas para disfrutar de su arte rupestre, ingresaba a la sierra por el único camino que en ese entonces existía: el que conduce al valle de Santa Marta, localizado en las estribaciones meridionales de la Sierra de San Francisco. Desde aquí los expedicionarios contrataban a los guías y rentaban las bestias de monta y carga que les permitían llegar a los cañones donde se concentra el Gran Mural. Sin embargo en 1984, la construcción del camino que conduce a la población de San Francisco de la Sierra, detonó un dramático cambio: poco a poco, el turismo prefirió la nueva vía ya que facilitaba el acceso a los arroyos norteños, donde se localizan los sitios y paisajes más espectaculares. Antes, alcanzar esos parajes requería de largas jornadas a lomo de mula; con el camino los tiempos se redujeron considerablemente pero la transformación de las comunidades y el entorno se agudizó. Un aspecto adicional que hace de este camino una vía muy atractiva, es que asciende gradualmente a las partes más altas de la sierra, lo que permite al visitante observar interesantes panorámicas de la planicie desértica del Vizcaíno, los sistemas lagunares del Pacífico, los cañones de la Ascensión y San Pablo y la Sierra de Santa Clara, cuyas solitarias cumbres se elevan hacia el este, casi colindando con el mar (Figura III.1.2).

La nueva situación generó que los habitantes de San Francisco de la Sierra experimentaran un apogeo en sus actividades como prestadores de servicios turísticos y una especialización en el oficio de guía-arriero, mientras que los de Santa Marta, padecieron una declinación en sus oportunidades laborales, a pesar de que ellos fueron los pioneros en este oficio y tuvieron el liderazgo durante años. Actualmente, la gran mayoría de estos guías-arrieros enfrentan una situación de escasez de trabajo y ausencia de incentivos para mejorar su actividad como guías, lo que se ha traducido en un mal servicio y falta de entrenamiento de las nuevas generaciones, quienes desconocen el oficio y las ubicaciones de los sitios rupestres.

Debido al aumento de visitantes y la falta de control, los sitios rupestres sufrieron el saqueo de elementos arqueológicos de superficie o bien recuperados a través de excavaciones informales. Algunas pinturas rupestres fueron dañadas, aunque afortunadamente poco. Las actividades de los visitantes se diversificaron, transgrediendo la legislación establecida, cuando, el arte rupestre empezó a ser objeto de investigaciones arqueológicas sin que existiera el conocimiento y control de las autoridades correspondientes. En diciembre de 1993 la sierra fue inscrita en la Lista de Patrimonio Mundial de la UNESCO, colocándola en el centro del interés internacional.

Implementación del Plan de Manejo

Un aspecto fundamental a lo largo de todos estos años ha sido la administración de este patrimonio cultural. La estrategia se forjó de manera gradual y paralela a la investigación arqueológica, consolidándose en 1994 con la cristalización y puesta en marcha del Plan de Manejo de la Sierra de San Francisco. Ese año coincidieron en la región dos proyectos de investigación en torno al arte rupestre de la sierra, uno arqueológico y otro de conservación (Stanley 1996): Proyecto Arte Rupestre de Baja California Sur (INAH, Fondo Nacional Arqueológico 1993-1994) y Conservation of Rock Art in Baja California, México (The Getty Conservation Institute 1994-1995). Fue entonces que se dieron las condiciones óptimas para generar una estrategia de protección en virtud de las nuevas circunstancias; diversas entidades interesadas en la preservación del arte

rupestre convinieron en la necesidad de unificar criterios y establecer un marco normativo: el Instituto de Conservación Getty, la asociación Amigos de Sudcalifornia y el INAH, unimos esfuerzos con el objetivo de diseñar y poner en marcha el Plan de Manejo. El modelo adaptado para el diseño de este Plan emana de The Burra Charter of Australia ICOMOS (1992; Pearson and Sullivan 1995) y enfatiza la importancia de definir, en primera instancia, el significado que tiene este lugar patrimonial, de manera que todas las estrategias de política y manejo sean consistentemente dirigidas hacia la preservación de los valores que lo hacen importante. Otro rasgo fundamental es la intervención total de todos aquellos grupos que tienen un interés en el área bajo discusión. Cabe destacar que esta participación en el proceso de planeación no tenía precedentes localmente.

De este modo se convocó a representantes de todos los sectores involucrados con el patrimonio cultural de la sierra, es decir: las comunidades serranas, ejidatarios, prestadores de servicios turísticos nacionales y extranjeros, Gobiernos Estatal y Municipal, Secretaría de Medio Ambiente y Recursos Naturales y la Reserva de la Biosfera El Vizcaíno. Esto permitió la conciliación de intereses y la toma de decisiones a través del *consenso*.

Las principales amenazas

Es necesario reconocer que el principal peligro lo constituye la presión que el turismo ejerce sobre los sitios Gran Mural. Al respecto la densidad, el patrón de distribución y la diversidad de los sitios prehistóricos en la región, nos enfrenta a una zona arqueológica sumamente expuesta, ya que los sitios se encuentran por todos lados, muchos de ellos a lo largo de los senderos que se siguen para acceder a ranchos y cañadas. Otro factor a considerar es la vulnerabilidad de los paneles rupestres, los cuales pueden sufrir daños irreversibles por actos vandálicos; a esto hay que agregar que los depósitos arqueológicos sufren un grave deterioro con el caminar constante de los visitantes y del abundante ganado caprino y bovino, el cual utiliza estos abrigos rocosos como refugio; la remoción del suelo limo-arenoso muy poco compactado, altera la información arqueológica y levanta partículas de ese depósito que se adhieren a las paredes pintadas, por solo mencionar algunos de los factores que deterioran el contexto general. Por lo anterior, en sus inicios, el Plan de Manejo se enfocó en mitigar el impacto de los visitantes en los sitios y su entorno y controlar y monitorear el acceso.

Desde los 1970s, los visitantes de la Sierra, establecieron *de facto* un circuito regular hacia los sitios Gran Mural más difundidos. Una de las prioridades inmediatas fue proporcionar medidas de protección directa en estos sitios para reducir su deterioro. Estas medidas consistieron en la instalación de andadores, barandales, cercos, senderos de acceso y señales informativas en seis de los sitios Gran Mural más visitados. En 2005 se habilitó un sitio más: Cuesta Palmarito. la habilitación de Cuesta Palmarito fue posible gracias al financiamiento otorgado por el Consejo Nacional Adopte una Obra de Arte A.C. y es el más popular en el sector sur de la Sierra (Figura III.1.4).

Políticas para el acceso de visitantes

Uno de los principales problemas que enfrentaba la zona era el acceso no controlado a los sitios, con o sin guías, y en consecuencia, la explotación de los sitios Gran Mural desde diversas perspectivas. La cantidad anual de visitantes hacia la Sierra había sido tradicionalmente baja, pero con la designación de Patrimonio Mundial el número se elevó substancialmente. Si continuaba el acceso no controlado, era de esperarse que algunos de los sitios raramente visitados, muy importantes por la integridad de sus depósitos arqueológicos, cayeran bajo una presión creciente.

La administración de una zona arqueológica como la que nos ocupa, con cientos de sitios arqueológicos esparcidos en miles de kilómetros cuadrados, precisó el diseño de una estrategia *sui generis*: ciertos conceptos y lineamientos generales fueron presentados como una propuesta preliminar y aprobados por consenso, estos son: la extensión de la zona arqueológica y el área rupestre; las rutas de acceso a la sierra; las zonas abiertas al público o de acceso restringido y diferentes niveles de visita (Gutiérrez Martínez y Hyland 2002).

LA ZONA ARQUEOLÓGICA Y EL ÁREA RUPESTRE

La mayoría de los sitios con pinturas rupestres y petroglifos se concentran en los cañones y mesas de la sierra, sin embargo, sus autores extendieron su territorio más allá de las estribaciones del macizo montañoso, hacia la costa del golfo y las planicies desérticas del Vizcaíno. En consecuencia tenemos la zona arqueológica y el área rupestre; la zona arqueológica, circunda prácticamente toda el área rupestre e incluye ambientes diversos como la costa del golfo, las vertientes de la sierra y las planicies desérticas del Vizcaíno, incluyendo su contacto con la laguna de San Ignacio; a su vez, la zona arqueológica se localiza totalmente dentro de la Reserva de la Biosfera el Vizcaíno (Figuras III.1.5 y III.1.6).

Vías de acceso

Se autorizaron dos caminos para el acceso del turismo a la sierra: el que conduce a San Francisco de la Sierra y el que conduce al Valle de Santa Marta. Ambos poblados se constituyen en los únicos puntos de partida permitidos para ingresar al área rupestre. Aquí se preparan las expediciones, se contratan los servicios de los guías/arrieros y en su caso se rentan las bestias de monta y carga (Figura III.1.7).

Figura III.1.4. Panel central de Cuesta Palmarito, Arroyo de Santa Marta, Sierra de San Francisco. La imagen muestra uno de los descansos del andador.

Niveles de visita

Las visitas a la Sierra se clasificaron en cuatro niveles. El Nivel I incluye aquellos sitios de fácil acceso por vehículo y caminatas limitadas; el Nivel II consiste en sitios seleccionados dentro del arroyo de San Pablo y el Arroyo del Parral que son accesibles a lomo de mula o caminatas extensivas, desde los poblados Santa Marta y San Francisco de la Sierra y que requieren acampar. Acampar es permitido solo en parajes designados. En orden de evitar la degradación ambiental de las áreas de acampado en los arroyos y para prevenir la saturación de los sitios Gran Mural, se han definido cantidades máximas de visitantes tanto para los sitios como para los campamentos. El Nivel III incluye otros sitios que se encuentran

en áreas menos frecuentadas tales como el Arroyo de San Gregorio, San Gregorito y el del Batequi, que pueden ser visitadas sólo tramitando un permiso con dos semanas de anticipación. Los grupos autorizados son acompañados por un custodio del INAH. El Nivel IV está diseñado para propósitos de investigación y el permiso solo se otorga a investigadores acreditados por el INAH y por la Reserva de la Biosfera El Vizcaíno (Figura III.1.7).

Este sistema permite al visitante la experiencia de un amplio rango de sitios y al mismo tiempo protege la mayoría de aquellos que están bastante bien conservados. En este sentido los sitios más populares han permanecido abiertos bajo este Plan.

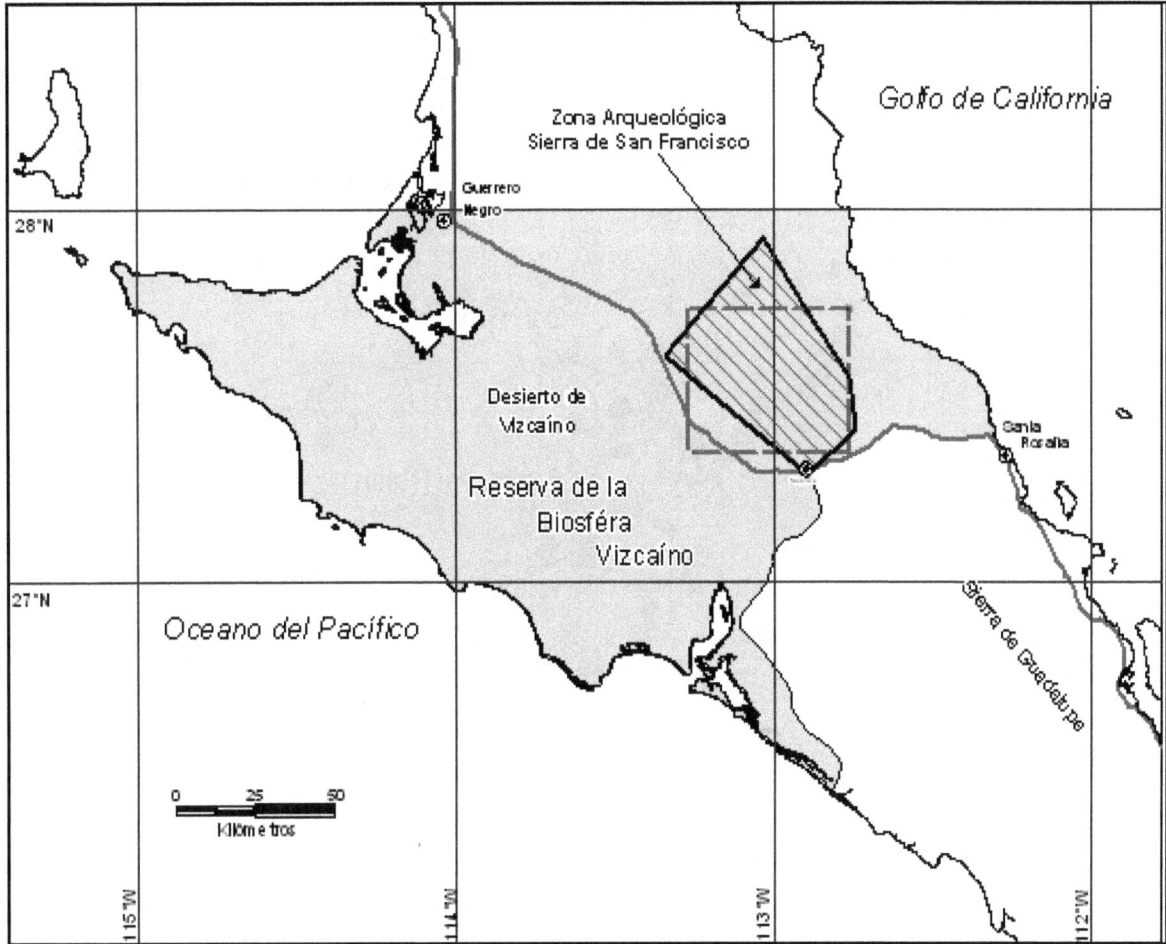

Figura III.1.5. Afortunadamente la Sierra de San Francisco se ubica totalmente dentro de la Reserva de la Biosfera El Vizcaíno, lo que coadyuva en la protección de sus recursos culturales.

Vigilancia

Como un asunto específico de la administración del turismo se ha establecido un proceso de monitoreo con base en la observación de la cantidad de visitantes que llegan a la sierra a lo largo del año, las rutas preferidas y los intereses detectados. El monitoreo involucra la inspección de las condiciones de los sitios y su entorno, así como la ejecución de las regulaciones concernientes a los visitantes y guías. Destacan las siguientes acciones:

Viajes periódicos de los custodios por rutas establecidas que cubren la totalidad del área rupestre;

Incremento de la vigilancia en todas las zonas durante la *temporada alta* (de octubre a mayo);

Inspecciones aleatorias a expediciones en zonas abiertas al público;

Participación de los custodios en la supervisión de las expediciones autorizadas para visitar áreas de acceso restringido.

En este sentido, un aspecto crucial fue el establecimiento de un Módulo de Información en San Ignacio, la población más próxima a la sierra. A través de éste se asegura la presencia

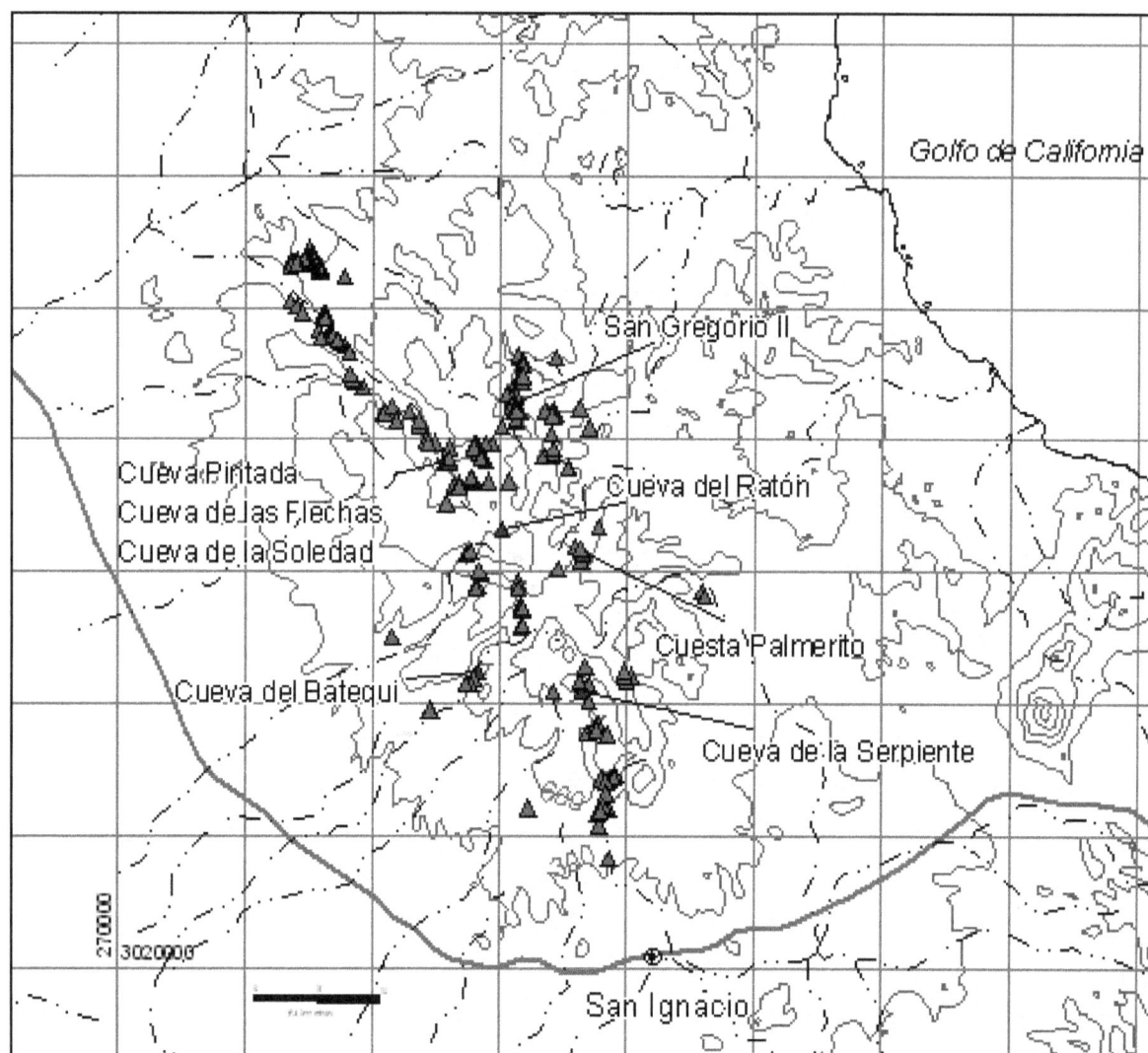

Figura III.1.6. Sitios Gran Mural en la Sierra de San Francisco. Se señalan algunos de los más populares.

permanente del INAH en la región, mientras que desempeña el doble papel para el público de ser un Centro de Interpretación y un centro de reservaciones y orientación para visitar la Sierra.

Requisito fundamental para el éxito en la conservación de las pinturas es la participación activa de la población local. La protección adecuada de los sitios depende de los guías locales que acompañan a los visitantes, y de tres custodios del INAH residentes en la sierra, los cuales se ocupan de la vigilancia de los sectores norte, centro y sur de la Sierra.

Evaluación del plan

Para asegurar el éxito del Plan de Manejo, el monitoreo y la revisión periódica son esenciales. Cada dos o tres años se realiza en San Ignacio una Reunión de Evaluación en la cual se hace un balance de los resultados obtenidos, así como una revisión de las problemáticas que han sido detectadas, para encontrar ante todo soluciones consensuadas. Hasta el momento se han realizado cuatro reuniones de evaluación.

Uno de los pilares fundamentales para el

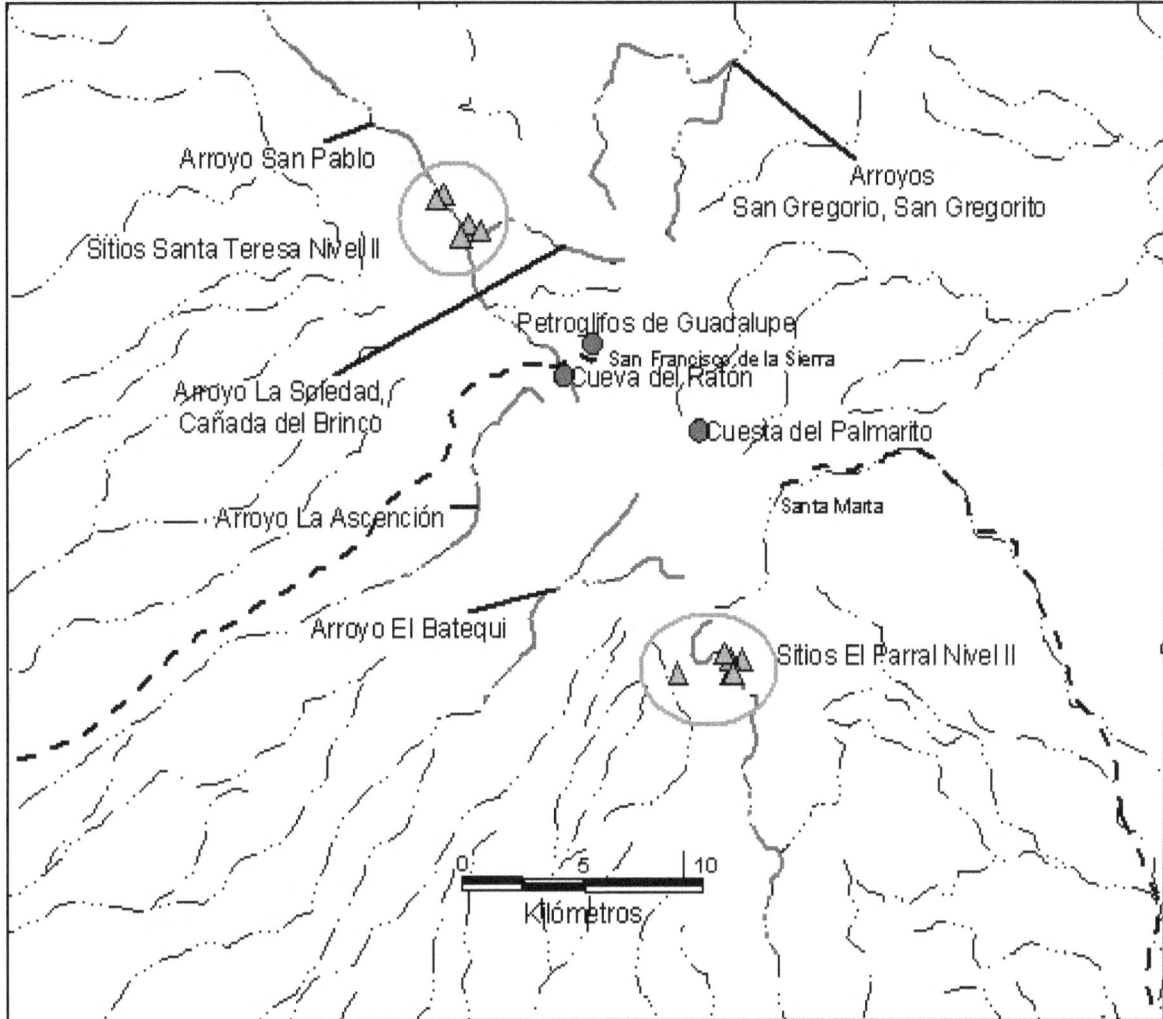

Figura III.1.7. Vías de Acceso autorizadas y Niveles de Visita.

éxito de este tipo de gestión y digamos, el espíritu que lo impulsa y hace válido, es el consenso, lo cual implica que ninguna decisión será tomada unilateralmente y por tanto, fuera de las reuniones de evaluación. Hay que recordar que esta es una estrategia flexible que puede evolucionar de acuerdo a las necesidades de desarrollo de la región, sin embargo hay aspectos medulares que no pueden cambiar, me refiero a aquellos que tienen que ver directamente con la estabilidad del arte rupestre; cambiarlos incidiría directamente en su deterioro y, entonces, el Plan de Manejo perdería su razón de ser.

A lo largo de estos años se han logrado avances significativos en torno a la administración y protección de esta herencia cultural. No obstante, ha habido sucesos que han vulnerado el Plan de Manejo, y ahora es el momento de hacer un balance acerca del estado actual de esta gestión.

PROBLEMAS RECIENTES

A partir del 2002 se desencadenaron una serie de acontecimientos que intentaron desequilibrar la estrategia. Estos sucesos se inician con la puesta en marcha de programas gubernamentales de desarrollo regional con cooperación estatal, nacional e internacional que fueron planteados a las comunidades de la sierra (*Proyecto Integral de Desarrollo Sostenible de la Reserva de la Biosfera el Vizcaíno*, Agencia Española de Cooperación Internacional. Proyecto Araucaria). Si bien las acciones emanadas de estos proyectos planteaban objetivos muy loables, sus responsables fallaron al ignorar los antecedentes en torno a la administración de los bienes culturales que el INAH había desarrollado en la región desde 1980 y, sobre todo, fue claro un desconocimiento absoluto de la idiosincrasia de los serranos y los visitantes, y la vulnerabilidad del arte rupestre. El INAH fue objeto de una campaña de desprestigio por parte de los responsables de estos programas quienes influyeron negativamente en las personas que hasta entonces habían sido nuestros aliados en la protección del patrimonio: los guías de la sierra.

Por presiones políticas, el director del INAH en Baja California Sur tomó la decisión unilateral de autorizar el ingreso de visitantes a la sierra sin mediar registro alguno. Esta decisión evidenció en ese momento, dos aspectos muy graves: 1) Se pasó por encima del espíritu del Plan de Manejo, el cual esgrime que cualquier cambio debe aprobarse por consenso y 2) dejó sentado un precedente de alto riesgo para el sostenimiento del Plan ya que cualquier otra inquietud por parte de la comunidad, del Gobierno del Estado o de organismos privados o públicos, por intermedio de la comunidad, se trasladaría al ámbito político. Desde entonces señalé el peligro de que a través de la coerción fuesen derrumbadas, una a una, todas aquellas medidas implementadas para la preservación del patrimonio, y desgraciadamente no me equivoqué.

En el 2006 el gobierno del estado de Baja California Sur dio a conocer un programa para la apertura de una red de caminos en la sierra de San Francisco. Casualmente, este programa surge paralelo al plan de desarrollo regional denominado Mar de Cortés, el cual fue diseñado a la sombra de intereses comerciales y políticos muy poderosos. Al amparo de estos planes, se manipulan las esperanzas de las comunidades, se generan enormes expectativas y el bien cultural se trasforma en un botín lucrativo y político que se puede explotar sin tomar en cuenta su vulnerabilidad y los valores que conlleva y que se deberían proteger.

Dadas las expectativas que generó el citado proyecto, no es difícil concluir que lo que se buscaba con estos caminos era generar la infraestructura indispensable para trasladar turistas en vehículos a los cañones de la sierra. De construirse muchas de éstas vías llegarían al núcleo del área rupestre donde el paisaje cultural es primigenio y cobija excepcionales sitios Gran Mural. Si se permite que este turismo de "entrada por salida" ingrese a los sectores donde actualmente se llega a través de eco-expediciones que tienen una duración de tres a cuatro días, la gran mayoría de los guías perderán la posibilidad de aprovechar racionalmente parte del patrimonio que hasta ahora ha sido dirigido a un turismo cultural.

Después de enfrentar presiones y situaciones muy desagradables con actores políticos de muy bajo perfil, y gracias a la oportuna intervención de las autoridades de la Reserva de la Biosfera El Vizcaíno, se logró detener el proyecto de apertura de caminos, aunque existen posibilidades de que tarde o temprano dicho proyecto se reactive. Habrá que estar muy alertas cada vez que se avecinen periodos electorales, pues es un hecho que eventos políticos como éste detonan o acentúan estas problemáticas. Lo que ya no fue posible detener fue la pavimentación de 10 de los 37 kilómetros del camino que conduce a San Francisco de la Sierra. En tres años más dicho camino estará totalmente asfaltado y es muy posible que con esta "facilidad" se ejerzan nuevas presiones sobre los sitios Gran Mural.

Todos sabemos lo que implica una carretera en una zona como esta, los riesgos son inminentes. Se está dotando a la sierra de la infraestructura esencial que podría, en un futuro no muy lejano, abrir la puerta a desarrollos urbanos que impactarían aquellos valores que, todavía, hacen de ésta una región excepcional. Esta imagen (Figura III.1.8) muestra claramente cómo el gobierno manipula la información con fines políticos y aunque no tengo la certeza, creo que se están preparando los nuevos escenarios: aquí se indica que esta carretera beneficiará a "9,000 personas para vivir mejor". Esto es falso y además absurdo. Sabemos por el censo mas reciente que la población total de la sierra no excede los 500 habitantes.

CONCLUSIONES

¿Cuáles han sido las fortalezas del Plan de Manejo a 16 años de su implementación? El modelo de administración ha demostrado ser una estrategia eficaz que ha contribuido a la conservación de los valores históricos, estéticos, científicos y simbólicos de la región. El paisaje, los sitios arqueológicos e históricos, los petroglifos y las pinturas rupestres se han mantenido estables. La investigación arqueológica se reguló y no ha habido saqueo de elementos arqueológicos como antaño.

¿Cuáles han sido las debilidades? El Plan de Manejo ha resultado ineficaz para coadyuvar en la preservación de los valores sociales de la región; por falta de espacio no es posible abundar acerca de como ha sido todo el proceso, pero debo decir que existe una gradual pérdida de las tradiciones y la identidad cultural. Mientras que el número de visitantes a la sierra se ha mantenido relativamente estable, la cantidad de guías se ha duplicado, lo que ha reducido las oportunidades de trabajo y ha enfrentado a las

Figura III.1.8. Camino a San Francisco de la Sierra. El letrero dice: "El Gobierno Federal moderniza un tramo de 9.5 kilómetros que beneficia a 9000 personas para vivir mejor" Sabemos que la población de la sierra no excede las 500 personas.

comunidades. Finalmente, es necesario señalar que el Plan de Manejo carece de un marco legal que le proporcione sustento y fuerza y queda claro que es débil ante los inminentes embates del "desarrollo y la modernidad"

¿Que lecciones hemos aprendido a lo largo de estos años? Durante el proceso de diseño e implementación del Plan de Manejo sabíamos de la importancia de conciliar intereses, tomar decisiones a través del consenso y, sobre todo, hacer partícipes a los representantes de todas las entidades que en aquel entonces se relacionaban con la sierra. Sin embargo, no previmos que al paso de los años, los entornos, las personas y los intereses cambiarían. Por citar algunos ejemplos: a) cuando se firmó este Plan de Manejo no se habían aprobado las reformas constitucionales que dieron origen a la enajenación de las tierras ejidales (Programa de Certificación de Derechos Ejidales, PROCEDE) convirtiendo a los ejidatarios de Baja California Sur en grandes latifundistas, ahora las mejores tierras están pasando a manos de empresarios y políticos; b) la principal limitante para fundar poblaciones grandes y desarrollos turísticos en la región era la escasez de agua, ahora existen las plantas desalinizadoras que producen agua potable de excelente calidad, esto ha elevado los precios de la tierra en toda la región; c) el gobierno del estado de Baja California Sur se transformó en estilo de administración cambiando democráticamente de partido, lo que implica un populismo desmedido como principal característica de la nueva administración. Todo esto ha incidido en las personas y sus intereses, lo que está llevando a la transformación irreversible de la cultura serrana, uno de los más importantes valores que hacían excepcional a la sierra de San Francisco e incluso a la región. Esta es una gran lección:

cuando en "áreas protegidas" existen núcleos de población marginados, es muy complicado mantener los escenarios en los que se generó el modelo de administración. Controlar el clamor por el "desarrollo" y el uso político del patrimonio es un trabajo arduo y en ocasiones casi imposible de lograr.

La abundancia de sitios rupestres localizados en las cordilleras centrales de la península de Baja California, la enorme extensión en donde se distribuyen y la escasez de recursos humanos y financieros, nos coloca como gestores ante una mega región arqueológica de difícil protección. La experiencia nos demuestra que sin la ayuda de la población local y sin la comprensión y apoyo de los tres sectores de gobierno, cualquier intento por preservar los valores culturales y naturales de ésta región fracasará. Es pues indispensable que los sectores privados y públicos sumemos esfuerzos para llegar a acuerdos que nos permitan establecer vínculos perdurables de amistad y alianzas estratégicas con las comunidades serranas que por generaciones han convivido con este patrimonio, y han sido la primera línea de defensa con la que contamos.

No obstante algunos tropiezos, seguiremos insistiendo tanto en la importancia de preservar este magnifico arte rupestre como en la trascendencia que tiene la investigación interdisciplinaria para lograr su gestión adecuada. Recordemos que el patrimonio adquiere un valor social desde el momento en que un grupo de personas lo reconocen como tal y es importante para su identidad, y es entonces cuando la arqueología trasciende entre las comunidades que coexisten con ese patrimonio, no solo porque aporta elementos para darles cohesión como sociedad, sino también porque puede contribuir a su desarrollo sustentable.

Part III, Chapter 2

Paquimé y el Museo de las Culturas del Norte en la construcción de una "nueva" identidad en el noroeste de Chihuahua

José Luis Punzo Díaz

RESUMEN

A partir de la construcción del Museo de las Culturas del Norte en 1996 y la declaratoria de la zona arqueológica de Paquimé como Patrimonio de la Humanidad por la UNESCO en 1998, se comenzó a forjar una identidad fuertemente enraizada en la exaltación del pasado prehispánico en el noroeste de Chihuahua, una zona fuertemente influenciada por la cultura mexicano-americana. Este proceso fue promovido por en primer lugar por la construcción del Museo de las Culturas del Norte, el cual mediante un discurso museográfico apologético nacionalista muy bien elaborado, se fundó como el centro para la formación de este orgullo comunitario. Así la declaratoria de la UNESCO y el otorgamiento del Premio Nacional de Ciencias y Artes en 1999, al ceramista del poblado de Mata Ortiz, Juan Quezada, volvió las miradas de las comunidades cultural mexicana y norteamericana a esta región. Eso convirtió al Centro Cultural Paquimé en preciado botín para las instituciones de cultura estatales y un punto importante para el desarrollo de programas de turismo cultural federal y estatal. Es en este marco que a través de la presente ponencia se trata de identificar cuáles han sido los elementos de formación identitaria en la región y como estos han repercutido de forma negativa y positiva en esa comunidad.

ABSTRACT

Since the construction of the Museo de las Culturas del Norte in 1996 and the declaration of the archaeological zone of Paquimé as a World Heritage site by UNESCO in 1998, a new identity strongly rooted in the exaltation of the pre-Hispanic past in Northwestern Chihuahua has been forged. This identity was first promoted by the creation of the Museo de las Culturas del Norte, which became the center of community pride. The recognition given by UNESCO and the National Award for Arts and Sciences in 1999 to the potter from the village of Mata Ortiz, Juan Quezada, focused the attention of the Mexican and American cultural communities to this region. These factors transformed the Paquimé Cultural Center into an important place for government cultural institutions as well as for the development of projects for cultural tourism at federal and state levels. In this paper I will identify which elements have impacted identity-formation in the region and if their impact has been negative and/or positive.

José Luis Punzo Díaz Centro INAH Durango

Parafraseando a Sian Jones (Jones 1997:1) me gustaría iniciar este trabajo diciendo que el rol que juega la arqueología en la construcción y legitimación de las identidades culturales es una de las tareas más importantes en la teoría y en la práctica arqueológica. Así en esta tarea, hoy día, sería muy ingenuo pensar que el quehacer arqueológico no está ligado o impacta en los programas políticos, culturales y económicos de los estados en todos sus niveles.

La región noroeste de Chihuahua y sus habitantes

Para ubicar el peculiar lugar donde se localiza el Museo de las Culturas del Norte y la zona arqueológica de Paquimé, quisiera cuando menos de manera general caracterizar su región inmediata.

Esta es la región noroeste de Chihuahua, la cual se compone de los municipios de Casas Grandes, Nuevo Casas Grandes, Janos, Galeana y Buenaventura. Se trata de una región eminentemente ganadera, donde también existen grandes extensiones cultivadas, ambos negocios muy productivos para muchos de sus dueños.

El centro poblacional de mayor envergadura es Nuevo Casas Grandes, el cual tiene un poco más de 50,000 habitantes, el conjunto de los cuatro municipios a los cuales nos referimos apenas cuentan con una población cercana a los 100,000 habitantes en un extenso territorio de 16,000 km², el cual es más grande que varios estados de la República Mexicana, como Tlaxcala o Querétaro.

El Museo de las Culturas del Norte y la zona arqueológica de Paquimé se ubican a las afueras del poblado de Casas Grandes, cercano al río del mismo nombre que irriga la región. Circundado por montañas y áridas extensiones de tierra, el verde del bosque de galería del río y sus huertas aledañas, forman un paisaje majestuoso.

En esta extensa y poco poblada región conviven distintos grupos sociales que se identifican a sí mismos como diferentes, asignándose un carácter étnico y/o religiosos: mormones, Lebarones, chinos, menonitas y tarahumaras que vienen como trabajadores temporales a la pizca; además de "mexicanos", como definen los "otros" al resto de la población. Cada uno de estos grupos sociales mantiene prácticas culturales continuas y restringidas muchas veces entre sí lo que genera fuertes sentimientos identitarios entre ellos y por supuesto los consabidos problemas xenófobos y racistas que tiene este tipo de convivencia, cuando a esa variabilidad se le correlacionan otras características como los son inteligencia o un carácter moral (Gosden 2006:3).

Paquimé antes de la declaratoria de Patrimonio Mundial

Como todos sabemos, el asentamiento arqueológico de Paquimé nunca se perdió en el tiempo, es decir siempre se supo de su existencia, así desde el primer grupo de españoles comandados por Francisco de Ibarra quienes llegaron a esta región en la década de 1560. Baltasar de Obregón, un soldado parte de dicha expedición, hace una extensa e interesante descripción de la ciudad abandonada de Paquimé, la cual compara con las ruinas romanas de España (Obregón 1988).

Será entrado el siglo XIX, cuando sobre todo viajeros norteamericanos describirán las ruinas de la ciudad de Paquimé. John Russell Bartlett (1854) y Adolph F. Bandelier (1880) y Carl Lumholtz (1902), son algunos de los viajeros que nos legaron sus descripciones. No obstante, en el imaginario de los habitantes del pueblo de Casas Grandes dichos sucesos pasaron prácticamente desapercibidos.

Sin embargo, otro hecho histórico cabe recalcar ya que forma parte importante hoy día de la identidad de los habitantes de Casas Grandes.

Durante la Revolución Mexicana se llevó a cabo una batalla para la toma del pueblo de Casas Grandes, los muertos en esa fueron sepultados en el hoy llamado Montículo de los Héroes de la Revolución, en Paquimé. Así todos los 6 de marzo, aniversario de la batalla, se realiza un acto cívico presidido por el presidente municipal y las autoridades del Centro Cultural Paquimé donde asisten un buen número de estudiantes de las escuelas del pueblo. En uno de los varios actos cívicos que enaltecen la importancia de la zona arqueológica en la identidad de los habitantes del pueblo de Casas Grandes.

Es muy interesante que en el transcurso de la investigación para elaborar este trabajo, es que en entrevistas con distintas personas del poblado de Casas Grandes todos coincidieron que fue la llegada de Di Peso en 1958 (Di Peso 1974). Sus trabajos lo que pudiera colocarse como el inicio de la revaloración de la zona arqueológica de forma más importante, no obstante también se comentó de forma reiterada que aun antes de la llegada de Di Peso las "tapias" de Paquimé servían de juego para todos los niños del pueblo. Desde entonces ya eran frecuentes las escapadas a buscar ollas o algún otro recuerdito de la antigua ciudad, cuestión ya notada por Lumholtz desde principios de siglo, quién menciona que los habitantes del pueblo habían encontrado vasijas y escudillas las cuales vendían a anticuarios o las dejaban para su propio uso. Dice el viajero noruego que los metates eran muy apreciados por los habitantes del valle y para él eran – sin disputa – los más bellos que había visto (Lumholtz 1945:87-88). Esto me parece relevante ya que cuando menos desde inicios el siglo XX, entre la gente de Casas Grandes, Paquimé existió en su vida cotidiana, dándole un valor otorgado socialmente, ya sea económico o utilitario por lo que fue significado e incorporado dentro de sus pautas de identidad.

Tras los trabajos de Di Peso, Paquimé regresó a su tranquilidad y continuó con su valor para sus habitantes, siendo zona de juegos de los estudiantes de la región, aunque ya hacia los años

setentas y ochentas muchas de las escuelas de Nuevo Casas Grandes, Galeana y Buenaventura y no sólo de Casas Grandes, acudían a visitar la zona arqueológica.

No obstante que la importancia o el conocimiento de Paquimé trascendió más allá de Casas Grandes en esta época, en lugares como Ciudad Juárez o Chihuahua el conocimiento de Paquimé era prácticamente nulo, de hecho eran más conocidos en Juárez los bares y las fiestas que había en Nuevo Casas Grandes por la gente que estudiaba en "la Juárez" en la colonia Juárez, que la zona arqueológica (llamada hoy, Academia Juarez Mexico Institute, manejada por la comunidad mormona que vive en ese poblado del municipio de Casas Grandes). Por otra parte, sabemos que ya desde estos años existían en Nuevo Casas Grandes varios negocios que utilizaban el nombre de Paquimé, tal vez el más famoso y que continua en operaciones hasta hoy es el Hotel Paquimé de la familia Piñón.

En ese marco se realizaban las visitas a la zona arqueológica, sobre todo por un público local y en muy baja escala por su lejanía de los grandes centros poblacionales. Pese a no tener una gran cantidad de datos sobre las estadísticas de visitantes antes de 1996, sabemos que a fines de los ochenta y principios de los años noventa, en Paquimé se recibía un promedio de 3,000 visitantes al año.

PAQUIMÉ DESPUÉS DE LA DECLARATORIA DE PATRIMONIO MUNDIAL

El Museo de las Culturas del Norte y la comunidad

Quisiera iniciar este apartado con un punto fundamental que resultó de este trabajo de investigación y es que todos los entrevistados coincidieron en que fue la creación del Museo de las Culturas del Norte entre 1992 y 1995 y su apertura al público el 26 de febrero de 1996 y no la declaratoria de Patrimonio Mundial en 1998, el punto que detonó en la comunidad la revaloración de Paquimé y la incorporación a la identidad de los habitantes de Casas Grandes y especialmente los de Nuevo Casas Grandes del pasado prehispánico. Así, en entrevistas entre la gente de Nuevo Casas Grandes, nos pudimos percatar, no solo eso, sino que incluso la mayoría no sabe que Paquimé es Patrimonio Mundial de la UNESCO.

De igual forma, el comentario general recabado en las entrevistas fue que el aporte más relevante que trajo consigo el Museo de las Culturas del Norte fue el incremento de turistas y que son solamente los empresarios dedicados del ramo los más beneficiados.

Veamos en la Tabla III.2.1 algunas cifras de visitantes al Museo en los últimos años para entender este fenómeno.

Desde la apertura del museo y la declaratoria, se registró una explosión de visitantes tremenda que llegó a su punto más alto a finales de los noventa y principios del año 2000. Estos datos se mantuvieron, más o menos constantes hasta 2005, cuando comenzó un retroceso en el número de visitantes, hasta el año pasado cuando llegó a su punto más bajo, creo esto debido a una serie de factores externos que han sucedido en la región.

Es importante recalcar que una de las funciones principales del Museo de las Culturas del Norte, no sólo ha sido la de promover la visita externa a éste, sino por el contrario, una de las estrategias fundamentales siempre fue la de promover una gran cantidad de proyectos de contribución social, como festivales, talleres, conciertos, obras de teatro, etc. que son la base fundamental de la vinculación con la comunidad, ya que estos participantes en talleres no se contabilizan como visitantes en las estadísticas, pero son niños con lo que trabajamos quienes generan ese sentido de pertenecía hacia el Museo y la zona arqueológica. Así por ejemplo en el último lustro han participado cerca de 200,000 personas. Por supuesto que muchísimos niños

Tabla III.2.1. Cifras de Visitantes al Museo de las Culturas del Norte

Año	Extranjeros	Total
2009	579	30,443
2008	2,272	46,047
2007	4,975	41,456
2006	10,782	51,929
2005	8,220	59,472
2004	13,450	71,784
2003	8,543	69,332
2002	13,118	70,961

de la región van varias veces al año al museo a distintas actividades, ya que este se ha convertido en el espacio cultural más importante de la región.

Pese a estas cifras, la trascendencia estatal del Museo de las Culturas del Norte y de Paquimé tiene un impacto limitado entre el grueso de la población. En Chihuahua pude percatarme que la gente pese a conocer la existencia de Paquimé y reconocer su importancia, en su gran mayoría, al preguntarles sobre lo que creían identificaba más a los chihuahuenses, daban cuenta que ese sentimiento se encuentra lejos del pasado prehispánico y se halla más ligado a otras cuestiones como la sierra tarahumara, Francisco Villa, o su herencia ranchera. Otro ejemplo que encontramos fue que preguntando entre el alumnado de UTEP en El Paso, Texas, muy pocos estudiantes sabían la existencia de Paquimé y del museo.

LA CONFORMACIÓN Y EL DISCURSO MUSEO DE LAS CULTURAS DEL NORTE

En el sexenio salinista se promovieron diferentes trabajos arqueológicos dentro de los llamados "megaproyectos", ya que contaron con recursos pocas veces vistos en la arqueología mexicana. La mayoría de estos recursos se aplicaron en zonas arqueológicas que fueron declaradas o ya eran Patrimonio Mundial por parte de la UNESCO. Así, desde las cúpula estatal se buscó revivir esa vieja tarea de la arqueología mexicana de exaltar la identidad nacional a través del pasado prehispánico (Fowler 1987:230), pero sobre todo y en una visión neoliberal, generar nuevos puntos de desarrollo turístico cultural que apoyara el ya floreciente turismo de sol y playa mexicano, uno de los motores más importantes de la economía mexicana después del petróleo.

En ese tenor uno de los megaproyectos del norte de México fue la construcción del Museo de las Culturas del Norte. Para este no se escatimó en recursos, se conjuntó a la investigadora emérita del INAH Beatriz Braniff para hacer el guión, Mario Schjetnan para hacer el diseño arquitectónico y a Jorge Agostoní para el diseño museográfico. Cabe analizar lo anterior desde esta perspectiva que presento.

Primero, el guión y la colección: Se trata de un guión realizado desde una perspectiva histórico-cultural sobre la Cultura Casas Grandes y en especial de Paquimé, basado en los estudios publicados por Charles Di Peso en los años setentas. Se trata de un guión que rebasa por mucho a un museo de sitio y reproduce un pasado histórico de 10,000 años desde cazadores de mamuts hasta grupos indígenas actuales en una vasta región que va desde Coahuila hasta Utah y Colorado. Así este discurso, una vez interpretado por los visitantes, posee una fuerte carga ideológica reflejada en los habitantes de la región de Casas Grandes. La colección que posee el museo es excelente, sobre todo en su parte de Paquimé, ya que además de la colección de las excavaciones de Di Peso, se ha enriquecido constantemente con distintas colecciones, especialmente repatriaciones que se han hecho desde el año 2000.

Segundo, el museo: El diseño arquitectónico del museo fue realizado por el afamado arquitecto mexicano Mario Schjetnan. Este edificio ha recibido premios internacionales. Se trata de un desarrollo circular que le permite al museógrafo generar remates visuales e isovistas muy interesantes que hacen que el visitante reciba una sorpresa a casi cada paso que da. De igual manera, tiene atrayentes detalles arquitectónicos como lo son alineamientos visuales entre los muros y por ejemplo la Atalaya de la cumbre del cerro Moctezuma en el patio cañón. Además de lo anterior tiene espacios muy bien diseñados para las tareas sustantivas del museo como son aéreas de servicios educativos, auditorio, áreas administrativas, bodegas, etc. Sin embargo, este magnífico edificio creo que tiene un problema importante y no tiene que ver con el diseño arquitectónico, sino con el diálogo arquitectónico con el sitio arqueológico, donde a mi juicio la escala del museo compite en demasía.

Tercero, la museografía: Jorge Agostoní ha sido uno de los referentes fundamentales de la museografía mexicana, participando en museos tan importantes como el Museo Nacional de Antropología, el museo de Historia Mexicana en Monterrey o el Museo Nacional de Arte. Por su diseño museográfico ha ganado varios premios, entre ellos en 1996 con el Museo de las Culturas del Norte: medalla de plata de la IV bienal de arquitectura mexicana. Por supuesto, que estos diseños museográficos han sido parte fundamental del estado mexicano para la creación de un sentimiento identitario nacional, cabe destacar la gran cantidad de paralelismos existentes entre los paneles que existen en el Museo Nacional de Antropología y los que se hicieron en el Museo de las Culturas del Norte. Así que desde mi punto de vista, los discursos museográficos de ambos museos tienen grandes puntos en común, pese a las décadas de diferencia en su creación: ambos cumplen con la misma función.

El turismo en la región noroeste de Chihuahua

Desde la creación del Museo de las culturas del Norte en 1996 y la declaratoria de Paquimé como Patrimonio Mundial en 1998, ha existido una transformación del sector turístico sobre todo en Nuevo Casas Grandes y en menor medida en Casas Grandes, para lo cual revisemos algunas cifras en las siguientes tablas. Esta información ha sido tomada del documento Proyecto turístico para la zona Noroeste, estrategia turística integral para la región noroeste de Chihuahua, elaborado por el Centro de Información Económica y Social de la Secretaría de Desarrollo Industrial del Gobierno del Estado de Chihuahua, de octubre a diciembre del año 2007.

Como podemos observar en la Tabla III.2.2, Casas Grandes no recibe sino una pequeña parte de los 2.66 millones de turistas que llegaron en el 2006. Sin embargo es importante destacar el impacto de éstos en una región tan poco poblada, que como hemos visto hace que destaque de manera importante.

Hablando ahora del Museo de las Culturas del Norte, tenemos que en ese mismo año, se recibió aproximadamente una visita de 43,000 personas, de los cuales el 65 por ciento fueron adultos y el 35 por ciento restante niños; el 24 por ciento fueron extranjeros, especialmente provenientes de los E.U.A, en un 93 por ciento. En las Tablas III.2.3 y III.2.4 podemos ver como se distribuyen por visitantes al museo por sus ciudades de origen.

Existen algunas operadoras turísticas norteamericanas especialmente Grand Circle travel quienes en conjunto con un par de prestadores de servicios de Nuevo Casas Grandes acaparan más del 90 por ciento de los turistas norteamericanos.

Se estima que desde la apertura del Museo de las Culturas del Norte se ha recibido a unos 350 mil turistas a la región, lo que podría significar una derrama económica directa de más de 25 millones de dólares para el sector turístico de Nuevo Casas Grandes y Casas Grandes.

Paquimé en la identidad de los habitantes del noroeste de Chihuahua

Como ya hemos mencionado, la identidad fundamentada en el orgullo de Paquimé se encuentra sobre todo entre los habitantes del pueblo de Casas Grandes desde hace muchísimos años, ejemplos patentes de ello los tenemos por todas partes, comenzando por el escudo del municipio, el cual incluye el Montículo de la Cruz.

Pero tenemos ejemplos de esto por todas partes en el pueblo, basta sentarse en la plaza y platicar con cualquier habitante para darnos cuenta. El ejemplo más reciente es el monumento a la "raza paquimeita" que se colocó a la entrada del pueblo en el nuevo par vial. Creo que retrata fehacientemente la idea apologética y etnocentrista que se ha usado para Paquimé a nivel de difusión y que se aprovecha en el guión del museo: el uso de ese gentilicio al que el discurso popular lo ha equiparado prácticamente como sinónimo de nación/grupo étnico, como ha pasado en muchas otras partes del mundo. (Díaz-Andreu 1996:57)

En cambio en Nuevo Casas Grandes el sentimiento identitario es más reciente y tiene que ver con la creación del museo y la declaratoria de Patrimonio Mundial. Aunque existían negocios como el Hotel Paquimé, tras estos eventos el uso de la palabra "Paquimé" se ha convertido en sinónimo de la región y se encuentra en más de 50 negocios de Nuevo Casas Grandes, así tenemos, Hotel, empacadora, cambios, lotes de autos, diversiones, insumos agrícolas, farmacia, etc. así como el uso de motivos prehispánicos en tiendas eléctricas, universidades, unión ganadera, entre muchísimas otras más.

Por si esto fuera poco existe una asociación de empresarios llamada Emprendedores Paquimé

Tabla III.2.2. Turismo En Chihuahua Por Región 2006 (expresado en miles)

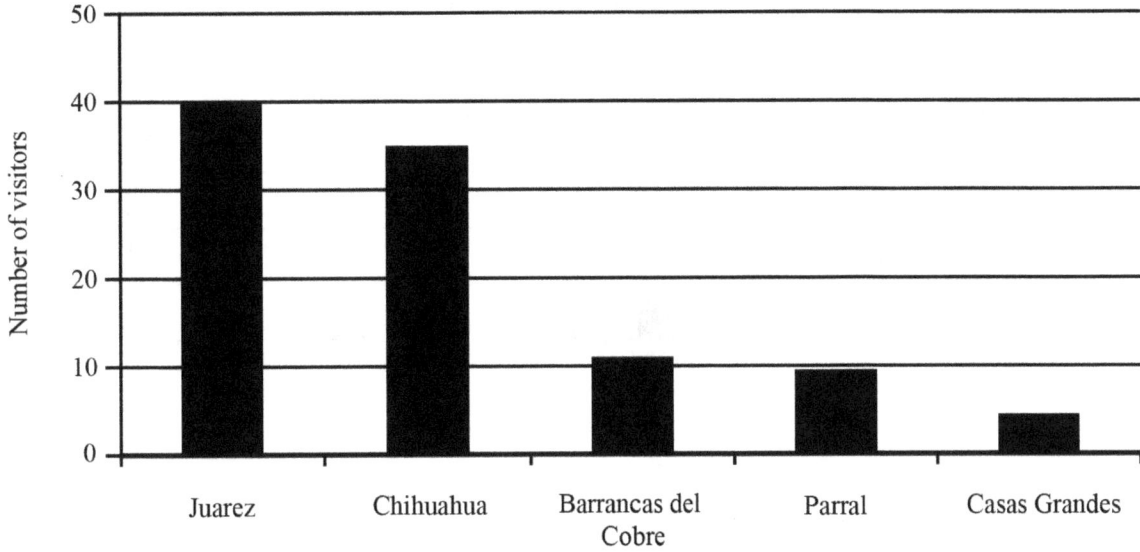

Tabla III.2.3. Visitantes Mexicanos al Museo de las Culturas del Norte Por Ciudad de Origen (expresado en miles)

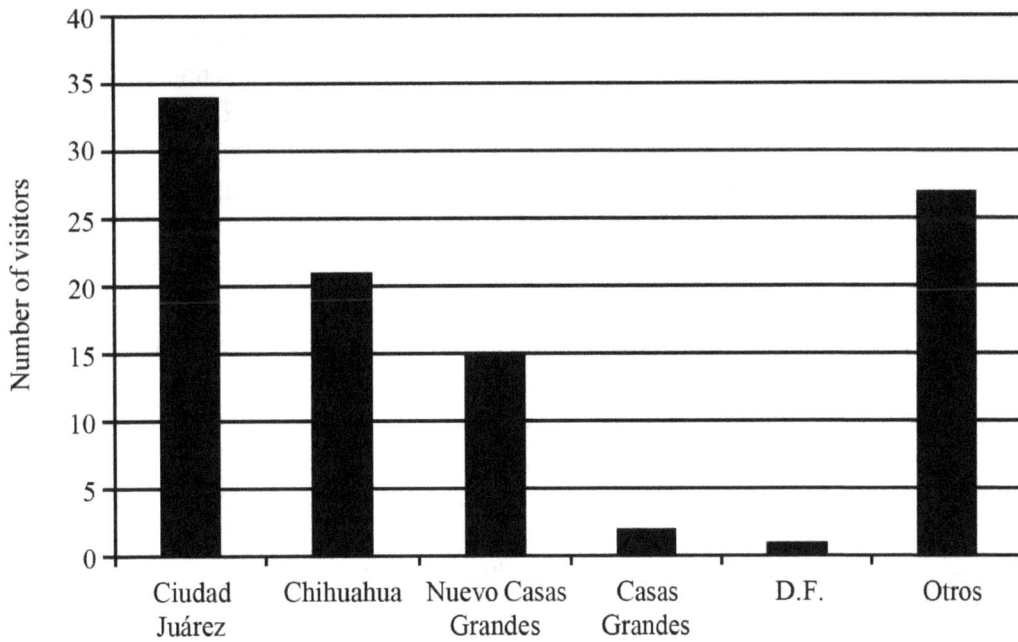

Tabla III.2.4. Visitantes Norteamericanos al Museo de las Culturas del Norte Por Ciudad de Origen
(expresado en miles)

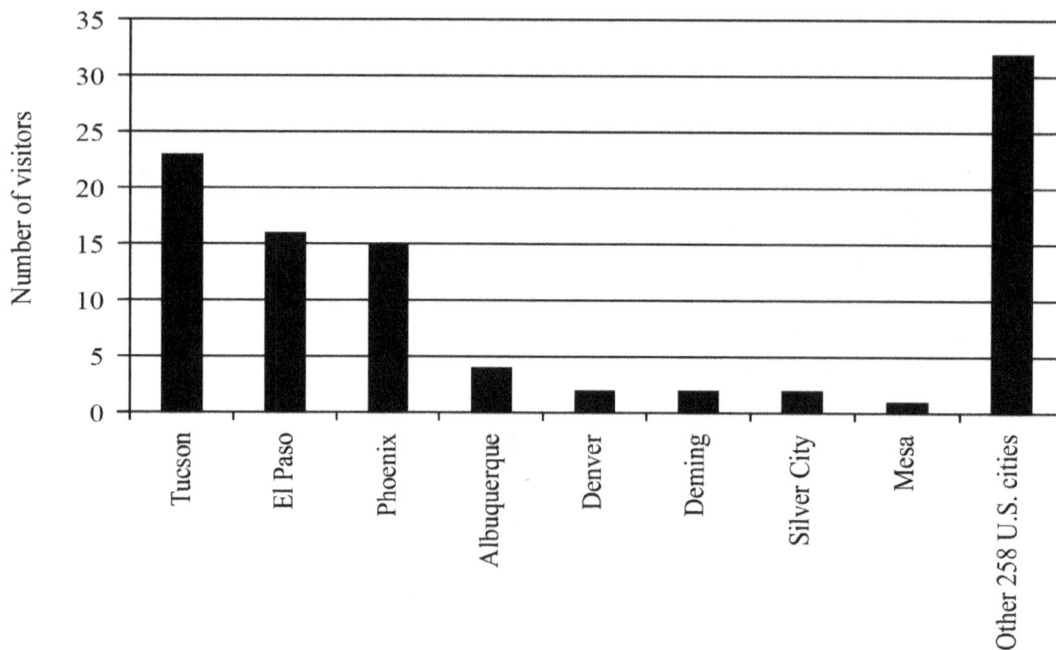

que fundaron un Festival Cultural llamado Nueva Paquimé que fomentan a los grupos de danza paquimeita, concursos de trajes regionales paquimeitas, concursos de pintura internacionales sobre temas de Paquimé e incluso construyeron en el rancho la victoria una pequeña reproducción de Paquimé en el 2003 para hacer un luz y sonido y distintos eventos que no les permitíamos en la zona arqueológica.

Incluso hoy día entre los jóvenes de Nuevo Casas Grandes hemos encontrado el uso del nombre de Paquime a ritmo de rap en la canción llamada Chantes longos, la cual puede ser vista en el internet. De igual forma pudimos ubicar una tortería de Phoenix llamada Paquimé, seguramente propiedad de alguien de la región.

PAQUIMÉ EN LA IDENTIDAD DE LOS CHIHUAHUENSES

En general entre la población del resto del estado no existe un fuerte sentimiento identitario que los relacione con su pasado indígena y por supuesto no con Paquimé. Sin embargo, entre la gente dedicada a la cultura, si Paquimé les parece uno de los elementos culturales más importantes del estado, lo cual no es de sorprender.

No obstante, en este sentido lo que me parce primordial mencionar es que es el gobierno del estado el que retoma más elementos de cultura Casas Grandes para identificarse y diferenciarse del resto de los gobiernos estatales. Ejemplo de ello fue la serie de vuelos en helicóptero que el exgobernador Patricio Martínez ordenara para la toma de imágenes aéreas las cuales iban a ser reproducidas en vajillas, las que se utilizarían en las comidas oficiales de dicho gobernador. Durante dicho sexenio se le dio mucho impulso a la región y se usaron de distintas maneras en las paginas oficiales motivos relacionados con la cultura Casas Grandes, en cambio en la presente administración de José Reyes Baeza, la mayoría de los motivos están relacionados con la sierra tarahumara.

Contrastante con Nuevo Casas Grandes

es que en Chihuahua sorprende lo poco que es usado el nombre de Paquimé en los distintos establecimientos comerciales, destacan solamente un criadero de perros chihuahuas, un desarrollo inmobiliario y una venta de tamales. Incluso encontramos un CD de música etno-tecno de Paquimé y Oasisamérica.

Y ENTONCES ¿PARA QUÉ SIRVEN LAS DECLARATORIAS DE PATRIMONIO MUNDIAL A NIVEL COMUNITARIO?

Claro que lo primero y más obvio que viene a la mente es que estas declaratorias de patrimonio mundial le dan un sentido de orgullo e identidad a los habitantes de esas regiones como hemos podido ver. Esa enorme cantidad de negocios y el uso y abuso de diseños Casas Grandes en muchísimos de los lugares de la ciudad lo atestiguan sin lugar a dudas.

No obstante, estas declaratorias de patrimonio mundial, tienen muchas más artistas que estos elementos visibles, es cuando las narrativas arqueológicas se encuentra y sirven a los políticos y burócratas de los estados. Así cabe preguntarse ¿quién o quienes pagaron por llevar a cabo el expediente y la consecuente declaratoria de patrimonio mundial? Atrás de todas estas declaratorias existe siempre un fuerte impulso económico que generalmente viene de los gobiernos estatales quienes son los que ponen el dinero para llevar a cabo los trabajos.

¿Quiénes son los especialistas que evalúan el sentido singular de la propuesta y sea una muestra del valor universal excepcional? Esa pregunta es aun más difícil de responder. Es este sentido me gustaría solamente agregar que como arqueólogo esa pregunta me parece careciente de sentido, ya que creo se premia más a la monumentalidad arquitectónica que al verdadero espíritu de la lista de Patrimonio Mundial. Esto en el sentido de que el genio humano está en todas las acciones que el hombre crea a través de agentes hábiles, entonces ¿porqué tiene más valor Chichen Itzá que un sitio de Sonora como el Cerro de Trincheras? A mí la respuesta me parece obvia, ninguno tiene más valor que el otro. En ese sentido creo yo que la lista de Patrimonio Mundial nació con una buena vocación de proteger algunos de los legados más relevantes de la humanidad, sin embargo en el camino se ha ido trastocando convirtiéndose en un botín político de los gobiernos nacionales, estatales y municipales que ha servido en muchos casos como parte de plataformas políticas en búsqueda de proyecciones a más altos puestos, además de convertirse en listas publicitaria impulsada por las oficinas de turismo, muchas de las veces dejando completamente de lado a las comunidades locales.

Finalmente, quisiera concluir diciendo que deberíamos trabajar más de cerca para que los sitios patrimonio de la humanidad se transformen en lugares donde las comunidades que viven en estos o cerca de ellos generen verdaderos lazos que lleven a establecer programas y proyectos vinculados a su conservación, investigación y difusión. Sería muy ingenuo pensar que nuestros trabajos arqueológicos no forman parte de una agenda mayor y que estos son utilizados de múltiples formas muchas veces no como nosotros quisiéramos.

Part III, Chapter 3

Arqueología, Turismo y Sitios Patrimonio de la Humanidad en México y Estados Unidos

César Villalobos

RESUMEN

El patrimonio arqueológico se ha convertido en el centro de un debate de múltiples alcances. Los reclamos por la propiedad y/o manejo de sitios arqueológicos por parte de estados nacionales, comunidades indígenas, minorías étnicas, arqueólogos, empresarios, turistas, y aún de saqueadores, son una pequeña muestra de que el pasado es un poderoso recurso ideológico siempre presente. Estos debates dejan entrever el intrínseco potencial que atesora el patrimonio arqueológico como materia prima, ya sea para la reproducción de ideologías, identidad, nostalgia y como generador de divisas. En la época neoliberal, los sitios arqueológicos parecen alejarse de las agendas nacionalistas y acercarse más a los intereses de explotación comercial. El postulado neoliberal implícito se comprueba en la medida en que los países turísticamente más visitados en el mundo, con algunas variantes, son también los que cuentan con mayor cantidad de sitios inscritos en la lista de UNESCO. En este capítulo discutiré la relación existente entre patrimonio arqueológico, UNESCO y turismo, y de qué forma dicha interacción afecta el manejo de los recursos arqueológicos. Bajo esta perspectiva serán comparados el Norte de México y Sur de Estados Unidos.

ABSTRACT

The ownership or stewardship of archaeological sites has been claimed by nation states, communities, ethnic minorities, archaeologists, executives, tourists, and even looters, demonstrating that the past is a powerful resource in the present. These struggles suggest that archaeological sites can be the raw material for the creation of ideology, identity, nostalgia, and as a generator generator of foreign exchange. In the "neoliberal" era, archaeological sites are being used less to support national agendas and more for commercial exploitation. Archaeological sites that have been the focus of this exploitation are located in countries whose economies are dependent upon tourism and often have multiple sites on the UNESCO list. In this chapter, I will discuss the relationship between archaeological resources, UNESCO and tourism. I will analyse the impact of these interactions in the management of archaeological resources in Northern Mexico and Southern United States.

INTRODUCCIÓN

El patrimonio arqueológico se ha convertido en el centro de un debate de múltiples matices. Los reclamos por el derecho a controlar el patrimonio arqueológico por parte de estados nacionales, comunidades indígenas, minorías étnicas, arqueólogos, empresarios, turistas, y aún de saqueadores, son una pequeña muestra de que el pasado es un poderoso recurso ideológico siempre presente. Estos debates dejan entrever el intrínseco potencial que atesora el patrimonio arqueológico como materia prima, ya sea para la reproducción de ideologías (Díaz-Andreu and Champion 1996), identidad (Silverman 2005), nostalgia (Hamilakis 2003) y como generador de divisas (Rowan and Baram 2004). En la época neoliberal, los sitios arqueológicos parecen

César Villalobos Durham University

alejarse de las agendas académicas y acercarse más a los intereses de explotación comercial. El postulado neoliberal implícito se comprueba en la medida en que los países turísticamente más visitados en el mundo, con algunas variantes, son también los que cuentan con mayor cantidad de sitios inscritos en la lista de sitios patrimonio de la humanidad de UNESCO. En el presente texto, discutiré la relación existente entre patrimonio arqueológico, UNESCO y turismo arqueológico y de qué forma dicha interacción afecta el manejo de los recursos arqueológicos.

Los sitios arqueológicos son susceptibles de ser explotados ideológicamente por su condición de antigüedad, recurso no renovable y siempre vigente. Los sitios arqueológicos tienen un papel fundamental en el imaginario de los turistas (Duke 2007). La reconstrucción y preservación de los restos arqueológicos juega un rol fundamental en la traducción o presentación de la historia para el consumo turístico (Hagen 2006). De hecho, la restauración de edificios en algunos casos parecería más una copia de arquitecturas aborígenes para ser consumidas por la audiencia turística. En otros casos los sitios arqueológicos son el escenario nocturno para presentar espectáculos de luz, sonido y agua, transformando en ello la función original de los propios sitios pero introduciéndolos sin duda en un nuevo conjunto de relaciones.

México junto con Egipto, Grecia y Perú han compartido una obsesión por sus antigüedades (Brading 2001; Hamilakis 2007; Silverman 2002; Wynn 2008). Han explotado las reliquias y monumentos en todas las variantes posibles, como materia de identidad, como sustento de ideologías, como carta de presentación al exterior, como las huellas imborrables de continuidades culturales, haciendo de los Museos verdaderos santuarios para una especie de peregrinaje moderno para la celebración de neo-rituales dedicados a los ancestros. Estos países también han puesto un interés bastante abultado para explotar el pasado con una orientación abiertamente turística.

ARQUEOLOGÍA PARA TODOS Y EN TODOS LOS LUGARES

En la actualidad la arqueología podría ser bastante mejor conocida en el mundo por su rol en la industria turística, cinematográfica y en la cultura popular que por su contribución a la ciencia y al conocimiento. Los productos de la investigación generalmente son conocidos por un público bastante reducido que compra los libros y que asiste a conferencias. Los medios tradicionales de divulgación académica arqueológica pierden terreno con la masiva propaganda de otros medios. Basta ver de reojo el concurso internacional que culmino el *siete de julio del dos mil siete*, titulado las Nuevas Siete Maravillas del Mundo Moderno, organizado por un empresario millonario Bernard Weber. Este magnate con la ayuda de los medios electrónicos y el Internet, y asociado con grandes cadenas nacionales y transnacionales contribuyeron a la difusión masiva de tal concurso alrededor del mundo. Una nominación de *nuevas maravillas* que en realidad, y en su momento, nadie supo explicar cuáles eran los fines de tan loable acción. Sin embargo, a tres años del evento, su objetivo ya parece ser lo que suponía seria: un negocio para la posteridad. Actualmente se ofrece a la venta un video sobre el proceso de nominación, así como souvenirs con imágenes de las *New 7 Wonders* que pueden ser adquiridos vía Internet sin cargo de envío (http://*www. new7wonders.com/en/index/*).

Este aparato publicitario masivo parecería ser desleal si se compara con tiraje de 1,000, 2,000 o 3,000 ejemplares que de editan bajo estrictos controles de revisión sobre lo que hacemos los arqueólogos, y de los cuales algunos ejemplares ciertamente van a parar a manos de lectores interesados, pero otro tanto a las bodegas de editoriales o se quedan atrapados en los anaqueles de bibliotecas que difícilmente serán leídos por más de tres lectores.

La idea que el público en la actualidad tiene

de la arqueología es en gran medida producida por el uso de la arqueología en la cultura popular y visitas directas a los sitios arqueológicos (Holtorf 2005) y claro por campañas como la de las Siete Nuevas Maravillas. El análisis del fenómeno turístico en arqueología ha abierto un importante campo de exploración que permite observar las divergencias y diferencias entre diversos actores que reclaman el manejo de los recursos arqueológicos. Los arqueólogos, el gobierno y las empresas privadas están en medio de una férrea batalla para demostrar quien tiene más derecho al manejo de los sitios. Debido a que es una característica global es interesante analizar esta problemática desde la perspectiva de los Sitios Patrimonio de la Humanidad (SPH) declarados por la UNESCO ya que éstos sin duda se encuentran en el centro del debate mundial.

En el presente texto originalmente me iba enfocar a discutir el caso de los SPH ubicados en el Noroeste-Suroeste de la frontera México-Estadounidense; sin embargo, a la luz del análisis es aun más interesante si a los SPH se les posiciona en el contexto general que guardan respecto a sus países. El manejo y función de los SPH depende directamente de las condiciones culturales y políticas de los respectivos países y en ello tanto Estados Unidos como México mantienen una relación con la UNESCO bastante diferente. Primero introduzco algunas cuestiones básicas precisamente sobre UNESCO y luego entro en materia de discusión acerca de lo que aquí nos ocupa, que es la comparación entre los dos países.

UNESCO y Turismo

A partir de 1950 se ha dado un crecimiento exponencial del sector turístico en el Mundo. De acuerdo a la Organización Internacional de Turismo en el 2008 hubo más de 900 millones de llegadas internacionales en el mundo. En 2007 este flujo de turistas produjo una ganancia total de 856 billones de dólares americanos en

viajes internacionales (UNWTO 2008a:3-5). Ello convierte al turismo internacional en la industria más grande de servicios en el mundo. El turismo se clasifica como una industria de servicios directos y no como una industria de adquisición de bienes materiales. En el contexto del capitalismo al que han llegado los países desarrollados, el turismo internacional se ha convertido en una industria masiva donde medianamente cualquier persona tiene la posibilidad de viajar al extranjero. Ello tiene una larga historia.

Tradicionalmente el viajar para conocer se limitaba al *Grand Tour* de las clases altas europeas. Se considera que el turismo moderno tiene su auge en la época posterior a la Revolución Industrial, pero es más claramente definido como turismo de masas inmediatamente después de la Segunda Guerra Mundial. Existe una buena cantidad de información que las primeras excursiones programadas en Inglaterra se efectuaron de Leicester a Loughborough – sur de Inglaterra – en 1841 organizadas por Thomas Cook, un incipiente empresario, cuya empresa ha sido perpetuada por sus herederos hasta la actualidad, y cuyo objetivo era distraer a los ingleses del excesivo consumo de alcohol (Brendon 1991).

A medida de que el capitalismo ha avanzado, las condiciones cambiaron y permitieron que grandes sectores del público tomaran parte en viajes que en la actualidad se conoce como turismo de masas (Cohen 1984, 1988). Hay diferentes elementos a considerar en el crecimiento prolongado de este fenómeno; por un lado, la relativa estabilidad en Europa Occidental y Estados Unidos, el incremento del tiempo de descanso, la creación de vías de comunicación y sobre todo el desarrollo de los viajes aéreos. El turismo internacional, que es el que en gran medida el que se refleja en las cifras económicas millonarias, es básicamente una práctica de las clases sociales con ingresos económicamente estables, y que puede incluir a funcionarios de alto perfil así como a otros sectores con ingresos más bajos como taxistas, choferes de autobuses y mano de obra no altamente calificada. Estados Unidos e Inglaterra así como otros países de primer mundo se han convertido en generadores masivos de turistas (UNWTO 2008a:9).

El análisis de la emergencia del turismo de masas durante la segunda parte del siglo XX es impensable sin la inclusión de las instituciones internacionales, que si bien, no son las que promueven propiamente el turismo, son un importante medio de regulación y observancia, por lo cual se hace imprescindible mencionarlas. La Organización de Naciones Unidas (ONU) por medio de la Organización de las Naciones Unidas para la Educación, la Ciencia y la Cultura (UNESCO) ha contribuido, indirectamente al desarrollo del turismo cultural a partir de la década de 1950.

La ONU en realidad fue creada como un organismo de mediación durante la Guerra Fría para construir la paz entre los hombres. La UNESCO como agencia especializada de la ONU fue creada también en 1945 y comparte los mismos objetivos. De los tratados en materia de regulación del patrimonio cultural emitidos por la UNESCO resaltan tres, la *Convención sobre la protección de los bienes culturales en caso de conflicto armado* (1954), la *Convención sobre las medidas que deben adoptarse para prohibir e impedir la importación, la exportación y a transferencia de propiedad ilícitas de bienes culturales* (1970) y la *Convención sobre la protección del patrimonio mundial, cultural y natural* (1972). Estas tres convenciones han tenido un fuerte impacto en la emergencia de lo que ahora conocemos como patrimonio cultural y natural.

De las tres, la que más influencia ha tenido en la emergencia del turismo arqueológico es la convención de 1972. La UNESCO en dicha convención lanzó la convocatoria a sus estados miembros para que realizaran un inventario de los sitios tanto naturales como culturales, o la combinación entre ambos, que se encontraran en su territorio y que de alguna manera tuviesen un valor único y excepcional (UNESCO 1972). De

ese inventario el Comité del Patrimonio Mundial definiría en base a los criterios de excepcionalidad cuales sitios se seleccionarían para conformar la Lista del Patrimonio Mundial. La lista se actualiza anualmente y para 2008 estuvo integrada por 878 propiedades, de las cuales 679 son culturales, 174 naturales y 25 mixtas. La lista tiene un fuerte componente de sitios arqueológicos, entre ellos se encuentran los Monumentos Nubios en Egipto, la Acrópolis de Atenas en Grecia, Pompeya en Italia, la Gran Muralla en China, Stonehenge en Inglaterra, el Taj Mahal en la India, Tikal en Guatemala y Teotihuacan en México, sólo por citar algunos ejemplos (WHC 2008).

Una de las actividades que ha fomentado la Convención de 1972, sin proponerlo originalmente, es precisamente el turismo masivo en sitios arqueológicos. En este sentido algo sumamente interesante que debe ser mencionado es la comparación de las listas de la UNESCO y de la Organización Mundial de Turismo (OMT). Comparado los diez países mas visitados según la lista de la OMT con los diez países con más sitios patrimonio según la UNESCO, resalta que prácticamente son los mismos. Es decir, los países más visitados por turistas son aquellos que cuentan con más sitios inscritos en la lista (UNWTO 2008b; WHC 2008). Lo que deja entrever que la inscripción de sitios en UNESCO no está desligada en absoluto de la presencia de turistas en los sitios arqueológicos.

Es necesario mencionar que UNESCO no escoge los sitios que formaran parte de la lista, el papel de UNESCO radica en evaluar su inclusión en la lista, los países participantes son los que nominan sus propios sitios (por ejemplo Aa (2005) compara el proceso de nominación en cinco países, entre ellos México y EEUU). La lista de UNESCO refleja los intereses del propio país en el que se encuentran los sitios, como se detallará a continuación; es claramente discernible que en México tienen un importancia sobresaliente los SPH asociados a la culturas prehispánicas, mientras que en los Estados Unidos el concepto de patrimonio natural y el patrimonio cultural contemporáneo – sin relación al pasado pre-colonial – tienen mucho más importancia. Este manejo y percepción es muy interesante puesto que representa dos visiones bien diferentes de manejo cultural que se hace en nuestros países y me parece un elemento interesante para la discusión y las implicaciones que tiene en la reproducción y creación de las ideologías.

MÉXICO Y SU OBSESIÓN POR EL PASADO

México es el país más visitado de América Latina y el octavo a nivel mundial que recibió alrededor de 21 millones de visitantes internacionales en 2008. El turismo en México es un indicador sumamente importante en la economía nacional (Clancy 1999). México cuenta con 29 SPH inscritos, 25 de los cuales son culturales y cuatro naturales. Dentro de los culturales, nueve son prehispánicos. Ellos son Monte Albán, Palenque, Teotihuacan, Chichén Itzá, El Tajín, Pinturas Rupestres de Baja California, Uxmal, Paquimé y Xochicalco (WHC 2008). Estos sitios en los años recientes han recibido en su conjunto alrededor de 5 millones de turistas al año concentrándose la mayoría de los visitantes en los sitios mesoamericanos (DataTur 2006). En el particular caso de los SPH en el Norte de México tenemos que Paquimé tan solo alcanza alrededor de 70,000 turistas por año (http://*www.arts-history.mx/banco/index.php?id_nota=12072004115037*), y ni que decir de la Sierra de San Francisco, que el conjunto de sitios fue visitado por 1,794 visitantes en 2006 (Gutiérrez Martínez 2009).

Estas cifras demuestran que ciertamente el turismo es masivo en sitios arqueológicos. Podría mencionarse que el turismo en sitios arqueológicos ha crecido paralelamente con el boom del turismo en general en México desde finales de la década de 1960 (Villalobos in preparation). La emergencia del turismo ha provocado una paulatina desestabilización en la relación que los arqueólogos mantienen con los sitios arqueológicos, con el estado y de hecho, con el resto de la sociedad. El aparente éxito del turismo masivo en las últimas dos décadas ha provocado inevitablemente tensiones institucionales, al interior de la academia y en sectores sociales tradicionalmente alejados del manejo cultural, todos reclamando acceso privilegiado y legítimo según justifican sus demandas.

A continuación proporcionaré algunas cifras interesantes (todas en pesos mexicanos) que reflejan una parte del origen de estas demandas por estos grupos en torno a lo que se precibe es un negocio millonario: el turismo arqueologico en los SHP mas exitosos. En Monte Albán durante el 2004 el ingreso por concepto de taquilla fue de $8,779,665 mientras que ese mismo año $3,953,959 fueron asignados como presupuesto al sitio (Robles 2005:18). Teotihuacan durante 2006 tuvo un ingreso por concepto de taquilla de $33,688,427 mientras que $10,524,400 fueron asignados al como presupuesto en 2007. Palenque durante 2006 tuvo un ingreso de $11,991,510 mientras que $4,347,995 fueron asignados como presupuesto en 2007. Finalmente para no hacer de estas cifras numeros interminables Tulum – que es el único que no es SPH de los que he mencionado – durante 2006 tuvo un ingreso de $35,399,235 mientras que únicamente $3,950,000 fueron asignados al como presupuesto sitio para el año 2007 (INAH 2008a, 2008b, 2008c). Estas cifras hay que tomarlas con cuidado puesto que en mis fuentes no se establece las partidas especificas de cada una de estos recursos. Estas cifras en bruto no incluyen salarios de investigadores adscritos a los sitios y tampoco presupuesto destinado a la investigación, sino que este presupuesto es usado principalmente para labores de mantenimiento y probablente en algunos casos algunos de esos recursos a labores menores de investigación. Sea como sea, los números no mienten, y la taquilla de estos SPH muestran que se produce mucho dinero por concepto de turismo.

Pese a estas cifras, hay que reconocer que

la gran mayoría de los sitios arqueológicos en el resto del país no son autosustentables por la sencilla razón de que no se encuentran abiertos al público. Eso genera precisamente que estos sitios económicamente más rentables sean la manzana de la discordia – los que todos quieren administrar – y aquellos otros sitios de menor impacto económico sean practicamente invisibles para las mayorias. Estas cifras – manejadas por el INAH – no representan el total de la derrama económica que se genera por concepto del turismo, recordemos que estas cifras representan el monto recuperado en las taquillas de los sitios arqueológicos correspondientes. Únicamente falta darse una vuelta, por ejemplo, a Teotihuacan—SHP—para darse cuenta de la cantidad de importantes relaciones sociales y económicas que se generan alrededor del turismo arqueológico. Hoteles, restaurantes, venta de artesanías, cobro de estacionamiento, venta de fruta, agua, cerveza, renta de vehículos, concesiones de taxis, espectáculos luz y sonido, y un sinnúmero de servicios correlativos son los que engrosan el interés de muchos grupos por los SPH.

Aquí hay un aspecto importante que me gustaría mencionar, más allá del valor evidentemente económico, la relación que se establece entre comunidades ya sean locales, nacionales o internacionales transforman el conjunto de percepciones sociales en torno a los sitios arqueológicos, y si bien el aspecto monetario es uno de ellos, la existencia social de los propios sitios depende de esas reciprocidades. Un claro ejemplo de ello se encuentra en Chichén Itzá, donde la mera existencia de los vendedores ambulantes, es parte de la propia constitución y composición del sitio arqueológico en el contexto local y global, y en conjunto con arqueólogos, turistas, políticos, comunidades indígenas y terratenientes se han creado las dinámicas redes sociales existentes en este sitio importante (Castañeda 1996, 2005).

Para ser más eficiente en expresarme acerca de lo que considero son problemas graves del

contexto político de la arqueología y que están relacionados con las cifras que proporcioné arriba – para lustrar la falta de claridad del uso y función de la arqueología para el presente gobierno – utilizaré una viñeta crítica que más se asemeja a una metáfora maliciosa. Supongamos un modelo hipotético en donde los políticos, inquietos por el gasto oneroso que representa la arqueología, pudieran escoger un número conveniente de sitios arqueológicos y símbolos del pasado a su libre albedrío. Sin duda escogerían sitios como Chichén Itzá, Templo Mayor, Tulum, Monte Albán, Xochicalco y Uxmal, la mayoría de ellos, los más taquilleros turísticamente hablando, como acabamos de ver, y los más rentables en términos de identidad nacional. Estos sitios en conjunto, por medio de su *appeal turistico* liberarían al estado de una pesada carga administrativa, y a la vez le proporcionarían permanentes ganancias económicas, además que le darían prestigio y tendría propiedad exclusiva sobre su usufructo sin necesidad de mediar decisiones con grupos indígenas, comunidades locales, y sectores críticos del sistema, y mucho menos con UNESCO o ICOMOS. En este sentido metafórico, sin duda el resto del patrimonio arqueológico estaría en manos ya sea de caciques locales (incluyendo a algunos arqueólogos), de rancheros-terratenientes, de empresas turísticas o de particulares, y en el mejor, pero el más improbable de los casos, bajo vigilancia de comunidades locales e indígenas.

Siguiendo el juego de la metáfora maliciosa, los arqueólogos bien podrían emular el sistema que existe en otros países y decidirse algunos por una vida profesional académica en las universidades, mientras que otros (seguramente en aumento permanente) se insertarían en la arqueología comercial de salvamento por las ventajas económicas que representaría; otros más, sin duda se solazarían en alimentar las necesidades de la arqueología oficial. Los sitios más rentables representarían lo que a los políticos les encanta promover, un país *lleno* de historia, orgullo de la nación y de *todos los mexicanos*. Los sitios arqueológicos serían perfectas reconstrucciones palaciegas para llevar a pasear a los presidentes y personalidades internacionales que visitan México, y ya de pasada se podrían organizar conciertos de rock o de música clásica. Como su usufructo seria total, podrían iluminar las pirámides ya sea para navidad, el día de reyes o colorearlas de blanco durante el equinoccio de primavera. De hecho, lo sitios podrían ser comprados parcialmente o en su totalidad por los gobiernos locales, la iniciativa privada o particulares. La legislación de 1972 si bien no se eliminaría o modificaría, sí se convertiría como un bello *survival* del nacionalismo postrevolucionario; de hecho, al no aplicarla quedaría como uno de esos lejano triunfos de la revolución al estilo priista. Pese a la grotesca caricatura que este juego verbal parece contener, esta conmovedora metáfora maliciosa, más que ser un ejercicio lúdico, es en gran medida la situación actual de la situación política en la que se encuentra la arqueología a principios del siglo XXI en México.

ESTADOS UNIDOS Y SU DISTANCIAMIENTO CON LA UNESCO

En 2006 Estados Unidos recibió casi 50 millones de turistas internacionales (cuarta posición a nivel mundial). Estados Unidos cuenta con 20 sitios declarados patrimonio de la humanidad – incluyendo dos sitios que se administran conjuntamente con Canadá, entre ellos, 8 son culturales y 12 naturales. Entre los culturales se encuentran sólo tres prehistóricos que son *Mesa Verde National Park, Cahokia Mounds State Historic Site y Chaco Culture National Historic Park* (WHC 2008). En Estados Unidos los SPH culturales prehistóricos en su conjunto captan alrededor de un millon de turistas al año. Mesa Verde registró una afluencia de 561,163 turistas en 2006 (http://*www.nps.gov/meve/ parkmgmt/statistics.htm*), Cahokia Mound recibe anualmente alrededor de 300,000 turistas

(http://*www.cahokiamounds.org/news-events/ blog/2009/07/23/boeing-helps-preserve-ancient-indian-site/*), mientras que Chaco recibe entre 60,000 y 80,000 visitantes al año (http://*home.nps. gov/chcu/parkmgmt/upload/EditedTrailEA.pdf*).

Es importante mencionar que una categoría fundamental ha sido la de Parque Nacional. Este se refiere a una reserva natural, o cultural-natural, declarada o bajo propiedad del gobierno. Se usan generalmente como áreas protegidas para la visita turística, para la protección de animales y de flora y fauna y en donde el desarrollo de infraestructura esta prácticamente prohibido. De acuerdo con Sellars para 1900 ya existían cuatro parques "naturales" nacionales en Estados Unidos (*Yellowstone, Sequoia, Yosemite y Mount Rainier*). De hecho *Yellowstone* es considerado la primera área conservada del mundo moderno (1872) (Sellars 2007:271). Uno de los parques naturales, que a la vez es SPH, mas visitados en Estados Unidos es *Great Smoky Mountains National Park*, cerca de 10 millones de turistas al año, sin embargo, la gente que lo visita difícilmente se percata de que se trata de un SPH (Aa 2005:110).

En los Estados Unidos los SPH naturales son más importantes que los SPH culturales prehistóricos. La presencia que el pasado tiene para Estados Unidos en la lista de la UNESCO es relativamente poca, menos de una cuarta parte de los sitios inscritos están relacionados con el pasado prehistórico. Los sitios arqueológicos en el Suroeste norteamericano han sido un elemento simbólico bastante problemático en términos políticos. Estos sitios intrínsecamente dejan entrever un doble colonialismo.

Primeramente porque en la invasión norteamericana de 1846-1848 México perdió más de la mitad de su territorio. Eso constituye la mayor cantidad de territorio que probablemente ningún país en el mundo ha perdido en la época moderna en un solo acto de agresión (Piñeira 1994:132), y resulta que los sitios arqueológicos más impactantes de todo el Suroeste están en dicha área. En segundo lugar, una vez siendo territorio de Estados Unidos, esas áreas se les confiscaron a las comunidades indígenas que se asentaban en los alrededores de los sitios, y aunque en el concepto de reservaciones se les asignaron ciertas áreas, estas fueron una mínima porción de lo que se consideraban originalmente como sus tierras. Anyon y Ferguson mencionan que a los Zuni sólo un 3 por ciento de las tierras originales les fueron concedidas (Anyon y Ferguson 1996:913).

En este contexto es bastante sencillo entender por qué el concepto predominante ha sido el patrimonio natural y no el cultural prehistórico. El mismo termino prehistoria, como generalmente se usa para definir en inglés lo que en México denominamos arqueología prehispánica, hace una marcada separación entre el pasado lejano – incluyendo los grupos indígenas – y el pasado reciente que inicia con la colonización, y por tanto la civilización europea en Norteamérica. Los sitios culturales prehispánicos y el pasado que representan una categoría que a la política exterior norteamericana no le interesa poner en la mesa de negociaciones. En este sentido, por ejemplo, es interesante resaltar que se han construido *patrimonios* culturales alejados de esa prehistoria incómoda, en aquellos lugares relacionados más directamente con el pasado reciente que fueron en los asentamientos originales de las 13 colonias inglesas. En las primeras décadas del siglo XX una nueva maquinaria ideológica se puso en marcha para la recreación de la identidad norteamericana sustentada en sus propias ideas mitológicas. Concentrémonos por instante en un interesante ejemplo.

En Dakota del Sur el área *Black Hills* contiene virtualmente todos los elementos de la mitología norteamericana del lejano oeste – cowboys, indios, mineros, cazadores de pieles, el tren de vapor, los salones y casinos. Obviamente la más importante atracción en *Black Hills* es el *Mount Rushmore National Memorial*. Esta consiste en los rostros de cuatro presidentes Norteamericanos tallados de forma monumental en la pared de un enorme frente rocoso. Las caras

de Washington, Jefferson, Lincoln y Roosevelt y cuyos logros sintetizan la historia reciente de los Estados Unidos anuncian en sí misma la historia por venir. Cada rostro corresponde a un pasaje de la historia, de la independencia y primer presidente norteamericano, se pasa a la Guerra Civil que culmina en la abolición de la esclavitud, se continúa con la declaración de la independencia y se finaliza con la expansión imperial del país. *Mount Rushmore* sintetiza los valores Norteamericanos, transforma las ficciones intangibles en una palpable representación (Pretes 2003:130-134). Otros atractivos turísticos en el esta área importantes en termino de identidad son la *Wall Drug Store* y el *Rapid City's Dinosaur Park*, que aunque sin las connotaciones políticas de *Mount Rushmore*, también son parte fundamental del imaginario cultural e ideológico de los norteamericanos.

Si bien *Mount Rushmore* no ha adquirido el estatus de SPH, es masivamente visitado lo que los hace ser particularmente importantes como sitios culturales. Asimismo solo mencionaré que la Estatua de la Libertad de Nueva York, es otro de los sitios culturales SPH que ha visto un incremento permanente de visitantes, hacia 1980 recibía un millón mientras que en el 2000 estaba recibiendo aproximadamente 5 millones de turistas. Esto debido a la restauración que se llevó a cabo a mediados de 1980, lo que eventualmente propició su nominación como SPH y que indudablemente ha provocado un aumento en visitas por turismo (Aa 2005:111).

Es relevante mencionar que estas producciones culturales proyectan valores y una versión hegemónica de la identidad nacional y de los aspectos políticos que se quieren fomentar que implícitamente callan los que se prefieren ocultar. Aunque con mayores posibilidades de análisis, en este sentido, me parece que queda demostrado el por qué los sitios culturales prehistóricos no figuran como predominantes en la lista de UNESCO en los Estados Unidos.

Además, el interés de los norteamericanos

en sus sitios SPH es bastante bajo debido a que es poco publicitado por un sentimiento contra las Naciones Unidas. Cabe recordar en que Estados Unidos fue miembro fundador de la UNESCO, se retiró en 1984 y reingresó hasta 2003 (Azzi 2005:773-775). Esto hace aun más compleja la percepción y uso de los sitios SPH declarados por la UNESCO por el ambiente anti-norteamericano provocado por otros países miembros de la UNESCO, contrarios a la política exterior intervencionista norteamericana. En su más puro postulado, las Naciones Unidas invita a todas las naciones a contribuir en la creación de la paz en la mente del ser humano y la política exterior norteamericana, como se puede observar ha sido el de un intervencionismo que no puede ser ocultado y ahí han estado los mayores desacuerdos de la nación norteamericana.

Discusión

El uso de los sitios arqueológicos en la sociedad contemporánea ha visto un cambio fundamental desde la segunda parte del siglo XX por la influencia del turismo. El crecimiento de la arqueología y de nuevos puestos asociados tanto académicos como privados así como a la atención de la prensa y la creación de organismos nacionales e internacionales ha cambiado la forma en que el público se acerca y aprende de la arqueología. Uno de estos medios ha sido la creación del concepto de SPH.

Como ha quedado asentado, no existe propiamente un concepto de Sitios Patrimonio de la Humanidad único y exclusivo, éste recae más bien en qué es lo que los países particulares quieran que se reconozcan como sus valores, ya sean naturales o culturales. Lo anterior como quedó demostrado, obedece a las condiciones particulares de cada país. Los sitios son incluidos en la lista por su excepcionalidad, y ese rasgo no es autoevidente ni universal, es un valor definido por las comunidades locales, gobiernos o instituciones que postulan sus propios sitios.

Los SPH son excelentes casos de estudio por su excepcionalidad, sin embargo, precisamente por ello, son un mal ejemplo de lo que pasa con el resto de los sitios arqueológicos. Los sitios prehistóricos o arqueológicos declarados por UNESCO representan un porcentaje muy bajo si se compara con los sitios registrados en los diferentes países. Por ejemplo en México hay 172 sitios arqueológicos abiertos al público y un estimado de 300,000 sitios registrados en todo el país.

Como se mencionó arriba, el turismo arqueológico en SPH en México, o sea nueve sitios atraen alrededor de cinco millones de visitantes al año; es decir más del 50 por ciento del turismo anual en sitios arqueológicos mexicanos y reciben mucho dinero por concepto de cobro de entrada. Por lo anterior, los SPH no son un buen indicador de cómo el turismo afecta a los sitios arqueológicos, ni son un indicador de las circunstancias reales por las que atraviesan otros sitios arqueológicos. Debido a su alto poder mediático, lo que pasa en los SPH se extrapola al resto de los sitios arqueológicos, lo que en muchos casos llega a generar una idea equivocada de lo que la arqueología es y lo que la arqueología representa.

En el caso de Estados Unidos los SPH culturales prehistóricos, se ubican sobre todo en el Suroeste norteamericano, un área que ha sido analizada desde diversas perspectivas y que ha sido un laboratorio de investigaciones por más de 100 años. Al no existir zonas prehistóricas declaradas en otras áreas, una comparación al interior de Estados Unidos se hace prácticamente imposible puesto que se carece de los parámetros para realizarla. Pero como se argumentó, la ausencia en el culto al pasado tiene sus raíces históricas en el culto por el pasado reciente de los Estados Unidos. Los SPH prehistóricos no son necesarios en términos políticos, de hecho, podría prescindirse de ellos.

Más allá de los límites de México o Estados Unidos el concepto de SPH precisamente se propone como un elemento que intenta aglutinar y *hablar* un lenguaje internacional, que con sus variantes permita la comunicación entre las naciones por medio de agendas comunes. El objetivo supremo de la ONU es "crear la paz en la mente de los hombres y mujeres del mundo". Precisamente uno de sus procesos instrumentales fue la creación de la Convención de 1972 y de la que se derivó la lista de SPH. Esta idea de patrimonio mundial ha sido criticado por su imperialismo implícito, es decir, por su apoyo en las primeras décadas de su existencia a los valores occidentales en detrimento de los de oriente, por ejemplo. También hay que mencionar que la Convención de 1972, aunque con muchos retos, ha contribuido a salvaguardar, proteger y difundir el conocimiento sobre sitios arqueológicos que de otra manera probablemente se hubieran destruido ya sea por causas naturales o por la directa destrucción de la mano del hombre.

CONCLUSIONES

Los SPH son tan visibles que contradictoriamente se vuelven invisibles. ¿En qué se parece Paquimé a la Estatua de la Libertad? o ¿Qué tiene de común la reserva de la biosfera *Sian ka'an* con el *Independence Hall*, de hecho, alguien sabe en qué países se encuentran estos lugares? Para darle sentido esta pregunta, invito a los lectores a hacer un cuestionario efímero e inmediato. Salgan al pasillo y escojan a un colega y pídanle que les nombre un solo sitio patrimonio de la humanidad en su país de residencia. Si nuestra entrevistada o entrevistado están relacionados con la temática, probablemente nombrarán alguno de ellos, con suerte a lo mejor a dos, pero difícilmente darán un listado preciso y mucho menos podrán citar cuáles son culturales y cuáles naturales.

Esta imposibilidad se encuentra en que la naturaleza misma del concepto Patrimonio de la Humanidad puesto que implica una gran diversidad de formas y contenidos desarrollados por las instancias políticas nacionales con vistas a su internacionalismo y no precisamente articulados con los problemas consuetudinarios que enfrentan las personas en los sitios como parte de la existencia cotidiana. El día en que realmente podamos dar una lista precisa de memoria, sin recurrir al Internet o a al Mapa anual de los SPH, es porque en realidad seremos ciudadanos universales y tendremos un patrimonio que compartimos como humanidad. Mientras tanto, seguiremos viviendo al interior de fronteras nacionales y nuestras identidades estarán determinadas en función de los valores asociados a tales naciones.

Part III, Chapter 4

Heritage Management in Mexico and the United States

Jeffrey H. Altschul and T. J. Ferguson

ABSTRACT

Archaeological sites, historic properties, and traditional cultural places in the borderlands area of Mexico and the United States are associated with many historical events and cultural processes that are common to both countries. The management of these heritage resources for research, preservation, and public interpretation, however, varies markedly depending on which side of the border they are situated. This presentation critically examines the heritage management programs of the United States and Mexico. First, we succinctly describe the laws and concepts that govern heritage management in each country. Next, we place these regulatory frameworks within a broader comparative context, with particular attention given the effects that a "polluter pays" approach to heritage management has on research and the resources. We then identify what we think are the strengths and weaknesses of each system. Heritage management in both countries is an evolving system, and as we continue to develop more effective means for protecting important cultural sites we think each country has something to learn from the other.

RESUMEN

Los sitios arqueológicos, monumentos históricos y otros lugares de interés cultural en la región fronteriza de México y Estados Unidos están ligados por medio de diversos eventos y procesos históricos comunes a ambos países. Sin embargo, pese a la proximidad territorial, el manejo de los recursos culturales, la investigación, conservación e interpretación varía sustancialmente dependiendo en que parte de la frontera se encuentre uno. En esta presentación examinamos críticamente los programas de manejo cultural tanto en Estados Unidos como en México. Primero, describiremos sucintamente las leyes y conceptos que guían—o gobiernan—el manejo de los recursos culturales en cada país. Posteriormente, ubicamos el marco legislativo en un contexto comparativo más amplio, ponemos especial atención a los efectos que el enfoque denominado "polluter pays" ejerce sobre la investigación y los propios recursos culturales. Finalmente, identificamos las ventajas y desventajas de cada sistema, sus puntos débiles y sus fortalezas. El manejo de los recursos culturales en ambos países es un sistema en continua evolución, y en la medida en que continuemos desarrollando más y mejores formas de proteger sitios de importancia cultural, consideramos que cada país, tendrá algo que aprender del otro.

Jeffrey H. Altschul Statistical Research, Inc. and the SRI Foundation
T. J. Ferguson University of Arizona

Franz Boas (1940) noted long ago every culture is the product of a unique and particular history. We keep this insight in mind as we compare the heritage management systems of Mexico and the United States. In examining how heritage sites are managed in our respective countries, we see that both managerial systems stem from a common, deep seated fascination with where we come from and how we got here. The two systems diverge, however, in how the particular histories of our countries have shaped our values, and how these values are expressed in the way we embrace, use, and impart heritage to our citizens and to others. We are less concerned with judging the relative success of differing management systems than we are in evaluating how these managerial frameworks provide a foundation to meet the challenges to heritage in the future and what we as archaeologists can do about it.

Comparisons of heritage management systems tend to focus on a set of arbitrary measures. How many sites have been recorded? Preserved? Excavated? Stabilized? Interpreted? Implicit in such measures is the assumption that heritage management has more to do with physical remains of the past than in how those remains affect the present. Most heritage programs, and certainly those of the United States and Mexico, are designed to provide public benefits, including information about history, spiritual or emotional connections with ancestors, and appreciation of artistic and technological achievements. To evaluate public benefits, therefore, we need to ask: What have we learned? What are we likely to learn by doing more survey or excavation? What places need to be preserved? How is information collected during heritage management shared with the public? Who decides what to do and how much of it to do? What rights do archaeologists, descendant communities and the public have in the decision-making process?

These are difficult questions to answer,

in part because the answers depend on how "information," "control," and "rights" are defined. These terms are deeply embedded in the value systems of our two countries. We explore the heritage systems of Mexico and the United States through three pairs of contrasting core values: private property versus national patrimony; centralized versus local control, and traditional versus scientific interpretive authority. It is not our contention that the two countries express opposite sides of these paired values; both heritage systems incorporate both sides of each pair in varying degrees. It is in how the conflicts between the competing sides of each value pair are resolved that distinguishes how our countries approach heritage and how we can expect our systems to evolve in the future.

PRIVATE PROPERTY VERSUS NATIONAL PATRIMONY

The core values of private property versus national patrimony are associated with the fundamentally different precepts that guide the legal systems of the U.S. and Mexico. Mexican jurisprudence derives from Roman law as it was interpreted and altered in medieval Spain (García-Bárcena 2007:14). United States jurisprudence, in contrast, is based on Saxon law, which evolved into English common law. In Mexico, ownership of the country's land and water was originally vested in the Crown, and then transferred to the newly formed nation of Mexico at independence in 1821. The nation has the right to transfer title of land parcels to private parties, although such transfer is only to be made for a public purpose. Even then, private ownership is restricted to the surface; everything below the surface, including archaeological sites, belongs to the nation. In contrast, land ownership in the United States is nearly absolute: property rights provide owners with control of both the surface and the subsurface. Private land owners in the United States own the archaeological sites and their contents (with the exception of human remains) located on and beneath their land.

It might be argued that treating archaeological sites as national patrimony as opposed to private property is the result of a historical sequence associated with the adoption and evolution of particular legal systems that have little, if anything, to do with archaeology. We believe such a narrow reading of history disguises significant differences between the two countries in the relation between their people and land.

In the United States, the notion that one's success is determined by individual achievement born of hard work, luck, and character is seared into the nation's consciousness. To a large extent, success is gauged by one's material wealth. Land is used both to achieve wealth and to mark accomplishment. The natural resources of a parcel of land – its timber, minerals, water, aesthetics, and other qualities – can be developed or sold either as a package or in parts. Land in the form of a home is not simply a residence, but a sign of one's achievement. Improving one's house and one's property is perceived as more than a right of ownership – it is a right of citizenship. Ideologically it is un-American to deprive the "king of his castle" the right to do what he wants to with his land.

In reality, however, private property rights are restricted all the time in the United States. Some restrictions deal with public safety, such as building codes. Other restrictions enforce community values, such as architectural codes for historic districts, or, in a slowly increasing number of cases in the southwestern United States, permits to develop land that are predicated on minimizing damage to archaeological sites. Importantly, the land owner bears the cost of meeting these restrictions. The United States, like many

countries throughout the world, has adopted a "polluter pays" approach to heritage. The individual or entity whose land development will disturb an archaeological site must pay to mitigate the effects of that action. When private companies are involved in projects on public land, many of the costs of heritage management are passed on to the project proponents.

Restrictions are placed on private property in the United States for the benefit of the public, although how a public benefit is defined and by whom is not clear. Public benefits tend to be at odds with private property rights. To the extent that these benefits are nebulous or serve the interests of only a small part of the public they tend to lose out to private property rights, which are clearly aligned with individual self interest. The history of heritage management in the United States tends to be one of hard fought battles between organizations representing private property rights and organizations contending that archaeological and historical resources represent the country's common heritage. The pendulum swings back and forth but the concepts of heritage and "polluter pays" have become firmly established. The current struggle between the competing values of private property and shared heritage are related to how we define the types of properties worth managing and the process by which we make preservation decisions.

The concept of national patrimony is poorly developed in the United States. Among the laws affecting archaeological resources, only the Native American Graves Protection and Repatriation Act (NAGPRA) specifically addresses patrimony, and then only to differentiate objects of Native American cultural patrimony from other types of archaeological, historical, and traditional objects that can be held as private property. The lack of a legal definition of national patrimony is reflected in how archaeological sites on public lands are perceived. In Arizona, for example, about 13 percent of the land is private property, with the remaining 87 percent under the control of federal, state, and local governments. Overwhelmingly, most archaeological sites in the state are located on public lands. One might think that they would be considered commonly owned. But such is not the case. Instead, we usually speak about sites as "owned" by a particular agency in a manner considered equivalent to private property, which the agency can develop or sell.

In Mexico, archaeological sites are viewed differently. The concept of national patrimony is deeply engrained in Mexican consciousness and has been enshrined in law for more than a century. In 1897, legislation made all archaeological and historical sites national property, and entrusted their protection and custody to the federal government (Kreutzer 2006:55). Article 73 of the Mexican constitution specifically reserves to the nation the right to legislate on archaeological resources whose preservation is of national interest. In 1939, the responsibility for historic and archaeological sites was entrusted to the Instituto Nacional de Antropología e Historia (INAH). The 1972 Ley Federal Sobre Monumentos y Zonas Arqueologicos, Artisticos e Historicos mandates the preservation of cultural patrimony and charges two agencies – INAH and the Instituto Nacional de Bellas Artes y Literatura (INBA) – to carry out that mandate.

In theory, funding for archaeological projects that stem from development in Mexico, what is termed cultural resources management (CRM) in the United States, should come exclusively from the federal government because safeguarding national patrimony is fundamentally a national responsibility. In practice, the situation is much more nuanced (Dore and López Varela 2009). The federal government provides INAH with funding for its programs, but this funding is augmented, particularly in the case of salvage projects,

by government controlled entities, such as Petróleos Mexicanos (PEMEX), Comisión Federal de Electricidad (CFE), or Comisión Nacional de Agua (CONAGUA), as well as private companies whose actions are causing disturbance to archaeological sites (Carballa Staedtler and Moguel Cos 2007; Martinez Muriel and Bader Rentería 2004). It is not only salvage projects that receive private funding; increasingly, the presentation of cultural heritage in museums is funded in part by private entities (Cesar Villalobos, personal communication 2010).

Whereas the United States has adopted an unapologetic, free-market framework to CRM, the Mexican system of heritage management is best described as a hybrid. Meeting the obligation to protect national patrimony requires greater funding than the federal government has thus far been willing to supply. Consequently, Mexico realizes that funding heritage management must include a "polluter pays" component. Yet Mexico is uneasy with a capitalistic approach to heritage management. Within Mexico, as with many other countries, there has been a long standing contentious debate about the influence of market forces on heritage management. Many countries feel strongly that safeguarding the nation's patrimony is incompatible with a heritage management system driven by a profit motive.

As government controlled entities and private businesses fund increasing amounts of archaeology, Mexico has tightened government control over heritage resource decisions. All decisions about heritage management are centralized in one federal agency. INAH decides how much work is done; INAH generally conducts the work; and INAH decides if the work has met professional quality standards. The Mexican approach is not unusual; many other countries have adopted a similar solution. The French system, for example, has been described by Willems (2008:287) as follows:

The French law has an archaeology tax, which is imposed on developers as compensation for the damage inflicted on the national heritage and which is used to pay for archaeological work. In France, it is the government that determines what the developer should pay and what he should comply with before the development can take place, and it is also the government that controls the archaeological work. This is being done by a public administrative institution called INRAP, and although there will in reality surely be contractual arrangements with the developer almost all archaeological work is a state monopoly.

This system does not have explicit standards and provides guarantees for the quality of the work being done because that is ascertained by INRAP. Moreover, there is no direct connection between the tax yield from any given development and the amount that INRAP will in practice spend on the excavation.

The Mexican system of heritage management shares with its French counterpart centralized government control of archaeology. Much like INRAP, INAH operates a state monopoly over archaeology and cultural heritage. The main difference is in funding. The French rely on a tax, which is spread over all developers, whereas the Mexican approach is to fund projects on an ad hoc basis.

Both INRAP and INAH have produced spectacular project results; they also have been marked by projects that have not been completed or have failed to meet expectations. The same can be said of free-market CRM in the United States. The main difference between the heritage management programs has less to do with the quality of the outcome than it does with control of the process. In the United States, the government ensures the public's interest by serving as a regulator, along with other interested parties, that oversees the work and certifies the quality of the results, whereas in Mexico, the government guarantees the desired benefit by actually doing the work. The United States system is designed to ensure that all "publics" (federal, state, local, and tribal) with an interest in a project can participate in shaping the direction and final results; the Mexican system assumes that the government has the best interest of all its citizens in mind.

CENTRALIZED VERSUS LOCAL CONTROL

In considering the core values of centralized versus local control of heritage management, an often raised question is "who owns the past?" Generally, this question is asked rhetorically when considering how decisions about heritage resources are made and who makes them. In Mexico the answer is simple for archaeological resources: the federal government "owns" the past. The federal government not only owns archaeological sites, it controls the decisions about how to manage and interpret them. All excavations must receive authorization from the Consejo de Arquelogía. The consejo is composed of 22 specialists, a president and his or her replacement, and ten members and their replacements who are picked by the director general of INAH (García-Bárcena 2007:14). Authorizations are for one year; multiyear projects must renew their authorization annually, and this requires a technical report containing results to date and proposed activities in the upcoming year. Upon completion a final report is required, as is the deposit of all project materials in a curatorial facility. In 2004, García-Bárcena (2007:14) reported that there were 626 archaeological projects in Mexico, of which 77 percent were from INAH, 10 percent from other Mexican institutions, and 13 percent from foreign institutions.

Contrast this amount of work with the United States, where the Secretary of the Interior reports that federal agencies performed more than 86,000 overviews and record searches, more than 103,000 archaeological field studies, and 518 archaeological excavations in 2008 (http://*www.nps.gov/archeology/SRC/index. htm, accessed 19 December 2009*). These figures do not include compliance projects sponsored by state or local government agencies, private companies, or non-compliance projects sponsored by government, universities, or private institutions, including those funded by the National Science Foundation, the National Geographic Society, or the Andrew W. Mellon Foundation. The fact that we do not know the exact number of projects in the United States is a reflection of the decentralized nature of heritage management. Each federal agency issues its own permits, or chooses not to issue permits, as do a myriad of state, local, and tribal government agencies across the country.

In Mexico, then, archaeologists decide which archaeological projects move forward. Decisions are tightly controlled by a small group with considerable power. In the United States, permits are issued by many agencies, some which employ archaeologists and some which do not, with the decision about who can perform the work and how they perform it made by agencies whose primary mission is not cultural heritage.

One might think that a system such as Mexico's, in which the direction and conduct of archaeology is tightly controlled by archaeologists, would result in the best public benefit. Certainly, the Mexican system is geared in that direction with great emphasis placed on stabilization, interpretation, and public education. But the control of archaeology by archaeologists means that other voices and interests, particularly those of descendant

communities, are not necessarily given appropriate attention (Lizama Aranda 2010). Robles García (2007:30) makes this point:

> the current tendency of projects submitted to the Council of Archaeology, whether by Mexicans or foreigners, is to virtually ignore the social context, treating sites as if they exist in a vacuum abstracted from any social reality.

Allowing archaeologists to retain control over archaeological decisions makes sense if the only value of these resources lies in their potential to help us understand the past from an empiricist and decidedly western scientific frame of reference. Such a system, however, has the effect of greatly restricting the ability to view archaeological materials using other worldviews, with the concomitant effect of constraining interesting and informative avenues of research. It also sets up a dynamic in which the archaeological establishment is closely aligned with the dominant power structure and government institutions. The interest of the federal government at times may be quite different than those of local communities. By minimizing how local communities influence the conduct of archaeology, archaeologists in Mexico risk being drawn into wider cultural disputes that may misread or undervalue the concerns of local communities for traditions, history, and culture which they perceive to be their "own" and of which they are the caretakers. For example, the demand by the Zapatistas in Chiapas to control archaeological sites in the region they claim were inhabited by their descendants was viewed by some not as a cultural heritage issue but as a simple fight for money. As Martínez Muriel (2007:19) wrote:

> Some people view the Zapatistas and other groups' claims on archaeological

sites as a sort of ethnic problem. In my opinion, this is not so much an ethnic and cultural problem as it is an economic struggle. In many communities, archaeological zones are thought to be a profitable business that can solve local economic problems. This is a false assumption, as most archaeological sites do not generate sufficient income and are in fact heavily subsidized by the Mexican Government.

We have no doubt that Martínez Muriel is right about the motives of some Zapatistas, but the experience of the United States suggests that this is not the entire story. In the decade following the passage of key laws governing cultural resources in the United States in the late 1960s, decisions about archaeological sites were largely left to archaeologists. Archaeologists representing government agencies, State Historic Preservation Offices (SHPO), the Advisory Council on Historic Preservation, and often the consultants who performed the fieldwork decided the fate of sites almost exclusively on the basis of the scientific importance of sites. Other interested parties, particularly Native American tribes and communities, were invited to voice their concerns, but not to participate in decision making as equals. Tribes argued that archaeological sites and other features of the landscape had cultural importance in addition to their scientific value, but these claims were rejected as being politically or economically driven. Non-Indians considered them to be inspired by a political struggle to be taken seriously in the nation-to-nation relationship with the federal government, or as part of a program to stop particular projects that ran counter to a tribe's economic interests.

As tribes pressed their claims to cultural heritage, archaeologists by and large resisted giving up control over decision making.

This situation changed in 1991 when the National Historic Preservation Act (NHPA) was amended to give tribes a role in the federal compliance process, and to recognize that traditional cultural properties are eligible for the National Register of Historic Places. The passage of the Native American Graves Protection and Repatriation Act (NAGPRA) the year before was also instrumental in fundamentally shifting how heritage is viewed in the United States These changes gave tribes a real "seat at the table" when decisions about archaeological, traditional, or sacred sites are made. Archaeologists, some of whom at first had resisted these changes, have for the most part found that their fears of losing control of how archaeology is conducted to be greatly overstated and more than compensated for by new avenues of research that have developed in collaboration with tribes and a renewed sense of social responsibility.

Returning to the issue raised in the Zapatista case of whether claims to control of archaeological materials are driven by cultural or economic factors, it is interesting to note that several tribes in the southwestern United States have established tribal museums. To our knowledge, none of these were designed solely for economic development. Instead, the impetus to create tribal museums, many of which required major investments by the tribes, was to take control of their heritage; to tell the public their version of their history, to be able to maintain archaeological and ethnographic collections from their ancestral sites, and to instill a sense of community pride by celebrating their proud past.

We recognize that the histories of the United States and Mexico have led to different legal views and cultural perceptions of the constituent groups that compose the citizenry of each country. Each country struggles with finding a balance between national and local interests in honoring their "common" heritage.

Archaeologists in both countries would do well to recognize their role in facilitating this discussion and to ensure that research performed in the public's interest actually recognizes the diversity and interests of all possible publics.

TRADITIONAL VERSUS SCIENTIFIC AUTHORITY IN ARCHAEOLOGICAL INTERPRETATION

This brings us to the final comparison of core values, which is traditional versus scientific authority in archaeological interpretation. In both Mexico and the United States, scientific authority provides the intellectual foundation for archaeological research and public interpretation. In both countries, however, there is a growing movement to expand this interpretive authority to include the traditional knowledge offered by indigenous groups. Be that as it may, there are significant differences in how traditional knowledge is used authoritatively, based on differences in the ideology of ancestry and descent in Mexico and the United States

In Mexico, the ideology of Mestizo ancestry means that the population is one and indivisible, with a multicultural composition derived from an admixture of indigenous occupants and Spanish immigrants (Alonzo 2004; Gamio 1916; Lomnitz 2001). Some scholars think the concept of mestizaje is a political tool used to create a national concept of a unique race, and criticize it because it silences both Indigenous and Spanish history and identity to create a monolithic state ideology (Gutierrez 1998). Nontheless, all Mexican citizens have a valid claim of descent from the original occupants of the ancient sites that now constitute the national patrimony and cultural heritage of the country. Politically, los indios de Mexico—the Indians of Mexico—are considered to be local communities that

may retain indigenous languages and cultural practices, but which have no greater claim of descent from ancient peoples than other citizens.

The situation in the United States is remarkably different. The Euro-american, Afro-american, and other immigrants are seen to be culturally and historically distinct from the Native peoples that were the original occupants of the country. Nonetheless, Native American archaeological sites have been appropriated as part of the national heritage providing an identity for the country, even if they are not historically related to most of the occupants (Colwell-Chanthaphonh 2005; Hinsley 2000). This appropriation has been accomplished by federal legislation, beginning with the Antiquity Act of 1906 and continuing through to the National Historic Preservation Act and the Archaeological Resources Protection Act. This legislation has converted the heritage sites of Native Americans into scientific resources to be used to advance the scientific interpretation of the past.

Native Americans, however, have a unique political status in the United States as sovereign but dependent nations, a status derived from the Marshall trilogy of Supreme Court decisions in the mid-nineteenth century. Native Americans value this political status and in the 1990s they convinced Congress to amend the NHPA and enact NAGPRA to provide federally recognized Indian tribes with a greater role in historic preservation decisions and control over ancestral human remains and funerary objects. The consultation between archaeologists and tribes mandated by federal legislation has led to increased participation of Native Americans in archaeological research, and an increasing number of collaborative projects in which traditional knowledge is arrayed in a complementary manner with scientific knowledge to produce a multi-vocal archaeology (Kuwanwisiwma

2008). This endeavor promises one day to develop an indigenous archaeology that uses native concepts and traditional theories in archaeological analysis and interpretation. We think expanding the intellectual foundation of archaeology to include non-Western concepts and theories is good for the intellectual health of our discipline.

Some people think that all citizens can claim an Indigenous heritage; other people conceptualize this in the reverse, that is, all Indigenous people are considered to be Mexican citizens. In either case, the twentieth century Mexican discourse on Indigenismo and Mestizaje marginalized Indigenous peoples and communities, in part because there were few Indian voices contributing to scholarship and Indians remained alienated from mainstream society (Brading 1988; Doremus 2001:401). Given this situation, the intellectual precepts of indigenous archaeology may need to be decoupled from their political context as found in the United States. When this is done, the incorporation of traditional authority in archaeological interpretation becomes community-based cultural heritage management (Hollowell and Nicholas 2009), and thus a dimension of local versus national control of heritage.

CONCLUSIONS

Each of our countries has something to learn from the other. With respect to private property versus national patrimony, we think the United States would benefit from the national ownership of heritage sites as is the case in Mexico. We think Mexico would benefit from a heritage management system with greater accountability. With respect to centralized versus local control, we think the Mexican system of heritage management with centralized control geared towards stabilization, interpretation, and public education has much to recommend it in terms of public benefit. However, the local control of managerial decisions found in the United States has an advantage in making sure the values and concerns of local communities and descendant groups are adequately considered in the decision making process. Finally, we think expanding the intellectual basis of archaeological research to include traditional as well as scientific authority is a positive development in Mexico and the United States because it makes archaeology a more democratic and multi-vocal enterprise that benefits local communities as well as the nation as a whole.

Acknowledgments An earlier version of this paper was presented at the 11th Southwest Symposium in Hermosillo, Mexico. The authors would like to thank Randy McGuire and Elisa Villalpando for organizing the conference and César Villalobos and Beth Bagwell for organizing the session "Archaeology and Society." Comments and assistance on the paper was gratefully received from Sandra Varela Lopez, César Quijada, and César Villalobos. The authors alone are responsible for any errors.

Part III, Chapter 5

O'odham Heritage, Sovereignty, and the Legal Conundrums of the U.S.-Mexico Boundary

Joseph T. Joaquin, Eric J. Kaldahl, and Peter Steere

ABSTRACT

The U.S.-Mexico boundary split O'odham ancestral lands in half. Since that time, Tohono O'odham and Hia-Ced O'odham communities have lived under two different legal frameworks. We review what U.S. and Mexican legal systems have meant for O'odham heritage protection. We also review the effect of U.S.-Mexican treaties, noting that the O'odham were never party to those treaties. The U.S. has developed a legal framework recognizing tribal sovereignty in heritage management, while O'odham communities in Mexico have confronted very different challenges. We consider two cases that occurred in the last decade at the O'odham village of Quitovac, Sonora. First a Mexican-government authorized research expedition removed ceremonial objects and human remains from Quitovac, while shocked O'odham families watched legally helpless. The mediation that resolved that situation involved Mexico, France, and the Tohono O'odham Nation. A few years later a proposed archaeological expedition engaged in advanced consultation with the Quitovac community resulting in greater dialogue. The U.S.-Mexican boundary will continue to pose vexing questions for O'odham communities and for materials recovered from O'odham ancestral lands. We believe that those future vexing questions can be resolved in respectful discussions among the various parties who care for the O'odham heritage.

RESUMEN

La frontera política México-Americana dividió en dos a las tierras ancestrales de los O'odham. Desde entonces, las comunidades Tohono O'odham y Hia-Ced O'odham han vivido bajo dos legislaciones diferentes. En este trabajo revisamos los marcos legales tanto de Estados Unidos como de México, enfocándonos en lo que han significado para la protección del patrimonio O'odham. Discutimos asimismo los efectos de los tratados México-Americanos, notando que las comunidades O'odham nunca han sido incluidas en la formulación de los mismos. En los Estados Unidos se ha desarrollado un marco legal en el cual se ha reconocido la soberanía indígena en la administración del patrimonio, mientras que las comunidades en México se han enfrentado a muy diferentes retos. Abordaremos dos casos que ocurrieron en la década pasada en la comunidad O'odham de Quitovac, Sonora. Primero, el gobierno Mexicano autorizó un proyecto de investigación arqueológica con permiso de remover y extraer restos humanos y objetos ceremoniales de Quitovac, en dicho caso, las familias O'odham miraban impresionadas la extracción de objetos sin posibilidad legal para detener el proyecto arqueológico. Para resolver la situación hizo falta la participación de México, Francia y la nación Tohono O'odham. Segundo, pocos años después, una propuesta de investigación arqueológica consultó previamente a la comunidad de Quitovac cuya intención resultó en un fructífero diálogo. La frontera México-Americana continuará representando inquietantes preguntas acerca de los objetos extraídos de las tierras ancestrales O'odham. Creemos que en el futuro, esta cadena de desconcertantes o inquietantes hechos, podrán ser resueltos en discusiones respetuosas entre los diferentes actores interesados en el patrimonio O'odham.

Joseph T. Joaquin (enrolled member of the Tohono O'odham Nation) Tohono O'odham Nation
Eric J. Kaldahl Amerind Foundation, Inc.
Peter Steere Tohono O'odham Nation

The traditional territory of the O'odham (the "People" in their language) was split in half by the creation of the present international boundary between the United States of America (U.S.) and los Estados Unidos Mexicanos (Mexico). The O'odham were not invited to the negotiating table for this decision, but they have lived with the consequences of O'odham families, villages, sacred sites, and ancient settlements governed by two non-O'odham nation states. Today the O'odham reside on both sides of the U.S.-Mexico border in the modern states of Arizona and Sonora, respectively. The Tohono O'odham Nation (the Nation) is a federally recognized tribal government within the U.S. The Nation has dealt with heritage management issues in the U.S. and Mexico on behalf of O'odham residing on both sides of the U.S.-Mexico border.

We present here case studies about the Nation's efforts to protect the O'odham heritage under two very different legal frameworks. There are many other problems that the U.S.-Mexico border has caused that we cannot address here, including disputes of citizenship, drug trafficking, drug violence, human trafficking, environmental degradation, and economic hardship. The Nation has seen their citizens threatened, killed, abused, and kidnapped. They have been harassed by government officials on both sides of the U.S.-Mexico border, and they have lost land and homes under duress. Although the Nation confronts many such serious border issues, we consider heritage protection to be an issue of equal importance (Castillo and Cowan 2001; Tohono O'odham Nation [the abbreviation "TON" will be used in citations hereafter] Executive Branch Administrative Plan 2004).

There is an essential connection between the well-being of today's people, O'odham land, and O'odham places both ancient and sacred. There is a word in O'odham "elid" that English speakers usually translate as "respect." *Elid* also encompasses the meaning of the English words "revere" and "value." O'odham believe that demonstrating *elid* for all people and all things in the world keeps communities healthy. Protecting O'odham heritage in all its forms (e.g., sacred places, archaeological sites, human burial grounds, songs, oral histories, etc.) is necessary for the well being of O'odham living today and for the O'odham of the future. Heritage protection is not an obscure academic subject to O'odham.

In addition to the documentary materials we will be referencing, the case studies presented here derive from the experiences of two of the authors: Joaquin and Steere. Joseph T. Joaquin is a member of the Tohono O'odham Nation. In our earliest case, Joaquin was an elected official serving on the Nation's Legislative Council. Later he became employed by the Nation's Cultural Affairs Division, experiencing the challenges of O'odham heritage protection in the field, in museums, in courts, and in conference rooms on both sides of the border. He has a long history representing the Nation's interests in repatriation and heritage management, from the early crafting of the U.S. Native American Graves Protection and Repatriation Act (NAGPRA) to the present.

Peter Steere is an archaeologist employed by the Nation. Today he works as the tribal government's first Tribal Historic Preservation Officer. For the last decade, he too has been engaged in the U.S. and Mexico's heritage protection legal frameworks through consultation, field direction, and legal cases.

Eric J. Kaldahl is an archaeologist who was employed by the Nation's Cultural Center & Museum as a curator. He worked closely with Joaquin and Steere and communities on both sides of the U.S.-Mexico border in creating the tribal museum. At the request of Joaquin and Steere, Kaldahl assisted in synthesizing the experiences of his co-authors with the documentary sources cited herein. Although no longer employed by the Nation, Kaldahl's participation here is based on his concern for the heritage protection challenges of the O'odham.

Critical to the content of this essay is

Graciela Barajas, who also completed the translation of our abstract into Spanish. She, too, was a firsthand witness to the events discussed here. She is a Mexican citizen who has played a crucial role as the Nation's translator and consultant during negotiations and consultations with Mexican officials.

A Few Historical Facts

Before we present our recent experiences in O'odham heritage protection, the reader should be made aware of a few historical facts. In the U.S. today, four federally recognized tribal governments with large O'odham populations control only a fraction of O'odham traditional lands. The four tribal governments are the Tohono O'odham Nation, the Ak Chin Indian Community, the Gila River Indian Community, and the Salt River Pima-Maricopa Indian Community. The ancestors of the O'odham lived in a much larger territory. The traditional lands of the O'odham were bounded by the Sonoran river and Sea of Cortez on the south, the Colorado river on the west, the Gila river on the north, and the San Pedro river on the east (Erickson 1994:12-18; Fontana 1989:36-38; Spicer 1962:118-121).

The arrival of the Spanish in the late-1600s changed the course of O'odham history forever. Mining interests, Spanish presidios, Catholic missionaries, and Spanish settlers pushed O'odham away from the best watered places. Sometimes the O'odham fought against the Spanish, and sometimes they fought alongside them. But gradually the traditional land base was lost, especially along the rivers of what is today Sonora (Erickson 1994:19-66; Spicer 1962:124-126).

After Mexico won its independence from Spain in 1821, the O'odham were declared to be Mexican citizens. The new framework of law and the Mexican courts did little to protect O'odham

citizens. Land and water continued to be a source for armed conflict between O'odham villagers and Mexican settlers (Booth 2000:61-62; Dobyns 1972:39; Erickson 1994:62-73, 84-85; Spicer 1962:133, 334-338).

The U.S. went to war with Mexico in 1846. In 1848 the Treaty of Guadalupe Hidalgo settled the peace between the two governments with a new international boundary established by that treaty at the Gila River. A few years later in 1854, the U.S. bought more land from Mexico in the Gadsden Purchase. The purchase created a new international boundary south of the Gila River (Erickson 1994:69, 78, 99-109). The new international boundary split O'odham traditional lands roughly in half. The O'odham were not party to the negotiations that established this international boundary.

In the U.S., the O'odham and the U.S. were never at war. No peace treaty settled the present O'odham land holdings. In the U.S. the protection of O'odham land was granted by U.S. Presidential Executive Orders and Acts of the U.S. Congress (Erickson 1994:78, 99-109; Kickingbird and Berkey 1977; TON Constitution 1986: Article I – Jurisdiction, Section 1). O'odham lands in the U.S. are administered by the four federally recognized tribal governments mentioned previously, the largest of which is the Tohono O'odham Nation which controls over 2.8 million acres. Under U.S. law, the Tohono O'odham formed their own constitutional government (Blaine 1981; Booth 2000; Erickson 1994:147-152, 160; Fontana 1989:121-122; Hall 1935a:20, 1935b:18; Spicer 1962:143-144; TON Constitution 1986). This set the foundation for the Nation to exert sovereignty over the Nation's land, patrimony, and citizens.

In Mexico, there are no tribal governments that speak for the O'odham, although a few O'odham communities have some local governance as *ejidos* (Spicer 1962:334-338). An *ejido* is an agricultural community that holds land communally.

The Nation has 28,000 enrolled members; roughly 1,500 enrolled tribal members live in Mexico (Castillo and Cowan 2001; TON Executive Branch Administrative Plan 2004).

O'ODHAM PATRIMONY

"Patrimony" and "Heritage" are terms that were used with great frequency at the Southwest Symposium in Hermosillo. We would like our readers to understand what these concepts mean to the O'odham. O'odham history is tied to their traditional territory. O'odham ancestors are buried here. There are sacred objects in O'odham traditional lands that O'odham believe help their people and communities to be healthy. When O'odham land is disturbed, when ancestors' graves are desecrated, when sacred objects are taken away – O'odham suffer. Former Nation Chairman Edward Manuel summarized this point quite well:

> According to our traditional O'odham way, we believe that many of the sufferings of our living people have their origin in the desecration of our dead, and it is affecting our traditional way of life. All O'odham people have a mission to preserve our cultural patrimony and to protect our territory and ancestors. All O'odham have a right to share in the traditional knowledge and wisdom of O'odham elders and their families who live in the lands described herein, regardless of where they live. The O'odham people have guarded and struggled to preserve their integrity and character as one people. (1 August 1997 letter to Instituto Nacional de Antropología e Historia Director M. C. Ramon Hinostroza from TON Chairman Edward Manuel, TON Cultural Center & Museum [CCM] archives, Topawa, Arizona)

The Papago Tribe of Arizona was the official designation of the Tohono O'odham tribal government from its first constitution adopted in 1937 until 1986. In 1986, the Tohono O'odham adopted a new constitution that designated their government as the Tohono O'odham Nation (Booth 2000:374-377, 398-410; Erickson 1994:148-151; TON Constitution 1986).

In the U.S., federal recognition of the Nation's sovereign powers provides legal tools to protect the O'odham heritage (Erickson 1994:147-149). The Archaeological Resources Protection Act (ARPA) helps the Nation prosecute looters and developers who damage tribal lands (U.S. ARPA of 1979, 16 U.S.C. 470aa-470m; Public Law 96-95).

Bridges, roads, schools, and houses are built on the Nation each year. The Nation realizes that other people who live on ancestral O'odham lands need these things, too. Thanks to the National Historic Preservation Act (NHPA), Arizona state laws, and local government law, the Nation is consulted when development occurs (U.S. NHPA, Public Law 89-665 and amendments; 16 U.S.C. 470 et seq.; U.S. Antiquities Act, 16 U.S.C. 431-433; State of Arizona State Historic Preservation Act of 1982 includes Arizona Revised Statues §41-862 through §41-864; State of Arizona Antiquities Act and its amendments includes Arizona Revised Statutes §41-841 through §41-845).

When the graves of O'odham ancestors must be taken from the ground, the Nation works with researchers to learn things from those remains (State of Arizona Revised Statues §41-844 and §41-865). After the studies are completed, these O'odham ancestors are reburied in a safe place with dignity and honor. In U.S. federal law, NAGPRA has given Native American governments a powerful tool to bring home sacred objects and the remains of ancestors, so that they can be respectfully cared for (U.S. NAGPRA, Public Law 101-601; 25 U.S.C.

3001-3013). Both Arizona state statutes and NAGPRA require Native American governments and researchers to consult with each other in the process of bringing ancestors and objects home.

Have these consultation processes always been smooth? No. But at least a legal framework exists that brings the interests of the Nation and the interests of others to the table for discussion. The O'odham believe that reasonable discussion can lead to good decisions among people acting in good faith.

The legal framework of Mexico is completely different. All pre-Spanish period antiquities and monuments are the property of the Mexican government by law. Most Spanish colonial period antiquities and monuments are also the property of the Mexican government (Lorenzo 1984; McGuire 2008:157-160; Mexico Federal Law on Archaeological Monuments and Zone published in 1972 with regulations published in 1975). The Mexican government has declared all these materials part of a national patrimony – and indigenous Mexican citizens do not have any special legal relationship to the materials and remains of their ancestors. There is no requirement to consult with Native people when graves will be disturbed. There is no special right of access to the remains of O'odham ancestors or sacred objects held in Mexico's museums. O'odham leaders in Mexico are rarely asked to participate in land management. When archaeological projects in O'odham ancestral territory are authorized by the *Instituto Nacional de Antropología e Historia* (INAH), no O'odham are consulted. No reports need to be sent to O'odham communities about what such projects might have learned.

Mexican O'odham leaders have been frustrated in their attempts to exercise their right to petition the federal government. O'odham communities in Mexico are poor. Taking long trips to Mexico City, finding lodging, getting meetings with appropriate government officials, hiring legal representation – these things are expensive. As enrolled members of the Tohono O'odham Nation, the O'odham of Mexico have worked with the Nation to help address problems (3 September 1990 Official Communication of the Council of Traditional O'odham of Mexico to the TON, TON CCM; Papago Tribal Council [PTC] Resolution no. 43-79, no. 44-79, and no. 20-83).

We turn now to two cases that illustrate the O'odham-Mexican experience. The final resolution of each case was not due to any law favoring the rights of O'odham to manage their own heritage. The resolution of these cases depended on Mexican officials of good conscience deciding to help O'odham communities.

THE QUITOVAC ETHNOARCHAEOLOGICAL PROJECT

In the mid-1980s, INAH authorized a group sponsored by France's Center for Mexican and Central American Studies (CEMCA) to conduct an archaeological and ethnoarchaeological project near Quitovac (*Gi'ito Wak*) (Rodríguez-Loubet et al. 1993:27-28). *Gi'ito Wak* is an ancient O'odham village. Located at a permanent water source in northern Sonora, geologists have said that the *Gi'ito Wak* lake has persisted since the last glacial advance at the end of the Pleistocene (Rodríguez-Loubet et al. 1993:53-56). Today *Gi'ito Wak* is the only O'odham community that holds a ceremony called the *wi:gita* each year (Bahr 1991; Davis 1920; Fontana 1987; Galinier 1991; Underhill 1946:153-161). People from all over the Nation, as well as from O'odham communities in Mexico, come to *Gi'ito Wak* for this ceremony. By holding this ceremony, O'odham believe that the community's health and land are improved and that the condition of all people throughout the entire world is also improved (18 May 1991 Position Statement of the Vigida Ceremony Officials, TON CCM; Testimony of the Vigida Delegation of the TON before Mexico's National Institute of Indigenous People [INI] September 19-20, 1991, Mexico City, TON CCM; TON Legislative Council Resolution no. 91-203). There are several differing dialects of O'odham spoken today (Hill 1992, 2001; Hill and Zepeda 1991; Joseph et al. 1949:66-71; Saxton et al. 1983:130-131; Underhill 1969:59-69).

"*Vigida*" is an alternate spelling of the ceremony held at *Gi'ito Wak* that represents one dialectical pronunciation of the ceremony. The spelling *wi:gita* represents the pronunciation of other dialectical groups and conforms to the official orthography adopted by the Nation (Zepeda 1983:5). The objects used in that ceremony are very powerful. Consequently they are stored away from the community, and only specially trained people care for those objects.

The French research project appeared in the village of *Gi'ito Wak*. Authorized to be there by authorities in Mexico City, no one in the community expected their arrival or understood their purpose. Nonetheless community members extended their hospitality to these visitors (Rodríguez-Loubet et al. 1993:28). Researchers surveyed the land and conducted excavations. They interviewed community members. The researchers went to places outside of the village where *wi:gita* ceremonial objects were stored. Several of these objects were taken by the researchers to Mexico City and Hermosillo. We also know human remains were taken to CEMCA laboratories. To this date, CEMCA has never provided a report of the French team's activities to the people of *Gi'ito Wak* or the Nation. A copy of the CEMCA team's report was obtained by the authors via interlibrary loan with the University of Pennsylvania.

We ask the reader to consider the O'odham perspective on these actions. Objects, actively being used in important community ceremonies were appropriated by foreign researchers. *Gi'ito Wak* members had opened their homes to these individuals, answered their questions, and toured them through the community. Their courtesy and trust was violated in the name of scholarship. Objects of great cultural importance to O'odham were treated as data to be taken at the pleasure of visiting foreigners, as were the human remains of O'odham ancestors. The damage was tremendous and trust has been hard to come by for later researchers working in the region (e.g., McGuire 2008:180-181).

Worse still, it was Mexican federal permits that authorized the removal of these materials from *Gi'ito Wak*, and Mexican law declares such findings to be part of a national patrimony that is to be held in the care and custody of INAH. There was no law in Mexico that the people of *Gi'ito Wak* could turn to. In the end, it was a few officials at INAH, at the Mexican government's National Indigenous Institute (INI), and at the French embassy who decided that returning the *Gi'ito Wak* materials was the right thing to do.

The Nation received a request for help from *Gi'ito Wak* (18 May 1991 Position Statement of the Vigida Ceremony Officials, TON CCM; TON Legislative Council Resolution 91-203). Local communities and councils of the Nation and the Nation's Legislative Council pledged their support (18 May 1991 Resolution of the TON Al Ce:k Community; 10 March 1992 Resolution of the TON Hia-Ceḍ O'odham Policy Board Supporting the Vigitha Elders on the Quitovac Issue; TON Legislative Council Resolution no. 91-203). The tribal government gathered the *wi:gita* ceremonial officials together. The Nation engaged legal counsel in Mexico City, and funded the travel of two *wi:gita* elders and their apprentices. In testimony before Mexico's INI, an agency similar to the U.S. Bureau of Indian Affairs, the *wi:gita* elders explained the importance of the sacred items seized by the researchers. They explained why the ceremony is important to O'odham, but also why they believe the ceremony is important to the welfare of everyone in the world (Testimony of the Vigida Delegation of the TON before INI, September

19-20, 1991, Mexico City, TON CCM; 16 December 1991 "On the Protection of Quitovac" a legal opinion prepared for the TON by Mexican Legal Consultant Isidro Asse, TON CCM).

This testimony took place in 1991, several years after the French expedition had left the field. The harsh light of the 500th anniversary of Columbus' arrival in the New World was shining on the Americas, and challenging every government to think about the lives of their indigenous people. The U.S. had just passed NAGPRA. Although no law compelled the Mexican or French governments to return those *Gi'ito Wak* sacred objects, a decision was made to do so. In 1992, CEMCA turned the *Gi'ito Wak* materials over to INAH. INAH released the materials to a representative of the Nation—Joseph T. Joaquin—to drive the sacred materials from Mexico City to *Gi'ito Wak* (16 December 1991 "On the Protection of Quitovac" a legal opinion prepared for the TON by Mexican Legal Consultant Isidro Asse, TON CCM; 7 September 1992 communication from the French Embassy to Mexico's *Consejo Nacional de Arqueología* conveying the material from the Quitovac Ethnoarchaeological Project to INAH, TON CCM; 14 October 1992 issuance of a Revocable Deposit from INAH to the Community of Quitovac, TON CCM; 16 October 1992 authorization by INAH to release materials from the Quitovac Ethnoarchaeological Project to the Quitovac Community, TON CCM).

Was this a repatriation? No. INAH has the authority to deposit collections with local or state governments (Mexico Federal Law on Archaeological Monuments and Zone published in 1972 with regulations published in 1975). Mexican law still asserts that these objects are federal property. The paperwork authorizing the release of the human remains and sacred objects from INAH to *Gi'ito Wak* would be similar to a "long term loan." The documents describe this action as a "revocable deposit" (*depósito revocable*). The authorization tells the

Gi'ito Wak community how to treat the returned materials, including those ceremonial objects that the *wi:gita* officials had maintained for untold years (14 October 1992 issuance of a Revocable Deposit from INAH to the Community of Quitovac, TON CCM). From the time the Quitovac Ethnoarchaeological Project ended in 1987, five years passed until the materials were returned in 1992. For five years objects important to the proper observance of the *wi:gita* ceremony were removed from the O'odham community.

The O'odham would have preferred that the French expedition never happened. We understand that the researchers had their work published in reports that no O'odham has ever been given (Rodríguez-Loubet et al. 1993). But we do appreciate the men and women at the French Embassy, at INAH, and at INI who helped to right this wrong. Perhaps this experience helped raise awareness prior to the next research expedition.

THE UNAM PROJECT

In 2003, the Nation received word that a researcher with the *Instituto de Investigaciones Antropológicas de la Universidad Nacional Autónoma de México* (UNAM) was planning a series of surveys and excavations in the *Gi'ito Wak* area. The research proposal states that human skeletal remains were to be analyzed (2003 *Proyecto Poblamiento Temprano del Noroeste de Sonora: Región de Quitovac, Instituto de Investigaciones Antropológicas de la UNAM*, submitted by Archaeologist Alejandro Terrazas Mata, TON CCM).

The Nation's first inquiry about the project was sent to the INAH center in Sonora. We learned that the project was being authorized by INAH officials in Mexico City. Officials with INAH Sonora were unaware of the proposed expedition (5 March 2003 letter to *Ingeniero* Joaquin Garcia Barcena of the *Consejo de Arqueología* from

TON Chairman Edward Manuel, TON CCM; 21 March 2003 Letter to Mexican Consul General Carlos I. Gonzalez from TON Chairman Edward Manuel, TON CCM).

With distant Mexico City officials involved, it fell to the Nation to use its resources to lobby for a halt to the project. By summer 2003, UNAM officials agreed to stop the proposed expedition. Again, we realize that all of the people involved were not legally compelled to do so. They listened to O'odham concerns and voluntarily brought an end to the project. We are grateful for that.

GOING FORWARD

As a people split by the U.S.-Mexico border, the O'odham confront several unique challenges. The O'odham experience with Mexican research and heritage law have been unnecessarily confrontational in recent years; whereas in the U.S., we have seen positive developments in heritage management law and practice that favors collaborations with Native people. The two Mexican case studies we have presented are stories of decisions made far away without any regard to their effect on the welfare of local people. We realize that Mexican law does not acknowledge Native people's unique relationship to the patrimony of Mexico. But we have seen that individual decision makers at INAH and in other federal institutions have acted on the side of indigenous human rights.

Our participation in the Hermosillo conference presented us with an opportunity to address practitioners in the fields of archaeology and anthropology whose research has led them to O'odham ancestral lands. It has taken many decades to achieve the level of collaboration that Native tribes now have with U.S. researchers. For those at work in Mexico, we urge INAH officials to bring local Native leaders to the table as permissions are granted for future research projects. Talking with Native people in no way

lessens INAH's authority to approve projects, but we believe such projects would gain much from collaboration. Researchers in the U.S. have certainly added depth to their archaeological interpretations through consultation with indigenous communities.

The Southwest Symposium and numerous publications have featured research projects conducted on O'odham ancestral lands, including projects at La Playa and Las Trincheras, both in Sonora. We have read studies that discuss the human remains taken from those places. The Nation would rather that the desecration of those graves had not occurred. O'odham believe that the disturbance of their ancestors hurts our living people and demonstrates great disrespect. In the State of Arizona, the removal of our ancestors' remains due to excavation requires a plan for repatriation and reburial; however, this procedure has not halted research (State of Arizona Revised Statues §41-844 and §41-865). In consultation with the Nation, the remains of O'odham ancestors are studied and documented by trained researchers prior to being given to the Nation for respectful reburial. The results of those studies are disseminated and shared with the scholarly community, as well as being archived with Native American communities.

We urge those working in Mexico to embrace this model. The Nation has asked INAH specifically to allow the human remains recovered at Las Trincheras and La Playa to be returned to a Mexican O'odham community like *Gi'ito Wak* for reburial (1 August 1997 letter to INAH Director M. C. Ramon Hinostroza from TON Chairman Edward Manuel, TON CCM). The Nation's requests have been denied (see also McGuire 2008:180-186). We do appreciate those researchers who have shown great sympathy and advocacy for the O'odham position in this matter. We hope that Mexico will use the precedent set by the Quitovac Ethnoarchaeological Project to make more *depósitos revocables* to local communities. We ask Mexico's elected officials and government agencies to allow O'odham ancestors to be at rest among their descendents. Respecting the remains of the dead, ensuring their care in a community of their descendents, demonstrates a basic support for the human rights of Mexico's indigenous people.

We ask that anthropologists in the field in northern Mexico work more closely with local indigenous people. Anthropologists have long held the belief that what they do is beneficial to the human community. No law compels a permitted project in Mexico to consult with Native communities or to report project findings to those communities. However, there is nothing preventing researchers from doing so. There is nothing preventing a researcher from designing a project to include consultation with Native people. There is nothing preventing a researcher from conducting public education about their studies in local communities. The careers of researchers tangibly benefit from successful scholarly studies. We ask researchers in the field to consider giving back to the people they study in their professional practice.

Unique to the O'odham situation, we consider U.S. museums, INAH, and the Tohono O'odham Nation. The Nation is aware that some U.S. museums have sacred objects and objects of cultural patrimony taken from O'odham ancestral lands in Mexico. The Nation has been rebuffed in its efforts to be consulted about the repatriation of these items, as U.S. museums have deferred to INAH. Some INAH officials have discouraged U.S. institutions from discussing such objects with the Nation's government. The present political environment in Mexico seems unfavorable to indigenous consultation (McGuire 2008:184-185). It is our position that U.S. museums that are hesitant to consult about sacred objects and objects of cultural patrimony are doing harm to collaborative relationships.

The two legal frameworks that O'odham live under will never be reconciled. But there is one thing that we find beneficial on both sides of the U.S.-Mexico border – that the people involved talk and listen to each other. U.S. law has compelled such discussions. Over time the benefits of consultation have become increasingly evident in anthropological practice. Although the law is very different, Mexican officials have talked with O'odham leaders and the Nation's government because those officials felt it was the right way to proceed. Unfortunately now we find ourselves in a time when discussions between O'odham communities and the Mexican government seem stifled. Let us not allow the large bureaucracies that we work within to prevent us from working together. There is much about our heritage and its management that will benefit through cooperation and understanding.

Part III, Chapter 6

Patrimonial Wasteland? Expanded Notions of Material Culture in the U.S.-Mexico Borderlands

Maribel L. Alvarez

ABSTRACT

The concept of "heritage" exerts a powerful influence in modern societies. Insofar as what is considered patrimonial is often associated with notions of kinship and authenticity, that which stands at the opposite end of this concept is often represented as threatening the integrity, sovereignty, and unity of the nation-state. In Mexico, discourses about patrimony have elaborated not only an objective record of protected archaeological and historical sites, cultural artifacts, and traditions but also a counter-discourse that condemns "mal gusto" (bad taste) and stereotypes. These discourses have been particularly acute in reference to the cultures and lifeways that emanate from the U.S.-Mexico border zones. The Border's cottage industries of "Mexican Curios" have been specifically targeted as examples of patrimonial degradation. In this paper, I propose an alternative framework for a consideration of the Border's material cultural inventory–one that acknowledges in objects of tourism and lowbrow ornamentation insightful traces of the political economy of the region and of the hybridity and contestation that informs Northern Mexican identities.

RESUMEN

El concepto de Patrimonio ejerce una ponderosa influencia en las sociedades modernas. En tanto que lo que se considera "patrimonial" es frecuentemente asociado a nociones filiales y de autenticidad nacional, todo aquello que se percibe en el polo contrario a estas ideas es representado como amenaza a la integridad, soberanía, y unidad del estado-nación. En México, los discursos sociales sobre el patrimonio han elaborado no solamente un inventario objetivo de zonas arqueológicas e históricas protegidas, artefactos culturales, y tradiciones sino también un contra-discurso que condena el "mal gusto" y los estereotipos. Estos discursos han sido especialmente agudos en referencia a las culturas y estilos de vida que parten de las zonas fronterizas con los Estados Unidos. Las pequeñas industrias autóctonas de la frontera que se dedican a la reproducción de los llamados "Mexican Curios" han sido especialmente señaladas como ejemplos de degradación al patrimonio nacional. En este trabajo, propongo un marco de referencia alternativo para una consideración del inventario material fronterizo–en esencia, un marco interpretativo que admite que se pueden encontrar trazos de valiosa información sobre la economía política de la región y sobre la hibridez y espíritu contestatario de las identidades Norteñas en los objetos de turismo y de cursilería clase-media que saturan el panorama visual de esta zona.

Maribel L. Alvarez Associate Research Social Scientist. The Southwest Center, University of Arizona

LEARNING FROM ARCHAEOLOGISTS

In an article published in the December 2009 issue of *Anthropology News*, Indiana University professor K. Anne Pyburn argues convincingly for why archaeologists "need to continue to be trained with an anthropologist's critique of the concept of culture." The critique referenced by Pyburn is familiar to anyone who attended graduate school in any of the social sciences after 1970. Parenthetically, I choose the year 1970 as benchmark because it was when Michel Foucault's book *The Order of Things: An Archaeology of the Human Sciences* first appeared in English. The reason for the book's significance is simple: Foucault's remarkable archaeological find consisted of a series of analytical artifacts, specifically one that he called an "episteme," that allowed in a manner more systematic than ever before a questioning of the bases of what we accept as knowledge.

The consequences of this questioning for anthropology were immediate and severe; its ravaging effect concentrated most dramatically in the concept that had been up to that moment anthropology's unique calling card and its focal claim to expertise: culture. Once a unifying theme in anthropology (albeit a unification that derived from the discipline's four fields' common ancestry in colonial ventures), the concept of "Culture" as a tidy place holder for a variety of human cognitive and behavioral expressions has irrevocably given way to a more complicated and contradictory understanding of human formations and processes. Whereas once anthropologists referred to "the" Culture of specific population groups with relative objectivity, confidence, and predictability, the critique of the concept of culture introduced variability, positionality, subjectivity, ideology, discourse, and representations as shifting variables of human experience that far from fixing in place any holistic notion of a group's Culture (with capital C) direct our attention instead to a multitude of cultural formations, negotiations, and modes of signification.

It is this nuanced, contextual understanding of "the cultural" that Pyburn argues archaeologists should heed. Pyburn believes that archaeologists should learn from cultural anthropologists to question the impulse to classify evidence of past human behavior according to static categories. Henceforth, to continue to be vital and relevant in an era of rapid change and globalization, Pyburn argues that the "future of archaeology" cannot be rationalized as anything else but "as anthropology."

I like Professor Pyburn's argument; it is totally consistent with how I think of and utilize the concept of culture. As a cultural anthropologist, too, it makes me happy to hear admonitions to other disciplines to emulate how *we* do things. But I want to direct my attention briefly to a curious paradox that Pyburn seems to have missed in her otherwise excellent exposition. Simply stated, anthropology has been learning more from archaeology lately than the other way around.

The claim that the critique of anthropology has made for complicating our understanding of culture has happened partly as a result of a newly found interest among anthropologists and other cultural studies scholars in the roles that objects, things, and artifacts play in constituting human meaning and organizing our social, sexual, political, emotional, domestic, leisure, and occupational lives. If anthropology has survived the "crisis" of its own postcolonial angst, one could argue that it has been partly because it has re-taken the discipline's primary interest in material cultures as a productive platform from which to analyze how today's borderless exchange of of iPods, cell phones, laptops, fashion sneakers, hybrid automobiles, and transgenic corn create social worlds and cultural "truths" worth examining, critiquing, and reimagining. In other words, "things are back" and with them, "a new fascination with the material stuff of life." (Trentmann 2009:283).

On this point, Professor Pyburn's argument invites an inversion: "the future of anthropology" seems predicated on the discipline's continued relevance as a kind of science of *excavation* – the dusting off and reassembling of fragments of meaning in a world where, as Arjun Appadurai noted with great success, things, too, possess "social lives." (Trentmann 2009:283). Across the social sciences, the role of everyday things in the process of constituting both structural relations and meanings is now undisputed (Candlin and Guins 2009). This renewed use of archaeology as a methodology helpful in unearthing human intentions and habits through artifacts is only partially metaphorical; it finds its ultimate application in the study of the commodity as the quintessential "thing" of contemporary consumer regimes.

As Foucault understood very well when he invoked the term to describe his exercise in un-doing what we take for granted, archaeology attends to both what is enduring and dissolving. "Things" are the stuff that stands opposite "words" to form systems of knowledge. And it is the "thing" aspect of objects that interest everyone – from Marxists and liberal capitalists to poststructuralists and positivists – precisely because objects are implicated tangibly in our social worlds in ways that previous theoretical turns to "discourse and signs" never quite managed to achieve (Trentmann 2009:283).

Still, before this turn to material culture devolves into a celebration of objects for mere materiality's sake, we are well advised to remember what every archaeologist that has ever found an interesting artifact in a pile of dust knows very well: the relationships between artifacts and their meanings are fraught with tensions, ambiguities, uncertainties, and slippages.

In his book *Material Cultures: Why Some Things Matter*, Daniel Miller reminds us that the predominant tendency in Western rationalism for more than five centuries has been to disregard objects as trivial components of real life (Miller 1998). Too much attention to objects, the logic goes, rapidly descends into fetishism. In their proper scale of value, objects should be regarded as nothing more than "background for living." The stigma of objectification pervades even those studies that take objects seriously; as a result many anthropological and cultural studies analysis of material practices tend to move their focus quickly from objects to society – it is, says Miller, as if these studies were trying to avoid the apparent embarrassment of "being caught gazing at mere objects" for too long (Miller 1998:9).

In the rush to move on to more weighty theoretical arguments, many cultural studies scholars tend to treat objects as little more than simply texts, representations, and symbols. Missing in many studies is often the *specificity* of the object's history of production, material qualities, form, metrics, style, technologies of reproduction and dissemination, and context. This extended and rigorous attention to details when examining objects is one area where anthropologists and other cultural scholars could stand to learn a great deal from archaeologists.

When we pass artifacts over quickly to move on to the theoretical points, we risk ignoring the complicated bits of information that are coded into the sociological DNA of objects – their histories of entanglement with other objects, locations, and epistemes. It is precisely because objects have had the definitive history of disregard in Western rationalism that Miller describes – because they saturate the spaces of the everyday without demanding great mental effort – that they are excellent locations where ideological processes can "hide" their biases, assumptions, claims to truth, and mechanics of power and knowledge. One only has to think about the pervasive use of cell phones, our attachments and dependence on them, for example, to appreciate how conjoined objects and ideologies of technological mastery, global communication, and individual choice can effectively become without even thinking twice about it. Archaeologists, of course, are trained to know these things. Or, they should be. What kind of understandings would emerge about how power holds things in place in our world today if our research were to dwell a little more extensively upon the more mundane qualities, experiences, and social textures of the objects that construct people's lives?

Border Artifacts

I have spent the last 15 years observing and documenting the flows and "social lives" of a particularly low-ranking type of artifact in the U.S.-Mexico border zone: plaster statuary produced from molds and sold under the label of "Mexican Curios" (souvenirs and/or adornments) to border residents and visitors. It goes without saying that one of the first issues my research confronts is the question of value. I am not speaking about the actual monetary or symbolic value of the figurines at hand, but of the "analytical" value that such mass-produced, kitschy, popular crafts can possibly hold for anthropological inquiry. Since Malinowski, anthropologists have been admonished by their mentors and teachers to focus on the substantial aspects of vernacular cultures and to disregard the products of mass culture that tend to homogenize and muddle or contaminate authentic local expressions. Despite the "crisis" and the "critique," this engrained operating principle of the discipline persists to this day (although one has to admit that considerable reflection on the anthropological dimensions of tourist's art have brought about some notable changes in perspective on this area. See for example Marcus and Myer 1995; Phillips and Steiner 1999).

My hope is that, at least on the matter of seeing some value on what others discard,

archaeologists can be sympathetic to the plight of my research interests. But in fact, sympathy is not exactly what I am seeking. Complicity, perhaps, is a better term. Nonetheless, let me reiterate the point. I believe there is great analytical value in establishing as a point of departure for any investigation of material culture in the U.S.-Mexico borderlands the following postulate: not all objects have been regarded worthy of analytical attention. Immediately, we are clued to a very fundamental piece of data: there are multiple regimes of objects and variable mechanisms of valuation operating simultaneously and, most importantly, off each other's circuits of logic, in the borderlands.

Myriad more questions pile up: What brought this about? How did the borderlands evolve through artifacts as a site of desire, exploitation, productivity, smuggling, convenience, pleasure, diversion, remembrance? Why are "marginal" objects found in "marginal" zones? What is the border the margin of? What is the opposite of "marginal"? and so forth (for answers to some of these questions see McCrossen 2009). Before I can even get to the objects that interest me, a sound research methodology would require that I map the coordinates of the divergent artifactual systems and historical/ideological constructs that have brought things to the present state of aesthetic evaluation in border towns.

To illustrate my argument, let me sketch what I call "the tale of the three little piggies."

On a corner of my office sit three different pig figurines made in Mexico. All three are piggy banks and in a story that would prove too long for this essay, I could explain how each represents a copy of the other across a span of approximately 75 years. Each pig was acquired in fundamentally distinct shopping expeditions at equally distinct sites: an antique shop in Tucson, Arizona; the Southwest Indian Art Fair at the Arizona State Museum also in Tucson; and a border curio shop in Nogales, Sonora. The first pig (Figure III.6.1) is made of clay, most likely manufactured in the 1930s; it's smaller than the rest and has the hues and colors of fading pastel paints mixed with purple and black.

It is exactly like another pig that a collector friend owns that was brought to him by his parents upon visiting Elizabeth Morrow in Cuernavaca, Mexico during the same decade. Morrow was the wife of Dwight Morrow, appointed U.S. ambassador to Mexico in 1927. She was an avid collector and enthusiastic promoter of Mexican folk arts. Her children's book *The Painted Pig* is considered a classic in Mexican folkways. Although certainly not unique, nor highly valuable, this little piggy is a desirable collector's item.

The second figure is also made of clay (Figure III.6.2). It was left unpainted to reflect the original reddish hues of the earthen material. It came with a label that attributed its making to an artisanal shop in Oaxaca, Mexico. No artist's name was provided. It was sold at the Southwest Indian Art Fair as an authentic imported folk art object manufactured by hand, most likely by an indigenous artisan. Although it is most likely produced serially, specifically for export and sales to tourists, the material, provenance, and implicit seal of authenticity granted by the anthropology museum where it was sold add special value to this object, even as it remains essentially a decoration. Small imperfections in the body of the figurine suggest traces of hand-molding and the square shape of the piggy's feet and snout suggest that it is an original vernacular interpretation of other more uniform pig shapes in Mexican folk arts.

The third piggy is made of plaster (Figure III.6.3), manufactured by mold at one of dozens of small petty commodity workshops in border towns

It is much larger than the previous two and its shape imitates the 1930s collectible perfectly, with the inclusion of a small handle on the top and the painterly decorations on each side. The form

Figure III.6.1. Pig from an antique shop in Tucson, Arizona.

Figure III.6.2. Pig from the Southwest Indian Art Fair.

Figure III.6.3. Pig from a curio shop in Nogales, Arizona.

of the piggy's face is also identical to the small collector's version. The flowers on each side have been airbrushed onto the surface, visibly exceeding the boundaries of the relief work. The flowers are bright yellow, painted most likely with commercial gloss paint for added shine. There's also a notable distinction in price from the other two piggies. While the antique piggy and the Oaxacan figure sold for approximately $30 USD, the larger plaster piggy commanded at best $5 USD. As a "border artifact," plaster piggies like this are *both* endearing to many Mexican families in or near the border who use them as yard decoration or as party favors for children's birthday parties and derided by some observers who reject them as nothing more than stereotypical, garish ornamentation.

While the taxonomies of "collectible," and "folk art" best describe the categories to which piggy 1 and piggy 2 can be assigned, piggy 3 is most likely to be associated with the group of border objects known as "curios" (short for "curiosities"). Dissecting in 1971 the universe of objects that constituted Mexican "artesanías" (handicrafts), the art critic Isabel Marin de Paalen wrote that those called "Mexican Curios" were the most debased because they were, bluntly, "objects without history" (Martin 1971). While I read Martin de Paalen's declaration as an invitation to inquire what could be behind such outright disdain (certainly even "bad" products can boast some kind of historical record concerning how they acquired their "badness"), it is fair to say that the intellectual and anthropological consensus in Mexico regards curios as simply "boorish derivations" of finer crafts and folk arts (Martínez Peñaloza 1988). As such, these objects can never be considered national patrimony for they lack that *natural* quality and immutable character that capture the innate essence of "Mexicanidad" (Mexican wholesomeness). In Mexico, since 1921 the canon of patrimony has been meticulously constructed around a preferred set of ideas:

Indian-made, rural, rustic, utilitarian, of lasting materials, anonymous, whimsical, based on precedent, or in defiance of all of the above as is the case of high-glazed pottery from Tonalá, Jalisco, simply of superb and exceptional craftsmanship and originality.

THE TROUBLE CURIOS MAKE

The Banamex collection of "Great Masters of Mexican Folk Arts" (Fomento 1998) includes only three northern Mexican handicrafts of serious pedigree: Mata Ortiz pottery, Raramuri pine needle baskets, and Seri iron wood sculpture. Yet, we know by sheer observation and experience as well as by a prevalent discourse of difference in the media and academic circles alike that northern Mexican bordertowns are characterized by unusually high levels of artifactual density. There is a lot of "stuff" that is either made on site, circulates through, or is dealt in the borderlands. Up until very recently, the very mention of the word "border" conjured up for most people the hyper crowded cabinets of curio stores at Avenida Revolucion in Tijuana, the over abundance of drinking establishments and tourist districts in Matamoros and El Paso, or the persistent sales pitch of ambulatory vendors in Nogales or Laredo.

More recently, especially since the passage of NAFTA, prescription drugs and agricultural commodities have joined curios, maquila-assembled goods, and service-oriented products such as upholstered furniture and junk auto parts in constituting a reliable system of border-specific artifacts. None of these mundane objects, however, can ever aspire to achieve the status of patrimony – they do not reflect what the Banamex folk art curators describe as the nation's "innate penchant for beauty and innovation." They are, simply, things – things that flow back and forth, things that embarrass, things that earn their purveyors a living, things that entertain, things that Gringos want, material things that have a definite function but that are incapable of producing meaning.

The class of objects known as "Mexican Curios" presents a singular kind of challenge to the stability of a patrimonial canon. Let's think back to the distinct attributes of that plaster piggy, the one with the emblazoned yellow flowers. Curios such as that plaster piggy bank display a promiscuity in colors, styles, and intentions that troubles the sense of order and efficiency to which national pride aspires. The beauty of first-grade folk arts (*artesanías finas*) after all – as evidenced in the extraordinary creations of a Talavera vase, a carved mask from Guerrero, a silk woven *rebozo* from Michoacan, or the elaborate silver jewelry from Taxco – resides precisely in their "quiet" dignity. That plaster piggy, on the other hand, was screaming for attention.

It is well known that since the 19th century the Mexican nation-state's construction of a canon of patrimony has always been contested. One need only recall the well-documented "invention" of the China Poblana to make the point. But Mexican Curios offer a particularly unwelcomed kind of contestation. Unlike other kinds of border goods and commodities, Curios present a double bind: their limitless reproduction *to reproduce the nation intentionally* ("take home a little bit of Mexico") is one of the most common sales spiels heard in bordertowns, yet at the same time they distort and undermine by their sheer existence the authenticity apparatus that produces the idea of the nation-state in the first place.

It is no wonder then, that Curios proliferate in environments where the "national culture" is allegedly diluted, contaminated, some would even say "prostituted." Curios can be found anywhere in Mexico today (most notably at airport souvenir shops run by the state), but their genesis and aesthetics of hybridity harkens back to the border, *el Norte*, the margin of the nation-state, the wasteland of patrimony.

And it is precisely this judgment of "lack" that brings us back to consider a resolutely *archaeological* type of question: is what we see all that there is? Because Curios are objects that straddle the line between "folkways" and "cultural debris," they probably hide very artfully deep deposits of social formations not immediately apparent to the plain eye. By this I mean that there are real lives, stories, functions to which Curios are connected that in turn manifest the failure of the nation-state in controlling a master narrative about its own legitimacy as the arbiter of culture. Curios embarrass the nation doubly: they improvise on the script as given and in doing so they point to the contingency of the script in the first place. There are, in other words, many ways to narrate Mexicanidad and Curios are evidence that not all the voices of "el pueblo" (the people) speak with the same aesthetic inflection.

Can archaeologists help anthropologists devise strategies to read borderlands material culture against the grain of the obvious, functional, and anecdotal? It would be a great accomplishment if we could start by seeing in the most debased of border artifacts – in Mexican Curios – traces of the histories of production and discourses of distinction that engendered the artifactual density that we so clearly associated with border economies and lifestyles. Can Curios perhaps offer evidence of what processes of state formation have been like in the outer edges of the national imaginary? My sense is that we are sitting on a treasure trove of good data that only our prejudices have prevented us from noticing. But to accomplish this we would need to dwell long enough on the Curios themselves – on their scandalous surfaces and celebratory gestures of fake authenticity. Anthropologists would need to think less like cultural experts who can discriminate a priori what is substantial from the mundane and appropriate instead the skepticism archaeologists assume before a strange object they have just pulled from the dry mud. It is, after all, not too farfetched to imagine an scenario, a few centuries from now, when some graduate student working on a dig in an area near the ancient border between the United States and Mexico would yell "Eurekas" of academic joy when she extracts from the side of a dirt mound fragments of a strange vessel decorated with bright yellow flowers.

References Cited/Bibliografía

Aa, Bart J.M. van der
    2005   *Preserving the Heritage for Humanity? Obtaining World Heritage Status and the Impacts of Listing.* Ph.D. dissertation, University of Groningen.

Abbott, David R.
    2003   The Politics of Decline in Canal System 2. In *Centuries of Decline During the Hohokam Classic Period at Pueblo Grande*, edited by David R. Abbott, pp. 201-227. University of Arizona Press, Tucson.

Abbott, David R., Alexa M. Smith, and Emiliano Gallaga
    2007   Ballcourts and Ceramics: The Case for Hohokam Marketplaces in the Arizona Desert. *American Antiquity* 72:461-484.

Abu-Lughod, Janet
    1989   *Before European Hegemony: The World System A.D. 1250-1350.* Oxford University Press, New York.

Acuña, Roberto (editor)
    1988   *Relaciones Geográficas del Siglo XVI: Nueva Galicia.* Tomo X, IIA-UNAM, México.

Adams, E. Charles and Andrew I. Duff (editors)
    2004   *The Protohistoric Pueblo World: A.D. 1275-1600.* University of Arizona Press, Tucson.

Adams, E. Charles, Vincent M. LaMotta, and Kurt Dongoske
    2004   Hopi Settlement Clusters Past and Present. In *The Protohistoric Pueblo World, A.D. 1275-1600*, edited by E. Charles Adams and Andrew I. Duff, pp. 128-136. University of Arizona Press, Tucson.

Adams, Richard E. W.
    2005   *Prehistoric Mesoamerica,* Third Edition. University of Oklahoma Press, Norman.

Adler, Michael A. (editor)
    1996   *The Prehistoric Pueblo World: A.D. 1150-1350.* University of Arizona Press, Tucson.

Aiton, Arthur S. (translator)
    1939   *Muster Roll and Equipment of the Expedition of Francisco Vazquez de Coronado.* William Clements Library, Ann Arbor, Michigan.

Akins, Nancy J.
    1986   *A Biocultural Approach to Human Burials from Chaco Canyon, New Mexico.* Reports of the Chaco Center No. 9. Branch of Cultural Research, National Park Service, Santa Fe.

Alonso, Ana María
    2004   Conforming Disconformity: "Mestizaje," Hybridity, and the Aesthetics of Mexican Nationalism. *Cultural Anthropology* 19(4):459-490.

Álvarez Palma, Ana María
    1982   Archaeological Investigations at Huatabampo. In *Mogollon Archaeology, Proceedings of the 1980 Mogollon Conference,* edited by Pat Beckett and Kira Silverbird, pp. 239-250. Acoma Books, Ramona, California.

    1990   Huatabampo: Consideraciones sobre una comunidad agrícola prehispánica en el sur de Sonora. *Noroeste de México* 9:9-93, Centro Regional del Noroeste INAH, Hermosillo.

Álvarez Palma, Ana María, Adriana Hinojo y Sergio Manterola
    2001   El Arcaico Sinaloense. Ponencia presentada en la XXVI Mesa Redonda de la Sociedad Mexicana de Antropología, del 28 de junio al 3 de agosto, Zacatecas.

Andersen, Ruth M.
    1979   *Hispanic Costume, 1480-1530.* Hispanic Society of America, New York City, New York.

Anyon, Roger and T. J. Ferguson
    1996   Cultural resource management at the Pueblo of Zuni, New Mexico, USA. *Antiquity* 69:913-930.

Ayres, James
    1970   An Early Historic Burial from the Village of Bac. *Kiva* 36(2):44-48.

Azzi, Stephen
    2005   Negotiating Cultural Space in the Global Economy: The United States, UNESCO, and the Convention on Cultural Diversity. *International Journal* 60(3):765-784.

Bahr, Donald M.
    1971   Who Were the Hohokam? The Evidence from Pima-Papago Myths. *Ethnohistory* 18(3):245-266.

    1991   Papago Ocean Songs and the *Wi:gita. Journal of the Southwest* 33(4):539-556.

Bahr, Donald M., Juan Smith, William Smith Allison, and Julian D. Hayden
    1994   *The Short, Swift Time of Gods on Earth: The Hohokam Chronicles.* University of California Press, Berkeley.

Bandelier, Adolph F.
    1884   Appendix: Reports by A. F. Bandelier on His Investigations in New Mexico During the Years 1883-1884. In *Fifth Annual Report of the Executive Committee, and the Third Annual Report of the Committee on the American School of Classical Studies at Athens, 1883-1884*, pp. 55-98. John Wilson and Son, Cambridge.

    1892   *Final Report of Investigations Among the Indians of the Southwestern United States, Carried on Mainly in the Years from 1880 to 1885, Part II.* Papers of the Archaeological Institute of America, American Series IV. John Wilson and Son, Cambridge.

del Barco, Miguel
    1988   *Historia natural y crónica de la antigua California.* Universidad Nacional Autónoma de México, México D.F.

Barrett, Elinore M.
    1997   The Geography of Middle Rio Grande Pueblos Revealed by Spanish Explorers, 1540-1598. In *The Coronado Expedition to Tierra Nueva. The 1540-1542 Route Across the Southwest,* edited by Richard Flint and Shirley C. Flint, pp. 195-208. University Press of Colorado, Boulder.

    2002   *Conquest and Catastrophe: Changing Rio Grande Pueblo Settlement Patterns in the Sixteenth and Seventeenth Centuries.* University of New Mexico Press, Albuquerque.

Baus Czitrom, Carolyn
   1982   Tecuexes y Cocas. Dos Grupos de la Región de Jalisco en el siglo XVI. Colección Científica, Serie Etnohistoria, No. 12, INAH, México.

   1985   The Tecuexes: Ethnohistory and Archaeology. In *The Archaeology of West and Northwest Mesoamerica,* edited by Michael S. Foster and Phil C. Weigand, pp. 93-117. Westview Press, Boulder, Colorado.

Bayman, James M.
   2002   Hohokam Craft Economies and the Materialization of Power. *Journal of Archaeological Method and Theory* 9:69-95.

Beals, Ralph
   1974   Relations Between Mesoamerica and the Southwest. In *The Mesoamerican Southwest: Readings in Archaeology, Ethnohistory, and Ethnography,* edited by Basil C. Hedrick, J. Charles Kelley, and Carroll L. Riley, pp. 58-63. Southern Illinois University Press, Carbondale.

Bell, Betty
   1974   Excavations at El Cerro Encantado, Jalisco. En *The Archaeology of West Mexico,* editado por Betty Bell, pp. 147-67. Sociedad de Estudios Avanzados del Occidente de México, Ajijic, Jalisco.

Bellwood, Peter
   1996   Phylogeny vs. Reticulation in Prehistory. *Antiquity* 70(270):881-890.

Beltrán, José C.
   2001   *La Explotación de la Costa del Pacífico en el Occidente de Mesoamérica y los contactos con Sudamérica y otras Regiones Culturales.* Universidad Autónoma de Nayarit, Tepic.

   2009   Playa del Tesoro y los intercambios con el Ecuador, *Memorias VI Coloquio Internacional de Occidentalistas.* Universidad de Guadalajara, Jalisco.

Beltrán, José C. y Lourdes González
   2007   Arqueología de la bahía de Banderas. En *El Occidente de México. Perspectiva Multidisciplinarias. Memorias del V Coloquio Internacional de Occidentalistas,* coordinado por Rosa Yáñez. Universidad de Guadalajara, Jalisco.

Benz, Bruce F.
   1999   On the Origin, Evolution, and Dispersal of Maize. In *Pacific Latin America in Prehistory: The Evolution of Archaic and Formative Cultures,* edited by Michael Blake, pp. 25-38. Washington State University Press, Pullman.

Bernal, Ignacio
   1979   *Historia de la arqueología en México.* Porrúa, México D.F.

   1980   *A History of Mexican Archaeology: The Vanished Civilizations of Middle America.* Thames and Hudson, London.

Blaine, Peter, Sr. and told to Michael S. Adams
   1981   *Papagos and Politics.* Arizona Historical Society, Tucson.

Blakeslee, Donald J.
   1997   Which Barrancas? Narrowing the Possibilities. In *The Coronado Expedition to Tierra Nueva. The 1540-1542 Route Across the Southwest,* edited by Richard Flint and Shirley C. Flint, pp. 252-266. University Press of Colorado, Boulder.

Blakeslee, Donald J. and Jay C. Blaine
2003   The Jimmy Owens Site: New Perspectives on the Coronado Expedition. In *The Coronado Expedition from the Distance of 460 Years,* edited by Richard Flint and Shirley C. Flint, pp. 203-218. University of New Mexico Press, Albuquerque.

Blanton, Richard et al.
1981   *Ancient Mesoamerica.* Cambridge University Press, United Kingdom.

Blanton, Richard and Gary Feinman
1984   The Mesoamerica World System. *American Anthropologist* 86 (3):673-682.

Boas, Franz
1915   Summary of the Work of the International School of American and Ethnology in Mexico. *American Anthropologist* 17(2):384-395.

1940   *Race, Language, and Culture.* The University of Chicago Press, Illinois.

Bolton, Herbert E.
1949   *Coronado: Knight of Pueblos and Plains.* University of New Mexico Press, Albuquerque.

Booth, Peter MacMillan
2000   *Creation of a Nation: The Development of the Tohono O'odham Political Culture, 1900-1937.* Ph.D. dissertation, Department of Philosophy, Purdue University. UMI Publications, Ann Arbor.

Bowen, Thomas G.
1976   *Seri Prehistory: The Archaeology of the Central Coast of Sonora, Mexico.* Anthropological Papers of the University of Arizona 27, The University of Arizona, Tucson.

Bradley, Ronna J.
1993   Marine Shell Exchange in Northwest Mexico and the Southwest. In *The American Southwest and Mesoamerica: Systems of Prehistoric Exchange*, edited by Jonathon E. Ericson and Timothy G. Baugh, pp. 121-151. Plenum Press, New York.

1999   Shell Exchange within the Southwest: The Casas Grandes Interaction Sphere. In *The Casas Grandes World,* edited by Curtis F. Schaafsma and Carroll L. Riley, pp. 213-228. The University of Utah Press, Salt Lake City.

Bradley, Ronna J. and Glen E. Rice
1996   Shell Artifacts from the Schoolhouse Point Mound, U:8:24/13a. In *The Place of the Storehouses, Roosevelt Platform Mound Study: Report on the Schoolhouse Point Mound, Pinto Creek Complex,* Roosevelt Monograph Series 6, Anthropological Field Studies 35, edited by Owen Lindauer, pp. 583-598. Arizona State University, Tempe.

1997   Shell Artifacts from the U:4:33/132, The Cline Terrace Mound. In *A Salado Platform Mound on Tonto Creek, Roosevelt Platform Mound Study: Report on the Cline Terrace Mound, Cline Terrace Complex,* Roosevelt Monograph Series 7, Anthropological Field Studies 36, edited by David Jacobs, pp. 455-464. Arizona State University, Tempe.

Brading, David A.
1988   Manuel Gamio and Official Indigenismo in Mexico. *Bulletin of Latin American Research* 7(1):75-89.

2001   Monuments and Nationalism in Modern Mexico. *Journal of the Association for the Sudy of Ethnicity and Nationalism* 7(4):521-531.

Brand, Donald D.
   1948   United States-Mexican Scientific and Cultural Relations. *Annals of the American Academy of Political and Social Science* 255:67-76.

Braniff C., Beatriz
   1972   Secuencias arqueológicas en Guanajuato y Cuenca de México: Intento de correlación. En *Teotihuacan*, XI Mesa Redonda, Sociedad Mexicana de Antropología 2:273-232, México.

   1974   Oscilación de la frontera septentrional mesoamericana. En *The Archaeology of West Mexico,* editada por Betty Bell, pp. 40-50. Sociedad de Estudios Avanzados del Occidente de México, Ajijic, Jalisco.

   1976   *Notas para la Arqueología de Sonora.* Cuadernos de los Centros No. 25. Instituto de Antropología e Historia, Dirección de Centros Regionales, Hermosillo.

   1992   *La Frontera Protohistórica Pima-Opata en Sonora, México: Proposiciones arqueológicas preliminares.* Vol. I. Colección Científica, INAH, Mexico D.F.

   1993   The Mesoamerican Northern Frontier and the Gran Chichimeca. In *Culture and Contact: Charles C. Di Peso's Gran Chichimeca*, edited by Anne I. Woosley and John C. Ravesloot, pp. 65-82. The Amerind Foundation, Inc., Dragoon, and The University of New Mexico Press, Albuquerque.

   1998   *Morales, Guanajuato y la tradición Chupícuaro.* Colección Científica, Serie Arqueología, INAH, México.

   2001   Introducción. En *La Gran Chichimeca: El Lugar de las Rocas Secas,* coordinado por Beatriz Braniff C., pp. 7-12. Consejo Nacional para la Cultura y las Artes, México, Jaca Book, Milán.

Braniff C., Beatriz (coordinadora)
   2001   La Gran Chichimeca: El Lugar de las Rocas Secas. Consejo Nacional para la Cultura y las Artes, México, Jaca Book, Milán.

Brasher, Nugent
   2007   The Chichilticale Camp of Francisco Vázquez de Coronado: The Search for the Red House. *New Mexico Historical Review* 82(4):433-468.

   2009   The Red House Camp and the Captain General: The 2009 Report on the Coronado Expedition Campsite of Chichilticale. *New Mexico Historical Review* 84(1):1-63.

   2010   Spanish Lead Shot of the Coronado Expedition: A Progress Report on Isotope Analysis of Lead from Five Sites. *New Mexico Historical Review* 85(1):79-81.

   2011a The Coronado Exploration Program: A Narrative of the Search for the Captain General. In *The Latest Word from 1540: People, Places, and Portrayals of the Coronado Expedition,* edited by Richard Flint and Shirley C. Flint, pp. 229-261. University of New Mexico Press, Albuquerque.

   2011b Francisco Vázquez de Coronado at Doubtful Canyon and on the Trail North: The 2011 Report Including Lead Isotopes, Artifact Interpretation, and Camp Description. *New Mexico Historical Review* 86(3):325-375.

   2013   The Francisco Vázquez de Coronado Expedition in Tierra Doblada: The 2013 Report on Artifacts and Isotopes of the Minnie Bell Site at Big Dry Creek, Catron County, New Mexico. *New Mexico Historical Review* 88(2):179-227.

Brendon, Piers
1991   *Thomas Cook. 150 Years of Popular Tourism.* Secker and Warburg, London.

Brew, Susan A. and Bruce B. Huckell
1987   A Protohistoric Piman Burial and a Consideration of Piman Burial Practices. *Kiva* 52(3):163-191.

Brown, R. Ben
1985 A Synopsis of the Archaeology of the Central Portion of the Northern Frontier of Mesoamerica. In *The Archaeology of West and Northwest Mesoamerica,* edited by Michael S. Foster and Phil C. Weigand, pp. 219-236. Westview Press, Boulder, Colorado.

Brown, David E.
1994   Appendix II. Scientific and Equivalent Common Names of Plants and Animals Arranged by Biomes. In *Biotic Communities of the Southwestern United States and Northwestern Mexico,* edited by David E. Brown, pp. 316-342. University of Utah Press, Salt Lake City.

Brunson, Judy Lynn
1989   *The Social Organization of the Los Muertos Hohokam: A Reanalysis of Cushing's Hemenway Expedition Data.* Ph.D. dissertation, Arizona State University, Tempe.

Brusca, Richard C.
1976   Evolución Geológica del Norte del Golfo de California y Comentarios sobre su Fauna. En *Sonora: Antropología del Desierto,* editado por Beatriz Braniff C., pp. 85-93. Colección Científica Diversa No. 27 INAH-SEP, México.

Buikstra, Jane E., Susan R. Frankenberg, and Lyle W. Konigsberg
1990   Skeletal Biological Distance Studies in American Anthropology: Recent Trends. *American Journal of Physical Anthropology* 82:1-7.

Buikstra, Jane E. and Douglas H. Ubelaker
1994   *Standards for Data Collection from Human Skeletal Remains.* Arkansas Archaeological Survey Research Series No. 44. Arkansas Archaeological Survey, Fayetteville.

2005   *El Hombre y sus instrumentos en la Cultura Bolaños.* Instituto de Investigaciones Antropológicas, UNAM, México.

Candlin, Fiona and Raiford Guins
2009   *The Object Reader.* Routledge, London.

Carballal Staedtler, Margarita and María Antonieta Moguel Cos
2007   Salvage and Rescue Archaeology in Mexico. The SAA Archaeological Record 7(5):23-25.

Caretta, Nicolás M.
2004   *Cerro de Santiago. Municipio de Pabellón de Arteaga, Aguascalientes.* Informe de la Prospección Arqueológica y diagnóstico. Centro INAH-Aguascalientes, Archivo de Monumentos Prehispánicos, INAH, México.

2006   *Proyecto Arqueológico Cerro de Santiago, Municipio de Pabellón de Arteaga, Aguascalientes.* Archivo de la Coordinación Nacional de Arqueología INAH, México.

Caretta, Nicolás M. y A. Motilla
2008   ¿Fuera o dentro de Mesoamérica? Sociedades y territorialidad en el centro norte de México en el Siglo XVI. En *Tiempo y Región: Estudios Históricos y Sociales,* pp. 335-348. Universidad de Querétaro-INAH.

Carpenter, John

1994   The Cahitan Connection: Modeling Mesoamerican-Southwestern Interaction in the Gran Chichimeca. Ponencia presentada en la 59 conferencia anual de la Sociedad de Arqueología Americana, 20-24 de abril de 1994, Anaheim, California.

1996   *El Ombligo en la Labor: Differentiation, Interaction and Integration in Prehispanic Sinaloa, México.* Unpublished Ph.D. dissertation, Department of Anthropology, University of Arizona, Tucson, University Microfilms Inc., Ann Arbor, Michigan.

2008   *Etnohistoria de Tierra Caliente: Los Grupos Indígenas de Sinaloa al Momento del Contacto Español.* Difocur/Cobaes/Cronistas, Culiacán, Sinaloa.

2009   Breve Historia Cultural Prehispánica del Valle del Río Fuerte. En *El Patrimonio Histórico y Arqueológico del Antiguo Fuerte de Montesclaros,* coordinado por Gilberto López, Alfonso Mercado Gómez y María de los Ángeles Heredia Zavala, pp. 46-64. INAH/Universidad Autónoma de Sinaloa/Ayuntamiento de El Fuerte.

Carpenter, John y Guadalupe Sánchez

2005   Proyecto Arqueológico Noreste de Sinaloa (Municipios de Choix y El Fuerte). Informe Técnico de la Primera Temporada. Reporte preliminar entregado al INAH, México, D.F.

2007   Nuevos Hallazgos Arqueológicos en La Región del Valle del Río Fuerte, Norte de Sinaloa. Diario de Campo 93 julio-agosto de 2007, pp. 18-29.

2008   Entre la Sierra Madre y el Mar: la Arqueología de Sinaloa. Arqueología 39:21-45. DEA-INAH, México.

Carpenter John, y Gilberto López

2009   Etnohistoria del momento de contacto y establecimiento de misiones jesuíticas. En El Patrimonio Histórico y Arqueológico del Antiguo Fuerte de Montesclaros coordinado por Gilberto López Castillo, Alfonso Mercado Gómez y María de los Ángeles Heredia Zavala pp. 89-106. INAH/Universidad Autónoma de Sinaloa/Ayuntamiento de El Fuerte.

Carpenter, John, Guadalupe Sánchez, and Haydee Chávez

2006   Informe Final del Proyecto Salvamento Arqueológico Álamo Dorado de la Minera Corner Bay S.A. de C.V. Informe técnico al Consejo de Arqueología INAH, México, D.F.

Carpenter, John, Guadalupe Sánchez y Julio Vicente

2008a   Informe Final del Proyecto Cerro de la Máscara. Informe técnico entregado a la Coordinación Nacional de Arqueología y al Consejo de Arqueología del INAH, México, D.F.

2008b   Informe Final del Proyecto Arqueológico de Salvamento Acueducto Alamo Dorado, Sonora. Informe técnico entregado a la Coordinación Nacional de Arqueología y al Consejo de Arqueología del INAH, México, D.F.

2009a   El sitio de petrograbados Cerro de la Máscara. En El Patrimonio Histórico y Arqueológico del Antiguo Fuerte de Montesclaros coordinado por Gilberto López Castillo, Alfonso Mercado Gómez y María de los Ángeles Heredia Zavala, pp. 65-88. INAH/Universidad Autónoma de Sinaloa/Ayuntamiento de El Fuerte.

2009b   Proyecto Arqueológico Norte de Sinaloa. Informe Técnico de la Temporada 2008 entregado al Consejo de Arqueología del INAH, México, D.F.

Carpenter, John, Guadalupe Sánchez, Julio Vicente y Haydee Chávez

2005   Informe Técnico del Estudio de Factibilidad de una Línea Eléctrica entre la presa Miguel Hidalgo,

Sinaloa y la Mina Álamo Dorado, Sonora, para la Minera Corner Bay S.A. de C.V. Reporte entregado al INAH, México, D.F.

Carpenter, John, Guadalupe Sánchez, and Elisa Villalpando
    2002   Of Maize and Migration: Mode and Tempo in the Diffusion of Zea mays in Northwest Mexico and the American Southwest. In Traditions, Transitions, and Technologies: Themes in Southwestern Archaeology, edited by Sarah Schlanger, pp. 245-258. University of Colorado Press, Boulder.

Carpenter, John and Julio Vicente
    2009   Fronteras Compartidas: La conformación social en el norte de Sinaloa y sur de Sonora durante el periodo cerámico. Espacio-tiempo 3:82-96.

Carpenter John, Julio Vicente, y Guadalupe Sánchez
    2008   Informe Final del Proyecto Arqueológico de Salvamento Acueducto Álamo Dorado, Sonora. Informe técnico entregado a la Coordinación Nacional de Arqueología y al Consejo de Arqueología del INAH, México, D.F.

Carr, Christopher
    1995a Building a Unified Middle-Range Theory of Artifact Design: Historical Perspectives and Tactics. In *Style, Society, and Person: Archaeological and Ethnological Perspectives,* edited by Christopher Carr and Jill E. Neitzel, pp. 151-170. Plenum Press, New York.

    1995b A Unified Middle-Range Theory of Artifact Design. In *Style, Society, and Person: Archaeological and Ethnological Perspectives,* edited by Christopher Carr and Jill E. Neitzel, pp. 171-258. Plenum Press, New York.

Carrera Stampa, Manuel
    1955   *Memoria de los servicios que había hecho Nuño de Guzmán, desde que fue nombrado Gobernador de Panuco en 1525.* José Porrúa e Hijos, México. D.F.

de las Casas, Gonzalo
    1936   Noticia de los Chichimecas y justicia de la guerra que les ha hecho por los españoles. In *Quellen zur Kulturgeschichte des präkolumbischen America,* edited by Hermann Trimborn, pp. 152-185. Stuttgart.

Caso, Alfonso
    1968   *A un Joven Arqueólogo Mexicano.* Colección de los Mensajes, Empresas Editoriales, México, D.F.

Castañeda, Queltzin
    1996   *In the Museum of Maya Culture. Touring Chichén Itzá.* University of Minnesota, Minneapolis.

    2005   Tourism "Wars" in the Yucatán. *Anthropology News: May.*

Castellanos, Eloy
    1992   Santiago. Inventario de Zonas Arqueológicas en Aguascalientes (Clave F-13-B-88-01-08). Subdirección de Registro Público de Monumentos y Zonas Arqueológicas, INAH, México, D.F.

Castillo, Guadalupe and Margo Cowan
    2001   *It is Not Our Fault: The Case for Amending Present Nationality Law to Make All Members of the Tohono O'odham Nation United States Citizens, Now and Forever.* Tohono O'odham Nation Executive Branch, Sells, Arizona.

Caywood, Louis R.
    1967   *The Zuni Mission Project: Zuni, New Mexico.* Southwest Archaeological Center, National Park Service.

Chase-Dunn, Christopher
  1998   *Global Formation: Structures in World Economy.* Rowman and Littlefield, Lanham, Maryland.

Chase-Dunn, Christopher and Thomas D. Hall
  1997   *Rise and Demise: Compraring World Systems.* Westview Press, Boulder, Colorado.

Chase-Dunn, Christopher and Kelly Mann
  1998   *The Wintu and Their Neighbors. A Very Small World-System in Northern California.* University of Arizona Press, Tucson.

Clancy, M. J.
  1999   Tourism and Development. Evidence from Mexico. *Annals of Tourism Research* 26(1):1-20.

Clark, Jeffery J.
  2001   *Tracking Prehistoric Migrations: Pueblo Settlers Among the Tonto Basin Hohokam.* Anthropological Papers of the University of Arizona No. 65. University of Arizona Press, Tucson.

Clark, Jeffery J., Deborah J. Huntley, J. Brett Hill, and Patrick D. Lyons
  2013   The Kayenta Diaspora and Salado Meta-Identity in the Late Pre-Contact U.S. Southwest. In *The Archaeology of Hybrid Material Culture,* edited by Jeb J. Card, pp. 399-424. Occasional Paper No. 39, Center for Archaeological Investigations, Southern Illinois University, Carbondale.

Clark, Jeffery J. and Patrick D. Lyons (editors)
  2012   *Migrants and Mounds: Classic Period Archaeology of the Lower San Pedro Valley.* Anthropological Papers No. 45. Archaeology Southwest, Tucson, Arizona.

Clark, Jeffery J., M. Steven Shackley, J. Brett Hill, Matthew A. Peeples, and W. Randall Haas, Jr.
  2012   *Long Distance Obsidian Circulation in the late Pre-Contact Southwest: Deviating from Distance-Decay.* Paper presented at the 77th Annual Meeting of the Society for American Archaeology, Memphis, Tennessee.

Cohen, Abner
  1979   Political Symbolism. *Annual Review of Anthropology* 8:87-113.

Cohen, Erik
  1984   The Sociology of Tourism: Approaches, Issues, and Definitions. *Annual Review of Sociology* 10:373-392.

  1988   Authenticity and Commoditization in Tourism. *Annals of Tourism Research* 15:371-386.

Colton, Harold S.
  1939   *Prehistoric Culture Units and Their Relationships in Northern Arizona.* Museum of Northern Arizona Bulletin No. 17. Northern Arizona Society of Science and Art, Flagstaff.

Colwell-Chanthaphonh, Chip
  2005   The Incorporation of the Native American Past: Cultural Extermination, Archaeological Protection, and the Antiquities Act of 1906. *International Journal of Cultural Property* 12(3):375-391.

Conkey, Margaret W.
  1984   To Find Ourselves: Art and Social Geography of Prehistoric Hunter-gatherers. In *Past and Present in Hunter-Gatherer Studies,* edited by Carmel Schrire, pp. 253-276. Academic Press, New York.

Cordell, Linda
  1997   *Archaeology of the Southwest,* Second edition. Academic Press, New York.

Corruccini, Robert S.
  1972   The Biological Relationships of Some Prehistoric and Historic Pueblo Populations. American Journal of Physical Anthropology 37(3):373-388.

Corruccini, Robert S. and Izumi Shimada
  2002   Dental Relatedness Corresponding to Mortuary Patterning at Huaca Loro, Peru. *American Journal of Physical Anthropology* 117:113-121.

Cowgill, George L.
  1990   Why Pearson's r is Not a Good Similarity Coefficient for Comparing Collections. *American Antiquity* 55(3):512-521.

Craig, Douglas B., James P. Holmlund, and Jeffery J. Clark
  1998   Labor Investment and Organization in Platform Mound Construction: A Case Study from the Tonto Basin of Central Arizona. *Journal of Field Archaeology* 25(3):245-259.

Creel, Darrell and Charmion McKusick
  1994   Prehistoric Macaws and Parrots in the Mimbres Area, New Mexico. *American Antiquity* 59:510-524.

Crosby, Alfred W.
  1972   *The Columbian Exchange.* Greenwood Publishing Company, Westport, Connecticut.

Crosby, Harry W.
  1997   *The Cave Paintings of Baja California: The Great Murals of an Unknown People.* Copley Books, Salt Lake City, Utah.

Crown, Patricia L.
  1994   *Ceramics and Ideology: Salado Polychrome Pottery.* University of New Mexico Press, Albuquerque.

Crown, Patricia L. and W. Jeffrey Hurst
  2009   Evidence of Cacao Use in the Prehispanic American Southwest. *Proceedings of the National Academy of Sciences* 106(7):2110-2113.

Cushing, Frank Hamilton
  1890   Preliminary Notes on the Origin, Working Hypothesis, and Primary Researches of the Hemenway Southwestern Archaeological Expedition. Paper presented at the Congres International des Americanistes, Compte-Rendu de la septieme session, Berlin 1888, Berlin.

  1896   Outlines of Zuñi Creation Myths. In *Thirteenth Annual Report of the Bureau of Ethnology for the Years 1891-1892,* pp. 321-447. Government Printing Office, Washington, D.C.

  1920   *Zuñi Breadstuff.* Indian Notes and Monographs, Vol. 8. Museum of the American Indian, Heye Foundation, New York.

Damp, Jonathan E.
  2005   The Battle of Hawikku: Archaeological Investigations of the Zuni-Coronado Encounter at Hawikku, the Ensuing Battle, and the Aftermath during the Summer of 1540. *Zuni Cultural Enterprise Research Series No. 13,* Zuni, New Mexico.

DataTur
  2006   *Compendio Estadístico del Turismo en México.* Secretaría de Turismo, México, D.F.

Davis, Edward H.
  1920   *The Papago Ceremony of the Víkíta.* Indian Notes and Monographs 3(4):157-177. Museum of the American Indian, Heye Foundation, New York.

Deagan, Kathleen
  2002   *Artifacts of the Spanish Colonies of Florida and the Caribbean, 1500-1800, Volume 2: Portable Personal Possessions.* Smithsonian Institution, Washington, D.C.

Dean, Jeffrey S.
  2000   Introduction: The Salado Phenomenon. In *Salado,* edited by Jeffrey S. Dean, pp. 3-16. Amerind Foundation, Dragoon, Arizona.

Dean, Jeffrey S., William H. Doelle, and Janet D. Orcutt
  1994   Adaptive Stress, Environment, and Demography. In *Themes in Southwest Prehistory,* edited by George J. Gumerman, pp. 53-86. School for American Research Press, Santa Fe, New Mexico.

Delgadillo, Rosalba y Sergio Sánchez
  1986   Inspección realizada sobre el derecho de vía del poliducto de Pemex. Tramo Aguascalientes-Zacatecas. Departamento de Salvamento Arqueológico, INAH, México.

DeMarrais, Elizabeth, Luis Jaime Castillo, and Timothy Earle
  1996   Ideology, Materialization, and Power Strategies. *Current Anthropology* 37(1):15-31.

Dewar, Robert E.
  1995   Of Nets and Trees: Untangling the Reticulate and Dendritic in Madagascar's Prehistory. *World Archaeology* 26(3):301-318.

Díaz-Andreu, Margara
  1996   Constructing Identities Through Culture. In *Cultural Identity and Archaeology: The Construction of European Communities,* edited by Paul Graves-Brown, Sian Jones, and Clive Gamble, pp. 48-61. Psychology Press, Routledge, London.

  2007   *A World History of Nineteenth-Century Archaeology. Nationalism, Colonialism and the Past.* Oxford University Press, Oxford.

Díaz-Andreu, Margarita and Timothy C. Champion (editors)
  1996   *Nationalism and Archaeology in Europe.* UCL Press, London.

Diguet, Leon
  1895   Note sur la pictographie de la Basse-Californie. L'Anthropologie 6:160-175.

Di Peso, Charles C.
  1953   The Sobaipuri Indians of the Upper San Pedro River Valley, Southeastern Arizona. The Amerind Foundation No. 6. The Amerind Foundation, Dragoon, Arizona.

  1955   Two Cerro Guaymas Clovis Fluted Points from Sonora, México. *Kiva* 21(2):13-15.

  1956   The Upper Pima of San Cayetano Del Tumacacori: An Archaeohistorical Reconstruction of the Ootam of the Pimeria Alta. The Amerind Foundation No. 7. The Amerind Foundation, Dragoon, Arizona.

  1958   The Reeve Ruin of Southeastern Arizona: A Study of a Prehistoric Western Pueblo Migration into the Middle San Pedro Valley. The Amerind Foundation No. 8. The Amerind Foundation, Dragoon, Arizona.

Di Peso, Charles C., cont'd
    1968   Casas Grandes: A Fallen Trading Center of the Gran Chichimeca. *Masterkey* 42:20-37.

    1974   *Casas Grandes: A Fallen Trading Center of the Gran Chichimeca.* Vols.1-3, The Amerind Foundation
            Series No. 9, Amerind Foundation Inc. – Norland Press, Flagstaff, Arizona.

    1979   Prehistory: O'otam. In Southwest, edited by Alfonso Ortiz, pp. 91-99. Handbook of North American
            Indians Volume 9, William C. Sturtevant, general editor. Smithsonian Institution, Washington, D.C.

    1980   The Hohokam and the O'otam. In Current Issues in Hohokam Prehistory: Proceedings of a Symposium,
            edited by David E. Doyel and Fred Plog, pp. 224-230. Anthropological Research Papers No. 23. Arizona
            State University, Tempe.

    1981   Discussion of Masse, Doelle, Sheridan, and Reff Papers from Southwestern Protohistory Conference. In
            The Protohistoric Period in the North American Southwest, A.D. 1450-1700, edited by David R. Wilcox and
            W. Bruce Masse, pp. 113-122. Anthropological Research Papers No. 24, Arizona State University, Tempe.

    1983   The Northern Sector of the Mesoamerican World System in Forgotten Places and Things: Archaeological
            Perspectives on American History. *Contributions to Anthropological Studies 3,* Center for Anthropological
            Studies, Albuquerque, New Mexico.

Di Peso, Charles C., John B. Rinaldo, and Gloria Fenner
    1974   Casas Grandes, A Fallen Trading Center of the Gran Chichimeca, Vol. 4-8. Northland Press, Flagstaff, Arizona.

Dobyns, Henry F.
    1966   An Appraisal of Techniques with a New Hemispheric Estimate. *Current Anthropology* 7:395-449.

    1972   *The Papago People.* Indian Tribal Series, Phoenix, Arizona.

    1976   *Native American Historical Demography.* Indiana University Press, Bloomington.

    1983   *Their Number Become Thinned.* University of Tennessee Press, Knoxville

    1989   Native Historic Epidemiology in the Greater Southwest. *American Anthropologist* 91(1):171-174.

Doelle, William H.
    1981   The Gila Pima in the Late Seventeenth Century. In *The Protohistoric Period in the North American
            Southwest, AD 1450-1700,* edited by David R. Wilcox and W. Bruce Masse, pp. 57-70. Anthropological
            Research Papers No. 24, Arizona State University, Tempe.

Dongoske, Kurt E., Michael Yeatts, Roger Anyon, and T. J. Ferguson
    1997   Archaeological Cultures and Cultural Affiliation: Hopi and Zuni Perspectives in the American Southwest.
            American Antiquity 62(4):600-608.

Dore, Christopher D. and Sandra L. López Varela.
    2009   The Future of Archaeology and Patrimony of Morelos. En *La Arqueología en Morelos: Dinámicas Sociales
            sobre las Construcciones de la Cultura Material,* editado por Sandra L. López Varela. Historia de Morelos,
            Tierra, gente, tiempos del Sur. vol. 2., Navarro Editores, Gobierno del Estado de Morelos, Cuernavaca.

Doremus, Anne
    2001   Indigenism, Mestizaje, and National Identity in Mexico during the 1940s and the 1950s. *Mexcan Stud-
            ies/Estudios Mexicanos* 17(2):375-402.

Doyel, David E.

1977 *Excavations in the Middle Santa Cruz River Valley, Southeastern Arizona.* Arizona State Museum Contribution to Highway Salvage Archaeology in Arizona No. 44. Arizona State Museum, University of Arizona, Tucson.

1981 *Late Hohokam Prehistory in Southern Arizona.* Contributions to Archaeology No. 2. Gila Press, Scottsdale.

1989 The Transition to History in the Northern Pimería Alta. In *Columbian Consequences, Volume 1: Archaeological and Historical Perspectives on the Spanish Borderlands West,* edited by David Hurst Thomas, pp. 139-158. Smithsonian Institution Press, Washington, D.C.

1991 Hohokam Cultural Evolution in the Phoenix Basin. In *Exploring the Hohokam: Prehistoric Desert Peoples of the Southwest,* edited by George J. Gumerman, pp. 231-278. University of New Mexico Press, Albuquerque.

Droessler, Judith B.

1981 *Craniometry and Biological Distance: Biocultural Continuity and Change at the Late-Woodland-Mississippian Interface.* Center for American Archaeology at Northwestern University, Evanston, Illinois.

Duff, Andrew I.

2002 *Western Pueblo Identities: Regional Interaction, Migration, and Transformation.* University of Arizona Press, Tucson.

Duffen, William A. and William K. Hartmann

1997 The 76 Ranch Ruin and the Location of Chichilticale. In *The Coronado Expedition to Tierra Nueva: The 1540-1542 Route Across the Southwest,* edited by Richard Flint and Shirley C. Flint, pp. 158-175. University Press of Colorado, Boulder.

Duke, Philip

2007 *The Tourist Gaze, the Cretans Glance: Archaeology and Tourism on a Greek Island.* Heritage, Tourism and Community. Left Coast Press, Inc., Walnut Creek, California.

Eisenberg, Leslie E.

1991 Mississippian Cultural Terminations in Middle Tennessee: What the Bioarchaeological Evidence Can Tell Us. In *What Mean These Bones?: Studies in Southeastern Bioarchaeology,* edited by Mary Lucas Powell, Patricia S. Bridges, and Ann Marie Wagner Mires, pp. 70-88. University of Alabama Press, Tuscaloosa.

Ekholm, Gordon

1939 Results of an Archaeological Survey of Sonora and Northern Sinaloa. *Revista Mexicana de Antropología* 3(1):7-11.

1940 The Archaeology of Northern and Western Mexico. In *The Mayas and Their Neighbors,* edited by C. L. Hay, pp. 307-320. Appleton-Century Company, Inc., New York.

1942 *Excavations at Guasave, Sinaloa, México.* Anthropological Papers of the American Museum of Natural History 38, Part 2, New York.

Ekholm, Kajsa and Jonathan Friedman

1982 Capital, Imperialism and Exploitation in Ancient World Systems. *Review 4* (1): 87-109.

Elera, Carlos
　1987　Inferencias socioeconómicas e ideológicas en torno a una tumba disturbada de la cultura Taicantin. Valle del Viru, Costa Norte del Perú. Cuicuilco 18: 62-78, ENAH-INAH, México.

El-Najjar, Mahmoud Y.
　1978　Southwestern Physical Anthropology: Do the Cultural and Biological Parameters Correspond? *American Journal of Physical Anthropology* 48:151-158.

Erickson, Winston P.
　1994　*Sharing the Desert: The Tohono O'odham in History.* University of Arizona Press, Tucson.

Ericson, Jonathon E. and Timothy G. Baugh (editors)
　1993　*The American Southwest and Mesoamerica: Systems of Prehistoric Exchange.* Plenum Press, New York.

Esquivel, Laura
　1995　Informe del Proyecto Arqueológico Sierra de Guadalupe. Temporadas de campo 1992/1993. Archivo Técnico del Consejo de Arqueología del INAH, México, D.F.

Ezell, Paul H.
　1963　Is There a Pima-Hohokam Culture Continuum? *American Antiquity* 29(1):61-66.

Farmer, James D.
　2001　Goggle Eyes and Crested Serpents of Barrier Canyon: Early Mesoamerican Iconography and the Archaic Southwest. In *The Road to Aztlan: Art from a Mythic Homeland,* edited by Virginia M. Fields and Victor Zamudio-Taylor, pp. 124-137. Los Angeles County Museum of Art, California.

Ferguson, T. J.
　1996　Native Americans and the Practice of Archaeology. *Annual Review of Anthropology* (25):63-79.

　2004　Academic, Legal, and Political Contexts of Social Identity and Cultural Affiliation Research in the American Southwest. In *Identity, Feasting, and the Archaeology of the Greater Southwest,* edited by Barbara J. Mills, pp. 27-41. University Press of Colorado, Boulder.

　2007　Zuni Traditional History and Cultural Geography. In *Zuni Origins: Toward a New Synthesis of Southwestern Archaeology,* edited by David A. Gregory and David R. Wilcox, pp. 377-403. University of Arizona Press, Tucson.

Ferguson, T. J. (compiler)
　2003　*Yep Hisat Hoopoq'yaqam Yeesiwa (Hopi Ancestors Were Once Here): Hopi-Hohokam Cultural Affiliation Study.* Hopi Cultural Preservation Office, The Hopi Tribe, Kykotsmovi, Arizona.

Ferguson, T. J. and Micah Lomaomvaya
　1999　*Hoopoq'yaqam niqw Wukoskyavi (Those Who Went to the Northeast and Tonto Basin): Hopi-Salado Cultural Affiliation Study.* Hopi Cultural Preservation Office, The Hopi Tribe, Kykotsmovi, Arizona.

Fernández, Gerardo
　2001　Proyecto Arqueológico Ojo Caliente, Estado de Zacatecas. Borrador del proyecto presentado ante el Consejo de Arqueología del INAH. Universidad Autónoma de Zacatecas.

Fewkes, Jesse W.
　1912　Casa Grande, Arizona. In *Twenty-eighth Annual Report of the Bureau of American Ethnology for the Years 1906-1907,* pp. 25-179. Government Printing Office, Washington, D.C.

Fields, Virginia M. and Victor Zamudio-Taylor (editors)
   2001   *The Road to Aztlan: Art from a Mythic Homeland.* Los Angeles County Museum of Art, California.

Firth, Raymond
   1973   *Symbols: Public and Private.* Allen & Unwin, London.

Fisher, Reginald
   1931   Second Report of the Archaeological Survey of the Pueblo Plateau, Santa Fe Sub-Quadrangle A. *The University of New Mexico Bulletin* Vol. 1 No. 1, Albuquerque.

Flint, Richard
   1992   The Pattern of Coronado Expedition Material Culture. Unpublished Ph.D. dissertation, Department of Behavioral Sciences, New Mexico Highlands University, Las Vegas, New Mexico.

   1997   Armas de la Tierra: The Mexican Indian Component of Coronado Expedition Culture. In *The Coronado Expedition to Tierra Nueva,* edited by Richard Flint and Shirley C. Flint, pp. 47-60. University Press of Colorado, Boulder.

   2003   What's Missing from this Picture? The Alarde, or Muster Roll, of the Coronado Expedition. In *The Coronado Expedition from the Distance of 460 Years,* edited by Richard Flint and Shirley C. Flint, pp. 57-80. University of New Mexico Press, Albuquerque.

   2008   *No Settlement, No Conquest. A History of the Coronado Entrada.* University of New Mexico Press, Albuquerque.

   2009   Without Them Nothing was Possible: The Coronado Expedition's Indian Allies. *New Mexico Historical Review* 84 (1):65-118.

   2011   Moho and the Tiguex War. In *The Latest Word from 1540. People, Places, and Portrayals of the Coronado Expedition,* edited by Richard Flint and Shirley C. Flint, pp. 348-366. University of New Mexico Press, Albuquerque.

Flint, Richard and Shirley C. Flint (editors, translators, and annotators)
   2005   *Documents of the Coronado Expedition, 1539-1542: "They Were Not Familiar with His Majesty, nor Did They Wish to Be His Subjects."* Southern Methodist University Press, Dallas, Texas.

Flint, Richard and Shirley C. Flint (editors)
   2011   *The Latest Word from 1540: People, Places, and Portrayals of the Coronado Expedition.* University of New Mexico Press, Albuquerque.

Flint, Shirley C.
   2003   The Financing and Provisioning of the Coronado Expedition. In *The Coronado Expedition from the Distance of 460 Years,* edited by Richard Flint and Shirley C. Flint, pp. 42-56. University of New Mexico Press, Albuquerque.

Fomento Cultural Banamex
   1998   *Great Masters of Mexican Folk Arts.* Harry N. Abrams, Inc., New York.

Fontana, Bernard L.
   1976   The Faces and Forces of Pimería Alta. In *Voices from the Southwest: A Gathering in Honor of Lawrence Clark Powell,* edited by Donald C. Dickinson, Margaret F. Maxwell, and W. David Laird, pp. 45-54. Northland Press, Flagstaff, Arizona.

Fontana, Bernard L., cont'd

1987   The *Vikita*: A Biblio History. *Journal of the Southwest* 29(3):259-272.

1989   *Of Earth and Little Rain.* University of Arizona Press, Tucson.

Fontana, Bernard L., William J. Robinson, Charles W. Cormack, and E. E. Leavitt, Jr.

1962   *Papago Indian Pottery.* University of Washington Press, Seattle.

Foster, John

1994   Notas sobre la arqueología de la Sierra Fría. En *Espacios: Cultura y Sociedad* 13:3-14, Enero-Febrero, Instituto Cultural de Aguascalientes, Aguascalientes.

Foster, Michael S.

1986   The Mesoamerican Connection: A View from the South. In *Ripples in the Chichimec Sea: New Considerations of Southwestern-Mesoamerican Interactions,* edited by Frances J. Mathien and Randall H. McGuire, pp. 55-69. Centre for Archaeological Investigations and Southern Illinois University Press, Carbondale and Edwardsville.

1988   The Early Ceramic Period in Northwest Mexico: An Overview. In *Mogollon V*, edited by Patrick H. Beckett. Coas Publishing Company, Las Cruces.

1995   The Loma San Gabriel Culture and its Suggested Relationship to other Early Plainware Cultures of Northwest Mexico. In *The Gran Chichimeca: Essays on the Archaeology and Ethnohistory of Northern Mesoamerica*, edited by Jonathan E. Reyman, pp. 179-207. *Avebury Worldwide Archaeology Series* 12. Ashgate Publishing Company, Brookfield, Vermont.

1999   The Aztatlán Tradition of West and Northwest Mexico and Casas Grandes: Speculations on the Medio Period Florescence. In *The Casas Grandes World*, edited by Curtis F. Schaafsma and Carroll L. Riley, pp. 149-163. The University of Utah Press, Salt Lake City.

2000   Archaeology of Durango. In *Greater Mesoamerica: The Archaeology of West and Norther Mexico*, edited by Michael S. Foster and Shirley Gorenstein, pp. 155-180. The University of Utah Press, Salt Lake City.

Foster, Michael S. and Shirley Gorenstein (editors)

2000   *Greater Mesoamerica: The Archaeology of West and Northwest Mexico.* The University of Utah Press, Salt Lake City.

Foster, Michael S. and Phil C. Weigand (editors)

1985   *The Archaeology of West and Northwest Mesoamerica.* Westview Press, Boulder, Colorado.

Fowler, Don D.

1987   Uses of the past: archaeology in the service of the state. *American Antiquity* 52(2): 229-248.

2000   *A Laboratory for Anthropology: Science and Romanticism in the American Southwest 1846-1930.* University of New Mexico Press, Albuquerque.

Frank, Andre Gunder and Barry K. Gills (editors)

1993   *The World System: Five Hundred or Five Thousand Years?* Routledge, London.

Frankenstein, Susan and Michael J. Rowlands

1978   The Internal Structure and Regional Context of Early Iron Age Society in Southwestern Germany. *Bulletin of the Institute of Archaeology* 15:73-112.

Frisbie, Theodore R.
 1983 Anazasi-Mesoamerican Relationships: From the Bowels of the Earth and Beyond. In *Proceedings of the Anazasi Symposium 1981,* edited by Jack E. Smith, pp. 215-227. Mesa Verde Museum Association, Mesa Verde National Park.

Fritz, Gordon
 1977 The Ecological Significance of Early Piman Immigration to Southern Arizona. Ms. on file, Arizona State Museum Library, Arizona State Museum, University of Arizona, Tucson.

 1989 The Ecological Significance of Early Piman Immigration to Southern Arizona. *The Artifact* 27(2):51-109.

Galaviz de Capdeville, María Elena
 1967 *Rebeliones Indígenas en el Norte de la Nueva España. Siglos XVI y XVII.* Editorial Campesina. México.

Galinier, Jacques
 1991 From Montezuma to San Francisco: The *Wi:gita* Ritual in Papago (Tohono O'odham) Religion. *Journal of the Southwest* 33(4):486-538.

Galván, Javier
 1976 *Rescate arqueológico en el fraccionamiento tabachines, Zapopan, Jalisco.* Cuadernos de los Centros 28. Dirección de los Centros Regionales INAH, México.

 1991 *Las tumbas de tiro del valle de Atemajac, Jalisco.* Colección Científica, Serie Arqueología 239, INAH, México.

Galván, Javier y Otto Schondube
 1975 Visita de inspección a Montesa, Zacatecas. Ms. Archivo del Centro Regional de Occidente, INAH, Guadalajara, Jalisco.

de Gaulejac, Vincent
 2002 Memoria e historicidad. *Revista Mexicana de Sociología* 64(2):31-46.

Gamio, Manuel
 1916 *Forjando Patria.* Librería de Porrúa Hermanos, México, D.F.

 1920 Las Excavaciones del Pedregal de San Angel y la Cultura Arcaica del Valle de México. *American Anthropologist* 22(2):127-147.

 1924 The Sequence of Cultures in Mexico. *American Anthropologist* 26(3):307-322.

García-Bárcena, Joaquín
 2007 Law and the Practice of Archaeology in Mexico. *The SAA Archaeological Record* 7(5):14-15.

García-Uranga, Baudelina
 1986 *Informe de los trabajos realizados durante la primera temporada de campo del proyecto localización, registro y estudio de sitios con pintura rupestre y/o petroglifos en la península de Baja California, México.* Archivo Técnico del Consejo de Arqueología del INAH, México, D.F.

Gardner, Erle S.
 1962 *The Hidden Heart of Baja.* Wm. Morrow, New York.

Gerald, Rex E.
1968   *Spanish Presidios of the Late Eighteenth Century in Northern New Spain.* Museum of New Mexico Research Records No. 7. Museum of New Mexico Press, Santa Fe.

Gilpin, Dennis and David A. Phillips, Jr.
1999   *The Prehistoric to Historic Transition Period in Arizona, circa A.D. 1519-1692: A Component of the Arizona Historic Preservation Plan.* Arizona State Historic Preservation Office, Arizona State Parks, Phoenix.

Gladwin, Harold S.
1937   *Excavations at Snaketown Volume II: Comparisons and Theories.* Medallion Papers XXVI. Gila Pueblo, Globe.

1957   *A History of the Ancient Southwest.* The Bond Wheelwright Company, Portland, Maine.

Gladwin, Harold S., Emil W. Haury, E. B. Sayles, and Nora Gladwin
1937   *Excavations at Snaketown: Material Culture, Volume I.* Medallion Papers XXV. Gila Pueblo, Globe, Arizona.

Gladwin, Winifred and Harold S. Gladwin
1929   *The Red-on-buff Culture of the Gila Basin.* Medallion Papers III. Pasadena, California.

1934   *A Method for Designation of Cultures and Their Variations.* Medallion Papers XV. Gila Pueblo, Globe, Arizona.

Gómez Gastelum, Luis
2003   Las conchas marinas durante el postclásico en el antiguo Occidente de México. *Eco.* Instituto Jaliscience de Antropología e Historia 4:13-19.

Gómez Gastelum, Luis y R. A. de la Torre
1996   Figuritas Cerrito de García en la Cuenca de Sayula, Jalisco. *Estudios del Hombre 3*, Universidad de Guadalajara, Jalisco, pp. 127-150.

Gómez, Sergio
2006   La Fragmentación del Patrimonio Cultural en Teotihuacán. *Memoria del IV Congreso Nacional de Investigadores del INAH*, Sindicato de Investigadores INAH, México, D.F.

González Leos, Brenda Elizabeth y Juan Ignacio Macías Quintero
2007   *Proyecto de prospección arqueológica en la región sur occidente del estado de Aguascalientes. Informe técnico correspondiente a la Primera Etapa de Investigación*, Diciembre 2005-Enero 2006, Catálogo de pinturas rupestres y petrograbados, El Colegio de Michoacán, Zamora, México.

Goodwin, Robert
2008   *Crossing the Continent 1527-1540.* HarperCollins, New York.

Gorenstein, Shirley and Michael S. Foster
2000   West and Northwest Mexico: The Ins and Outs of Mesoamerica. In *Greater Mesoamerica: The Archaeology of West and Northwest Mexico,* edited by Michael S. Foster and Shirley Gorenstein, pp. 3-19. The University of Utah Press, Salt Lake City.

Green, William and John F. Doershuk
1998   Cultural Resource Management and American Archaeology. *Journal of Archaeological Research* 6(2):121-168.

Gregory, David A.
  1991   Form and Variation in Hohokam Settlement Patterns. In *Chaco and Hohokam: Prehistoric Regional Systems in the American Southwest*, edited by Patricia L. Crown and W. James Judge, pp. 159-193. School of American Research Press, Santa Fe, New Mexico.

Grosscup, Gordon L.
  1976   The Ceramic Sequence at Amapa. *The Archaeology of Amapa, Nayarit.* Monumenta Archaeologica, 2: 208-272, University of California, Los Angeles.

Guevara Sánchez, Arturo
  1987   Vestigios Prehistóricos del Estado de Sinaloa. Dos Casos. *Arqueología* 1:9-29. Revista de Monumentos Prehispánicos, Instituto Nacional de Antropología e Historia, México.

Gutiérrez Martínez, María de la Luz
  1991   Informe de los trabajos realizados durante la segunda temporada de campo del proyecto localización, registro y estudio de sitios con pintura rupestre y/o petroglifos en la Sierra de San Francisco, B.C.S. Archivo Técnico del Consejo de Arqueología del INAH, México, D.F

  2003   Segundo Informe Técnico Anual del Proyecto Identidad Social, Comunicación Ritual y Arte Rupestre: El Gran Mural de la Sierra de Guadalupe, B.C.S. Archivo Técnico del Consejo de Arqueología del INAH, México, D.F.

  2009   Visitantes a la Sierra de San Francisco. Estadísticas INAH, Compendio Digital en posesión del autor, México.

Gutiérrez Martínez, María de la Luz y Baudelina García-Uranga
  1990   *Análisis Contextual de Pintura Rupestre: Un Caso de Estudio en la Baja California.* Tesis de Licenciatura en Arqueología, Escuela Nacional de Antropología e Historia. SEP - INAH.

Gutiérrez Martínez, María de la Luz y Justin R. Hyland
  2002   *Arqueología de la Sierra de San Francisco: Dos décadas de investigación del fenómeno Gran Mural.* Colección Científica, no. 433. Primera edición, Instituto Nacional de Antropología e Historia, México, D.F.

Gutiérrez, María de la Luz, Enrique Hambleton, Justin R. Hyland, and Nicholas Stanley Price
  1996   The Management of World Heritage sites in remote areas. In *Conservation and Management of Archaeological Sites* 1(4):209-225, James & James, London.

Gutiérrez, Natividad
  1998   What Indians Say about Mestizos: A Critical View of a Cultural Archetype of Mexican Nationalism. *Bulletin of Latin American Research* 17(3):285-301.

Gosden, Chris
  2006   Race and Racism in Archaeology: Introduction. *World Archaeology* 38(1):1-7, Taylor & Francis, Ltd.

Gregory, David A. and David R. Wilcox
  2007   Revising the Mogollon Concept. In *Zuni Origins: Toward a New Synthesis of Southwestern Archaeology*, edited by David A. Gregory and David R. Wilcox, pp. 165-209. University of Arizona Press, Tucson.

Hadley, Diana and Thomas E. Sheridan
  1995   *Land Use History of the San Rafael Valley, Arizona (1540-1960).* USDA Forest Service General Technical Report RM-GTR-269. Rocky Mountain Forest and Range Experiment Station, U.S. Department of Agriculture, Fort Collins.

Hagen, Joshua
  2006   *Preservation, Tourism and Nationalism.* Heritage, Culture and Identity. Ashgate, Gateshead.

Hale, Kenneth and David Harris
  1979   Historical Linguistics and Archaeology. In *Southwest*, edited by Alfonso Ortiz, pp. 170-177. Handbook of North American Indians Volume 9, William C. Sturtevant, general editor. Smithsonian Institution, Washington, D.C.

Hall, T. B. (editor)
  1935a   *Aw-O-Tahm Ah-Pa-Tac* 1(5). Bureau of Indian Affairs, Sells Agency, Sells, Arizona.

  1935b   *Aw-O-Tahm Ah-Pa-Tac* 1(6). Bureau of Indian Affairs, Sells Agency, Sells, Arizona.

Hambleton, Enrique
  1979   *La Pintura Rupestre de Baja California.* Fomento Cultural Banamex, México D.F.

Hamilakis, Yanis
  2003   Lives in Ruins: Antiquities and National Imagination in Modern Greece. In *The Politics of Archaeology and Identity in a Global Context,* edited by S Kane, pp. 51-78. Colloquia and Conference Papers 7. Archaeological Institute of America, Boston, Massachusetts.

  2007   *The Nation and Its Ruins: Antiquity, Archaeology, and National Imagination in Greece.* Classical Presences. Oxford University Press, Oxford.

Hammond, George P. and Agapito Rey
  1940   *Narratives of the Coronado Expedition,* University of New Mexico Press, Albuquerque.

Hargrave, Lyndon L.
  1970   *Mexican Macaws: Comparative Osteology and Survey of Remains from the Southwest.* University of Arizona Press, Tucson.

Harmon, Marcel
  2005   Centralization, Cultural Transmission, and "the Game of Life and Death" in Northern Mexico. Ph.D. dissertation, Department of Anthropology, University of New Mexico, Albuquerque.

  2006   Religion and the Mesoamerican Ball Game in the Casas Grandes Region of Northern Mexico. In *Religion in the Prehispanic Southwest,* edited by Todd L. VanPool, Christine S. VanPool, and David Phillips, pp. 185-218. AltaMira Press, Walnut Creek, California.

Hartmann, William K. and Betty Graham Lee
  2003   Chichilticale: A Survey of Candidate Ruins in Southeastern Arizona. In *The Coronado Expedition from the Distance of 460 Years,* edited by Richard Flint and Shirley C. Flint, pp. 81-108. University of New Mexico Press, Albuquerque.

Haury, Emil W.
  1945   *The Excavation of Los Muertos and Neighboring Ruins in the Salt River Valley, Southern Arizona, Based on the Work of the Hemenway Southwestern Archaeological Expedition of 1887-1888.* Papers of the Peabody Museum of American Archaeology and Ethnology Vol. 24, No. 1. Harvard University, Cambridge, MA.

  1950   Final Discussion. In *The Stratigraphy and Archaeology of Ventana Cave,* edited by Emil W. Haury, Kirk Bryan, Edwin H. Colbert, Norman E. Gabel, Clara Lee Tanner, and T. E. Buehrer, pp. 521-548. University of Arizona Press, Tucson.

1958   Evidence at Point of Pines for a Prehistoric Migration from Northern Arizona. In *Migrations in New World Culture History*, edited by Raymond H. Thompson, pp. 1-6. University of Arizona Bulletin Vol. 29(2). Social Science Bulletin No. 27. University of Arizona Press, Tucson.

1976   *The Hohokam, Desert Farmers and Craftsmen: Excavations at Snaketown, 1964-1965.* University of Arizona Press, Tucson.

1980   On the Discovery of Ventana Cave. In *Camera, Spade, and Pen: An Inside View of Southwestern Archaeology*, edited by Marnie Gaede, pp. 123-130. University of Arizona Press, Tucson.

1984   The Search for Chichilticale. *Arizona Highways* 60(4):14-19.

Hayden, Julian D.
1970   Of Hohokam Origins and Other Matters. *American Antiquity* 35(1):87-93.

Hays-Gilpin, Kelley and Jane H. Hill
1999   The Flower World in Material Culture: An Iconographic Complex in the Southwest and Mesoamerica. *Journal of Anthropological Research* 55:1-37.

2000   The Flower World in Prehistoric Southwest Material Culture. In *The Archaeology of Regional Interaction: Religion, Warfare, and Exchange across the American Southwest and Beyond Proceedings of the 1996 Southwest Symposium*, edited by Michelle Hegmon, pp. 411-428. University Press of Colorado, Boulder.

Helms, Mary W.
1993   *Craft and the Kingly Ideal: Art, Trade, and Power.* University of Texas Press, Austin.

Hill, J. Brett, Jeffrey J. Clark, William H. Doelle, and Patrick D. Lyons
2004   Prehistoric Demography in the Southwest: Migration, Coalescence, and Hohokam Population Decline. *American Antiquity* 69(4):689-716.

2010   Depopulation of the Northern Southwest: A Macroregional Perspective. In *Leaving Mesa Verde: Peril and Change in the Thirteenth-Century Southwest*, edited by Timothy A. Kohler, Mark D. Varien, and Aaron M. Wright, pp. 34-52. Amerind Studies in Archaeology, vol. 5. University of Arizona Press, Tucson.

Hill, Jane H.
1992   Fast and Slow in Tohono O'odham. Paper presented to the *II Encuentro de Lingüística en el Noroeste*, Hermosillo, Sonora, Mexico. Manuscript on file, Tohono O'odham Nation Cultural Center & Museum Archives, Topawa, Arizona.

1992   The Flower World of Old Uto-Aztecan. *Journal of Anthropological Research* 48:117-145.

2001   Languages on the Land: Toward and Anthropological Dialectology. In *Archaeology, Language, and History: Essays on Culture and Ethnicity,* edited by John Edward Terrell, pp. 257-282. Bergin & Garvey, Westport, Connecticut.

Hill, Jane H.
2007   The Zuni Language in Southwestern Areal Context. In *Zuni Origins: Toward a New Synthesis of Southwestern Archaeology,* edited by David A. Gregory and David R. Wilcox, pp. 22-38. University of Arizona Press, Tucson.

Hill, Jane H. and Ofelia Zepeda
1991   "Some People say I sound just like I'm from around here:" The Speech of Tohono O'odham "dialect

outsiders." Draft paper presented at Annual Meeting of the Southwestern Anthropological Association, Tucson, Arizona. Manuscript on file, Tohono O'odham Nation Cultural Center & Museum archives, Topawa, Arizona.

Hinsley, Curtis M.
    2000   Digging for Identity, Reflections on the Cultural Background of Collecting. In *Repatriation Reader, Who Owns American Indian Remains,* edited by Devon A. Mihesuah, pp. 37-55. University of Nebraska Press, Lincoln.

Hinton, Thomas B.
    1959   *A Survey of Indian Assimilation in Eastern Sonora.* Anthropological Papers of the University of Arizona 4. University of Arizona Press, Tucson.

Hodge, Frederick W.
    1937   *History of Hawikuh, New Mexico: One of the So-Called Cities of Cibola.* Ward Ritchie Press, Los Angeles.

Hollowell, Julie and George Nicholas
    2009   Using Ethnographic Methods to Articulate Community-Based Conceptions of Cultural Heritage Management. *Public Archaeology* 8(2-3):141-160.

Holtorf, Cornelius
    2005   *From Stonehenge to Las Vegas.* AltaMira Press, Oxford.

Hordes, Stanley M.
    1989   Historical Context of LA 54147. In *A Sixteenth Century Spanish Campsite in the Tiguex Province,* edited by Bradley J. Vierra, pp. 207-222. Laboratory of Anthropology Notes No. 475, Museum of New Mexico, Santa Fe.

Hosler, Dorothy
    1994   Arqueología y metalurgia en el Occidente de México. El Bronce Mesoamericano orígenes, desarrollo y difusión. *Transformaciones mayores en el Occidente de México,* coordinado por Ricardo Ávila, Colección Fundamentos, pp.13-39. México.

Howell, Todd L.
    1994   *Leadership at the Ancestral Zuni Village of Hawikku.* Ph.D. dissertation, Arizona State University, Tempe.

    2003   700 Years of Flaked Stone Use at Zuni Pueblo. Paper presented at the Amerind Foundation Advanced Seminar: Colonialism and Culture Change at Zuni A.D. 1300-1900, Manuscript on file at Zuni Heritage and Historic Preservation Office.

Howell, Todd L. and Keith W. Kintigh
    1996   Archaeological Identification of Kin Groups Using Mortuary and Biological Data: An Example from the American Southwest. *American Antiquity* 61(3):537-554.

Hrdlička, Aleš
    1931   Catalogue of Human Crania in the United States National Museum: Pueblos, Southern-Utah Basketmakers, Navajo. *Proceedings of the U.S. National Museum* 78(2):1-95.

Huckell, Bruce B.
    1984   Sobaipuri Sites in the Rosemont Area. In *Miscellaneous Archaeological Studies in the ANAMAX-Rosemont Land Exchange Area*, edited by Martyn D. Tagg, Richard G. Ervin, and Bruce B. Huckell, pp. 107-130. Arizona State Museum Archaeological Series No. 147(4). Arizona State Museum, University of Arizona, Tucson.

Hu-DeHart, Evelyn
1981 *Missionaries, Miners and Indians*. University of Arizona Press, Tucson.

Hudson, Charles
1990 *The Juan Pardo Expeditions: Exploration of the Carolinas and Tennessee, 1566-1568*. The University of Alabama Press, Tuscaloosa.

Huntington, Ellsworth
1911 The First Americans. *Harper's Monthly Magazine* 122(729):451-462.

1914 *The Climatic Factor as Illustrated in Arid America*. Carnegie Institution of Washington Publication No. 192. Carnegie Institution of Washington, Washington, D.C.

Hulse, Frederick
1945 Skeletal Material. In *Excavations at Culiacan, Sinaloa*, edited by Isabel Kelly, pp. 187-198. Ibero-Americana:25.

Huntley, Deborah L. and Keith W. Kintigh
2004 Archaeological Patterning and the Organizational Scale of Late Prehistoric Settlement Clusters in the Zuni Region of New Mexico. In *The Protohistoric Pueblo World: A.D. 1275-1600*, edited by E. Charles Adams and Andrew I. Duff, pp. 62-74. University of Arizona Press, Tucson.

Huntley, Deborah L., Jeffery Clark, Robert Jones, Katherine Dungan, and J. Brett Hill
2010 Get Back: Kayenta and Salado Migrations into Southwest New Mexico. In *The Collected Papers from the 15th Biennial Mogollon Conference, Silver City, New Mexico, 2008*, edited by Lora Jackson Legare, pp. 51-72. Special Report No. 12. El Paso Archaeological Society, Texas.

INAH
1972 *Ley Federal Sobre Monumentos y Zonas Arqueológicos*. Instituto Nacional de Antropología e Historia, México, D.F.

2008a Monto por Taquilla y Otros Ingresos: IFAI 1115100008208, http://*www.ifai.org.mx/*. INAH, México.

2008b Presupuesto Autorizado 2007: IFAI 1115100028107, http://*www.ifai.org.mx/*. INAH, México.

2008c Presupuesto Ejercido: IFAI 1115100034607, http://*www.ifai.org.mx/*. INAH, México.

Jacobs, David and Glen E. Rice
1997 The Function of U:4:33/132, The Cline Terrace Mound. In *A Salado Platform Mound on Tonto Creek, Roosevelt Platform Mound Study: Report on the Cline Terrace Mound, Cline Terrace Complex*, Roosevelt Monograph Series 7, Anthropological Field Studies 36, edited by David Jacobs, pp. 577-586. Office of Cultural Resource Management, Arizona State University, Tempe.

Jenkins, Richard
1997 *Rethinking Ethnicity*. Sage, London.

Jiménez Betts, Peter F.
1988 La Arqueología en Zacatecas. En *La Antropología en el Norte de México*, editado por Carlos García Mora y Martín Villalobos Salgado, pp. 345-365. Col. Biblioteca del INAH, Vol. 12, INAH, México.

1989 Perspectivas sobre la arqueología de Zacatecas. En *Arqueología* 5:7-50, Dirección de Monumentos Prehispánicos, INAH, México.

Jiménez Betts, Peter F., cont'd

1992   Una red de interacción del noroeste de México: Una interpretación. En *Origen y desarrollo de la civilización en el Occidente de México: Homenaje a Pedro Armillas y Angel Palerm*, editado por Brigitte B. de Lameiras y Phil C. Weigand, pp. 177-204. El Colegio de Michoacán, Zamora.

1998   Áreas de interacción del noreste mesoamericano. En *Memoria, VI Coloquio de Occidentalistas*, editado por Ricardo Ávila, Jean P. Emphoux, Luis G. Gastelum, Susana Ramírez, Otto Schöndube y Francisco Valdez, pp. 295-303. ORSTOM, Universidad de Guadalajara, CEMCA, UNAM, Jalisco.

2007   The Relevance of Ethics in the Archaeology of Mexico as Pertaining to its Northern Neighbors. *The SAA Archaeological Record* 7(5):32-34.

Jiménez Betts, Peter F. and J. Andrew Darling

2000   Archaeology of Southern Zacatecas: The Malpaso, Juchipila, and Valparaiso-Bolaños Valleys. In *Greater Mesoamerica: The Archaeology of West and Northern Mexico*, edited by Michael S. Foster and Shirley Gorenstein, pp. 155-180. The University of Utah Press, Salt Lake City.

Jiménez Moreno, Wigberto

1943   Tribus e idioma. *Reunión de Mesa Redonda sobre Problemas Antropológicos de México y Centro América.* Sociedad Mexicana de Antropología, México, pp. 121-132.

Joseph, Alice, Rosamond B. Spicer, and Jane Chesky

1949   *The Desert People: A Study of the Papago Indians.* University of Chicago Press, Illinois.

Keen, Myra

1971   *Sea Shells of Tropical West America. Maritime Mollusks from Baja California to Peru.* Stanford University Press, California.

Kelley, J. Charles

1966   Mesoamerica and the Southwestern United States. In *The Handbook of Middle American Indians,* edited by Gordon Willey and Gordon Ekholm, pp. 95-111. University of Texas Press, Austin.

1974   *Pictorial and Ceramic Art in the Chichimec Cultural Littoral of the Chichimec Sea,* Special Publications of the Museum of Texas Tech University, Vol. 7:23-54, Texas.

1975   An Alternative Hypothesis for the Explanation of Anasazi Culture History. In *Collected Papers in Honor of Florence Hawley Ellis*, edited by Theodore Frisbie, pp. 178-223. Papers of the Archaeological Society of New Mexico No. 2, Albuquerque.

1986   The Mobile Merchants of Molino. In *Ripples in the Chichimec Sea: New Considerations of Southwestern-Mesoamerican Interactions*, edited by Frances J. Mathien and Randall H. McGuire, pp. 81-104. Southern Illinois University Press, Carbondale and Edwardsville.

1991   The Known Archaeological Ballcourts of Durango and Zacatecas. In *The Mesoamerican Ballgame,* edited by Vernon L. Scarborough and David R. Wilcox, pp. 87-100. University of Arizona Press, Tucson.

1993   Zenith Passage: The View from Chalchihuites. In *Culture and Contact: Charles C. Di Peso's Gran Chichimeca,* edited by Anne I. Woosley and John C. Ravesloot, pp. 83-104. The Amerind Foundation, Inc., Dragoon, and The University of New Mexico Press, Albuquerque.

1995   Trade Goods, Traders and Status in Northwestern Greater Mesoamerica. In *The Gran Chichimeca: Es-*

says on the Archaeology and Ethnohistory of Northern Mesoamerica, edited by Jonathon E. Reyman, pp. 102-145. Avebury, Hampshire.

2000   The Aztatlán Mercantile System. Mobile Traders and the Northwestward Expansion of Mesoamerican Civilization. In *Greater Mesoamerica: The Archaeology of West and Northwest Mexico,* edited by Michael S. Foster and Shirley Gorenstein, pp. 137-154. The University of Utah Press, Salt Lake City.

Kelley, J Charles, Walter Taylor y Pedro Armillas
  1961-1963   Studies of the North-Central Frontier of Mesoamerica. Archaeological and Ecological Investigation of the Northe Central Frontier of Mesoamerica and the Relationships of the Cultures of Central Mesoamerica, the Gran Chichimeca, and the American Southwest, September 1, 1961-August 31, 1963 (2 years), ms., Submitted by the Southern Illinois University Carbondale, Illinois.

Kelley, J. Charles and Ellen Abbott Kelley
  1975   An Alternative Hypothesis for the Explanation of Anasazi Culture History. In *Collected Papers in Honor of Florence Hawley Ellis,* edited by Theodore R. Frisbie, pp. 178-223. Papers of the Archaeological Society of New Mexico 2. Archaeological Society of New Mexico, Santa Fe.

Kelley, David H.
  1964   Knife-wing and Other Man-eating Birds. En *Sobretiro del XXXV Congreso Internacional de Americanistas* 1962:589-590. México.

Kelly, Isabel
  1938   *Excavations at Chametla, Sinaloa.* Ibero Americana 14. University of California Press, Berkeley.

  1945   *Excavations at Culiacan, Sinaloa.* Ibero Americana 25. University of California Press, Berkeley.

  1980   *Ceramic Sequence in Colima: Capacha, an Early Phase.* Anthropological Papers of the University of Arizona 37, University of Arizona Press, Tucson.

Kickingbird, Lynn and Curtis Berkey
  1977   *Executive Orders Establishing the Papago Reservations with a Brief Chronological History.* Institute for the Development of Indian Law, Publications Department, Vienna, Virginia.

Kidder, Alfred V.
  1932   *The Artifacts of Pecos.* Yale University Press, New Haven.

Kintigh, Keith W.
  1985   *Settlement, Subsistence, and Society in Late Zuni Prehistory.* Anthropological Papers of the University of Arizona 44. University of Arizona Press, Tucson.

  2000   Leadership Strategies in Protohistoric Zuni Towns. In *Alternative Leadership Strategies in the Prehispanic Southwest,* edited by Barbara J. Mills, pp. 95-116. University of Arizona Press, Tucson.

Kohl, Philip L.
  1979   "The World Economy" of West Asia in the Third Millennium B.C. In *South Asian Archaeology 1977,* edited by Maurizio Taddei, pp. 55-85. Naples.

  1998   Nationalism and Archaeology: On the Constructions of Nations and Reconstructions of the Remote Past. *Annual Review of Anthropology* 27:223-46.

Kohn, Lucy Ann P., Steven R. Leigh, and James M. Cheverud
  1995   Asymmetric Vault Modification in Hopi Crania. *American Journal of Physical Anthropology* 98:173-195.

Konigsberg, Lyle W.
  2006   A Post-Neumann History of Biological and Genetic Distance Studies in Bioarchaeology. In *Bioarchaeology: The Contextual Analysis of Human Remains*, edited by Jane E. Buikstra and Lane A. Beck, pp. 263-279. Elsevier, New York.

Konigsberg, Lyle W. and Stephen D. Ousley
  1995   Multivariate Quantitative Genetics of Anthropometric Traits from the Boas Data. *Human Biology* 67:481-498.

Kreutzer, Daniel D.
  2006   Privatising the Public Past: The Economics of Archaeological Heritage Management. Archaeologies 2(2):52-66.

Kristiansen, Kristian
  1998   *Europe Before History.* New Studies in Archaeology Series, Cambridge University Press, United Kingdom.

  2009   Contract Archaeology in Europe: An Experiment in Diversity. *World Archaeology* 41(4):641-648.

Kroeber, Alfred Louis
  1948   *Anthropology: Race, Language, Culture, Psychology, Prehistory.* Revised. Harcourt, Brace, and World, Inc., New York.

Kuwanwisiwma, Leigh J.
  2008   Collaboration Means Equality, Respect, and Reciprocity, A Conversation about Archaeology and the Hopi Tribe. In *Collaboration in Archaeological Practice,* edited by Chip Colwell-Chanthaphonh and T. J. Ferguson, p. 151-169. AltaMira Press, Lanham, MD.

Lahr, Marta M. and J. E. Bowman
  1992   Paleopathology of the Kechipawan site: Health and disease in a Southwestern Pueblo. *Journal of Archaeological Science* 19(6):639-654.

Le Blanc, Steven
  1986   Aspects of Southern Prehistory: A. D. 900-1400. In *Ripples in the Chichimec Sea: New Considerations of Southwestern – Mesoamerican Interactions*, edited by Frances Joan Mathian y Randall H. McGuire. pp. 105-134. Southern Illinois University Press, Carbondale.

Lekson, Stephen
  1999   *The Chaco Meridian: Centers of Political Power in the Ancient Southwest.* AltaMira Press, Walnut Creek, California.

  2000   Salado in Chihuahua. In *Salado,* edited by Jeffrey S. Dean. Amerind Foundation New World Studies. University of New Mexico Press, Albuquerque.

  2005a Chaco and Paquimé: Complexity, History, Landscape. In *North American Archaeology,* edited by Timothy R. Pauketat and Diana DiPaolo Loren, pp. 235-272. Blackwell, Malden.

  2005b Complexity. In *Southwest Archaeology in the Twentieth Century,* edited by Linda S. Cordell and Don D. Fowler, pp. 157-173. University of Utah Press, Salt Lake City.

2008   *A History of the Ancient Southwest.* School of Advanced Research Press, Santa Fe, New Mexico.

Lelgemann, Achim
    2001   El cañón de Juchipila como corredor de comunicaciones entre Occidente y Norte de México: Nuevas evidencias de Tepisuazco, Zacatecas. Ponencia presentada en el Congreso Piña Chan: Nuevos aportes arqueológicos en el Norte y Occidente de México, Museo Nacional de Antropología e Historia, México.

Lindauer, Owen (editor)
    1996   *The Place of the Storehouses, Roosevelt Platform Mound Study, Report on the Schoolhouse Point Mound, Pinto Creek Complex,* Parts 1 and 2. Office of Cultural Resource Management, Arizona State University, Tempe.

Linton, Adelin
    1955   Preface. In *The Tree of Culture*, edited by Ralph Linton, pp. v-viii. Alfred A. Knopf, New York.

Lister, Robert H.
    1961   Twenty-five Years of Archaeology in the Greater Southwest. *American Antiquity* 27:39-45.

Lister, Robert H. and Agnes M. Howard
    1955   The Chalchihuites Culture of Northwestern Mexico. *American Antiquity* 21:122-129.

Lizama Aranda, Lilia
    2010   Heritage Values and Mexican Cultural Policies: Dispossession of the "Other's" Culture by the Mexican Archaeological System. In *Heritage Values in Contemporary Society,* edited by George S. Smith, Phyllis M. Messenger, and Hilary A. Soderland, pp. 225-238. Left Coast Press, Walnut Creek, California.

Loendorf, Chris
    2012   *The Hohokam-Akimel O'odham Continuum: Sociocultural Dynamics and Projectile Point Design in the Phoenix Basin, Arizona.* Gila River Indian Community Anthropological Research Papers No. 5. Gila River Indian Community Cultural Resource Management Program, Sacaton.

Loendorf, Chris, Craig M. Fertelmes, and Barnaby Lewis
    2013   Hohokam to Akimel O'odham Obsidian Acquisition at the Historic Period Sacate Site (GR-909), Gila River Indian Community, Arizona. *American Antiquity* 78(2):266-284.

Lomnitz, Claudio
    2001   *Deep Mexico Silent Mexico: An Anthropology of Nationalism.* University of Minnesota Press, Minneapolis.

López-Mestas, Lorenza et al.
    1994   Sitios y materiales: Avances del proyecto Altos de Jalisco. En *Contribuciones a la Arqueología y Etnohistoria del Occidente de México,* editado por Eduardo Williams, pp. 279-296. El Colegio de Michoacán, Zamora.

López-Mestas, Lorenza y Jorge Ramos de la Vega
    1992   *Investigaciones arqueológicas en Sierra de La Comaja, Guanajuato.* Tesis de Licenciatura en Arqueología. Universidad de Guadalajara, Jalisco.

    1998   Investigaciones arqueológicas en el valle de Cihuatlán, Barra de Navidad. *El Occidente de México: arqueología, historia y medio ambiente.* Actas del IV Coloquio de Occidentalistas. Universidad de Guadalajara-ORSTOM, México.

Lorenzo, José Luis
    1984   Mexico. In *Approaches to the Archaeological Heritage*, edited by Henry Cleere, pp. 89-100. Cambridge University Press, Massachusetts.

    1998   *La Arqueología y México.* Instituto Nacional de Antropología y Historia, México D.F.

Lorenzo, José Luis y Lorena Mirambell
    1983   *La Cerámica: un documento arqueológico.* Instituto Nacional de Antropología e Historia, Cuaderno de Trabajo No. 23, INAH, México, D.F.

Lynott, Mark J.
    1997   Ethical Principles and Archaeological Practice: Development of an Ethics Policy. *American Antiquity* 62(4):589-599.

Lyons, Patrick D.
    2003a   *Ancestral Hopi Migrations.* Anthropological Papers of the University of Arizona No. 68. University of Arizona Press, Tucson.

    2003b   Hopi Ethnoarchaeology in Relation to the Hohokam. In *Yep Hisat Hoopoq'yaqam Yeesiwa (Hopi Ancestors Were Once Here): Hopi-Hohokam Cultural Affiliation Study,* compiled by T. J. Ferguson, pp. 123-163. Hopi Cultural Preservation Office, The Hopi Tribe, Kykotsmovi, Arizona.

    2004a   José Solas Ruin. *Kiva* 70(2):143-181.

    2004b   Cliff Polychrome. *Kiva* 69(4):361-400.

    2013   "By their fruits ye shall know them" The Pottery of Kinishba Revisited. In *Kinishba Lost and Found: Mid-Century Excavations and Contemporary Perspectives,* edited by John R. Welch, pp. 145-208. Arizona State Museum Archaeological Series No. 206. Arizona State Museum, University of Arizona, Tucson.

Lyons, Patrick D. and Jeffery J. Clark
    2008   Interaction, Enculturation, Social Distance, and Ancient Ethnic Identities. In *Archaeology Without Borders: Contact, Commerce, and Change in the U.S. Southwest and Northwestern Mexico,* edited by Laurie D. Webster and Maxine McBrinn, pp. 185-207. University Press of Colorado, Boulder, and INAH, Chihuahua.

    2012   A Community of Practice in Diaspora: The Rise and Demise of Roosevelt Red Ware. In *Potters and Communities of Practice: Glaze Paint and Polychrome Pottery in the American Southwest A.D. 1250 – 1700,* edited by Linda S. Cordell and Judith Habicht-Mauche, pp. 19-33. Anthropological Papers of the University of Arizona No. 75. University of Arizona Press, Tucson.

Lyons, Patrick D., J. Brett Hill, and Jeffery J. Clark
    2008   Demography, Agricultural Potential, and Identity among Ancient Immigrants. In *The Social Construction of Communities: Agency, Structure, and Identity in the Prehispanic Southwest,* edited by Mark D. Varien and James Potter, pp. 191-213. AltaMira Press, Lanham, Maryland.

    2011   Irrigation Communities and Communities in Diaspora. In *Movement, Connectivity, and Landscape Change: The 20th Anniversary Southwest Symposium,* edited by Margaret C. Nelson and Colleen Strawhacker, pp. 375-401. University Press of Colorado, Boulder.

Lyons, Patrick D. and Alexander J. Lindsay, Jr.
    2006   Perforated Plates and the Salado Phenomenon. *Kiva* 72(1):5-54.

Lyons, Patrick D. and Anna A. Neuzil
2006   Research on the Mills Collection. *Archaeology Southwest* 20(2):17.

Macías Quintero, Juan Ignacio
2006   *Prospección arqueológica en la región sur occidente de Aguascalientes*. Tesis de Licenciatura. Unidad de Antropología, Universidad Autónoma de Zacatecas, Zacatecas, México.

2007   *Arqueología de Aguascalientes,* Primer Libro, ICA, México.

Manzo Oguín, Enriqueta
1983   *Ornamentos arqueológicos de concha del norte de Jalisco*. Tesis de Licenciatura en Arqueología. Escuela Nacional de Antropología e Historia, México.

Marcos, Jorge
1995   El Mullu y el Pututo. La articulación de la ideología y el tráfico a larga distancia en la formación del Estado Huancavilca. *Primer encuentro de Investigadores de la costa Ecuatoriana en Europa: Arqueología, Etnohistoria, Antropología Sociocultural.* Ediciones ABYA YALA, Quito.

Marcus, George E. and Myers, Fred R.
1995   *The Traffic in Culture: Refiguring Art and Anthropology.* University of California Press, Berkeley.

Markussen, Christine
2006   Applying recent advances in geophysics to the American Southwest. Report prepared by Statistical Research, Inc. for the City of Albuquerque. Copies available from City of Albuquerque.

Markussen, Christine, Matthew F. Schmader, Christopher D. Dore, Clay Mathers, and Jessica Ogden
2007   Probing the Past, Resisting Excavation: Results of Resistivity Surveys at Piedras Marcadas Pueblo, Albuquerque, New Mexico. Poster presented at the 72nd Annual Meeting of the Society for American Archaeology, Austin.

Marshall, Michael P.
1986   National Register of Historic Places nomination for LA 290 (Mann Site) for the Rio Medio project. Cibola Research Consultants, Corrales NM. Nomination prepared for and copies available from the New Mexico Historic Preservation Division, Santa Fe.

1987   An Archaeological Survey of the Mann-Zuris Pueblo Complex (LA 290), A Southern Tiwan Settlement of the Middle Rio Grande District. Cibola Research Consultants, Corrales NM. Report prepared for and copies available from City of Albuquerque.

1988   An Archaeological Survey of the Mann-Zuris Pueblo Complex, Phase II. Cibola Research Consultants, Corrales, NM. Report prepared for and copies available from City of Albuquerque.

Martin, Paul S. and John B. Rinaldo
1960   *Table Rock Pueblo, Arizona.* Fieldiana: Anthropology 51(2). Chicago Natural History Museum, Chicago.

Martin de Paalen, Isabel
1971   *Arte Popular Mexicano.* Banco Nacional de Comercio Exterior, México.

Martínez Muriel, Alejandro
2007   The State Control on Archaeology in Mexico. *The SAA Archaeological Record* 7(5):16-19.

Martínez Muriel, Alejandro and Cipactli Bader Rentería
   2004   Dos décadas de arqueología en México. *Mexican Studies/Estudios Mexicanos* 20(2):187-220.

Martinez-Peñaloza, Porfirio
   1988   *Arte Popular y Artesanías Artísticas en México.* SEP, México.

Masse, W. Bruce
   1981   A Reappraisal of the Protohistoric Sobaipuri Indians of Southeastern Arizona. In *The Protohistoric Period in the North American Southwest, AD 1450-1700,* edited by David R. Wilcox and W. Bruce Masse, pp. 28-56. Anthropological Research Papers No. 24, Arizona State University, Tempe.

Mathers, William
   2011   Tangled Threads, Loose Ends, and Knotty Problems: The Place of Moho in Tiguex Archaeology, Geography, and History. In *The Latest Word from 1540. People, Places, and Portrayals of the Coronado Expedition,* edited by Richard Flint and Shirley C. Flint, pp. 367-397. University of New Mexico Press, Albuquerque.

Mathers, William and Charles Haecker
   2011   Between Cibola and Tiguex: A Vázquez de Coronado Presence at El Moro National Monument, New Mexico. In *The Latest Word from 1540. People, Places, and Portrayals of the Coronado Expedition,* edited by Richard Flint and Shirley C. Flint, pp. 286-307. University of New Mexico Press, Albuquerque.

Mathien, Frances Joan
   1986   External Contacts and the Chaco Anasazi. In *Ripples in the Chichimec Sea: New Considerations of Southwestern – Mesoamerican Interactions,* edited by Frances Joan Mathien and Randall H. McGuire, pp. 220-242. Centre for Archaeological Investigations and Southern Illinois University Press, Carbondale and Edwardsville.

   1993   Social Stratification among the Chaco Anasazi. In *The American Southwest and Mesoamerica,* edited by Jonathon E. Ericson and Timothy G. Baugh, pp. 27-63. Plenum Press, New York.

Mathien, Frances Joan and Randall H. McGuire (editors)
   1986a *Ripples in the Chichimec Sea: New Considerations of Southwestern – Mesoamerican Interactions.* Southern Illinois University Press, Carbondale and Edwardsville.

Mathien, Frances Joan and Randall H. McGuire
   1986b Adrift in the Chichimec Sea. In *Ripples in the Chichimec Sea: New Considerations of Southwestern – Mesoamerican Interactions,* edited by Frances Joan Mathien and Randall H. McGuire, pp. 1-8. Southern Illinois University Press, Carbondale and Edwardsville.

Mathiowetz, Michael
   2008   *The Sun Youth of Mesoamerica and the Greater Southwest: Mesoamerican Religion and Cosmology at Paquimé, Chihuahua.* Paper presented at the 73rd Annual Meeting of the Society for American Archaeology, Vancouver, Canada.

Matos Moctezuma, Eduardo
   1983   *Manuel Gamio: La Arqueología Mexicana. Argumentos.* Ideas de Nuestro Tiempo. UNAM, Mexico

Meacham, J. Lloyd
   1926   The Second Spanish Expedition to New Mexico. *New Mexico Historical Review* 1:265-291.

Meighan, Clement
1972   *Archaeology of the Morett Site, Colima.* Publications in Anthropology, Vol. 7, University of California Press, Berkeley.

1976   *The Archaeology of Amapa Nayarit.* Monumenta Archaeologica 2, The Institute of Archaeology, University of California, Los Angeles.

Mera, Harry P.
1933   A Proposed Revision of the Rio Grande Glaze Paint Sequence. *Laboratory of Anthropology Technical Series, Bulletin No. 5,* Santa Fe, New Mexico.

1940   Population Changes in the Rio Grande Glaze-paint Area. *Laboratory of Anthropology Technical Series, Bulletin No. 9,* Santa Fe, New Mexico.

McCrossen, Alexis (editor)
2009   *Land of Necessity: Consumer Culture in the United States-Mexico Borderlands.* Duke University Press, Durham.

McKusick, Charmion R.
1982   Avifauna from Grasshopper Pueblo. In *Multidisciplinary Research at Grasshopper Pueblo, Arizona,* edited by William A. Longacre, Sally J. Holbrook, and Michael W. Graves, pp. 87-96. University of Arizona Press, Tucson.

McGee, W. J.
1895   The Beginning of Agriculture. *American Anthropologist* 8(4):350-375.

McGuire, Randall H.
1980   The Mesoamerican Connection in the Southwest. *Kiva* 46:3-38.

1982   A History of Archaeological Research. In *Hohokam and Patayan: Prehistory of Southwestern Arizona,* edited by Randall H. McGuire and Michael B. Schiffer, pp. 101-152. Academic Press, New York.

1986   Economies and Modes of Production in the Prehistoric Southwestern Periphery. In *Ripples in the Chichimec Sea: New Considerations of Southwestern – Mesoamerican Interactions,* edited by Frances Joan Mathian and Randall H. McGuire, pp. 243-269. Southern Illinois University Press, Carbondale.

1989   The Greater Southwest as Periphery of Mesoamerica. In *Centre and Periphery: Comparative Studies in Archaeology,* edited by Tim C. Champion, pp. 40-66. Unwin Hyman, London.

1991   On the Outside Looking In: The Concept of Periphery in Hohokam Archaeology. In *Exploring the Hohokam: Prehistoric Desert Peoples of the American Southwest,* edited by George J. Gumerman, pp. 347-382. Amerind Foundation New World Studies Series No. 1. Amerind Foundation, Dragoon, and University of New Mexico Press, Albuquerque.

1992   Archaeology and the First Americans. *American Anthropologist* 94(4):816-836.

1993a Charles C. Di Peso and the Mesoamerican Connection. In *Culture and Contact: Charles C. Di Peso's Gran Chichimeca,* edited by Anne I. Woosley and John C. Ravesloot, pp. 23-38. The Amerind Foundation, Inc., Dragoon, and The University of New Mexico Press, Albuquerque.

1993b The Structure and Organization of Hohokam Exchange. In *The American Southwest and Mesoamerica,* edited by Jonathon E. Ericson and Timothy G. Baugh, pp. 95-119. Plenum Press, New York.

McGuire, Randall H., cont'd
2008   *Archaeology as Political Action.* University of California Press, Berkeley, California.

McGuire, Randall H. and Elisa Villalpando C.
1993   *An Archaeological Survey of the Altar Valley, Sonora, Mexico.* Arizona State Museum Archaeological Series 184. Arizona State Museum, University of Arizona, Tucson.

2007   The Hohokam and Mesoamerica. In *The Hohokam Millennium,* edited by Suzanne K. Fish and Paul R. Fish, pp. 56-64, School for Advanced Research Press, Santa Fe, New Mexico.

Mendiola, Francisco
1994   *Petroglifos y Pinturas Rupestres en el Norte de Sinaloa.* Tesis de Licenciatura en Arqueología, Escuela Nacional de Antropología e Historia, México, D.F.

Miller, R. Wick
1983a   Uto-Aztecan Languages. In *Handbook of North American Indians,* Vol. 10, edited by Alfonso Ortiz, pp. 113-124. Smithsonian Institution, Washington, D. C.

1983b   A Note on Extinct Languages of Northwest Mexico of Supposed Uto-Aztecan Affiliation. *International Journal of American Linguistics* 49(3):328-334.

Mills, Barbara J.
1995   The Organization of Protohistoric Zuni Ceramic Production. In *Ceramic Production in the American Southwest,* edited by Barbara J. Mills and Patricia L. Crown, pp. 200-230. University of Arizona Press, Tucson.

2007   A Regional Perspective on Ceramics and Zuni Identity, A.D. 200-1630. In *Zuni Origins: Toward a New Synthesis of Southwestern Archaeology,* edited by David A. Gregory and David R. Wilcox, pp. 210-238. University of Arizona Press, Tucson.

2008   How the Pueblos Became Global: Colonial Appropriations, Resistance, and Diversity in the North American Southwest. *Archaeologies: Journal of the World Archaeological Congress* 4(2):218-232.

Mills, Barbara J., Jeffery J. Clark, Matthew A. Peeples, W. R. Haas, Jr., John M. Roberts, Jr., J. Brett Hill, Deborah L. Huntley, Lewis Borck, Ronald L. Breiger, Aaron Clauset, and M. Steven Shackley
2013   Transformation of Social Networks in the Late Pre-Hispanic US Southwest. *Proceedings of the National Academy of Sciences of the United States of America* 110(15):5785-5790.

Mills, Barbara J. and T. J. Ferguson
2008   Animate Objects: Shell Trumpets and Ritual Networks in the Greater Southwest. *Journal of Archaeological Method and Theory* 15(4):338-361.

Mills, Jack P. and Vera M. Mills
1969a   *The Kuykendall Site: A Prehistoric Salado Village in Southeastern Arizona.* Special Report No. 6. El Paso Archaeological Society, El Paso.

1969b   Burned House: An Additional Excavation at the Kuykendall Site. *The Artifact* 7(3):21-32.

1971   The Slaughter Ranch Site: A Prehistoric Village near the Mexican Border in Southeastern Arizona. *The Artifact* 9(3):23-52.

1978   *The Curtis Site: A Pre-Historic Village in the Safford Valley.* Privately Published by Jack P. Mills and Vera M. Mills, Elfrida, Arizona.

Minar, C. Jill and Patricia L. Crown
  2001   Learning and Craft Production: An Introduction. *Journal of Anthropological Research* 57(4): 369–380.

Minnis, Paul
  1989   The Casas Grandes Polity in the International Four Corners. In *The Sociopolitical Structure of Prehistoric Southwestern Societies,* edited by Steadman Upham, Kent G. Lightfoot, and Roberta A. Jewitt, pp. 269-305. Westview Press, Boulder, Colorado.

Minnis, Paul E. and Michael Whalen
  1992   El Sistema Regional de Casas Grandes, Chihuahua. Informe al Consejo de Arqueología. Archivo Técnico del Consejo de Arqueología INAH, México.

  1993   Casas Grandes: Archaeology in Northern Mexico. *Expedition* 35 (I):34-43.

  2010   The First Prehispanic Chile (Capsicum) from the U.S. Southwest/Northwest Mexico and Its Changing Use. *American Antiquity* 75(2):245-257.

Minturn, Penny Dufoe
  2006   *The Biogeography of Tonto Basin in Central Arizona.* Ph.D. dissertation, Arizona State University, Tempe.

Mitchell, Douglas R. and Judy L. Brunson-Hadley
  2001   An Evaluation of Classic Period Hohokam Burials and Society: Chiefs, Priests, or Acephalous Complexity? In *Ancient Burial Practices in the American Southwest,* edited by Douglas R. Mitchell and Judy L. Brunson-Hadley. University of New Mexico Press, Albuquerque.

Montané, Julio César
  1996(1985)   "Desde los orígenes hasta 3000 años antes del presente". En *Historia General de Sonora, Tomo I: Periodo Prehistórico y Prehispánico,* (segunda edición), pp. 151-195. Gobierno del Estado de Sonora, Hermosillo.

Moore, John H.
  1994   Putting Anthropology Back Together Again: The Ethnogenetic Critique of Cladistic Theory. *American Anthropologist* 96(4):925-948.

  2001   Ethnogenetic Patterns in Native North America. In *Archaeology, Language, and History: Essays in Culture and Ethnicity,* edited by John E. Terrell, pp. 31-56. Bergin and Garvey, Westport, Connecticut.

Mountjoy, Joseph
  1990   El desarrollo de la cultura Aztatlán visto de su frontera suroeste. En *Mesomérica y el Norte de México: Siglo IX-XI,* editado por Sodi Miranda, pp. 541-564. INAH, México.

  2000   Prehispanic Cultural Development Along Southern Coast of West Mexico. *Greater Mesoamerica: The Archaeology of West and Northwest Mexico,* edited by Michael S. Foster and Shirley Gorenstein, pp. 81-106 University of Utah Press, Salt Lake City.

Nakayama, Antonio
  1974   *Relación de Antonio Ruiz (La Conquista en el Noroeste).* Colección Científica 18, INAH, México, D.F.

Nelson, Ben A.
  1994   Outpost of Mesoamerican Empire and Architectural Patterning at La Quemada, Zacatecas. In *Culture and Contact: Charles C. Di Peso's Gran Chichimeca,* edited by Anne I. Woosley and John C. Ravesloot, pp. 173-179. Amerind Fundation New World Studies Series: No. 2, University of New Mexico Press, Albuquerque.

Nelson, Ben A., cont'd
  1995   Complexity, Hierarchy, and Scale: A Controlled Comparison between Chaco Canyon, New Mexico, and La Quemada, Zacatecas. *American Antiquity* 60:597-618.

  2000   Aggregation, Warfare, and the Spread of the Mesoamerican Tradition. In *Archaeology of Regional Interaction,* edited by Michelle Hegmon, pp. 317-338. University Press of Colorado, Boulder.

  2006   Mesoamerican Objects and Symbols in Chaco Canyon Contexts. In *The Archaeology of Chaco Canyon: An Eleventh-Century Pueblo Regional Center,* edited by Stephen H. Lekson, pp. 339-371. School of American Research Press, Santa Fe, New Mexico.

Nelson, Ben A., J. Andrew Darling, and David A Kice
  1992   Mortuary Practice and Social Order at La Quemada, Zacatecas, Mexico. *Latin America Antiquity* 3(4):298-315.

Nelson, Richard I.
  1986   Pochteca and Prestige: Mesoamerican Artifacts in Hohokam Sites. In *Ripples in the Chichimec Sea: New Considerations of Mesoamerican-Southwestern Relationships,* edited by Frances J. Mathien and Randall H. McGuire, pp. 154-182. Southern Illinois University Press, Carbondale.

Neuzil, Anna A.
  2008   *In the Aftermath of Migration: Renegotiating Ancient Identity in Southeastern Arizona.* Anthropological Papers of the University of Arizona No. 73. University of Arizona Press, Tucson.

Neuzil, Anna A. and Patrick D. Lyons
  2006   *An Analysis of Whole Vessels from the Mills Collection Curated at Eastern Arizona College, Thatcher, Arizona.* Technical Report No. 2005-001. Center for Desert Archaeology, Tucson, Arizona.

Newell, Gillian
  1999   American and Mexican Archaeology: Differences in Meaning and Teaching. *The SAA Bulletin* 17(5).

Noyola, Andrés
  1994   Análisis preliminar de la cerámica del fraccionamiento San Juan Atoyac, Jalisco. En *Contribuciones a la arqueología y etnohistoria del Occidente de México,* editado por Eduardo Williams, pp. 55-92. El Colegio de Michoacán, Zamora.

de Obregón, Baltasar
  1988   *Historia de los Descubrimientos Antiguos y Modernos de la Nueva España Escrita por el Conquistador en el Año de 1584.* Editorial Porrúa, S.A., México.

Olivé, Julio César
  1980   Reseña Histórica del Pensamiento Legal Sobre Arqueología. En *Arqueología y Derecho en México,* editado por Jaime Litvak King, Luis González R. y María del Refugio González, pp. 19-46. Antropológia 25. UNAM-IIA-IIJ, México.

  2003 [1988]   El Instituto Nacional de Antropología e Historia. En *INAH: Una Historia. Volumen I. Antecedentes, Organización, Funcionamiento y Servicios,* editado por Julio César Olivé Negrete y Bolfy Cottom, vol. 1, pp. 33-108. 3 vols. INAH, México.

Ortman, Scott G.
  2009   *Genes, Language, and Culture in Tewa Ethnogenesis, A.D. 1150-1400.* Ph.D. dissertation, Arizona State University, Tempe.

2012   *Winds from the North: Tewa Origins and Historical Anthropology.* University of Utah Press, Salt Lake City.

Pailes, Richard A.
1972   *Archaeological Reconnaissance of Southern Sonora and Reconsideration of the Rio Sonora Culture.* Ph.D. dissertation, Department of Anthropology, Southern Illinois University, Carbondale.

1976a Recientes investigaciones arqueológicas en el sur de Sonora. In *Sonora: Antropología del Desierto, Colección Científica Diversa* No. 27, INAH-SEP, pp. 137-155. México.

1976b Relaciones Culturales Prehistóricas en el Noroeste de Sonora. In *Sonora: Antropología del Desierto. Colección Científica Diversa* No. 27, INAH-SEP, pp. 213-228. México.

Pailes, Richard A. and Joseph W. Whitecotton
1979   The Greater Southwest and the Mesoamerican "World" System: An Explanatory Model of Frontier Relationships. In *The Frontier: Comparative Studies.* Vol. 2, edited by William W. Savage, Jr. and Stephen I. Thompson, pp. 105-121. University of Oklahoma Press, Norman.

1995   The Frontiers of Mesoamerica: Northern and Southern. In *The Gran Chichimeca: Essays on the Archaeology and Ethnohistory of Northern Mesoamerica,* edited by Jonathan E. Reyman, pp. 13-45. Avebury Press, Aldershot, United Kingdom.

Palacios Díaz, Mario
2010   *Aguascalientes Prehispánico. Las pinturas rupestres del Ocote.* Licenciatura en Historia, Centro de Ciencias Sociales y Humanidades, Departamento de Historia, Universidad Autónoma de Aguascalientes.

Patterson, Thomas
1999   The Political Economy of the Archaeology in the United States. *Annual Review of Anthropology* 28:155-174.

Paulsen, Allison C.
1977   Patterns of Maritime Trade between South Coastal Ecuador and Western Mesoamerica 1500 B.C.-A.D 600. In *The Sea in the Pre-Columbian World,* edited by Elizabeth P. Benson, pp. 141-160. Dumbarton Oaks, Washington.

Pendergast, David M.
1962   Metal Artifacts in Prehispanic Mesoamerica. *American Antiquity* 27:520-545.

Pennington, Campbell W.
1963   *The Tarahumar of Mexico: Their Environment and Material Culture.* University of Utah Press, Salt Lake City.

Peregrine, Peter and Gary Feinman
1996   *Pre-Columbian World Systems.* Monographs in World Archaeology 26, Prehistory Press, Madison, Wisconsin.

Pérez Bedolla, Raúl Gerardo
1985   Geografía de Sonora. En *Historia General de Sonora, Vol I: Periodo Prehistórico y Prehispánico,* pp. 111-172. Gobierno del Estado de Sonora, Hermosillo, México.

Pérez de Ribas, Andrés
1944   *Historia de los Triunfos de Nuestra Santa Fe entre Gentes las Más Bárbaras y Fieras del Nuevo Orbe* (1645). Tres volúmenes. Editorial Layac, México.

Phillips, David A., Jr.
   1992   *Archaeological Monitoring and Data Recovery at the Paloparado Site, Santa Cruz County, Arizona.* SWCA Archaeological Report No. 92-46. SWCA, Inc. Environmental Consultants, Tucson, Arizona.

Phillips, Ruth B. and Christopher B. Steiner
   1999   *Unpacking Culture: Art and Commodity in Colonial and Postcolonial Worlds.* University of California Press, Berkeley.

Piñeira, David
   1994   La Historia de la Frontera México-Estados Unidos en el Contexto de las Fronteras de Iberoamérica. *Frontera Norte* 6(11):123-133.

Plog, Stephen
   1983   Political and Economic Alliances on the Colorado Plateaus AD 400 to 1450. *Advances in World Archaeology* 2:289-330.

Plog, Stephen, Steadman Upham, and Philip C. Weigand
   1982   A perspective on Mogollon-Mesoamerican Interaction. In *Mogollon Archaeology: Preceedings of the 1980 Mogollon Conferences,* edited by Patrick Beckett, pp. 227-238. Acoma Books, Ramona, California.

Pretes, Michael
   2003   Tourism and Nationalism. *Annals of Tourism Research* 30(1):125-142.

Pohl, John M. D.
   2001   Chichimecatlalli: Strategies for Cultural and Commercial Exchange between Mexico and the American Southwest, 1100-1521. In *The Road to Aztlan: Art from a Mythic Homeland,* edited by Virginia M. Fields and Victor Zamudio-Taylor, pp. 86-101. Los Angeles County Museum of Art, California.

Rakita, Gordon F. M.
   2006   Hemenway, Hrdlička, and Hawikku: A Historical Perspective on Bioarchaeology Research in the American Southwest. In *Bioarchaeology: The Contextual Analysis of Human Remains,* edited by Jane E. Buikstra and Lane A. Beck, pp. 95-111. Academic Press, New York.

Ramírez Urrea, Susana
   1997   El papel interregional de la cuenca de Sayula, Jalisco, en el Epiclásico y Postclásico temprano: Observaciones preliminares. Conferencia IV Coloquio Bosch-Gimpera, Guadalajara, Jalisco.

Ravesloot, John C. and Stephanie M. Whittlesey
   1987   Inferring the Protohistoric Period in Southern Arizona. In *The Archaeology of the San Xavier Bridge Site (AZ BB:13:14), Tucson Basin, Southern Arizona,* edited by John C. Ravesloot, pp. 8-98. Arizona State Museum Archaeological Series No. 171 (parts 1 and 2). Arizona State Museum, University of Arizona, Tucson.

Razo Zaragoza, José Luis
   1963   *Crónicas de la Conquista del Nuevo Reyno de Galicia.* México: IJAH, INAH, Universidad de Guadalajara, Gobierno del Estado de Jalisco.

Rea, Amadeo M.
   1997   *At the Desert's Green Edge: An Ethnobotany of the Gila River Pima.* University of Arizona Press, Tucson.

Reed, Erik K.
   1955   Painted Pottery and Zuni History. *Southwestern Journal of Anthropology* 11(2):178-193.

Reff, Daniel T.
1987 The Introduction of Smallpox in the Greater Southwest. *American Anthropologist* 89(3):704-708.

1989 Disease Episodes and the Historical Record: A Reply to Dobyns. *American Anthropologist* 91(1):174-175.

1991 *Disease, Depopulation and Culture Change in Northwestern New Spain, 1518-1764.* University of Utah Press, Salt Lake City.

1997 The Relevance of Ethnology to the Routing of the Coronado Expedition in Sonora. In *The Coronado Expedition to Tierra Nueva: The 1540-1542 Route Across the Southwest,* edited by Richard Flint and Shirley C. Flint, pp. 137-146. University Press of Colorado, Boulder.

Reid, J. Jefferson
2008 History of the Papaguería Project, 1938-1942. In *Fragile Patterns: The Archaeology of the Western Papaguería,* edited by Jeffery H. Altschul and Adrianne G. Rankin, pp. 105-120. SRI Press, Tucson, Arizona.

Relethford, John H.
2002 Apportionment of Global Human Genetic Diversity Based on Craniometrics and Skin Color. *American Journal of Physical Anthropology* 118:393-398.

2004 Boas and Beyond: Migration and Craniometric Variation. *American Journal of Human Biology* 16:379-386.

Relethford, John H. and John Blangero
1990 Detection of Differential Gene Flow from Patterns of Quantitative Variation. *Human Biology* 62(1):5-25.

Relethford, John H., Michael H. Crawford, and John Blangero
1997 Genetic Drift and Gene Flow in Post-Famine Ireland. *Human Biology* 69(4):443-465.

Relethford, John H. and Francis C. Lees
1982 The Use of Quantitative Traits in the Study of Human Population Structure. *Yearbook of Physical Anthropology* 25:113-132.

Reyman, Jonathan E.
1978 Pochteca Burials at Anasazi Sites? In *Across the Chichimec Sea. Papers in Honor of J. Charles Kelley,* edited by Carroll L. Riley and Basil C. Hedrick. pp. 242-259. Southern University Press, Carbondale.

Reyman, Jonathan E. (editor)
1995 *The Gran Chichimeca: Essays on the Archaeology and Ethnohistory of Northern Mesoamerica.* Avebury Press, Aldershot, United Kingdom.

Rice, Anna
2010 The Potential for Tlaloc Images on Prehistoric Pottery and Rock Art in the Mimbres Region of the North American Southwest. Unpublished Honor's Thesis, Department of Anthropology, University of Oklahoma, Norman.

Rice, Glen E.
1998 Migration, Emulation, and Tradition in Tonto Basin Prehistory. In *A Synthesis of Tonto Basin Prehistory: The Roosevelt Archaeology Studies, 1989-1998,* Roosevelt Monograph Series 12, Anthropological Field Studies 41, edited by Glen E. Rice, pp. 231-242. Office of Cultural Resource Management, Arizona State University, Tempe.

Rice, Glen E., cont'd

2000 Hohokam and Salado Segmentary Organization: The Evidence from the Roosevelt Platform Mound Study. In *Salado*, edited by Jeffrey S. Dean, pp. 143-166. University of New Mexico Press, Albuquerque.

Riley, Carroll L.

1976 *Sixteenth Century Trade in the Greater Southwest.* Mesoamerican Studies No. 10. Southern Illinois University Museum, Carbondale.

1985 The Location of Chichilticale. In *Southwestern Culture History: Collected Papers in Honor of Albert H. Schroeder,* edited by Charles H. Lange, pp. 153-162. Papers of the Archaeological Society of New Mexico No. 10. Archaeological Society of New Mexico, Albuquerque.

1986 An Overview of the Greater Southwest in the Protohistoric Period. In *Ripples in the Chichimec Sea: New Considerations of Southwestern-Mesoamerican Interactions,* edited by Frances J. Mathien and Randall H. McGuire, pp. 45-54. Center for Archaeological Investigations and Southern Illinois University Press, Carbondale.

1987 *The Frontier People: The Greater Southwest in the Protohistoric Period.* University of New Mexico Press, Albuquerque.

2005 *Becoming Aztlán: Mesoamerican Influence in the Greater Southwest, AD 1200-1500.* The University of Utah Press, Salt Lake City.

Riley, Carroll L. and Basil C. Hedricks (editors)

1978 *Across the Chichimec Sea: Papers in Honor of J. Charles Kelley,* Southern Illinois University Press, Carbondale and Edwardsville.

Rinaldo, John B.

1959 *Foote Canyon Pueblo, Eastern Arizona.* Fieldiana: Anthropology 49(2). Field Museum of Natural History, Chicago, Illinois.

1964 Notes on the Origins of Historic Zuni Culture. *Kiva* 29(4):86-98.

Robb, John E.

1998 The Archaeology of Symbols. *Annual Review of Anthropology* 27:329-346.

Robinson, William J.

1958 A New Type of Ceremonial Pottery Killing at Point of Pines. *Kiva* 23(3):12-14.

Robinson, William J. and Roderick Sprague

1965 Disposal of the Dead at Point of Pines, Arizona. *American Antiquity* 30(4):442-453.

Robles García, Nelly M.

2007 The Practice of Archaeology in Mexico: Institutional Obligations and Scientific Results. *The SAA Archaeological Record* 7(5):9-10.

2007 Management and Conservation of Archaeological Sites. *The SAA Archaeological Record* 7(5):29-31.

Robles Ortíz, Manuel

1974 Distribución de artefactos Clovis en Sonora. *Boletín* 2:25-32, Instituto Nacional de Antropología e Historia, México.

Rhodes, Diane
  1997   Coronado Fought Here: Crossbow Boltheads as Possible Indicators of the 1540-1542 Expedition. In *The Coronado Expedition to Tierra Nueva,* edited by Richard Flint and Shirley C. Flint, pp. 37-46. University Press of Colorado, Boulder.

Rodríguez, Ignacio
  2000   Mesoamérica, ese oscuro Objeto del Deseo. *Dimensión Antropológica* 19:http://www.dimensionantropologica.inah.gob.mx/?cat=76.

Rodríguez-Loubet, Francois, Michel Antochiw, and Elizabeth Araux
  1993   *Quitovac 1: Ethnoarchéologie du Désert de Sonora, Mexique.* Centro de Estudios Mexicanos y Centroamericanos, Editions Recherches sur les Civilisations, Paris, France.

Roseman, Charles C. and Timothy D. Weaver
  2004   Multivariate Apportionment of Global Human Craniometric Diversity. *American Journal of Physical Anthropology* 125:257-263.

Rowan, Yorke M. and Uzi Baram (editors)
  2004   *Marketing Heritage. Archaeology and the Consumption of the Past.* Altamira Press, California.

Russell, Frank
  1908   The Pima Indians. In *Twenty-Sixth Annual Report of the Bureau of American Ethnology for the Years 1904-1905,* pp. 3-389. Government Printing Office, Washington, D.C.

Rutsch, Mechthild
  2001   Ramón Mena y Manuel Gamio. Una mirada oblicua sobre la antropología mexicana en los años veinte del siglo pasado. *Relaciones* 88(XXII):81-118.

Rzedowski, Jerzy
  1981   *Vegetación de México.* Editorial Limusa, México, D.F.

Sánchez, Guadalupe
  2001   A Synopsis of Paleo-Indian Archaeology in Mexico. *Kiva* 67(2):120-136.

  2010   Los Primeros Mexicanos: Late Pleistocene/Early Holocene Archaeology of Sonora, Mexico. Unpublished Ph.D. dissertation, School of Anthropology, University of Arizona, Tucson.

Sánchez, Joseph P.
  1988   *The Rio Abajo Frontier, 1540-1692: A History of Early Colonial New Mexico.* History Monograph Series, Albuquerque Museum, Albuquerque.

  1997   A Historiography of the Route of the Expedition of Francisco Vázquez de Coronado: Compostela to Cíbola. In *The Coronado Expedition to Tierra Nueva: The 1540-1542 Route Across the Southwest,* edited by Richard Flint and Shirley C. Flint, pp. 115-123. University Press of Colorado, Boulder.

Santoscoy, Alberto
  1903   *Historia de Nuestra Señora de San Juan de los Lagos.* Mexico: Tip. de la Compañía Editorial Catolica.

Sauer, Carl
  1932   *The Road to Cibola.* Ibero-Americana:3, University of California Press, Berkeley.

  1935   *Aboriginal Population of Northwestern Mexico.* Ibero-Americana:10, University of California Press, Berkeley.

Sauer, Carl and Donald Brand
  1932   *Aztatlán, Prehistoric Mexican Frontier on the Pacific Coast.* Ibero-Americana:1, University of California Press, Berkeley.

Saxton, Dean, Lucille Saxton, and Susie Enos
  1983   *Tohono O'odham/Pima to English, English to Tohono O'odham/Pima Dictionary,* 2nd edition. University of Arizona Press, Tucson.

Sayles, Edith Booth
  1936   *An Archaeological Survey of Chihuahua Mexico,* Medallion Papers XXII. Gila Pueblo, Globe, Arizona.

Scarborough, Vernon L., and David R. Wilcox (editors)
  1991   *The Mesoamerican Ballgame.* University of Arizona Press, Tucson.

Schaafsma, Curtis F. and Carroll L. Riley
  1999   The Casas Grandes World: Analysis and Conclusion. In *The Casas Grandes World,* edited by Curtis F. Schaafsma and Carroll L. Riley, pp. 237-249. The University of Utah Press, Salt Lake City.

Schaafsma, Curtis F. and Carroll L. Riley (editors)
  1999   *The Casas Grandes World.* The University of Utah Press, Salt Lake City.

Schaafsma, Polly
  1994   The Prehistoric Kachina Cult and Its Origins as Suggested by Southwestern Rock Art. In *Kachinas in the Pueblo World,* edited by Polly Schaafsma, pp. 63-79. University of New Mexico Press, Albuquerque.

  1998   The Paquimé Rock Art Style, Chihuahua, Mexico. *Rock Art of the Chihuahuan Desert Borderlands,* edited by Sheron Smith-Savage and Robert J. Mallouf, pp. 33-44. Center for Big Bend Studies, Sul Ross State University, Alpine, and the Texas Parks and Wildlife Department.

  1999   Tlalocs, Kachinas, Sacred Bundles, and Related Symbolism in the Southwest and Mesoamerica. In *The Casas Grandes World,* edited by Curtis F. Schaafsma and Carroll L. Riley, pp. 164-192. The University of Utah Press, Salt Lake City.

  2001   Quetzalcoatl and the Horned and Feathered Serpent of the Southwest. In *The Road to Aztlan: Art from a Mythic Homeland,* edited by Virginia M. Fields and Victor Zamudio-Taylor, pp. 138-149. Los Angeles County Museum of Art, California.

Schachner, Gregson
  2006   The Decline of Zuni Glaze Ware Production in the Tumultuous Fifteenth Century. In *The Social Life of Pots: Glaze Wares and Cultural Dynamics in the Southwest, A.D. 1250-1680,* edited by Judith A. Habicht-Mauche, Suzanne A. Eckert and Deborah L. Huntley, pp. 124-141. University of Arizona Press, Tucson.

Schávelzon, Daniel
  1999   The Origins of Stratigraphy in Latin America: The Same Question, Again and Again. *Bulletin of the History of Archaeology* 9(2):1-10 (http://www.danielschavelzon.com.ar/estratigraf.pdf).

Schillaci, Michael A.
  2003   The Development of Population Diversity at Chaco Canyon. *Kiva* 68(3):221-245.

Schillaci, Michael A., Joel D. Irish, and Carolan C.E. Wood
  2009   Further Analysis of the Population History of Ancient Egyptians. *American Journal of Physical Anthropology* 139:235-243.

Schillaci, Michael A., Erik G. Ozolins, and Thomas C. Windes
    2001   Multivariate Assessment of Biological Relationships Among Prehistoric Southwest Amerindian Populations. In *Following Through, Papers in Honor of Phyllis S. Davis,* edited by Regge N. Wiseman, Thomas C. O'Laughlin and Cordelia T. Snow. Papers of the Archaeological Society of New Mexico No. 27. Archaeological Society of New Mexico, Albuquerque.

Schillaci, Michael A. and Christopher M. Stojanowski
    2002   A Reassessment of Matrilocality in Chacoan Culture. *American Antiquity* 67(2):343-356.

    2003   Postmarital Residence and Biological Variation at Pueblo Bonito. *American Journal of Physical Anthropology* 120:1-15.

    2005   Craniometric Variation and Population History of the Prehistoric Tewa. *American Journal of Physical Anthropology* 126:404-412.

Schmader, Matthew F.
    1986   Archaeological Resources of the Piedras Marcadas Arroyo Area. Rio Grande Consultants, Albuquerque. Report prepared for and copies available from City of Albuquerque.

    2008a Nailing Down Coronado: Assemblage and Tactics of a sixteenth Century Spanish Entrada in the Tiguex Province of Nuevo Mexico. Paper presented at the 73rd Annual Meeting of the for American Archaeology, Vancouver.

    2008b Summary of Research Activities at Piedras Marcadas Pueblo (LA 290). Open Space Division, City of Albuquerque. Report prepared for Historic Preservation Division, Santa Fe. Copies available from the City of Albuquerque.

    2009   Summary of Research Activities at Piedras Marcadas Pueblo (LA 290)—Second Annual Report. Open Space Division, City of Albuquerque. Report prepared for Historic Preservation Division, Santa Fe. Copies available from the City of Albuquerque.

    2011   Thundersticks and Coats of Iron: Recent Discoveries at Piedras Marcadas Pueblo, NM. In *The Latest Word from 1540. People, Places, and Portrayals of the Coronado Expedition,* edited by Richard Flint and Shirley C. Flint, pp. 308-347. University of New Mexico Press, Albuquerque.

    2012a "The Peace that was Granted had not been Kept": Coronado in the Tiguex Province, 1540-1542. Paper presented at the 77th Annual Meeting of the Society for American Archaeology, Memphis.

    2012b Summary of Research Activities at Piedras Marcadas Pueblo (LA 290)—Third Annual Report. Open Space Division, City of Albuquerque. Report prepared for Historic Preservation Division, Santa Fe. Copies available from the City of Albuquerque.

Schmader, Matthew F. and Joseph P. Sánchez
    2009   Spanish Exploration of la Nueva Mexico: Comparing Sixteenth Century Expeditions of the American Southwest and Continental Interior. Paper presented at the 74th Annual Meeting of the Society for American Archaeology, Atlanta.

Schmidt, Robert H.
    1976   A Geographical Survey of Sinaloa. *Southwestern Studies, Monograph* No. 50. Texas Western Press, University of Texas, El Paso.

Schmidt, Robert H., cont'd
   1978   The Climate of Sinaloa. *Climatological Publications, Mexican Climatology Series No. 2.* Office of the State Climatologist, Laboratory of Climatology, Arizona State University, Tempe.

Scholnick, Jonathan
   2003   Ceramics and Zuni Chronology. Paper presented at the Amerind Foundation Advanced Seminar: Colonialism and Culture Change at Zuni A.D. 1300-1900, Manuscript on file at Zuni Heritage and Historic Preservation Office.

Schöndube, Otto
   1980   Época prehispánica. En *Historia de Jalisco: Vol. 1, Desde los tiempos prehistóricos hasta fines del siglo XVII,* editado por José M. Muría, pp. 113-257. Unidad Editorial del Gobierno de Jalisco, Guadalajara.

   1982   El Occidente de México hasta la época tolteca. En *Los orígenes de México,* pp. 271-298. Ediciones Salvat Mexicana, México.

   1983   Hallazgos en el Hospital de Belén. *PANTOC* 5: 51-68. Universidad Autónoma de Guadalajara, Jalisco.

Schöndube, Otto y Javier Galván V.
   1978   Salvage Archaeology at El Grillo-Tabachines, Zapopán, Jalisco, México. In *Across the Chichimec Sea: Papers in Honor of J. Charles Kelley,* edited by Carroll L. Riley and Basil C. Hedrick, pp. 144-164. Southern Illinois University Press, Carbondale.

Schroeder, Albert H.
   1955   Fray Marcos de Niza, Coronado, and the Yavapai. *New Mexico Historical Review* 30(4):265-296.

Scott, Stuart
   1974   Archaeology and the Estuary: Researching Prehistory and Paleoecology in the Marismas Nacionales, Sinaloa and Nayarit, Mexico. En *The Archaeology of West Mexico,* editado por Betty Bell, pp. 51-56. Sociedad de Estudios Avanzados del Occidente de México, Ajijic, Jalisco.

Searcy, Michael T.
   2010   *Symbols and Sociopolitical Organization: Mesoamerican Iconography in the U.S. Southwest/Northwest Mexico.* Ph.D. dissertation, Department of Anthropology, University of Oklahoma, Norman.

Sebastian, Lynn
   2007   Good Colleagues, Good Neighbors. *The SAA Archaeological Record* 7(5):11-13.

Segunda Relación Anónima
   1955   Segunda Relación Anónima de la Jornada que hizo Nuño de Guzmán á la Nueva Galicia. In *Memoria de los servicios que había hecho Nuño de Guzmán desde que fue nombrado gobernador de Pánuco en 1525,* anotado por Manuel Carrera Stampa, pp. 165-176. José Porrua e Hijos, México, D.F.

Sellars, Richard W.
   2007   A Very Large Array: Early Federal Historic Preservation-The Antiquities Act, Mesa Verde, and the National Park Service Act. *Natural Resources Journal* 47:267-328.

Seltzer, Carl C.
   1944   *Racial Prehistory in the Southwest and the Hawikuh Zunis.* Papers of the Peabody Museum of Archaeology and Ethnology 23. Harvard University, Cambridge, Massachusetts.

Seymour, Deni J.

1989   The Dynamics of Sobaipuri Settlement in the Eastern Pimería Alta. *Journal of the Southwest* 31(2):205-222.

1993a *Piman Settlement Survey in the Middle Santa Cruz River Valley, Santa Cruz County, Arizona.* Report submitted to State Historic Preservation Office, Arizona State Parks, Phoenix. Mariah Associates, Inc., Albuquerque.

1993b In Search of the Sobaipuri Pima: Archaeology of the Plain and Subtle. *Archaeology in Tucson* 7(1):1-4.

1997   Finding History in the Archaeological Record: The Upper Piman Settlement of Guevavi. *Kiva* 62(3):245-260.

2002   *Conquest and Concealment: After the El Paso Phase on Fort Bliss.* Lone Mountain Report 525/528. Lone Mountain Archaeological Services, Inc., El Paso, Texas.

2003   Sobaipuri-Pima Occupation in the Upper San Pedro Valley: San Pablo de Quiburi. *New Mexico Historical Review* 78(2):147-166.

2004   A Ranchería in the Gran Apachería: Evidence of Intercultural Interaction at the Cerro Rojo Site. *Plains Anthropologist* 49(190):153-192.

2007a A Syndetic Approach to Identification of the Historic Mission Site of San Cayetano del Tumacácori. *International Journal of Historical Archaeology* 11(3):269-296

2007b Delicate Diplomacy on a Restless Frontier: Seventeenth-Century Sobaípuri-O'odham Social and Economic Relations in Northwestern New Spain, Part 1. *New Mexico Historical Review* 82(4):469-499.

2007c An Archaeological Perspective on the Hohokam-Pima Continuum. *Old Pueblo Archaeology* 51:1-7.

2008   Delicate Diplomacy on a Restless Frontier: Seventeenth-Century Sobaípuri-O'odham Social and Economic Relations in Northwestern New Spain, Part 2. *New Mexico Historical Review* 83(2):171-199.

2009a Evaluating Eyewitness Accounts of Native Peoples along the Coronado Trail from the International Border to Cíbola. *New Mexico Historical Review* 84(3):399-435.

2009b The Canutillo Complex: Evidence of Protohistoric Mobile Occupants in the Southern Southwest. *Kiva* 74(4):421-446.

2009c Distinctive Places, Suitable Spaces: Conceptualizing Mobile Group Occupation Duration and Landscape Use. *International Journal of Historical Archaeology* 13(3):255-281.

2010a Beyond Married, Buried, and Baptized: Exposing Historical Discontinuities in Engendered O'odham Households. In *Engendering Households in the Prehistoric Southwest,* edited by Barbara J. Roth, pp. 229-259. University of Arizona Press, Tucson.

2010b Contextual Incongruities, Statistical Outliers, and Anomalies: Targeting Inconspicuous Occupational Events. *American Antiquity* 75(1):158-176.

2011a *Where the Earth and Sky are Sewn Together: Sobaipuri-O'odham Contexts of Contact and Colonialism.* University of Utah Press, Salt Lake City.

2011b Mats, Multiple Stories, and Terraces: Earliest Documentary Accounts of Indigenous Sonorans. In *The Latest Word from 1540: People, Places, and Portrayals of the Coronado Expedition,* edited by Richard Flint and Shirley C. Flint, pp. 154-193. University of New Mexico Press, Albuquerque.

Shaul, David Leedom and Jane H. Hill
   1998   Tepimans, Yumans, and Other Hohokam. *American Antiquity* 63(3):375-396.

Shennan, Stephen
   2000   Population, Culture History, and the Dynamics of Culture Change. *Current Anthropology* 41(5):811-835.

Shreve, Forrest
   1937   The Vegetation of Sinaloa. *Bulletin of the Torrey Botanical Club* 64:605-613.

Silverman, Helaine
   2002   Touring Ancient Times: The Present and Presented Past in Contemporary Peru. *American Anthropologist* 104(3):881-902.

   2005   Embodied Heritage, Identity Politics, and Tourism. *Anthropology and Humanism* 30(2):141-155.

Simon, Arleyn and David Jacobs
   2000   Salado Social Dynamics Networks and Alliances. In *Salado*, edited by Jeffrey Dean, pp. 193-218. Amerind Foundation, Dragoon, Arizona.

Simpson, James H.
   1871   Coronado's March in Search of the "Seven Cities Of Cibola" and Discussion of their Probable Location. In *Annual Report of the Board of Regents of the Smithsonian Institution Showing the Operations, Expenditures and Condition of the Institution for the Year 1869*, pp. 309-340. Government Printing Office, Washington, D.C.

Skeates, R.
   2000   *Debating the Archaeological Heritage*. Duckworth Debates in Archaeology. Duckworth, London.

Smith, Watson, Richard B. Woodbury, and Nathalie F. S. Woodbury
   1966   *The Excavation of Hawikuh by Frederick Webb Hodge: Report of the Hendricks-Hodge Expedition, 1917-1923.* Contributions from the Museum of the American Indian Heye Foundation No. 20, Museum of the American Indian, New York.

Somerville, Andrew D., Ben A. Nelson, and Kelly J. Knudson
   2009   Isotopic Investigation of Pre-Hispanic Macaw Breeding in Northwest Mexico. *Journal of Anthropological Archaeology* 29:125-135.

Spicer, Edward H.
   1962   *Cycles of Conquest: The Impact of Spain, Mexico, and the United States on the Indians of the Southwest, 1533-1960.* University of Arizona Press, Tucson.

Spier, Leslie
   1917   *An Outline for a Chronology of Zuni Ruins.* Anthropological Papers of the American Museum of Natural History 18, part 3. American Museum of Natural History, New York.

   1918   *Notes on Some Little Colorado Ruins.* Anthropological Papers of the American Museum of Natural History 18, part 4. American Museum of Natural History, New York.

Steadman, Dawnie Wolfe
   2001   Mississippians in Motion? A Population Genetic Analysis of Interregional Gene Flow in West-Central Illinois. *American Journal of Physical Anthropology* 114:61-73.

Stojanowski, Christopher M.
    2004   Population History of Native Groups in Pre- and Postcontact Spanish Florida: Aggregation, Gene Flow and Genetic Drift on the Southeastern U.S. Atlantic Coast. *American Journal of Physical Anthropology* 123:316-332.

    2005   Spanish Colonial Effects on Native American Mating Structure and Genetic Variability in Northern and Central Florida: Evidence from Apalachee and Western Timucua. *American Journal of Physical Anthropology* 128:273-286.

Stojanowski, Christopher M. and Michael A. Schillaci
    2006   Phenotypic Approaches for Understanding Patterns of Intracemetery Biological Variation. *Yearbook of Physical Anthropology* 49:49-88.

Strouhal, Evžen
    1992   Anthropological and Archaeological Identification of an Ancient Egyptian Royal Family (5th Dynasty). *International Journal of Anthropology* 7:43-63.

Suárez Diez, Lourdes
    1988   Historia de las investigaciones de concha en México. *Antropología en Mexico,* vol. 6, coordinado por Carlos García Mora, Instituto Nacional de Antropología e Historia, México.

    1989   *Conchas prehispánicas en México,* BAR International Series, No. 514, Oxford.

    2007   *Conchas y caracoles: ese universo maravilloso.* Instituto Nacional de Antropología e Historia, México.

Talavera, Jorge Arturo y Ruben Manzanilla Lopez
    1991   Proyecto de Investigación y Salvamento Arqueológico en Mochicahui, Sinaloa. *Antropología* 34:22-27.

Taube, Karl
    2001   The Breath of Life: The Symbolism of Wind in Mesoamerica and the American Southwest. In *The Road to Aztlan: Art from a Mythic Homeland,* edited by Virginia M. Fields and Victor Zamudio-Taylor, pp. 102-123. Los Angeles County Museum of Art, California.

Teague, Lynn S.
    1993   Prehistory and the Traditions of the O'odham and Hopi. *Kiva* 58(4):435-454.

Tello, Fray Antonio
    1942   *Crónica miscelánea de la Sancta Provincia de Xalisco,* T. III, Editorial Font, Guadalajara, México.

    1945   *Libro segundo de la crónica miscelánea de la provincia de Xalisco (1650-51).* Gobierno del Estado de Jalisco, Universidad de Guadalajara, INAH, Jalisco.

Terrell, John E.
    2001   Introduction. In *Archaeology, Language, and History: Essays on Culture and Ethnicity,* edited by John E. Terrell, pp. 1-10. Bergin and Garvey, Westport, Connecticut.

Thibodeau, Alyson M., John T. Chesley, and Joaquin Ruiz
    2012   Lead Isotope Analysis as a New Method for Identifying Material Culture Belonging to the Vázquez de Coronado Expedition. *Journal of Archaeological Science,* Volume 39, Issue 1: 58-66.

Thomas, Noah and Barbara J. Mills
    2003   Zuni Ceramics, Identity, and Colonialism. Paper presented at the Amerind Foundation Advanced Seminar:

Colonialism and Culture Change at Zuni A.D. 1300-1900, Manuscript on file at Zuni Heritage and Historic Preservation Office.

Thompson, Marc

1999   *Mimbres Iconology: Analysis and Interpretation of Figurative Motifs.* Ph.D. dissertation, Department of Archaeology, University of Calgary, Alberta, Canada.

2000   Knife-wing: A Prominent Mesoamerican, Mimbres, and Pueblo Icon. In *Sixty Years of Mogollon Archaeology: Papers from the Ninth Mogollon Conference, Silver City, New Mexico, 1996,* edited by Stephanie M. Whittlesey, pp. 145-150. SRI Press, Tucson, Arizona.

Tierney, Michael

1996   The Nation, Nationalism and National Identity. In *Nationalism and Archaeology,* edited by John A. Atkinson, Iain Banks and Jerry O'Sullivan, pp. 12-21. Cruithne Press, Glasgow.

Trentmann, Frank

2009   Materiality in the Future of History: Things, Practices, and Politics, *Journal of British Studies* 48 (April).

Trigger, Bruce G.

1984   Alternative Archaeologies: Nationalist, Colonialist, Imperialist. *Man* 19(3):355-370.

Turner, Christy G., II

1987   Affinity and Dietary Assessment of Hohokam Burials from the Site of La Ciudad, Central Arizona. In *Specialized Studies in the Economy, Environment, and Culture of La Ciudad Part I and II,* edited by JoAnn Kisselburg, Glen E. Rice, and Brenda L. Shears, pp. 215-230. Anthropological Field Studies No. 20. Office of Cultural Resource Management, Arizona State University, Tempe.

1993   Southwest Indian Teeth. *National Geographic Research and Exploration* 9(1):32-53.

Turner, Christy G., II and Joel D. Irish

1989   Further Assessment of Hohokam Affinity: The Classic Period Populations of the Grand Canal and Casa Buena Sites, Phoenix, Arizona. In *Archaeological Investigations at the Grand Canal Ruins: A Classic Period Site in Phoenix Arizona,* volume 2, edited by Douglas R. Mitchell, pp. 775-792. Soil Systems Publications in Archaeology No. 12. Soil Systems, Inc., Phoenix, Arizona.

Turner, Victor

1975   Symbolic Studies. *Annual Review of Anthropology* 4:145-161.

Underhill, Ruth M.

1939   *Social Organization of the Papago Indians.* Columbia University Contributions to Anthropology No. 30, Columbia University Press, New York.

1946   *Papago Indian Religion.* Columbia University Press, New York.

Undreiner, George J.

1947   Fray Marcos de Niza and His Journey to Cibola. *The Americas* 3(4):415-486.

UNESCO

1972   *Convention Concerning the Protection of the World Cultural and Natural Heritage.* UNESCO, Paris.

UNWTO

2008a   *Tourism Highlights.* 2008 ed. World Tourism Organisation. Annual Publication, Spain.

2008b World Tourism Organisation. Official Site, United Nations, Spain. http://*www.unwto.org/index.php.*

Upham, Steadman
1982 *Polities and Power.* Academic Press, New York.

1986 Imperialists, Isolationists, World Systems, and Political Realities: Perspectives on Mesoamerican-Southwestern Interactions. In *Ripples in the Chichimec Sea: New Considerations of Southwestern-Mesoamerican Interactions,* edited by Frances Joan Mathien and Randall H. McGuire, pp. 205-219. Centre for Archaeological Investigations and Southern Illinois University Press, Carbondale.

1986 Smallpox and Climate in the American Southwest. *American Anthropologist* 88(1):115-128.

Utermohle, Charles J., Stephen L. Zegura, and Gary M. Heathcote
1983 Multiple Observers, Humidity, and Choice of Precision Statistics: Factors Influencing Craniometric Data Quality. *American Journal of Physical Anthropology* 61:85-95.

Valencia Cruz, Daniel
1992 Arqueología de Aguascalientes. En *Arqueología.* No. 39, pp. 12-23.

1993 Arqueología de Aguascalientes. En *Espacios: Cultura y Sociedad.* Instituto Cultural de Aguascalientes, No. 11, pp. 3-11. Septiembre-Octubre.

1994 Identificación, catalogación y conservación de sitios con pintura rupestre en el estado de Aguascalientes. Ms. Informe al Centro Regional INAH Aguascalientes, México.

VanPool, Christine S.
2003 *The Symbolism of Casas Grandes.* Ph.D. dissertation, Department of Anthropology, University of New Mexico, Albuquerque.

VanPool, Christine S. and Todd L. VanPool
2007 *Signs of the Casas Grandes Shamans.* University of Utah Press, Salt Lake City.

VanPool, Christine S., Todd L. VanPool, and Marcel J. Harmon
2008 Plumed and Horned Serpents of the American Southwest. In *Touching the Past: Ritual, Religion, and Trade of Casas Grandes,* edited by Glenna Nielson-Grimm and Paul Stavast, pp. 47-58. Museum of Peoples and Cultures, Brigham Young University, Provo, Utah.

VanPool, Todd L., Craig T. Palmer, and Christine S. VanPool
2008 Horned Serpents, Tradition, and the Tapestry of Culture, In *Cultural Transmission and Archaeology: Issues and Case Studies,* edited by Michael J. O'Brien, pp. 77-90. Society for American Archaeology Press, Washington, D.C.

VanPool, Todd L., Christine S. VanPool, and David A. Phillips, Jr.
2006 The Casas Grandes and Salado Phenomena: Evidence for a Religious Schism in the Greater Southwest. In *Religion in the Prehispanic Southwest,* edited by Christine S. VanPool, Todd L. VanPool, and David A. Phillips, Jr., pp. 235-252. AltaMira Press, New York.

Vargas, Victoria D.
1995 *Copper Bell Trade Patterns in the Prehispanic U.S. Southwest and Northwest Mexico.* Arizona State Museum Archaeological Series, no. 187. University of Arizona Press, Tucson.

2001 Mesoamerican Copper Bells in the Pre-Hispanic Southwestern United States and Northwestern Mexico.

In *The Road to Aztlan: Art from a Mythic Homeland,* edited by Virginia M. Fields and Victor Zamudio-Taylor, pp. 196-211. Los Angeles County Museum of Art, California.

Vázquez León, Luis
  2003   *El Leviatán Arqueológico: Antropología de una Tradición Científica en México.* CIESAS, México

Vicente, Julio and John Carpenter
  2008   The Protohistoric Period and Cultural Continuity of Cahitan-Speaking Groups in Northwest Mexico. Paper presented in the Recent Research in Northwest Mexico symposium, 73 Annual Meeting of the Society for American Archaeology, March 25-29th, 2008, Vancouver, Canada.

Vierra, Bradley J. (editor)
  1989   A Sixteenth Century Spanish Campsite in the Tiguex Province. *Laboratory of Anthropology Notes No. 475,* Museum of New Mexico, Santa Fe.

Vierra, Bradley J. and Stanley M. Hordes
  1997   Let the Dust Settle: A Review of the Coronado Campsite in the Tiguex Province. In *The Coronado Expedition to Tierra Nueva: The 1540 – 1542 Route Across the Southwest,* edited by Richard Flint and Shirley C. Flint, pp. 209-219. University Press of Colorado, Boulder.

Villalobos, César
  2011   *Heritage Tourism and Archaeology in the History of Archaeology. Mexico Case Study.* Ph.D. dissertation, Durham University.

Villalpando, Elisa
  2000   The Archaeological Traditions in Sonora. In *Greater Mesoamerica: The Archaeology of West and Northern Mexico,* edited by Michael S. Foster and Shirley Gorenstein, pp. 241-254. The University of Utah Press, Salt Lake City.

Villalpando, Elisa (editor)
  2002   *Boundaries and Territories: Prehistory of the U.S. Southwest and Northern Mexico.* Anthropological Research Papers 54, Arizona State University, Tempe.

Vivian, Gordon
  1932   A Restudy of the Province of Tiguex. Unpublished Masters of Arts Thesis, University of New Mexico, Albuquerque.

Wallace, Henry D., James M. Heidke, and William H. Doelle
  1995   Hohokam Origins. *Kiva* 60(4):575-618.

Wallerstein, Emmanuel
  1974   *The Modern World System I.* Academic Press.

  1978   Civilization Modes of Production. *Theory and Society* 5:1-10.

  1980   *The Modern World System II.* Academic Press, New York.

Watkins, Joe E.
  2003   American Indians, First Nations, and Archaeology in North America. *American Antiquity* 68(2):273-285.

Webster, Laurie D., Maxine A. McBrinn, and Eduardo Gamboa Carrera (editors)
  2008   *Archaeology Without Borders: Contact, Commerce, and Change in the U.S. Southwest and Northwestern Mexico.* University Press of Colorado, Boulder.

Weigand, Phil C.
  1982   Mining and Mineral Trade in Prehistoric Zacatecas. *Anthropology* VI (1 & 2): 87-134.

  1985   Evidence for Complex Societies during Western Mesoamerican Classic Period. In *The Archaeology of West and Northwest Mesoamerica,* edited by Michael S. Foster and Phil C. Weigand, pp. 47-92. Westview Press, Boulder, Colorado.

  1995   Minería prehispánica en las regiones noroccidentales de Mesoamérica, con énfasis en la turquesa. En *Arqueología del Occidente y del Norte de México,* editado por Eduardo Williams y Phil C. Weigand. El Colegio de Michoacán, Zamora.

  1999   El sitio arqueológico: Cerro de Tepisuazco (Jalpa, Zacatecas) y sus relaciones con la tradición Teuchitlán. En *Tercer simposium: Los Altos de Jalisco a fin de siglo,* editado por C. González Pérez, pp. 241-274. Sistema de Educación Media Superior, Universidad Autónoma de Guadalajara, Jalisco.

Weigand, Phil C. and Acelia García de Weigand
  2001   A Macroeconomic Study of the Relationships Between the Ancient Cultures of the American Southwest and Mesoamerica. In *The Road to Aztlan: Art from a Mythic Homeland,* edited by Virginia M. Fields and Victor Zamudio-Taylor, pp. 184-195. Los Angeles County Museum of Art, California.

Weigand, Phil, Acelia García de Weigand y J. Andrew Darling
  1999   "El sitio arqueológico de Tipisuazco (Jalpa, Zacatecas) y sus relaciones con la tradición Teuchitán." En *Tercer simposium: Los Altos de Jalisco a fin de siglo,* editado por C. González Pérez, pp. 241-274. Sistema de Educación Media Superior, Universidad Autónoma de Guadalajara, Jalisco.

Wells, E. Christian
  2006   *From Hohokam to O'odham: The Protohistoric Occupation of the Middle Gila River Valley, Central Arizona.* Gila River Indian Community Anthropological Research Papers No. 3. Gila River Indian Community Cultural Resource Management Program, Sacaton.

WHC
  2008   UNESCO World Heritage Centre. Official Site, http://*whc.unesco.org/*. UNESCO, Paris.

Whalen, Michael E. and Paul E. Minnis
  1996a Studying Complexity in Northern Mexico: The Paquimé Regional System. In *Debating Complexity: Proceedings of the 26th Annual Chacmool Conference,* edited by Daniel A. Meyer, Peter C. Dawson, and Donald T. Hanna, pp. 161-168. Archaeological Association and the Department of Archaeology, University of Calgary, Alberta, Canada.

  1996b Ball Courts and Political Centralization in the Casas Grandes Region. *American Antiquity* 61 (4):732-46.

  1996c The Context of Production around Paquimé, Chihuahua, Mexico. In *Interpreting Southwestern Diversity: Underlying and Overarching Patterns,* edited by Paul R. Fish and J. Jefferson Reid, pp. 173-184. Anthropological Research Paper 48, Arizona State University, Tempe.

  2000   Leadership at Casas Grandes, Chihuahua, Mexico. In *Alternative Leadership Strategies in the Prehispanic Southwest,* edited by Barbara J. Mills, pp.168-179. University of Arizona Press, Tucson.

Whalen, Michael E. and Paul E. Minnis, cont'd
2001   *Casas Grandes and its Hinterland: Prehistoric Regional Organization in Northwest Mexico.* University of Arizona Press, Tucson.

2003   The Local and Distant in the Origin of Casas Grandes, Chihuahua, Mexico. *American Antiquity* 68:314-332.

2009   *The Neighbors of Casas Grandes: Excavationg Medio Period Communities of Northwest Chihuahua, Mexico.* University of Arizona Press, Tucson.

Whitecotton, Joseph and Richard Pailes
1986   New World Pre-Columbian World Systems. In *Ripples in the Chichimec Sea: New Considerations of Southwestern-Mesoamerican Interactions,* edited by Frances Joan Mathien and Randall H. McGuire, pp. 183-204. Centre for Archaeological Investigations and Southern Illinois University Press, Carbondale.

Whittlesey, Stephanie M.
1995   Mogollon, Hohokam, and O'otam: Rethinking the Early Formative Period in Southern Arizona. *Kiva* 60(4):465-480.

Wilcox, David R.
1985   Preliminary Report on New Data on Hohokam Ballcourts. In *Proceedings of the 1983 Hohokam Conference,* edited by Alfred E. Dittert, Jr. and Donald E. Dove, pp. 641-654. Arizona Archaeological Society Occasional Paper 2. Phoenix.

1986   A Historical Analysis of the Problem of Southwestern-Mesoamerican Connections. In *Ripples in the Chichimec Sea: New Considerations of Southwestern-Mesoamerican Interactions,* edited by Frances Joan Mathien and Randall H. McGuire, pp. 9-44. Southern Illinois University Press, Carbondale and Edwardsville.

1986b Tepiman Connection: A Model of Mesoamerica – Southwestern Interaction. In *Ripples in the Chichimec Sea: New Considerations of Southwestern-Mesoamerican Interactions,* edited by Frances Joan Mathien and Randall H. McGuire, pp. 135-153. Centre for Archaeological Investigations and Southern Illinois University Press, Carbondale.

1991   The Mesoamerican Ballgame in the American Southwest. In *The Mesoamerican Ballgame,* edited by Vernon L. Scarborough and David R. Wilcox, pp. 101-125. University of Arizona Press, Tucson.

Wilcox, David R. and W. Bruce Masse
1981   A History of Protohistoric Studies in the North American Southwest. In *The Protohistoric Period in the North American Southwest, A.D. 1450-1700,* edited by David R. Wilcox and W. Bruce Masse. Anthropological Research Papers No. 24, Arizona State University, Tempe.

Wilcox, David R., William H. Doelle, and J. Brett Hill
2003   Coalescent Communities GIS Database: Museum of Northern Arizona, Center for Desert Archaeology, Geo-Map Inc. On file, Archaeology Southwest, Tucson.

Wilkerson, S. Jeffery K.
1991   And Then They Were Sacrificed: The Ritual Ballgame of Northeastern Mesoamerica Through Time and Space. In *The Mesoamerican Ballgame,* edited by Vernon L. Scarborough and David R. Wilcox, pp. 45-71. University of Arizona Press, Tucson.

Willems, Willem J.H.
2008   Archaeological resource management and preservation. In *Preserving archaeological remains in situ. Proceedings of the 3rd conference 7-9 December 2006. Vol. 10. Geoarchaeological and Bioarchaeological*

Studies, edited by Henk Kars and Robert M. van Heeringen, pp. 283-289. Institute for Geo- and Bioarchaeology, Free University, Amsterdam.

Willey, Gordon R. and Jeremy A. Sabloff
  1980   *A History of American Archaeology.* 2nd edition, W. H. Freeman and Co., San Francisco, California.

Williams-Blangero, Sarah and John Blangero
  1989   Anthropometric Variation and the Genetic Structure of the Jirels of Nepal. *Human Biology* 61:1-12.

Woodson, M. Kyle
  1999   Migrations in Late Anasazi Prehistory: The Evidence from the Goat Hill Site. *Kiva* 65(1):63-84.

Woosley, Anne I. and John C. Ravesloot (editors)
  1993   *Culture and Contact: Charles C. Di Peso's Gran Chichimeca.* The Amerind Foundation, Inc., Dragoon, and The University of New Mexico Press, Albuquerque.

Wyckoff, Kristina C.
  2009   Mimbres-Mesoamerican Interaction: Macaws and Parrots in the Mimbres Valley, Southwestern New Mexico. Unpublished Master's thesis, Department of Anthropology, University of Oklahoma, Norman.

Wynn, Lisa L.
  2008   Shape Shifting Lizard People, Israelite slaves, and Other Theories of Pyramid Building: Notes on Labor, Lationalism, and Archaeology in Egypt. *Journal of Social Archaeology* 8(2):272–295.

York, Robert and Gigi York
  2011   *Slings and Slingstones: The Forgotton Weapons of Oceania and the Americas.* Kent State University Press, Ohio.

Zepeda, Ofelia
  1983   *A Tohono O'odham Grammar.* University of Arizona Press, Tucson.